Canonical Marriage Preparation in the Igbo Tradition in the Light of Canon 1063 of the 1983 Code of Canon Law

AFRICAN THEOLOGICAL STUDIES

Etudes Théologiques Africaines

Edited by Gerhard Droesser and Chibueze Udeani

KIRCHENRECHT

VOLUME 4

Zur Qualitätssicherung und Peer Review der vorliegenden Publikation

Die Qualität der in dieser Reihe erscheinenden Arbeiten wird vor der Publikation durch einen Herausgeber der Reihe geprüft.

Notes on the quality assurance and peer review of this publication

Prior to publication, the quality of the work published in this series is reviewed by one of the editors of the series.

Paulinus Chibuike Nwaigwe

Canonical Marriage Preparation in the Igbo Tradition in the Light of Canon 1063 of the 1983 Code of Canon Law

Canonical Norms and Inculturation

PETER LANG
EDITION

Bibliographic Information published by the Deutsche Nationalbibliothek
The Deutsche Nationalbibliothek lists this publication in the Deutsche Nationalbibliografie; detailed bibliographic data is available in the internet at http://dnb.d-nb.de.

Zugl.: Würzburg, Univ., Diss., 2012

Library of Congress Cataloging-in-Publication Data

Nwaigwe, Paulinus Chibuike, 1975- author.
Canonical marriage preparation in the Igbo tradition in the light of Canon 1063 of the 1983 Code of Canon Law : canonical norms and inculturation / Paulinus Chibuike Nwaigwe.
pages cm. — (African theological studies ; v. 4)
"Würzburg, Univ., Diss., 2012."
ISBN 978-3-631-64778-3 — ISBN 3-631-64778-6 1. Marriage (Canon law) 2. Igbo (African people)—Rites and ceremonies. 3. Marriage—Religious aspects—Catholic Church. 4. Marriage customs and rites—Nigeria. 5. Catholic Church. Codex Juris Canonici (1983). Canon 1063. 6. Christianity and culture—Nigeria. I. Title.
KBU3110.N93 2013
262.944008996332—dc23

2013038186

D 20
ISSN 2196-0615
ISBN 978-3-631-64778-3 (Print)
E-ISBN 978-3-653-03573-5 (E-Book)
DOI 10.3726/978-3-653-03573-5

Peter Lang Edition is an Imprint of Peter Lang GmbH.

Peter Lang – Frankfurt am Main · Bern · Bruxelles · New York · Oxford · Warszawa · Wien

This book is part of the Peter Lang Edition list and was peer reviewed prior to publication.

www.peterlang.com

Dedication

To my beloved and cherished parents
Mr. Festus Nwaigwe (late) and Mrs. Catherine Nwaigwe
Towards adequate and effective marriage preparation in Igboland.

Acknowledgements

Human life is a gift which is realised most in love and mutual understanding since man is a being for others. Hence, I am grateful to God for his manifold blessings on me. My profound gratitude goes to my former Superior General, Very Rev. Fr. Dr. James Michael Okpalaonwuka whose permission to further my studies abroad, made the realization of this work possible. My present Superior General, Very Rev. Fr. Dr. George Okorie is worthy of mention for his paternal care, unflinching support and encouragement in the pursuit of my studies.

My unalloyed appreciation goes to my chief supervisor Prof. Dr. Heribert Hallermann who handed me a lot from his scholarly insight and erudition with his simplicity and humility. His painstaking effort, diligent moderation, and steadfastness in correcting this work notwithstanding his other tight schedules inside and outside the University campus cannot be equated with anything. I cannot thank him enough for his guidance and dedication not only during this doctoral thesis but more also for his continued interest in me and support for my future endeavours. The ideas he imparted in me will ever remain indelible and evergreen. He is simply a friend to me.

I equally thank Prof. Dr. Ottmar Meuffels, my second supervisor for his constructive criticisms and useful corrections. My appreciation goes also to Rev. Fr. Dr. Fintan Garvin, a priest from the Archdiocese of Dublin, Ireland, who not only made some insights into this work but also gave me some useful materials that guided me throughout my writing of this dissertation. I sincerely thank Mrs Birgit Liebler for organizing and formatting the manuscript of this work. I thank also Fr. Godswill Agbagwa for the materials he provided me. I am also indebted to the entire members of Staff most especially of the theology faculty of the University of Würzburg, Germany.

My profound appreciation goes to my congregation; Sons of Mary Mother of Mercy, through whose foundation, this work was made possible. I am equally indebted to the entire members of this religious family. My deepest gratitude goes to Rev. Fr. Dr. Christopher Agoha, whose contribution has helped in shaping my life and personality in this my noble congregation. His scholarly insights, love, care, support and encouragement are not to be left out. I thank members of the German region of my congregation, especially those with whom I have lived very closely here in Germany – Frs. Christogonus Keke, Basil Ezechukwu, Mcdonald Nwandu, Uche Iheke and Vitalis Emesi for their brotherly care and support.

This work would not have seen the light of the day without the support of the diocese of Würzburg, Germany, who offered me scholarship to study in the University of Würzburg and also incorporated me into the pastoral activities of the diocese. I am sincerely grateful.

I am ever grateful to the entire Egenhausen community, Germany, who not only sheltered me but provided me support financially and encouraged me. I am indebted to you all. I thank in a especial way the families of Mr and Mrs Horst and Anita Conze, Norbert Dedat, Mrs Ruth Schulwitz (late), and Mrs Brigitte Neuwirth, for their support and encouragement.

To be mentioned are my good friends who stood by me with words of encouragement – Frs. Bede Nwadinobi, Matthew Anyanwu, Augustine Nzekwe, Rowland Onyenali, Tony Chimaka and Damian Ikejiama. I sincerely thank my bossom friend Johnson Nani, for his support and assistance in this very work. You are a good friend. I thank in a special way my Anty Queen O. for her support, care and encouragement in seeing to the realisation of this work. I also thank immensely Dr and Mrs Kevin Anyanwu, Mr and Mrs Ralph Obiyo for their care and support in my academic pursuit.

To my parents, Mr. Festus Nwaigwe (late) and Mrs Catherine Nwaigwe who made me what I am today, I remain ever grateful and indebted to them for their care, support, and encouragement all these years. I equally express my profound gratitude to my brothers and sisters, relations, benefactors and benefactresses for their care and support. To all those who have always supported and encouraged me in my field of academics, I say thank you and God bless you all.

Vorwort

P. Nwaigwe Paulinus Chibuike SMMM, der als Priester einer nigerianischen Ordensgemeinschaft angehört, geht aus von der pastoralen Situation, die in seinem Heimatland im Blick auf die Ehe festzustellen ist, und zielt auf die Verbesserung der Ehepastoral und namentlich der Ehevorbereitung bzw. Ehebegleitung. Zu diesem Zweck untersucht er sowohl die traditionelle institutionalisierte Ehevorbereitung bei den Igbo als auch die diesbezüglichen kanonischen Normen und lehramtlichen Weisungen mit der Absicht, beide im Sinne der Inkulturation christlicher Lebenspraxis in eine fruchtbare Beziehung zu bringen.

Die Untersuchung, die am 22.10.2012 von der Katholisch-Theologischen Fakultät der Julius-Maximilians-Universität Würzburg als Inauguraldissertation angenommen wurde, wird in fünf Hauptkapiteln entfaltet:

Kapitel eins untersucht die kanonisch vorgeschriebene Ehevorbereitung während der Geltungsdauer des CIC/1917 und erstreckt sich insofern zeitlich auch über die Zeit des II. Vatikanischen Konzils und die Nachkonzilszeit, die – kirchenrechtlich gesehen – mit der Promulgation des CIC/1983 endet. Im CIC/1917 stand die Frage nach der Gültigkeit und der Erlaubtheit der Eheschließung im Mittelpunkt. Auch wenn dieser Codex noch keine systematische Norm zur Ehevorbereitung enthält, bietet er diesbezügliche Anknüpfungspunkte in den Verpflichtungen, die der zuständige Pfarrer im Blick auf die Brautleute hatte: Belehrung über die Heiligkeit des Ehesakraments, die gegenseitigen Rechte und Pflichten der Eheleute sowie die Aufgaben der christlichen Eltern. Ebenso sollte der Pfarrer die Brautleute in kluger Weise über die Ehehindernisse belehren und ganz allgemein für deren christliche Unterweisung sorgen. Die Enzyklika „Casti Connubii" P. Pius XI. legt mit der Unterscheidung zwischen der entfernten und der unmittelbaren Ehevorbereitung in gewisser Weise das Fundament für die weitere Entwicklung in diesem Bereich. P. Pius XII. hat sich in einer ganzen Reihe von Ansprachen mit der Vorbereitung junger Menschen auf die Ehe befasst und bezeichnete eine sorgfältige Ehevorbereitung als Schlüssel für eine gelungene Ehe. P. Johannes XXIII. wünschte eine entsprechende Katechese schon von Kindheit an. Das II. Vatikanische Konzil erneuert zum einen die Theologie des Ehesakraments, zum anderen sieht es die Ehevorbereitung nicht mehr nur als Aufgabe der Pfarrer an, sondern verpflichtet die gesamte kirchliche Gemeinschaft, an dieser wichtigen Aufgabe mitzuwirken. Das Instrumentum Laboris für die Bischofssynode von 1980 enthält fünf Paragraphen, die sich ausdrücklich mit der entfernteren und der unmittelbaren Ehevorbereitung befassen. In diesem Zusammenhang wird wertschätzend darauf verwiesen, dass in manchen Teilen der Welt Familien mittels überlieferten Brauchtums junge Menschen auf die Ehe und das Familienleben vorbereiten; dies ist in gewisser Weise ein Anknüpfungspunkt für die weiteren Ausführungen des Verfassers zur Situation in seinem Heimatland. Als Frucht der Bischofssynode wurde von P. Johannes Paul II. das Apostolische Schreiben „Familiaris Consortio" veröffentlicht, in dem die Ehevorbereitung als ein von Kindheit an dauernder Prozess konzipiert wird, der die entfernte, die nähere und die unmittelbare Ehevorbereitung umfasst.

Kapitel zwei legt das kanonische Eheverständnis des geltenden CIC/1983 dar, das erkennbar das durch das Konzil erneuerte theologische Konzept der Ehe entfaltet. So wird beispielsweise die hierarchische Ordnung der Ehezwecke überwunden und die Ehe als eine umfassende Lebensgemeinschaft verstanden, die auf das Wohl der Ehegatten sowie die Zeugung und Erziehung von Nachkommenschaft hingeordnet ist. Das Verständnis der Ehe als Bund schließt deren Charakter als Vertrag ein und nicht aus. Die Lehre von der Sakramentalität der Ehe erhält einen ekklesiologischen Akzent, indem die christlich gelebte Ehe als ein wichtiges Aufbauelement der Kirche verstanden wird. Als Wesenseigenschaften der Ehe normiert der CIC/1983 die Einheit und die Unauflöslichkeit, was sich im Hinblick auf das Eheverständnis der Igbo insbesondere bei kinderlos bleibenden Ehen als besonderes Problem erweist. Auch der ehestiftende Konsens, der ausschließlich von den beiden Partnern zu leisten ist, kann unter Umständen in Konflikt zum traditionellen Konsens bei den Igbo geraten, der auch eine Zustimmung der Familie und des Stammes umfasst, jedoch keine Ehe ohne den Konsens der Brautleute kennt.

Kapitel drei stellt vor diesem Hintergrund ausführlich die Ehevorbereitung und die Ehebegleitung vor, die in c. 1063 CIC/1983 normiert ist. Die ausführliche Darlegung der Redaktionsgeschichte lässt erkennen, wie die diesbezüglichen Weisungen des Konzils konsequent in geltendes Recht umgesetzt wurden. Gestützt wird die in c. 1063 CIC/1983 ausgesprochene Verpflichtung der Pfarrer durch die diesbezügliche Ordnungs- und Aufsichtspflicht des Ordinarius (c. 1064 CIC/1983) sowie durch die in c. 1067 CIC/1983 ausgesprochene Verpflichtung der nationalen Bischofskonferenzen, Normen für das so genannte Brautexamen, das Aufgebot usw. zu erlassen. Im Interesse, dass Ehen gültig geschlossen werden, ist in spezifischen pastoralen Situationen eine besondere Erlaubnis des zuständigen Ortsordinarius erforderlich. Vor diesem Hintergrund wird schließlich der c. 1063 CIC/1983 selbst ausführlich erörtert, der die gesamte christliche Gemeinde zur vorbereitenden und begleitenden Hilfe für die Braut- und Eheleute verpflichtet und dabei dem zuständigen Seelsorger eine besondere Verantwortung zuweist. Auch den christlichen Eheleuten kommt in diesem Zusammenhang eine besondere Rolle zu. Im Sinne eines Prozesses umfasst die Ehevorbereitung die entfernte und allgemeine Vorbereitung der Kinder und Jugendlichen durch Erziehung und Katechese, die unmittelbare und persönliche Vorbereitung der Brautleute, die fruchtbringende liturgische Feier der Eheschließung sowie die dauernde Begleitung der Eheleute. Im Anschluss an diese gründlichen und ausführlichen Darlegungen weist der Verfasser auf besondere Problemfälle bei der Ehevorbereitung hin.

Kapitel vier präsentiert das Eheverständnis und das traditionelle System der Ehevorbereitung bei den Igbo. Nach einigen grundlegenden Informationen ethnographischer und sozio-politischer Art werden Grundzüge der Religion der Igbo sowie ihrer religiösen und moralischen Werte erläutert. Die Ehe ist stark auf die Zeugung von Nachkommenschaft, insbesondere von männlichen Nachkommen ausgerichtet und stellt nicht nur eine Verbindung zwischen zwei Individuen, sondern zwischen zwei Familien oder Gemeinschaften dar. Die Ehe gilt aufgrund göttlicher Stiftung als heilig. Polygamie wird aus sozialen Statusgründen toleriert und ist ebenso ein Mittel, um die als Schande empfundene Kinderlosigkeit zu heilen. Eine große Kinderzahl wird angestrebt, Kinder werden wertgeschätzt und eine Frau wird erst als Mutter zum vollwertigen Glied der Familie. Dem traditionellen Eheverständnis der Igbo sind auch eine Reihe von Ehehindernissen bekannt wie das Fehlen des Mindestalters, Blutsverwandtschaft, Schwägerschaft, Impotenz, öffentlich bekannte Kriminalität, die Zugehörigkeit zur Kaste der Osu (Sklaven, Unreine) sowie chronische Krankheiten wie beispielsweise AIDS. Während der Ehevorbereitung werden diese Faktoren durch die jeweiligen Familienclans einer eingehenden Prüfung unterzogen. Schon von Kindheit an werden Jungen und Mädchen von Eltern und Familien auf ihre jeweilige künftige Rolle in Ehe und Familie hin erzogen. Zu den Initiationsriten gehört die Beschneidung von Mädchen und Jungen, die in der Regel acht Tage nach der Geburt stattfindet. Weitere Initiationsriten sind für Mädchen die Fattening Ceremony und für Jungen die Wearing Cloth Ceremony. Für die Eheschließung selbst kommt dem Konsens hohe Bedeutung zu: Der Konsens der Partner konstituiert die Ehe; er wird allerdings umfasst von der Zustimmung der Eltern. Die vorausgehende Partnerwahl und die Nachforschung bezüglich möglicher Ehehindernisse und des sozialen Status der Partnerfamilie liegen in der Verantwortung der beiden Großfamilien. Auf den obligatorischen Besuch bei der Familie der Braut folgt ein erster längerer Aufenthalt der Braut in der Familie des Bräutigams. Die formale Übergabe der Braut und der Mitgift bildet den Abschluss der zahlreichen Etappen der Eheschließung. Vor diesem Hintergrund stellt der Verfasser ein Dokument der Westafrikanischen Bischofskonferenzen zur Ehevorbereitung und Familienpastoral vor, das jedoch zum einen in der Praxis wenig bekannt ist oder zumindest wenig Beachtung findet, und das zum anderen viel zu allgemein gehalten ist.

In Kapitel fünf entwickelt der Verfasser ein eigenes Programm der Ehevorbereitung und der Ehebegleitung, das auf diözesaner Ebene angesiedelt und durchgeführt werden soll. Es soll von einer diözesanen Kommission getragen werden, der unter Leitung eines Priesters sachverständige Laien und insbesondere erfahrene Ehepaare angehören sollen, um die gestufte Ehevorbereitung und die Ehebegleitung im Sinne des c. 1063 CIC zu gestalten. Das Ehevorbereitungsprogramm soll einen hohen Grad an Verbindlichkeit für die Brautleute besitzen, die Nichtteilnahme kann aber kein kirchliches Ehehindernis konstituieren. Im Folgenden wird das Programm differenzierter nach den einzelnen Stufen der kanonischen Ehevorbereitung entwickelt mit dem Anspruch, diese Stufen im Sinne einer Inkulturation des christlichen Eheverständnisses in der Igbo-Kultur zu gestalten. In diesem Zusammenhang werden mehrere Workshops mit den Verlobten durchgeführt, bei denen u.a. auch eine Unterweisung in den Formen der natürlichen Familienplanung stattfindet. Bei der unmittelbaren Ehevorbereitung wird großer Wert auf eine fruchtbare Gestaltung der liturgischen Feier gelegt und es soll auch Raum sein für ein Besinnungswochenende, das insbesondere der Feier der Versöhnung dient. Die Begleitung der Ehepaare durch verschiedene Gruppen wird ebenfalls als wichtige Aufgabe thematisiert. In einem weiteren Abschnitt werden einzelne Umstände angesprochen, die eine besondere pastorale Aufmerksamkeit beanspruchen: Frühe Eheschließungen, Hochzeiten älterer Paare, konfessions- und religionsverschiedene Eheschließungen, voreheliche Schwangerschaft, Gültigmachung einer Ehe, unverheiratetes Zusammenleben, schwere Krankheiten wie vor allem AIDS. Abschließend präsentiert der Verfasser Überlegungen, wie die Ehevorbereitung und Eheschließung und somit das christliche Eheverständnis in die Kultur der Igbo inkulturiert werden könnte und schlägt im Wesentlichen eine Synchronisierung der traditionellen Ehevorbereitung der Igbo mit der kanonischen Ehevorbereitung vor. Letztere könnte notwendige Korrekturen am traditionellen Eheverständnis erreichen und gleichzeitig die erforderliche Rechtssicherheit herstellen, die in der traditionellen Form nicht in dem Maße gegeben ist.

Auch wenn es sich primär um eine kirchenrechtliche Arbeit handelt, hat P. Nwaigwe Paulinus Chibuike SMMM auch weitere, übergreifende Perspektiven entwickelt und sich mit einer grundlegend pastoralen Haltung, die auf einem sicheren theologischen und kirchenrechtlichen Fundament ruht, den praktischen Fragen der Kirche seines Heimatlandes gestellt. Die Beschäftigung mit den Fragen der Ehevorbereitung und Ehebegleitung lässt ein hohes Maß an Wertschätzung gegenüber der eigenen Herkunftskultur erkennen, ohne dass diese verklärt wird; das vom Verfasser überzeugend und ausgewogen dargelegte sakramententheologische und kanonische Eheverständnis auf der Grundlage des II. Vatikanischen Konzils entfaltet diesbezüglich ein kritisches und heilendes Potential. Der vom Verfasser entwickelte eigenständige Lösungsvorschlag zur Ehevorbereitung und Ehebegleitung ist sehr überzeugend, auch wenn er der Bewährung und der eventuell daraus resultierenden Verbesserung in der Praxis bedarf.

Als Betreuer und Begleiter der vorliegenden Doktordissertation durfte ich in den Jahren gemeinsamer Arbeit nicht nur den wissenschaftlichen Eifer, sondern auch den sympathischen Menschen und glaubwürdigen Priester Nwaigwe Paulinus Chibuike kennenlernen. Ich wünsche der vorliegenden Untersuchung eine breite und wohlwollende Rezeption und verbinde damit die Hoffnung und den Wunsch, dass das Engagement das Verfassers für eine gute Ehevorbereitung in seiner Heimat reiche Frucht trägt.

Würzburg, 11. Juni 2013
Univ.-Prof. Dr. theol. Heribert Hallermann
Inhaber des Lehrstuhls für Kirchenrecht an der Julius-Maximilians-Universität Würzburg

Table of Contents

General Introduction

Background

The institution of marriage as a sacrament is a serious and sacred commitment that unites a man and a woman together in the most profound and permanent way. This bond between a man and a woman serves as the basic unit of human society and of the Church. Their mutual love is a total reminder of the love of Jesus Christ to his bride, the church. In this unique union, they make a solemn commitment to be totally for each other[1]. Hence, this unique relationship between a man and a woman requires the most careful attention and preparation.

Emphasizing the importance of preparation for marriage PCF opines: "The starting point for an itinerary of marriage preparation is the awareness that the marriage covenant was taken up and raised to a sacrament of the New Covenant by the Lord Jesus Christ, through the power of the Holy Spirit. The sacrament joins the spouses to the self-giving love of Christ the Bridegroom for the Church, his Bride… by making them the image of, and sharers in this love"[2].

Since the Second Vatican Council characterizes the institution of marriage as an "intimate partnership of life and love"[3], it is imperative that adequate and effective marriage preparation for prospective couples expressing the desire to marry in the church be given special attention. This marriage preparation has a wider dimension as it penetrates people's culture. PCF in affirming this asserts: "Marriage preparation must be set within the urgent need to evangelize culture-by permeating it to its roots… – in everything that concerns the institution of marriage: making the Christian Spirit penetrate minds and behaviour, as well as the laws and structures of the community where Christians live…. This preparation, both implicitly and explicitly, constitutes one aspect of evangelization, so much so that it can deepen the strength of the Holy Father's affirmation: "The family is the heart of the New Evangelization"[4]. It is through this culture permeation that we arrived at the topic of this work since Christianity itself has the primary function of meeting and examining the cultures and customs of the

1 Cfr. Diocese of Shreveport, Sacramental Guidelines, p.128.
2 PCF, n.9.
3 GS, 48 §1.
4 PCF, n.20.

people with the intentions of mainly enriching such cultures while at the same time being enriched by such cultures[5].

The Igboman who embraces Christianity wants also to be fully Christian but without rejecting his Igbo identity and culture. The Church itself recognizes and enhances what is most suitable in the cultures of the people, receiving from them "everything that is able to express better the unsearchable riches of Christ. Only with the help of all the cultures will it be possible for those riches to be manifested ever more clearly and for the Church to progress towards a daily more complete and profound awareness of the truth, which has already been given to her in its entirety by the Lord"[6].

In view of this, there is an urgent need to foster and promote marriage preparation in Igboland as a way of rediscovering the Christian and traditional values of marriage as an institution. To be married in the Catholic Church is much more than having the wedding ceremony in a church building. While marriage as a contract is legally binding, so also a covenant is spiritually and morally binding. It means two individuals are joined together in a lasting union of love as God has willed it. The marriage bond between a man and a woman is indissoluble. God who instituted this sacrament has also affirmed it, "what therefore God has joined together, let no man put asunder"[7]. So it should be the primary task of the Church and that of the society to adequately and effectively give unflinching support to prospective couples and young people by instructing and catechizing them in the values and norms of both Christian and traditional marriage. "Besides, it is important to equip and educate prospective couples with the cultural and Christian values necessary to mould their mentality in a positive direction which will in turn give expression to those crucial values of marital life. Such Christian values of marriage may include mutual love and lasting bond, unity and indissolubility, procreation and education of children granting that these will seek to make their marital lives fruitful and acceptable to the church and the society"[8].

It is pertinent to note that since the promulgation of the 1917 Code, there has been progress in the meaning and understanding of the institution of marriage as a sacrament both in theology and canon law. Marriage preparation during this period focused on assuring that the institution of marriage was protected against what might make for an invalid and illicit celebration of marriage[9].

5 Cfr. B.K. Nwakonobi, Igbo System of Kinship: Christian Response, A Study of One of the Important Pastoral Moral Challenges in Africa, A Dissertation, Rome 1997, p.4.

6 FC, 10§1.

7 Mt, 19:6.

8 P.K. Amevor, New Approaches to Marriage Preparation in the 1983 Code of Canon Law: Challenges to the Particular Church in Ghana, Doctoral Dissertation, Regensburg 2009, p.4.

9 Cfr. C.1019 §1 CIC/1917.

While embracing the spirit of the Second Vatican Council, the 1983 Code calls for pastoral care of prospective couples entering into marriage, the involvement of the local ordinary, priests and the ecclesial community in the preparation of marriage to provide adequate and effective assistance to young people and those entering marriage.

In his Apostolic Exhortation, Familiaris Consortio, John Paul II affirms marriage and the family as constituting "one of the most precious of human values"[10]. The Pope examines how "the family in the modern world, as much as and perhaps more than any other institution, has been beset by the many profound and rapid changes that have affected society and culture"[11]. He concludes that "the Church must therefore promote better and more intensive programs of marriage preparation in order to eliminate as far as possible the difficulties that many married couples find themselves in, and even more in order to favour positively the establishing and maturing of successful marriages. Marriage preparation has to be seen and put into practice as a gradual and continuous process"[12].

The Code of 1983 includes a requirement for prospective couples to participate in marriage preparation prior to their wedding by stating that there should be "personal preparation for entering marriage, so that the spouses are disposed to the holiness and the obligations of their new state"[13]

The Pontifical Council for the Family emphasises that "preparation for marriage, for married and family life, is of great importance for the good of the Church. In fact, the sacrament of marriage has great value for the whole Christian community and, in the first place, for the spouses whose decision is such that it cannot be improvised or made hastily"[14]. The PCF goes further to define marriage as that which "implies a real vocation to a particular state and a life of grace. In order to be brought to its maturation, this vocation requires adequate, particular preparation and a specific path of faith and love, all the more so because this vocation is given to a couple for the good of the Church and society"[15].

In this regard, as an implementation to its renewed meaning and understanding of marriage, the Church recognizes the necessity for effective and adequate marriage preparation and pastoral care of marriage. This study attempts to give the influence of theological and canonical enrichments in the meaning and understanding of the matrimonial sacrament upon the legal provisions for marriage preparation in the Igbo dioceses of Nigeria.

---

10 FC,1§2.

11 Ibid,1§1.

12 Ibid, 66§2&3.

13 C.1063, 2° CIC/1983.

14 PCF, n. 1.

15 PCF, n. 9.

Statement of the Problem

Christian marriage forms the basis of the family which is adequately identified as the foundation of the society. Such institution requires certain values and principles because marriage is a vocation and a sacrament of the Church[16]. Nowadays, the institution of marriage has become just another way of life for many people in Igboland as well as other parts of the world, and not the Christian calling to holiness and perfection. One notices that we are now living with the reality in our society of today that quite a huge number of prospective couples prepare for the wedding ceremony but not for married life itself[17]. In Igboland today, the high rate of divorce, the common practice of traditional marriage without the church wedding, and a growing lack of healthy attitude toward a firm commitment of couples to each other are on the increase. Affirming this, Burke stresses: "The breakdown of marriages in our society today gives us matter for study and for great sadness. So many couples are in marriage for what they can get from it not for what they can put into it. Husbands and wives look upon one another as objects to be used not as persons to be loved. The great example of this is when a woman has no child, observe the language; it is the woman who is to blame not the couple! For some things the man and the woman are one but not for this"[18].

Today many of our people are unwilling to enter a Church marriage while they are still in their prime of life. Some are reluctant to put themselves in a relationship which they view as demanding, prohibiting and permanent. There are many cases of marital disharmony and rupture and reluctance of so many to wed in the Church. This has resulted to sadness and grave concern about the good of our Catholic young people and the future of the Church and the stability of marriage in Igboland[19]. These problems should alert pastors of souls to the dangers of prospective couples entering marriage without adequate and thorough preparation for marriage. Adequate and effective marriage preparation will assist the prospective couple to appreciate the meaning and understanding of Christian marriage, and to live out their commitment to each other in faith and love in accordance with the example of Christ and the teachings of the Church.

Therefore, as a panacea to these problems, we need a more dynamic, systematic and thoughtfully planned marriage preparation in the Igbo dioceses. "The family urgently needs to be helped and supported.... For her part, the Church

16 Cfr. Diocese of Shreveport, Sacramental Guidelines, p.128.

17 Cfr. J. Burke, The Pre-Marriage Investigation by the Priest, Lagos 1998, p. v.

18 J. Burke, Marriage Today, Lagos 1990, p.3.

19 Cfr. A.O. Gbuji, The Pastoral Care of Marriage and Family Life in Nigeria, St. Paul Press Training School, Ibadan 2006, p.21.

must untiringly promote a plan of pastoral care for families, capable of making every family rediscover and live with joy and courage its mission to further the Gospel of Life"[20].

Aim of the Work

This work studies the canonical marriage preparation in the culture of the Igbo people with its canonical norms and chance for inculturation. The ecclesial community in Igboland need to assist prospective couples prepare for life together, a life that is sacramental in character and attitude. Hence, our primary aim in choosing this topic is to present and evaluate the canonical provisions and its juridical importance for an adequate and effective marriage preparation in Igbo dioceses. By so doing we aim at providing the ambience and opportunity for prospective couples to establish successful marriages and their stability in Igboland.

Through this way, the engaged couples in Igboland will be able to grasp the unique and multi-faceted nature of marriage made holy in Christ which is beyond its purely social or legal demands. Thus it is made evident on the ecclesial community guided by the parish priest, to provide and promote marriage preparation for prospective couples[21].

In response to this need, we will in this study formulate a positive approach to marriage preparation by attempting to show how the Igbo people can better prepare their children and youth for marriage and family life. The guidelines we shall propose will apply to all marriages in the dioceses of Igboland in which a Catholic is taking part. This will no doubt help in making the marriage and the family life more meaningful and acceptable to the Igbo people.

Scope of the Work

The scope of this work is evident from the title. It concerns canonical marriage preparation in the Igbo tradition, canonical norms and inculturation. Hence, we do not intend to study in its entirety the Igbo culture, custom and tradition in their complex and far reaching understanding. This work limits itself to the study of

20 John Paul II, Evangelium Vitae, Libreria Editrice Vaticana, Roma 1995, n.94.

21 Cfr. Diocese of Norwich, Marriage Preparation, 2011. http://www.ccfsn.org/pdffiles/marriage-prep.2011.pdf (Accessed: 7.11.2011).

canonical marriage preparation in Igbo dioceses as contained in the 1983 Code of Canon Law as well as in particular laws and also Igbo traditional marriage preparation as it is practiced in Igbo culture by the Igbo people.

We do not pretend to have an all treatment about this topic. We embarked on this topic of marriage preparation because it will provide for the prospective couples and those already married in Igboland a lasting union where Christ is ever-more present thereby making the couples ministers of Christ's love to one another and to the whole world. Also the outcome of this marriage preparation will determine and enhance the future permanence of marriage and family life in Igboland.

The work is also extended to inculturating the sacrament of marriage with that of the traditional Igbo marriage most especially in the areas of preparation for marriage and rite of marriage celebration. This will make the Church marriage more meaningful to the Igbo people and help promote their cultural values as Christians. "It is by means of "inculturation" that one proceeds towards the full restoration of the covenant with the wisdom of God, which is Christ Himself. The whole Church will be enriched also by the cultures which, though lacking technology, abound in human wisdom and are enlivened by profound moral values"[22].

All along there have been many writers in Igboland who have written immensely about marriage in the Christian and Igbo tradition – its similarities and differences. Some have also written on inculturating the two marriage rites together but there has not been a work written with regard to inculturating the canonical preparation of marriage and the Igbo traditional preparation of marriage. This is our task in this work; to find a possible way of bringing the two preparations together in a process of inculturation so that it will be meaningful to the Igbo people without them loosing their Igbo identity and their Christian doctrine.

Christianity takes the risk of rejecting some important elements of Igbo culture and this makes it hard for prospective couples in Igboland to embrace canonical marriage preparation. Inculturation is needed. How can it be provided? People still get married and form families. How are they prepared for this life-long union? Many participate only on traditional marriage preparation while others do not prepare at all. There is therefore an urgent need for an improvement upon Igbo Christians positive attitudes towards canonical marriage preparation in the form of inculturation which could put a stop to the present dichotomy between the canonical marriage preparation and the traditional marriage preparation in Igboland.

22 FC, 10§3.

Argument of the Thesis

Marriage and family life constitute the biggest challenges facing the Catholic Church today. What are their chances of survival? Polygamy, separation, divorce, trial marriages and observing only traditional marriage are sometimes the order of the day in Igboland. Must that be the case? Is there anything we can do to change this trend? This is the argument of this work. One of the most meaningful arguments contributing for a successful marriage is preparation. Nothing must be ignored by the dioceses in Igboland to ensure that every prospective couple who wants to enter marriage is properly prepared. Preparing adequately will definitely go a long way towards ensuring successful marriages and towards the quality of life of those already married.

Therefore, what is needed, according to John Paul II, "is a serious preparation of young people for marriage, one which clearly presents Catholic teaching on this sacrament at the theological, anthropological, and spiritual levels"[23]. Adequate marriage preparation is provided through pastors of souls and the ecclesial community. The 1983 Code represents a new approach in norms concerning marriage preparation and the way marriage preparation and pastoral care in marriage preparation are to be organised and implemented[24].

Furthermore, since there is a level of obligation attached to this marriage preparation and pastoral care of marriage, pastors of souls and the ecclesial community are bound to assist in preparing prospective couples in Igbo dioceses for marriage in accordance with the law of the Church[25]. To this view, the work also argues that collaboration and co-responsibility among the agents of pastoral care of marriage in the Igbo dioceses of Nigeria and the effective implementation of the general norms of the Code concerning marriage preparation and pastoral care will undoubtedly lead to a good, adequate, effective, and efficient preparation of prospective couples for marriage and help them understand the true meaning of Christian marriage in its canonical and sacramental aspect.

Method of Research

Our method will be theological, canonical, pastoral, historical, expository, exegetical, evaluative, critical, and comparative so as to achieve the purpose of this work which is above all, presenting some guiding principles and policies for

23 CA, 46.

24 Cfr. CC.1063-1072 CIC/1983.

25 Cfr. C.1063 CIC/1983.

structuring a process of preparation, formation and catechesis for the sacrament of marriage in Igbo dioceses. In applying these methods we will focus our studies primarily on the appropriate canons and norms, and their commentaries. We shall also use the method of library research for the work. This method will incorporate the use of both primary and secondary sources and also other literatures that are appropriate to such a canonical work.

Motivation of the Work

Some years ago the institution of marriage was accorded the respect it deserved because of its stability. It was held in high esteem and seen as sacred which called a couple to each other in the most profound and permanent way. Before its celebration it was preceded by a well-drawn out process of preparation.

But today marriage in Igboland as well as other parts of the world faces a variety of problems and challenges especially in this area of stability. Marriage preparation and pastoral care of marriage in Igboland are still lacking adequate structures. There are still no set-up policies and guidelines for marriage preparation in Igbo dioceses.

In view of this, there is urgent need for marriage preparation and pastoral care of marriage in Igboland. There is the necessity to set-up a comprehensive diocesan and parish policies and guidelines concerning marriage preparation that will take into account the situation of marriage in the various dioceses and parishes in Igboland. Hence, the motivation of this work.

Structure of the Work

In order to accomplish the aim of this work, we systematically structured it into five chapters with general introduction and conclusion. The general introduction introduces the work by giving the background information, stating the problem, revealing the aim, scope of the work, and methodology of the work. It also discusses the argument of the work. The work argues that cooperation and responsibility among the various agents of marriage preparation and pastoral care of marriage in Igboland, and the proper execution of the norms of the Code concerning marriage preparation will lead to a good, fruitful and effective preparation of prospective couples for marriage in Igbo dioceses of Nigeria.

Chapter one deals with the study of the general norms about marriage preparation in the Code of 1917. In studying these norms there is no doubt that they will provide a more fertile ground for a deeper and systematic study of the canonical norms which exerted powerful influence on marriage preparation in the revised Code of Canon Law. A number of vital developments will be dealt with in this chapter that gave important shape to marriage preparation, such as the two instructions issued by the Sacred Congregation for the Discipline of the Sacraments in 1921 and 1941.

This chapter examines also some elements of the response of the Church on marriage preparation starting with Pope Pius XI's encyclical Casti Connubii (1931), some writings of Pope Pius XII, some addresses of Pope John XXIII. We shall also turn our attention to the document of the Second Vatican Council, Gaudium et Spes, to see how it really influenced our understanding on the meaning of marriage today especially with regard to marriage preparation. The chapter will also explore what the 1980 Synod of Bishops on the Family discussed and proposed and proposed about marriage preparation, as well as John Paul II's apostolic exhortation, Familiaris Consortio (1981).

Chapter two treats purely the meaning and canonical understanding of marriage in the Code of 1983. Here, the nature, ends, properties and what marital consent means are going to be explored in this very chapter, to see what must be transmitted into the very understanding of marriage in Igbo tradition, and the fundamental principles and values underlying the more pertinent norms and texts.

Chapter three studies the various stages of the development of what was to be seen as canon 1063 of the Code of 1983. We shall look at the changes in its formulation and the arguments that preceded these changes. The influence the 1975 Schema exerted on the formulation of this very canon will also be examined. The exegesis and analysis of the canon will be treated in details to know exactly what the canon is establishing, drawing tremendously on the apostolic exhortation, Familiaris Consortio and the Pontifical Council for the Family on preparation for the sacrament of marriage. We shall also turn our attention on some of the difficult situations that arise in the marriage preparation and pastoral care for marriage.

Chapter four examines the nature of Igbo traditional marriage, the essential qualities, its impediments, Igbo traditional marriage procedures, consent in Igbo traditional marriage, and marriage preparation in Igbo tradition. The Igbo people do not contract marriage without traditionally preparing adequately for it. During such preparation great attention is given to parental role, community role and initiation into adulthood. The preparation in question will consist of remote and proximate and it takes sometimes a long process before it is concluded. In this traditional marriage preparation we shall see whether there is something similar to that of canonical marriage preparation in the Code. In this chapter we shall first consider the Igbo worldview as numerous factors contribute to the worldview of the Igbo people. The Igbo traditional marriage is both procreation and community oriented.

We shall also in this chapter take a cursory look at the AECAWA overview on marriage preparation in West Africa. The bishops of this region of the continent recognise that the most pressing needs of the Church in West Africa and other parts of Africa is preparing the Christian faithful more properly and effectively for marriage.

The final chapter will explore how the provisions of canon 1063 of the new Code will help us to propose a pastoral guidelines and policies for marriage preparation in Igbo dioceses. To achieve this objective, we shall use the provisions of canonical doctrine on marriage and the good cultural values in Igboland to suggest these pastoral guidelines and policies. The frame work of this proposal will draw heavenly on the approach adopted by the General Synod of the Dioceses in the Federal Republic of Germany as well as some Archdioceses and Dioceses in the United State of America. We find this framework very suitable to our own situation as it permeates and appeals to both diocesan and parish level as a comprehensive marriage preparation that involves everybody and carries everybody along.

We shall also in this last chapter suggest and propose the inculturation of traditional and Church marriages in the celebration of sacramental marriage. We shall do this, by integrating the positive values of Igbo culture especially as it regards traditional marriage preparation and Igbo traditional rite of marriage into the principles of Christian marriage so that the Igbo people will be glad to perform the two ceremonies together without loosing their cultural identity and the Christian doctrine.

Chapter One: Legal marriage preparation during the validity of the Code of 1917

1. Marriage Preparation in the Code of 1917

1.1. Introduction

The concern in this chapter is to study the norms in general concerning marriage preparation in the code of 1917. The study of the prevailing canonical doctrines involved during this period will provide more fertile ground for a deeper and systematic study of the canonical norms which undoubtedly exerted considerable influence on the preparation of marriage in the 1983 code of canon law. The main elements involved in marriage preparation of 1917 code were principally the canonical investigation by the parish priest of those intending to marry, and the publication of the marriage banns[26] as we shall see when analyzing the general norms concerning marriage preparation in the 1917 code. The 1917 code however, stressed maintaining the freedom of the parties to marry, with some concern for the proper instruction about marriage. The focus was more of juridical than a strictly pastoral nature, with a pre-occupation to ensure that those wishing to marry were free from any impediment and were aware of those basic elements of their faith and what the church understood by the sacrament of marriage.

1.2. The General Norms Concerning Marriage Preparation

The first chapter in the title on marriage in the 1917 code concerns what need to be done before the celebration of marriage, most especially the banns of marriage[27]. The initial canons on the title matrimony deal with the general canonical and theological nature of marriage. These canons describe marriage as being elevated by Christ our Lord between two baptized persons to the dignity of a

26 Cfr.F.Gavin, Pastoral Care in Marriage Preparation(can.1063).History,Analysis of the Norm and its Implication by Some Particular Churches,Rome 2004,p.22.

27 Cfr.1917 Code,Book III,Part 1 De Sacramentis,Title IV De Matrimonio,chapter I De iis quae matrimonii celebration praemitti debent et praesertim de publicationibus matrimonialibus,cc.1019-1034.

sacrament.[28] For this elevation to take place in any concrete instance, it is necessary and sufficient that both parties be validly baptized and validly married. Marriage has this sacramental character from the moment of its celebration, if both parties are already validly baptized. Canon 1013 deals with the ends and essential properties of marriage. Canon 1014 establishes a presumption in favour of the validity of marriage in all cases where there is a positive and probable doubt, that is, reason both for validity and against it. Canon 1015 differentiates between merely ratified, ratified and consummated, legitimate and putative marriage. It asserts the presumption in favour of the consummation of the marriage once the parties have cohabited together. Canon 1016 determines the areas of competence of divine law, canon law and civil law as regards marriages of baptised persons .Canon 1017 treats the act of betrothal[29] or formal engagement. This is a promise of marriage made either unilaterally (by one party) or bilaterally (by both parties) which must be made in writing. The object of the promise is future marriage.[30]

The most important canon on the parish priest's obligation to instruct his people on the sacrament of marriage and its impediments is canon 1018.[31] This canon addresses the general instruction by the parish priest on marriage. The general instruction on marriage is to be addressed not only to those about to be married but also to all the parishioners. This canon however, does not enumerate when and how this instruction is to be given and does not also go into details with regard to the content of the instruction. However, the general instruction is to be understood in the context of canon 1332 which urges parish priests to hold a catechetical instruction for adults on Sundays and holydays of obligation,[32] and canon 1344 which obliges the parish priest to announce the word of God in the customary homily.[33] While these are clearly two different obligations, they have much in common.[34] Major consideration in the canons was given in canon 1019

28 Cfr.c.1012 CIC/1917: §1."Christus Dominus ad sacramenti dignitatem evexit ipsum contractum matrimonialem inter baptizatos"; §2. "Quare inter baptizatos nequit matrimonialis contractus validus consistere,quin sit eo ipso sacramentum".

29 Cfr.P.C. Augustine, A Commentary on the New Code of Canon Law, London 1935,p.35.

30 Cfr.F.Gavin, Pastoral Care in Marriage Preparation,p.24.

31 Cfr.c.1018 CIC/1917: „ Parochus ne omittat populum prudenter erudire de matrimonii sacramento eiusque impedimentis".

32 Cfr.c.1332 CIC/1917: „ Diebus dominicis aliisque festis de praecepto, ea hora quae suo iudicio magis apta sit ad populi frequentiam,debet insuper parochus catechismuim fidelibus adultis, sermone ad eorum captum accommodato, explicare."

33 Cfr. c.1344 CIC/1917: „ Diebus dominicis caterisque per annum festis de praecepto proprium cuiusque parochi officium est, consueta homilia, praesertim intra missam in qua maior soleat esse populi frequentia, verbum Dei populo nuntiare."

34 Cfr. F.Gavin, Pastoral Care in Marriage Preparation,p.29.

§ 1[35] to assuring that nothing stood in the way of the valid or licit celebration of the marriage. This canon asserts that before a marriage is celebrated it must appear with moral certainty from a careful investigation, that there is no obstacle to its validity.[36] The canon indicates that the legislator does not presume a readiness for marriage on the part of all who request it. The moral certitude mentioned in this canon is analogous to that required of the judge before declaring the invalidity of a marriage. In other words, if the ensuing investigation leads the parish priest or other priests to the well-founded conclusion that in all probability the proposed marriage will be invalid, he has no choice but to refuse to witness it.[37] Hence, the parish priest must determine the free state of those about to marry, meaning that they must be free of that which would prevent the marriage from being valid or licit in the external forum.[38] The parish priest has a grave obligation to examine the method of reaching moral certitude and states before he admits people to marriage. This certitude is arrived at by means of positive and morally certain arguments and not merely conjecture or negative arguments.[39]

Canon 1019 § 2 declares that in danger of death, if other proofs cannot be had, and in the absence of indications to the contrary, the sworn statement of the contracting parties that they have been baptized and are under no impediment is sufficient. This implies that the danger of death which is one of the conditions for being content with less rigid proof, means a probability of death affecting either party, from any cause whether intrinsic or extrinsic. The fact that only one exception is mentioned seems to suggest that, in the mind of the legislator, those prescriptions are not to be dispensed with except for really grave reasons.[40]

The preliminary investigation in canon 1019 § 1 consists chiefly of two procedures: the personal investigation of the parties by the parish priest, and the publication of the banns. The norms regarding this first procedure are stipulated in canon 1020. This canon states that it is the responsibility of the parish priest to carry out this personal investigation, even when another priest is to perform

---

35 Cfr. C. 1019 § 1 CIC/1917: „ Antequam matrimonium celebretur, constare debet nihil eius validae ac licitae celebrationi obsistere."

36 Cfr. T.L. Bouscaren – A.C. Ellis, Canon Law: A Text and Commentary, Milwaukee 1957,p.457. See also, M. F. Capello, De matrimonio,n. 145,p.140; F.X. Werns – P. Vidal, Ius matrimonial, n. 122, p.140.

37 Cfr. T.P. Doyle, The Canonical Foundations for Pre-marriage Guidlines, in: T.P. Doyle, ed; Marriage studies,1, Washington D.C. 1980,p.67.

38 Cfr. F. Capello, De Sacramentis, vol. v; De Matrimonio, edition quinta,Taurino 1947,p.147. "Status liber sponsorum est eorum libertas seu immunitas ab iis omnibus quae in ford externo validate ac licitae matrimonii celebrationi obstare possent, praesertim immunitas ab omni matrimonio impedimento." Cfr.T.P. Dolyle ,The Canonical Foundations.pp.67 and 75.

39 Cfr. F.X. Wernz – P. Vidal, Ius matrimoniale, Rome 1946, n.112, p.140.

40 Cfr. H.A. Ayrinhac, Marriage legislation in the Code of Canon Law, London 1932, p.25.

the marriage.[41] The parish priest who has the right to assist at the marriage is determined according to canon 1097.[42] This personal investigation by the parish priest is to take place before the Banns are published and before the parties are issued the required instruction on the nature of the marriage.[43] The parish priest must question the parties separately about the freedom of their consent. No priest is to assist at a marriage if there is any reasonable ground of suspicion regarding the freedom of consent on both sides. The conversation, however, should be conducted cautiously, that is, with tact and prudence.[44] The aim of this personal investigation consists of: 1.To determine freedom from impediments. 2. To ensure that the parties have sufficient knowledge of Christian doctrine. 3. To ensure freedom of consent.[45] In Igbo traditional marriage, this freedom of consent is not only limited to the two parties involved but it is also subject to parental approval so as to guarantee the progress of the family and to ensure the handing on of a well-organized marriage tradition to their posterity. Matrimonial consent is in fact much more than a mere act of the will. It must be noted that the three areas of investigation are separate. However, it should be noted that freedom from canonical impediments does not necessarily mean freedom of consent.[46] An instruction stressing the need to assure the parties freedom to marry was first issued in 1911 by the Sacred Congregation for the Sacraments. The same purpose was spelled out in a more detailed – instruction in 1921. A later instruction on June 29, 1941,

41 Cfr. c. 1020 CIC/1917:§1. „Parochus cui ius est assistendi matrimonio, opportuno antea tempore, diligenter in, vestiget num matrimonio contrahendo aliquid obstet." §2. "Tum sponsum tum sponsam etiam seorsum et caute interroget num aliquot detineantur impedimento, an consensum libere, praestent, et an in doctrina Christiana sufficienter instructi sint, nisi ob personarum qualitatem haec ultima interrogation inutilis appareat." §3. "Ordinarii loci est peculiares normas pro huiusmodi parochi investigatione dare."

42 Cfr.c.1097 CIC/1917: §1.„Parochus autem vel loci Ordinarius matrimonio licite assistunt:
1° Constito sibi legitime de libero statu contrahentium ad norman iuris;
2° Constito insuper de domicilio vel quasi-domicilio vel menstrual commoratione aut, si de vago agatur, actuali commoratione alterutrius contrahentis in loco matrimonii;
3° Habita, si conditions deficient de quibus n.2, licentia parochi vel Ordinarii domicilii vel quasi domicilii aut menstruae commorationis alterutius contrahentis, nisi vel de vagis actu itinerantibus res sit, qui nullibi commorationis sedem habent, vel gravis necessitas intercedat quae a licentia petenda excuset."
§ 2: "In quolibet casu pro regula habeatur ut matrimonium coram sponsae parocho celebretur, nisi iusta causa excuset; matrimonia autem catholicorum mixti ritus, nisi aliud particulari cautum sit, in ritu viri et coram eiusdem parocho sunt celebranda."
§ 3: "Parochus qui sine licentia iure requisite matrimonio assistit, emolumenta stolae non facit sua, eaque proprio contrahentium parocho remittat."

43 Cfr.F.X. Wernz – P. Vidal, Ius matrimoniale, n.112, p.144.

44 Cfr. T.L. Bouscaren – A.C. Ellis, Canon Law, p.458.

45 Cfr. F.X. Wernz – P. Vidal, Ius matrimoniale, n.112, p.143.

46 Cfr. T.P. Doyle, The Canonical Foundations, p.68.

went into much greater detail and even adds new safeguards of reporting as a way of implementing its directives.[47] The Code Commission added that if the parties are ignorant of the Christian doctrines, that it is the duty of the priest to instruct them at least in the rudiments of the Christian doctrine and not refuses to wed them as provided in the case of public sinners or persons notoriously under a censure according to canon 1066.[48] The diocesan bishop could issue more special rules or norms for this investigation.

Canon 1021 states that unless baptism was administered in the parish priest own church, he is to require a baptismal certificate of each party or of the catholic party only, if the marriage is to be contracted with a dispensation from disparity of cult. From the catholic party a baptismal certificate is required before the date of the marriage. This is designed to prove not only that the person is baptized, but also to prove the freedom from certain public impediments such as public vows, previous marriage, etc, which are required by law to be recorded there. Only in case an official certificate cannot be obtained can it be supplied by other proof.[49] This requirement of a certificate is also applicable to a baptized non- catholic.[50] The practice of being contented with an ordinary assurance from a baptized non-catholic is clearly contrary to what the code says, and exposes the marriage to the danger of objective nullity unless a dispensation from disparity of cult has been obtained ad cautelam.[51]

The norms regarding the publication of Banns cover over half of the canons concerning marriage preparation in the 1917 code (cc.1022 – 1030). This publication of marriage banns has already been stated and discussed at the Council of Trent.[52] The parish priest has the mandatory obligation to announce publicly the

---

47 Cfr.S. Congregatio de Sacramentis, Instructio ad Ordinarios circa statum liberum ac Denunciationem initi matrimonii,March 6,1911: AAS3(1911) 102-103; S. Congregatio de Disciplina Sacramentorum, instruction ad Ordinarios locorum super probatione status liberi ac denuntiatione initi matrimonii,July 4, 1921: AAS13, pp.348- 349.Cfr.J.H.Provost – K.Walf, ed; Studies in Canon Law, Leuven 1991,p.175.

48 Cfr.c. 1066 CIC/1917: „ Si publicus peccator aut censura notorie innodatus prius ad sacramentalem confessionem accedere aut cum Ecclesia reconciliari recusaverit, parochus euis matrimonio ne assistat, nisi gravis urgeat causa, de qua, si fieri possit, consulat Ordinarium.“ For a more detail on the response by the code Commission concerning knowing the Christian doctrine by the parties, see: Pontificia Commissio ad Codics Canones Authentice Interpretandos, Dubia 1918,IV, 3:AAS 10,p.345.Cfr. J.H. Provost –K.Walf, ed; Studies in Canon Law, p.175.

49 Cfr. T.L. Bouscaren – A.C. Ellis, Canon Law, p.459.

50 Cfr. M.F. Capello, De matrimonio, n.149, p.142. Cfr. F.Gavin, Pastoral Care in Marriage Preparation, p.26.

51 Cfr. T.L. Bouscaren – A.C. Ellis, Canon Law, p.459.

52 „Hence, following in the footsteps of the holy council of the Lateran held under Innocent III, this council orders that henceforth, before a marriage is contracted, an announcement of those intending to marry shall be made publicly during the mass by the parish priest of the contracting parties on three successive feast days. After these announcements have been made, and if

names of those who are about to marry (c.1022).[53] The obligation to announce publicly the names is grave and remains binding even though the parish priest is certain that no impediment exists. The necessity of the Banns affects, not the validity, but only the licitness of marriage.[54] The publication of the Banns must be made by the parties' own parish priest in the parish where the parties or either of the parties has a domicile or quasi-domicile (c.1023). Canon 1024 stipulates that the publications should be made for three successive Sundays or other days of obligation, in the church, during the solemnities of the mass or during other divine services attended by many of the people. Here, the time, place and form of publication are to be taking into consideration.

The local ordinary of the place may, for his own territory, substitute for the publications the public posting of the names of the contracting parties at the doors of the parochial or other church for a period of at least eight days, provided, that two feast days of obligation are included within the period (c. 1025). Canon 1026 states cases in which the Banns of marriage are omitted. The Banns are not to be made for marriages contracted with a dispensation from the impediment of disparity of cult or mixed religion. Their publication may be permitted by the local ordinary under the conditions: (1) that there be some prudent reason there for; (2) that there be no danger of scandal; (3) that the dispensation from the impediment has been obtained beforehand; (4) that the religion of the non-catholic party be omitted from the announcements.[55] The reason behind the omission of the Banns was a fear that the church might have been seen as implicitly approving of or encouraging mixed marriages.[56] All the faithful are bound to make known of any impediment they know to the parish priest or the local ordinary of the place before the celebration of the marriage (c. 1027). The canonical obligation[57]

---

no legitimate impediment is raised in objection, the celebration of the marriage must then take place in open church." Cfr.Council of Trent, sess. XXIV, de ref. matrim; c.I,Cfr. Tanner, pp.755 – 756.Cfr. F.Gavin, Pastoral Care in Marriage Preparation, p.26.

53 Cfr. C. 1022 CIC/1917: „ Publice a parocho denuntietur inter quosnam matrimonium sit contrahendum."

54 Cfr. T.L. Bouscaren – A.C. Ellis, Canon Law, p. 460; F.X. Wernz – P. Vidal, Ius matrimonial, n. 122, p. 150; M. F. Cappello, De matrimonio, n. 161, pp. 154 – 155; H.A. Ayrinhac, Marriage legislation, p. 33.Cfr. F.Gavin, Pastoral Care in Marriage Preparation, p. 26.

55 Cfr. T. L. Bouscaren – A. C. Ellis, Canon Law, p. 462.

56 Cfr.J.A. Abbo – J.D. Hannan, The Sacred Canons: A Concise Presentation of the Current Disciplinary Norms of the Church, II, St. Louis 1960, p. 202; J.B. Roberts, The Banns of Marriage: An Historical Synopsis and Commentary, Washington 1931, pp. 44 – 56.Cfr. F.Gavin,Pastoral Care in Marriage Preparation, p.27.

57 This Obligation arises from the natural and divine law, in as much as all are obliged to the extent of their power to prevent irreverence to the sacrament, sin, and harm to the neighbour, some or all of which evils necessarily result from illicit or invalid marriage. However, it is also binding as an ecclesiastical law in accordance to the terms of this canon, on all persons who

is a grave one in conscience, to reveal the impediment to the parish priest or to the local ordinary of the place, and as soon as possible.[58] Canon 1028 speaks of dispensation from the Banns.[59] This dispensation is to be given for just cause by the local ordinary of the parties (loci Ordinarius proprius) of the place where the parties, or either of them, have a domicile or quasi- domicile. The local ordinary can as well dispense from the Banns even outside his own diocese. The dispensing power given to the local ordinary here is attached to his office by the law itself and therefore, it is ordinary jurisdiction.[60] If another parish priest conducted the investigation he must immediately by authentic document[61] send information as to the result of the same to the parish priest who is to assist at the marriage (c.1029). This investigation by the parish priest starts with the examination of the parties as stated in canon 1020 and involves any further investigation that may be necessary to establish a moral certainty that they are free to marry. The parish priest should not assist at the marriage after the investigations and publications until he has received all the necessary documents, and unless there is reasonable cause to the contrary, until three days have elapsed after the last publication (1030). The necessary documents are: (a) reports from other parish priests on the result of any investigation or publication which they may have carried out; (b) the prescripts containing any dispensations which may be required.[62]

Procedure in doubt or certainty regarding impediment is recorded in canon 1031. In order that the necessary moral certainty is established, this canon states that when a doubt[63] arises about the existence of an impediment, the parish priest

---

know (with certainty or at least serious probability) of any impediment. For more details on this, see: T. L. Bouscaren – A.C. Ellis, Canon Law, p. 463; H.A. Ayrinhac, Marriage Legislation, p.41; J.A. Abbo – J.D. Hannan, The Sacred Canons, p.202.

58 Cfr. T.L. Bouscaren – A. C. Ellis, Canon Law, p.463.

59 Cfr. c. 1028 CIC/1917: §1."Loci Ordinarius proprius pro suo prudenti iudicio potest ex legitima causa a publicationibus etiam in aliena dioecesi faciendis dispensare."

§ 2. "Si plures sint Ordinarii proprii, ille ius habet dispensandi, in cuius dioecesi matrimonium celebratur; quod si matrimonium extra proprias ineatur dioeceses, quilibet Ordinarius proprius dispensare potest."

60 Cfr. c.197 CIC/1917:§1. "Potestas iurisdictionis ordinaria ea est quae ipso iure adnexa est officio; delegate, quae commissa est personae."

§ 2. "Potestas ordinaria potest esse sive propria sive vicaria."

61 An authentic document in this context means a letter properly signed by the parish priest and sealed with the parish seal. Therefore, the report is authentic when these conditions are met, and that is all that the code explicitly requires.

62 Cfr.T.L. Bouscaren – A.C. Ellis, Canon Law, p.466.

63 A doubt here could be positive or negative. A positive doubt is one in which there are some reasons both for and against the existence of the impediment. A negative doubt is one that is not based on reasons or one based on weak or negligible reasons. Cfr. J.J. Donovan, The Pastor's Obligation in Pre-nuptial Investigation: A historical Synopsis and Commentary, Washington 1938, p.107.

shall investigate the matter more thoroughly by questioning at least two witnesses under oath, provided the impediment in question would not bring dishonor or injure the parties. Furthermore, if necessity requires it, the parish priest may interrogate the parties themselves in the same way. If for any reason the doubt still persists after the investigation, the parish priest should endeavor to consult the local ordinary before going on with the marriage. If a certain impediment is discovered; if it is occult, in order to get a dispensation, the parish priest should refer the matter, without mentioning names, either to the local ordinary or to the sacred penitentiary. If it is public, the parish priest must proceed with the publication until the impediment is removed. Canon 1032 deals with marriage of persons without fixed abode.[64] A parish priest should not assist at the marriage of persons who are Vagi except in cases of necessity as described in canon 91, unless after obtaining a permission to assist from the local ordinary of the place or from a priest delegated by him. It is obvious from the words of this canon that the church is very cautious about admitting Vagi to marriage. The fact about the instability of their place of residence, it is quite easy for them to conceal impediments to marriage, particularly the impediment of ligament. Therefore, the legislation of canon 1032 is a precaution against illicit and invalid unions.[65]Even before this legislation the Council of Trent mandated parish priests not to assist at the marriages of Vagi or of those with no fixed abode, until they had first made a diligent investigation about them and upon referring the matter to the local ordinary, had obtained from him permission to assist at the marriage.[66]

Canon 1033 addresses the parish priest role in instructing the prospective Spouses concerning the sanctity of the sacrament of marriage, the mutual obligations of spouses, parents and sacramental preparation (penance and eucharis) before the celebration of the wedding ceremony. We shall return to this very canon when dealing with the general and particular instructions.

The last canon on the 1917 Code about marriage preparation is canon 1034 and it deals with marriage of minors.[67] This canon states that the parish priest must seriously dissuade minor sons and daughters from contracting marriage without the knowledge or against the reasonable wishes of their parents, and should they refuse to obey, he should not assist at their marriage without consulting the local ordinary. The validity of the marriage of minors, even against the wishes of their

64 Vagi are defined in Canon 91 of 1917 Code as persons who have neither a domicile nor a quasi-domicile anywhere.

65 Cfr. J.J. Donovan, The Pastor's Obligation, p.259.

66 Cfr. Council of Trent, Sess. XXIV, de ref. matrim; c. 7; T.L. Bouscaren – A.C. Ellis, Canon Law, p. 469.

67 Minors in this context are those who have not completed their twenty-first year, and who are not legally emancipated from parental authority.cfr. c. 88 §1 CIC/1917.

parents, provided they have reached the canonical age,[68] is no longer mentioned and has not been since the Council of Trent.[69]Parents have no right to control absolutely the marriages of their children by imposing or forbidding either marriage in general or a particular marriage, because children are not subject to parental authority in the choice of a state of life, and because the right transferred in marriage is intimately personal and outside the scope of parental authority. Yet minor children should, even in this matter, consult their parents and follow their reasonable advice.[70]

1.3. The Instruction

The 1917 Code speaks of marriage instruction in two different places. The first is a general instruction stated in canon 1018, and the second is a particular instruction for those planning marriage which is dealt with in canon 1033. We shall now briefly take a look at them.

1.3.1. The General Instruction

Under the general instruction, canon 1018 instructs the parish priests to teach their people concerning marriage and its impediments. Although this canon refers to two subjects of instruction; the sanctity of marriage and impediments, the force of the legislation is that there be such instruction. The content can and should be modified to suit present-day needs.[71] According to Bouscaren and Ellis, the general instruction involves, "the nature of marriage, it's beautiful elevation to the dignity of a sacrament, its graces, the jurisdiction of the church, necessity of observing her laws, the primary purpose of marriage, the sin and social plague of birth prevention, mutual helpfulness of husband and wife, marriage as a state

68 Cfr.c. 1067 CIC/1917: §1. "Vir ante decimum sextum aetatis annum completum, mulier ante decimum quartum item compltum, matrimonium validum inire non possunt."
§ 2. "Licet matrimonium post praedictam aetatem contractum validum sit, current tamen animarum pastores ab eo avertere iuvenes ante aetatem, qua, secundum regionis receptos mores, matrimonium iniri solet." It should be noted that what this canon presented is a restriction on the right to marry and was challenged a year after the promulgation of the Code. The reply from the Congregation of the Council held that general capacity to marry with regard to age is not a vested right and therefore, the Code did not infringe on or unduly limit the basic right. Cfr. S.C. Concilii, 6-18, 1919.Cfr. Canon Digest, vol.1, p.508.

69 Cfr. Council of Trent, Sess. XXIV, de, ref. matrm; c.1, in Tanner 755.Cfr. F.Gavin, Pastoral Care in Marriage Preparation, p.28.

70 Cfr. T.L. Bouscaren – A.C. Ellis, Canon Law, p.472.

71 Cfr. T.P. Doyle, The Canonical Foundations, p.71.

of consecration to duty and to God, Christian example the best antidote for prevalent vices against marriage, catholic education of children, the impediments, especially that of mixed religion."[72] The manner of this general instruction is to be given prudently as a gentle reminder to avoid alike sensationalism and pale aloofness, but to give the people the instruction they so solely need and want. In other words, a general instruction that is clear, sympathetic and practical.[73]Some authors interpret this instruction as something broader, In other words, as a course of instruction in secondary or tertiary education.[74]This very instruction should start with children's catechesis so as to help them understand the meaning of family life education based on Christian values in accordance to the age and status of the children, and then continue with adults in a more ordered and developed way. Pope Pius XI began his encyclical Casti Connubii of 1931 with a strong statement on the necessity of instruction on the Christian principles concerning marriage. We shall return to Pius XI when treating some ecclesial documents on marriage preparation. In accordance to this, every Pope in modern times has also spoken often of the necessity for general instruction on marriage. This shows that the obligation to offer general instruction on marriage is to be taken seriously.

1.3.2. Particular Instruction

After the canonical investigation into freedom to marry, the parish priest is obliged to instruct the parties about the nature of marriage. The place of the relevant canon 1033[75] establishes the fact that the instruction is quite different from the investigation, and not to be confused with the general instruction on marriage in canon 1018, or with the previous examination of the parties in canon 1020. The subject matter of this particular instruction is the sanctity of marriage, the mutual obligations of husband and wife, and the duties of parents to their children. It is pertinent to say here that because of the experience, prudence and tactfulness which this particular instruction requires, it is highly recommended and encouraged that the parish priest himself performs this investigation. It must also be added that this instruction be treated from the context of marriage as a sacrament. If the parish priest finds the parties, or either of them, totally ignorant of the conjugal obligation, he should make sure that they are fully instructed about this

72 T.L. Bouscaren – A.C. Ellis, Canon Law, p.457.

73 Cfr. Ibid.

74 Cfr. H.A. Ayrinhac, Marriage Legislation, p.22.

75 Cfr.c.1033 CIC/1917:"Ne omittat parochus, secundum diversam personarum conditionem, sponsos docere santitatem sacramenti matrmonii, mutuas coniugum obligationes et obligationis parentum ergo prolem; eosdemque vehementer adhortetur ut ante matrimonii celebrationem sua peccata diligenter confiteantur, et sanctissimam Eucharistiam pie recipiant."

obligation. A few words on love, mutual forbearance, patients and the education of children in accordance to the catholic doctrine will always be proper if the parties are found to be fully instructed. In the words of Capello: " The pastor should explain the obligations of married life, mutual love, mutual fidelity, protection on the part of the husband, submission on the part of the wife, the licitness of the conjugal act, the mutual obligation of rendering the debitum, the licitness of all acts which are ordained toward generation, the illicitness of others, that in doubt the parents confessor should be consulted. He should also explain and seriously inculcate the obligations of parents toward their children, that baptism is to be conferred as soon as possible, catholic education attended to from the earliest years, moral and physical care to be provided."[76]

With regard to the manner and circumstances of this particular instruction, Wernz – Vidal have this to say: "This instruction is to be given in a positive manner so as not to discourage or intimidate the engaged couple. The reason for the instruction is to ensure that the sacrament of matrimony will be received in pious and worthy manner and that the parties will live out their marriage in a Christian fashion. In addition, the commentary makes it very clear that the instruction is not to be deffered to the days just before the wedding, as a kind of afterthought or distasteful necessity."[77] Canon 1033 states further that the instruction in question should be "secundum diversam personarum conditionem. The personal instruction to be given here by the parish priest is to take into consideration the condition of the persons involved. In Igboland the instruction takes place at least before the period of the Banns elapses. Allowance is made for a couple who live at a great distance from each other, or whose work schedules make it difficult or impossible for one or both to attend the regular catechetical program of particular instruction."This allows the parish priest the discretion to decide in the case of each individual couple the content and extent of the instruction that he deems necessary. However, the obligation on the parish priest to give the instruction would, according to most of the commentators, seem to be grave"[78].

The canon ends with the obligation on the part of the parish priest to earnestly exhort the parties to receive the sacraments of penance and holy eucharis before the wedding. Matrimony is a sacrament of the living therefore, should be received

---

76 M.F. Capello, De matrimonio, n. 184, p.176.Cfr. T. L. Bouscaren – A.C. Ellis, Canon Law, p.470.

77 F.X. Wernz – P. Vidal, Ius matrimoniale,n. 122, p.146. „ Quae instructio non videtur differenda usque ad ultimos dies ante nuptias, sed vel immediate ante proclamationes vel primo proclamationum tempore est absolvenda." On the manner and circumstances of this instruction,see also: T.L Bouscaren – A.C. Ellis, Canon Law, p.470.

78 M.F.Capello, De matrimonio, n.184. pp.176-177; P.H. Jone, Commentarium, p.239; T.L. Bouscaren – A.C. Ellis, Canon Law, p.470; F. Blanco Najera, El Codigo de derecho canonico, p.271. Cfr. F. Gavin, Pastoral Care in Marriage Preparation, p.33.

in a state of grace for those intending to wed in the Catholic Church. This exhortation is also found in the decree Tametsi of the Council of Trent[79] as well as in other documents such as the Roman Ritual.[80] The Praenotanda of the revised rite of marriage which was promulgated on March 19, 1969, states that "the couples should be instructed on the church's teaching concerning marriage and the family. This instruction is directly related to the faith dimension of the sacrament: Priests should first of all strengthen and nourish the faith of those about to be married, for the sacrament of marriage presupposes and demands faith."[81]

1.4. Conclusion

The legislation in the 1917 Code included a number of juridical requirements that tended to guarantee a valid and lawful celebration of marriage. In addition to this, some other recommendations and requirements that were pastoral in nature were also included. The couples intending to marry were invited to become aware if the responsibility they were taking on and the sanctity of the sacrament they were celebrating.[82] The Code was chiefly concerned about the validity and liceitness of marriage celebration. In the words of J. Provost: " In effect, preparation of a couple for marriage – at least as it was presented in the code – focused on assuring that the institution of marriage would be safeguarded. It needed to be protected against what might make for an invalid or illicit celebration and had to be shielded from possible sin."[83] In addition to being concerned about licit and valid celebration of marriage, the Code of 1917 was also interested in other matters as regards marriage preparation. The parish priest was obliged "ne omittat parochus" stated in canon 1033, to instruct the parties carefully on the sanctity of the sacrament of marriage, the mutual obligations and the obligation of parents toward their children. The Code also imposed upon the parish priest the duty to instruct people tactically and prudently about the sacrament of marriage and the impediments (c.1018), and to discover whether the parties were adequately instructed in Christian doctrine (c.1020 § 2). From what we have said so far, it is

79 Cfr. Council of Trent, Sess:XXIV, de ref. matrim; c.1, Cfr. Tanner, p. 756.

80 Cfr. Paul V, Rituale Romanum, n.17, p.276.

81 The Rite of Marriage Introduction, n.7, in Rites, New York 1976, p.535, Cfr. T. P. Doyle, The Canonical Foundations, p. 72.

82 Cfr. T. Rincon-Perez, "Commentary on canons 1063-1072, Pastoral Care and the Prerequisites for the Celebration of Marriage", in: A. Marzoa – J. Miras – R. Rodriguez-Ocana, eds; Exegetical Commentary on the Code of Canon Law, Vol. III/2, Montreal 2004, p. 1110.

83 J.H.Provost, Marriage Preparation in the New Code: Canon 1063 and the Novus Habitus Mentis, pp.174 – 175. Cfr. J.H.Provost – K. Walf, eds; Studies in Canon Law Presented to P.J.M. Huizing, Leuven 1991, p.173-192.

reasonable to say that the canons on marriage preparation in the 1917 Code were models with regard to preparation for marriage.

2. Marriage Preparation in Some Papal and Ecclesial Documents before the II. Vatican Council

2.1. Introduction

In part one of chapter one, we studied some canons that treated marriage preparation in the 1917 Code. From what we have seen, the 1917 Code, no doubt exerted an unmistakable influence on the canonical doctrine of marriage preparation. It is pertinent to say that from these canons we have seen some factors pertaining to contemporary marriage which renders tactful and prudent marriage preparation all the more urgent today. In this part two of chapter one, we shall now study the importance which some of the papal and ecclesial documents of the Magisterium placed on a sound understanding of marriage preparation before the Second Vatican Council with a view to examining some elements of the response of the church to this very need.

2.2. Encyclical letter Casti Connubii of Pius XI

The most important and far-reaching contribution of the pontificate of Pius XI in the field of marriage preparation was his encyclical letter, Casti Connubii of 31st December 1930[84]. In this encyclical, the Pope was dismayed by the assaults which seemed to be launched against marriage from every side. While writing to the bishops of the world, he says: "We observe- and you, venerable Brethren, cannot but share our sorrow as you also observe – that there are many unmindful of this divine work of renewal, who are totally ignorant of the sanctity of marriage, who imprudently deny, who even allow themselves to be led by principles of a modern and perverse ethical doctrine to repudiate it with scorn…. These pernicious errors and degraded morals have begun to spread even among the faithful"[85]. In the first section of the encyclical Pius reminded us that if marriage was an objec-

84 Cfr. Pius XI, Encyclical Casti Connubii, „ De Matrimonio Christiano spectatis praesentibus familiae et societatis condicionibus, necessitatibus, erroribus vitis," 31.12. 1930: AAS 22 (1930) pp.539-592.

85 Cfr. Pius XI, Casti Connubii, p.581.

tive reality created by God it should be able to be defined. He did this by turning to St. Augustine's De bono Coniugii, which speaks of the marital goods of the offspring, fidelity and sacrament. There Augustine explained the three goods that make marriage good in its entirety: "By fidelity the spouses take care not to have intercourse with partners outside. By the good of offspring the spouses take care to accept children lovingly.... By the sacramentum they take care not to separate the marriage, and if dismissed, not to remarry even for the sake of children"[86].

The Pope, in the second section of his encyclical outlines some evils threatening marriage and sins against conjugal life which sounds remarkably contemporary. These errors he mentioned as contraception, abortion, sterilization, adultery, trial marriages, cohabitation, mixed marriages and divorce. In the third section of the encyclical the Pope sets out some remedies to restore Christian marriage to its proper dignity. These remedies consist of a return to the divine plan and submission to the divine will. He goes on to talk about the instruction which parish priests must give to the faithful in view of marriage. It is in this context that the Pope goes on to deal specifically with marriage preparation, after which he outlines the necessity for public aid to support marriage and the relationship between church and states."Wherefore, those who have the care of the State and of the public good cannot neglect the needs of married people and their families, without bringing great harm upon the State and on the common welfare. Hence, in making the laws and in disposing of public funds they must do their utmost to relieve the needs of the poor, considering such a task as one of the most important of their administrative duties"[87].

Pius XI in outlining the remedies necessary to restore the Christian marriage to its proper state speaks about the two stages of marriage preparation – remote and proximate. He adds: "All these things however,...depend in large measure on the due preparation remote and proximate, of the parties for marriage"[88]. He opines that remote preparation for marriage should begin in childhood as to inculcate and foster Christian values. He goes on to say that, "for it cannot be denied that the basis of a happy wedlock, and the ruin of an unhappy one, is prepared and set in the souls of boys and girls during the period of childhood and adolescence."[89] This entails, in other words, that a long program of marriage preparation and family life should be inculcated in the religions education and pastoral activities of children and the youth so as to deepen their Christian faith and religious knowledge and most importantly, to teach them the meaning of

86 T.Mackin, Marriage in the Catholic Church: The Marital Sacrament, New Jersey 1989, p.526.

87 Pius XI, Casti Connubii, p.587.

88 Pius XI, Casti Connubii, p.584. " Haec omnia, magnam partem a debita coniugum pendent tam remota quam proxima ad matrimonium praeparatione".

89 Ibid.

Christian marriage and its demands. This process of remote preparation must continue so that "those who are about to enter on married life, approach that state well disposed and well prepared, so that they will be able, as far as they can, to help each other in sustaining the vicissitudes of life, and yet more in attending to their eternal salvation and in forming the inner man unto the fullness of the age of Christ."[90] It is pertinent to know that in both phases the long term program of marriage preparation recommended here by Pope Pius XI, is in accordance with the general instruction of canon 1018 of 1917 Code. This is in view of the fact that the general instruction is to be addressed not only to those intending to marry but to the whole parish.

Pius XI moves on to admonish those wanting to enter married life and also those whose duty is to educate the Christian youth to take cognizance of the future by preparing what is good in marriage preparation. He urges: " Consequently, both those who are now thinking of entering upon this sacred married state, as well as those who have the charge of educating Christian youth, should, with due regard to the future, prepare that which is good, obviate that which is bad."[91] The Pope recalls what he stated in his encyclical on education, Divini illus Magistri of December 1929: "The inclinations of the will, if they are bad, must be repressed from childhood, but such as are good must be fostered, and the mind, particularly of children, should be imbued with doctrines which begin with God, while the heart should be strengthened with the aid of divine grace, in the absence of which, no one can curb evil desires, nor can his discipline and formation be brought to complete perfection by the church. For Christ has provided her with heavenly doctrines and divine sacraments, that he might make her an effectual teacher of men."[92]

Turning to proximate preparation of a good married life belongs to the care of choosing a rightful partner for the future happiness of the would-be couple. The Pope urges those about to enter into married life to "keep before their minds the thought first of God and of true religion of Christ, then of themselves, of their partner, of the children to come, as also of human and civil society, for which wedlock is a fountain head."[93] In making this choice the prospective partners should pray diligently for divine help so that their choice will be in accordance

90 Pius XI, Casti Connubii, p.585.

91 Ibid.

92 Pius XI, Enc. Divini illius Magistri, 31 Dec. 1929, p.69. "A pueritia igitur voluntatis inclinations, si pravae, cohibendae, sin autem bonae, promovendae sunt, ac praesertim puerorum mens imbuatur doctrinas a Deo profectis et animus divinae gratiae auxiliis roboretur oportet, quae si defuerint, nec suis quisque moderari cupiditatibus poterit neque ad absolutionem perfectionemque disciplina atque informatio ab Ecclesia adduci, quam ideo Christus caelestibus doctrinis ac divinis Sacramentis instruxit, ut efficax omnium hominum esset magistra."

93 Pius XI, Casti Connubii, p.586.

with Christian prudence, not indeed led by the blind and unrestrained impulse of lust, nor by any quest for wealth, rather by an upright love and a sincere affection for the would-be partner.[94] Pius admonishes the prospective partners not to omit to ask the prudent advice of their parents as regards choice of partner, whose mature knowledge, experience and judgment may safeguard them from making a disastrous choice.[95]

The encyclical Casti Connubii of Pope Pius XI made a remarkable and positive contribution on the importance of marriage preparation in the church for prospective partners, those already married and the entire people of God. Although the encyclical did not spell out in detail the form this marriage preparation is to take, it lays the basic foundation for future developments.[96]

2.3. Some Allocutions of Pius XII on Marriage Preparation

The contribution of Pope Pius XII to the theology of marriage with regard to marriage preparation is well-known. Though he never wrote any encyclical specifically addressed to marriage preparation, he is to be regarded as the Pope who spoke more extensively concerning marriage and the family than any other Pope in modern era.[97] Pius XII is to be noted for having reaffirmed the traditionally accepted values of marriage in the wake of a swiftly changing world. His doctrine on marriages is to be gleaned from the various discourses and radio-messages he pronounced.[98]

The Pope was chiefly concerned with upholding the sacredness and validity of marriage in the wake of secularism. During his first three years of pontificate, from 1939 through 1942, he discoursed most frequently to newly wedded couples who had come to his audiences in the Vatican Palace.[99] One of the most helpful

94 Cfr. Ibid.

95 Cfr. Ibid.

96 Cfr. T.J. Groarke, Marriage Preparation in Contemporary Theology and Canon Law, Rome 1991, p.33.

97 For a fuller understanding of his writings and various discourses on marriage and family, see: M.J. Byrnes, Papal Teachings: Marriage, transl; New York 1963, pp.301-526.

98 Cfr. C.J. Scicluna, The Essential Definition of Marriage according to the 1917 and 1983 Codes of Canon Law: An Exegetical and Comparative Study, Lanham 1995, p.93.

99 Cfr.M.J. Byrnes, Papal Teachings, pp.301-526. Quotes from such discourses delivered on May 24, 1939; July 12, 1939; Nov.8,1939; Dec.6, 1939; Jan.17, 1940; June 26, 1940; Oct. 23,1940; Jan.15,1941; Jan.29,1941; March 5,1941; March 19,1941; August13,1941; August 20,1941; March 18,1942; April 22,1942; and April 29,1942. After the last date, Pius' discourses were directed to various national and international associations and to such Catholic groups as the Roman Rota and the Clergy of Rome. For more details on this, see: T. Mackin, The Marital Sacrament, New Jersey 1989, p.573.

of Pius discourse is found in his address to newly wedded couples of October 21, 1942, where he took up the problem of fidelity, probably because World War II had by then forced prolonged separation of spouses. He sees the crisis in fidelity as a crisis in the history of love in a marriage: "Then, for true and faithful love, begins the struggle, and at the same time the challenge. No longer blind, it becomes perfectly aware of these failings, but accepts them with affectionate patience, conscious as it is of its own defects ... Love is ready to perceive what brings together and unites, and not what divides .... Far from showing off its own superiority, it tactfully asks advice of the partner, letting it be known that if it has something to give, it is also happy to receive. It is in this way, obviously, that a spiritual union is established in the wedded couple, an intellectual and practical cooperation which makes them both to rise toward the truth in which there is unity, toward the supreme truth, toward God. What else is this fidelity but the mutual gift of their mind"[100].

From all his discourses and radio- messages on marriage we see the Pope's clarion call to prepare the young people adequately for marriage. In his address to the Women of Catholic Action in October 1941, he observes that many young people enter into married life without thinking of the duties and obligations involved in bringing up children. To this, he adds that a serious and proper preparation for marriage is the key to a successful marriage.[101] The Pope's extensive discourse on marriage preparation is to be found in his address to the pupils and teachers of schools for adult education in March 1953. He says that the foundation of society and the basis for education and of every culture is the family. He goes on to highlights the obligations of parents with regard to marriage preparation: "The mother should possess:(a) the elementary knowledge necessary for the government of a family; (b) the art of keeping the house in order; (c) the ability to deal with statements of accounts; (d) useful ideas about bringing up children; (e) above all, enough understanding of the rules of pedagogy to profit by the experience of others. The father, should possess the ability: (a) to procure for his wife and children the financial means indispensable for life; (b) to be the enlightened and wise guide, strong in his personal experience; (c) to be a prudent counselor in matters regarding the important laws of life; (d) to be a counselor with regard to the intimate aspirations and difficulties of those dear to him, to whom he gives spiritual support, more important and needful than material protection"[102]. It should be

100 M.Chinigo, eds; The Pope Speaks: The Teachings of Pope Pius XII, New York 1957, p.24.

101 Cfr. Pius XII, Address to the Women of Catholic Action, 26 October,1941. Cfr. Discorsie Radiomessaggi di sua Santita Pio XII, III, Milano 1942, pp.223-235. Cfr. F.Gavin, Pastoral Care in Marriage Preparation, p.43.

102 Pius XII, Address to the Students and Teachers of Schools for adult Education, March 19,1953. Cfr. Discorsi e Radiomessaggi di Sua Santita Pio XII , XV, Tipografia Poliglotta Vaticana 1954,pp.7-17.Cfr. F.Gavin, Pastoral Care in Marriage Preparation, pp.44-45.

noted here that these obligations of parents with regard to marriage preparation was seen by Pope Pius XI from the point of view of the European culture. In Igbo culture the content of the obligation is a family as well as extended family affairs. The attention here is not only on the process of giving birth to children but more especially on the relationship of the mother and her husband to the children. The relationship of love between the wife and the husband should be extended to the children and this should guide their relationship to other members of the extended family. In most cases, this obligation in Igbo culture is formulated to concentrate on the wife as the centerpiece of the family. The motive is that if the wife should know her duty and that of her husband then it would be easy for her to make amendment to her husbands' reactions to the daily activities in the family.

Pope Pius XII was also particularly concerned with the education of young people most especially in matters relating to chastity. It was on this matter that he spoke of the importance of education in preparing for marriage. In 1944, he underlined the importance of bringing young people up in matters pertaining to chastity and affections as a prelude to marriage.[103] The young people must also be educated in obedience and respect towards authority. This is easy when people recognize themselves as subjects of God and his commandments.[104] Pius XII views the education of young people as part of the remote preparation for marriage. It is by forming the young people as responsible and mature persons from an early age that they will be ready for the duties and obligations that marriage brings when the time comes. The Pope enjoins Pastors of souls to guide and instruct with the light of faith a whole generation so that the two "cancers" of the family – the abuse of matrimony and the violation of marital fidelity – may be healed.[105]

The Pope in his allocution to the Italian Association of Catholic Teachers reiterated the clarion call of preparing young people for marriage: "It is essential that adult education should not lose sight of the importance of preparing young people for marriage and of the serious obligations of fathers and mothers of families …. Adult education should enlighten them (young adults) on the needs and difficulties of marriage and the setting up of a home"[106].

Pope Pius XII had on previous instances talked about the role of parents in educating their children on matters concerning Christian doctrine and married

103 Cfr.Pius XII, Allocution to the Parish Priests and Lenten Preachers of Rome, February 22, 1944. Cfr. M.J.Brynes, Papal Teachings, p.356.

104 Cfr. Pius XII, Address to the Women of Italian Catholic Action Women's Apostolate, 24 July ,1949, p.162. Cfr. F.Gavin, Pastoral Care in Marriage Preparation, p.46.

105 Cfr. Pius XII, Allocution to the Parish Priests and Lenten Preachers of Rome, February 22, 1944. Cfr. M.J. Byrnes, transl; Papal Teachings, p.447.

106 Pius XII, Allocution to the Italian Association of Catholic Teachers, March 19, 1953. Cfr. M.J. Byrnes, transl; Papal Teachings, p.356.

life. He insisted that the family is the first school which cannot be substituted, a school that covers all types of education right from the cradle.[107] He opined that the education of their children is both a right and an obligation on the part of parents given to them directly by God.[108] By so doing, parents educate through their own words and example in this way, instructing their children in Christian doctrine and its daily practice.[109]

From the on-going we can confidently say that Pope Pius XII saw marriage preparation as a collaboration between the entire ecclesial community which involves pastors of souls, parents, lay faithful and those whose duty is to educate young people.

2.4. John XXIII's Address to the Prelates of the Sacred Rota

Pope John XXIII was a decisive driving force behind the convocation and preparation of Vatican Council II. Although the Pope did not go into details like the other two Popes already discoursed with regard to marriage preparation, he nevertheless recognized the importance of marriage preparation and catechesis to the young people intending to marry and to the engaged couples. In his 1961 allocution to the Rota, John XXIII declared: "What is needed then, what is irreplaceable, is a vast work of catechesis and of illustration of the truth: by the traditional means which the church has at her disposal, and also by those which are made available by the press and the new audio – visual techniques. New forms must be sought to bring this teaching to those who are contemplating marriage in particular to young people and to engaged couples"[110]. The Pope's encyclical, Pacem in Terris of 1963 includes a short comment on the family as origin of human society, which arises from marriage freely contracted.[111]

107 Cfr. Pius XII, Radio Message addressed to the fourth Congress of Catholic Education of Central America, p.207. Cfr. Discorsi e Radiomessaggi di Sua Santita Pio XII, XIII, Tipografia Poliglotta Vaticana 1952, pp.203-209.

108 Cfr. Pius XII, Radio Message for the Day of the Family, p.19. Cfr. Discorsi e Radiomessaggi di Sua Santita Pio XII, XIV, Tipografia Poliglotta Vaticana 1953, pp.17-27.

109 Cfr. Pius XII, Address to the Men of Catholic Action of Portugal, p.363. Cfr. Discorsi e Radiomessaggi di Sua Santita Pio XII, XII, Tipografia Poliglotta Vaticana 1951, pp.359-365. See also, Address to Jeunesse Independante Catholique Feminine of Belgium, p.196. Cfr. Discorsi e Radiomessaggi di Sua Santita Pio XII, XVII, Tipografia Poliglotta Vaticana 1956, pp.193-197.

110 John XXIII, Address to the Prelates of the Sacred Rota, E anzitutto, nelle incertezze dottrinali, December 13, 1961. Cfr. M.J.Byrnes, transl; Papal Teachings, p.538.

111 Cfr. John XXIII, Enc; Pacem in Terris, April 11, 1963, AAS 55, p.261. " Quod ad familiam attinet, quae in matrimonio nititur, libere nimirum contracto, uno, indissolubili, ipsam existi-

2.5. Conclusion

From what we have seen so far, marriage preparation in some Papal and Ecclesial documents of the church before the II. Vatican Council cannot be overemphasized. Pope Pius XI's encyclical, Casti Connubii brings out in a very systematic manner the church's teaching on marriage.[112] The Pope sees marriage preparation as both remote and proximate, spanning a lifetime yet with particular emphasis on the period immediately prior to the marriage. He views it as involving the collaboration of bishops, priests and laity.

In the nineteen years of his pontificate, Pope Pius XII frequently drew attention to the family and the pastoral care problems involved in marriage preparation. He was of the opinion that people had to be prepared from an early age for marriage and the responsibilities it involved. He made this known in many of his allocutions addressed to various associations and people at various times.

Although Pope John XXIII did not speak extensively on marriage preparation as the two other Popes previously discoursed, he nevertheless recognized the importance of marriage preparation in his address to the Prelates of the Sacred Rota.

3. Innovation of Marriage Preparation in the II. Vatican Council and the following Period

3.1. Introduction

Having examined marriage preparation in some Papal documents of the church, our main thrust here is on the innovation of marriage preparation in the Second Vatican Council and in the 1980 Synod of Bishops about the family. It is appropriate to say that the Second Vatican Council teachings on marriage marked a watershed in the church's understanding of marriage.[113] Although the Council Fathers in their discussions made little emphasis on marriage preparation, the document nevertheless greatly influenced how the church subsequently approached mar-

---

mari opus est tamquam humane societatis primum et natural semen." Cfr. C.J. Scicluna, The Essential Definition of Marriage, p.96.

112 The church's teaching on marriage had already been outlined by Pope Leo XIII in his encyclical Arcanum Divinae Sapientiae of 1880. Cfr. Leo XIII, Enc; Arcanum Divinae Sapientiae, 10 February 1880.

113 Cfr. J.P. Beal, "Marriage: Commentary on Historical Overview and canons 1055-1062", in: J.P. Beal – J.A. Coriden – T.J. Green, ed; New Commentary on the Code of Canon Law, Bangalore 2004, 1239.

riage preparation programs. Also the 1980 Synod of Bishops made remarkable achievements on marriage preparation programs in their various proposals during the Synod. These achievements of Second Vatican Council and that of the 1980 Synod of Bishops on marriage preparation are what we are to examine now.

3.2. Marriage Preparation in Gaudium et Spes

The Second Vatican Council dedicated paragraphs 47 to 52 of its Pastoral Constitution on the Church in the Modern World to marriage.[114] It is pertinent to know that the Dogmatic Constitution on the Church, Lumen Gentium, provided the context for the Council's approach to Christian marriage most especially with regard to the vocation of the married couple to a life of holiness.[115]

The personalist approach was made manifest in the Council's treatment of marriage as an intimate sharing (communitas) of married life and love and in its respected emphasis on the importance of conjugal love.[116] It views marriage as a freely chosen, lifelong bonding of equal partners. In this regard, it places love rather than law as the norm for the relationship and the growing spiritual life of the husband and wife as a goal which is also important as the biological life of children. The document sees the spouse's love as the very essence of the relationship, a love that is God-given, expressed in and securing its stability by the conjugal act of mutual self-giving.[117] The Council Fathers, however, did not deny that marriage is also an institution rooted in the creation itself of human persons as man and woman.[118]

The Council in referring indirectly to marriage preparation observes: "It is imperative to give suitable and timely instruction to young people, above all in the heart of their own families, about the dignity of married love, its role and

114 Cfr.Ibid.

115 Cfr. LG, 11 § 2. "Finally, in virtue of the sacrament of Matrimony by which they signify and share (cf.Eph.5:32) the mystery of the unity and faithful love between Christ and the Church, Christian married couples help one another to attain holiness in their married life and in the rearing of their children." LG,41 §1."The forms and tasks of life are many but holiness is one – that sanctity which is cultivated by all who act under God's Spirit and, obeying the Father's voice and adoring God the Father in spirit and in truth, follow Christ, poor, humble and cross-bearing, that they may deserve to be partakers of his glory."

116 Cfr. GS, 48.

117 Cfr. T.A.Salzman,et al; eds; Marriage in the Catholic Tradition: Scripture, Tradition, and Experience, New York 2004, p.113.

118 Cfr. P.J.Huizing, Council Implication of the Conception of Marriage in the Concilar Constitution Gaudium et Spes, in: W.P.Roberts, Commitment to Partnership, eds; New York 1987, pp.106-107.

its exercise; in this way they will be able to engage in honorable courtship and enter upon marriage of their own"[119]. Here lies the difference between 1917 Code and that of 1983 Code with regard to the instruction of young people and those intending to marry. While canon 1018 of 1917 Code admonishes parish priest not to fail to instruct the people on the sacrament of matrimony and its impediments as his sole obligation, canon 1063 of 1983 Code on the other hand asserts that it is not only the prerogatives of pastors of souls to instruct young people on marriage but also the obligations of all the ecclesial community to do so. This ecclesial community includes the family, for it is here that children first learn the objects of relationship which will later influence their own married lives. We shall return to this in chapter three when treating marriage preparation in canon 1063 of 1983 Code. In paragraph 52 the Council underscores the importance of education for children and highlights the responsibility of the parents and teachers in preparing young people to married state. "The education of children should be such that when they grow up they will be able to follow their vocation … and choose their state of life with full consciousness of responsibility; and if they marry they should be capable of setting up a family in favorable moral, social and economic circumstances. It is the duty of parents and teachers to guide young people with prudent advice in the establishment of a family; their interest should make young people listen to them eagerly; and they should beware of exercising any undue influence, directly or indirectly, to force them into marriage or compel them in their choice of partner"[120]. It is not without reason, in the thoughts of Häring, that the Council Fathers dealt with well-timed marriage instruction in pre-marital and marital chastity in the perspective of conjugal love. In this way, education in sexual matters receives its definitive orientation from the mystery of love.[121]

There is a clarion call on all who exercise an influence in the community and in social groups to dedicate themselves effectively and diligently to the welfare of marriage and the family. Particular attention is given to civil authority to consider it a sacred duty to recognize the true nature of marriage and the family, to protect and foster them and at the same time, safeguarding them in public morality and to promote domestic prosperity.[122]

Having outlined the duty of all who exercise influence in the community and that of Civil authority to promote the values of marriage and the family, attention is drawn to experts in other sciences, most especially biology, medicine, social science and psychology to be of help to the welfare of marriage and the family

119 GS, 49 §3.

120 GS, 52 §1.

121 Cfr. B.Häring, Fostering the Nobilty of Marriage and the Family, in: H.Vorgrimler, eds; Commentary on the Documents of Vatican II, V, New York 1969, p.239.

122 Cfr. GS, 52 §2.

and the peace of mind of people, if by pooling their findings they try to clarify thoroughly the different conditions favoring the proper regulation of births.[123]

The Council Fathers made emphasis on the proper and adequate training of priests so as to be able to offer adequate pastoral services to marriage and to deal with family matters and to nurture the vocation of married people in their married and family life by the preaching of the word of God, by liturgy, and other spiritual assistance. They should also sympathetically and patiently strengthen them in their difficulties and comfort them in charity with a view to the formation of truly radiant families.[124] Various organizations such as family associations are encouraged to champion their programs of instruction and activities to strengthen young people, and especially young married couples, and to prepare them for family, social and apostolic life.[125]

The Council finally, urges married couples to witness through the living out of their conjugal love, so that in the footsteps of Christ, the principle of life, they will bear witness by their faithful love in the joys and sacrifices of their calling, to that mystery of love which the Lord revealed to the world by his death and resurrection.[126]

In the decree on the apostolate of lay people (Apostolicam Actuositatem), there is a list of a number of works of family apostolate, such as assisting engaged couples to make adequate preparation for marriage, supporting of adolescents with advice and help, taking part in the teaching of Catechism and supporting married couples and families in difficult situations.[127]

Judging from what we have seen and discoursed about marriage preparation, Vatican II Council does not provide a comprehensive program for marriage preparation, rather, it stresses the necessity of it and encourages its implementation. It is of utmost importance to note here that the task of its implementation as regards marriage preparation is not confined completely to the pastors of souls. The responsibility of the family is strongly emphasized and the contribution of the laities and experts in other fields of human endeavour and of married couples is highly recommended. We shall see these encouragement and implementation well-developed in the 1980 Synod of Bishops and Pope John Paul's Apostolic Exhortation, Familiaris Consortio.

123 Cfr. GS, 52 §4.
124 Cfr. GS, 52 §5.
125 Cfr. GS, 52 §6.
126 Cfr. GS, 52 § 7.
127 Cfr. AA, 11 §2.

3.3. The 1980 Synod of Bishops about the Family

3.3.1. The Synod

The 1980 Synod of Bishops started its work on 26 September and was officially ended on 25 October 1980. There were changes in the exact formation of the theme for the 1980 Synod under three Popes – starting from De Familia in Mundo Hodierno of Paul VI to De Familia Christiana of John Paul I and finally to De Muneribus Familiae Christianae in Mundo Hodierno of John Paul II.[128] It is worthy of note that the changes in the titles suggested also a shift of emphasis.[129] Although the 1980 Synod was devoted to the role of the Christian Family in the Modern World, it was also compelled to deal with the pastoral issues about the lived experience of marriage. What was important to John Paul II in reshaping this title was not to bring forth the questions of conjugal morality; rather his greatest concern was in the valorization of the Christian family as ecclesia domestica in order to lend credence for the future of Christianity and to compensate for the languishing of other supportive structures.[130]

The first preparatory document for the 1980 Synod was the Lineamenta of March 1979 sent to all the Episcopal Conferences of Bishops to seek their comments and approval in preparation for the Synod. The official Latin text contains 50 pages, including 4 pages of index. It consists of three parts namely: situating the problems, doctrinal issues, and the roles of the Christian family.[131] It is worthy of note that some of the Bishops in their response to the Lineamenta circulated to them underscored the necessity of marriage preparation. The Bishops from Indonesia spoke of the obligation of the church toward families with regard to marriage preparation, giving greater attention to cultivating husband-wife relationships, and helping parents. They demanded credible approach to the pastoral care of the family.[132] The Indian Bishops in their response stressed the need

128 The precise formulation of the theme for the 1980 Synod of Bishops went through meaningful changes under three Popes. The first was during the meeting of the Concilium of the Secretariate for the Synod on May 18, 1978, it was suggested that the theme should be "The Family in the Modern World". The proposal was accepted by Pope Paul VI. On September 26, 1978, another proposal with the theme "The Christian Family" was approved by Pope John Paul I two days before his sudden death. On 17 November 1978, the suggested theme was once again approved by Pope John Paul II and was renamed with the title "The Role of the Christian Family in the Modern World". Cfr. J.Grootaers – J.A.Selling, The 1980 Synod of Bishops on the Role of the Family, Leuven 1983, p.70.

129 Cfr. F.Gavin, Op. Cit; p.56.

130 Cfr. J.Grooters – J.A.Selling, Op. Cit; pp.70-72.

131 Cfr. J.Grooters – J.A.Selling, Op. Cit; p.203.

132 Cfr. J.Grooters – J.A.Selling, Op. Cit; p.39

for marriage education. They emphasized the importance of family catechesis, through which family members share their faith experiences and seek renewal; and the preparation for family life, including sex education in the context of a communication of the right values. In addition to pre-marital preparation, follow-up programs for newly-wedded are also a crying need of the time.[133]

The Brazilian Bishops started in their own response by analyzing the major factors which determine the types of family present in their country. In response to these factors, they propose that the family should exercise those functions which seem to be truly essential, namely, formation, affectivity, social, consciousness, catechesis and family liturgy.[134] The Bishops applauded family pastoral initiatives which have contributed to the Christian formation of families. These activities include various types of movements of married couples and courses of preparation for engaged couples, parents and godparents. They were of the opinion that these initiatives should be integrated among themselves and with organic pastoral planning so that all dimensions of pastoral life may be enriched by them and them, in turn enriched. They recommended that the church ought to purify marriage celebrations and adopt other means so that religious weddings be more than simple social events. The Church should also organize "Family Counseling Centers", with the cooperation of universities and other centers of high learning. Also care should be given to the remote and immediate preparation for marriage, the celebration itself, pastoral care for special situations, and an adequate preparation for priests and married couples who work in family movements.[135]

The second document produced by the Secretariat of the Synod, Instrumentum Laboris, was issued on 16 June, 1980 as a working paper in preparation for the Synod. This document was presented only as a vehicle for meditation and discussion during the Synod itself as a Schema for the outcome of that meeting.[136] After a brief introduction (1-8), the document has three parts: The situation of the family in the world (9-26); God's plan for the contemporary family (27-50); and pastoral problems (51-95). The document itself has five paragraphs dedicated to marriage preparation (86-90).

Paragraph 86 under the general heading of Pastoral Problems of sub-heading VI, emphasis the importance of preparing young people for marriage. It adds that in some parts of the world preparing young people for marriage is taken care of by families themselves who, through antique customs and traditions, teach the

---

133 Cfr. J.Grooters – J.A.Selling, Op. Cit; p.41.

134 Cfr.J.Grooters – J.A.Selling, Op. Cit; p .51.

135 Cfr.J.Grooters – J.A.Selling, Op.Cit; pp.55-56.

136 Cfr. Synod Secretariat, De muneribus familiae christianae in mundo hodierno: Instrumentum laboris ad usum sodalium Quinti Coetus Generalis, Typis Polyglottis Vaticanis 1980, pp.258-270.

young people about the social and religious aspects of marriage and family life itself. It suggests that experience teaches that those young people who are well prepared for family life have a better chance of living a healthier family life.[137]

The document (IL) argues that in the catechesis which young people receive from early infancy, they should be introduced to the doctrine of the church on the family, and by so doing they come to understand marriage as a sacramental state. They must be encouraged to appreciate sexuality as a part of every person, and the need to respect each woman's dignity as potential mother and each man as a potential father. Above all, they need to be helped to understand the value of virginity before marriage.[138]

Paragraph 88 speaks of remote preparation of engaged couples. This remote preparation takes place in different regions in accordance with local custom and practice. Preparation must include a complete formation of family life, dealing with the day to day problems of marriage. Engaged couples must be encouraged to get involved in family apostolate and be supported by the fraternity and co-operation of other families.[139] The document linked immediate preparation for marriage to the pre-nuptial inquiry. It suggests that this pre-nuptial inquiry needs to be looked at with the help of experts in different disciplines in order to help couples avoid the danger of instability in marriage.[140]

3.3.2. The Different Phases

The 1980 Synod of Bishops at its beginning was divided into three major phases. The first phase was dedicated to interventions by the bishops meeting in general sessions. The second phase was divided into eleven small language groups to discuss the principle themes which had been put forth. The final phase was the gathering together and voting on the fourty-three propositions presented to the Pope at the end of the Synod which was based upon the results of their discussions. We shall now analyse them one by one as they relate to marriage preparation.

3.3.2.1. Phase One: The General Exchange of Ideas

The first phase of the Synod started with the preliminary report of the Relator, Cardinal Ratzinger. This report was based upon the second document produced by the Secretariat of the Synod, Instrumentum Laboris, and upon the reactions which had been received from the different Episcopal Conferences. In line with

137 Cfr.F.Gavin, Pastoral Care in Marriage Preparation, p.57.

138 Cfr. Ibid.

139 Cfr. F.Gavin, Pastoral Care in Marriage Preparation, p.58.

140 Cfr. Ibid.

the three-fold style of the preparatory documents – description of the situation, the family in the place of God, and pastoral problems, he enumerated the principle aspects of the general theme to which the Synod was to address itself.[141] There were ten plenary sessions held during which the vast majority of speeches were delivered which culminated to no less than 162 oral interventions delivered out of 216 participants. There were also 51 written interventions which were handed over to the Secretariat.[142]

During this first phase, marriage preparation was not one of the major themes discussed, but the issue, did surface on a number of occasions. Analysis of the interventions in terms of marriage preparation shows some bishops describing the situation in their own countries and moving further to highlight the need for adequate marriage preparation in their different dioceses. For example, Mons. Pietro Fiordelli, bishop of Prato in Italy, highlighted the different stages of marriage preparation and emphasized that the church needs to see the period of engagement as a special time of grace for the engaged couples and for the church community who must accompany them. He commended what he described as the courageous decision of the Italian bishops to introduce the idea that couples who intend to marry engage in at least a year-long journey of faith, an aspect of catechumenate in preparation for the sacrament.[143]

The Relatio Altera of the Relator, Cardinal Ratzinger, in his report at the end of the first phase, came to be a pivotal point of the Synod.[144] The Relatio Altera included also an eight page appendix of sound and coherent questions about the six themes which were later handed over to the discussion groups to pave way for the second phase to go forth with a certain amount of consideration of the many views which had been expressed from so many bishops. The Relator made two direct references to marriage preparation. Under the heading dealing with the relation between faith and the sacrament (including marginal believers or baptized non-believers), he spoke about the great attention that was given to the call for mandatory marriage preparation programs.[145] Also under the heading dealing with pastoral action for the family, Cardinal Ratzinger touched upon the need for graduated phases of preparation for marriage, pastoral action in helping marital life, the useful role of small communities including the parish or associations. He

141 Cfr. J.Grooters – J.A. Selling, Op.cit; p.73.

142 Cfr. J.Grooters – J.A.Selling, Op.cit; p.74.

143 Cfr. Conferenza Episcopale Italiana, Evangelizzazione e Sacramenti, n.87. Cfr. F.Gavin, Pastoral Care in Marriage Preparation, pp.59-60.

144 Cfr. Synodus Episcoporum 1980 Relatio Altera (16 pages with an 8 page appendix comprising of detailed proposals intended for the circuli minores). A condensed version of the text came into light in Osservatore Romano,120 (8 October,1980), French edition, p.31,(21 October,1980). Cfr. J.Grooters – J.A.Selling, Op.cit; p.106.

145 Cfr. J.Grooters – J.A.Selling, Op.cit; p.109.

also noted with eagerness the desire of many bishops to draw up a directory for the pastoral care of the family.[146]

3.3.2.2. Phase Two: The Small Discussion Groups

The second phase of the Synod lasted the whole of the week from 6 to 10 October during which the eleven circuli minors discussed the principle themes which had been put forward.[147] During this second phase, some discussion groups spoke about the need for a gradual approach to marriage preparation with different stages, and the basic role that the family and the whole church community should play. One of the English language groups led by Cardinal Hume emphasized that greater importance needs to be placed upon marriage preparation through the education and catechesis of young persons, in the long term, and in the short term for those who are about to marry.[148] The group felt that the local ordinary has the right to determine the length and method of immediate preparation, but at the same time, it is equally recommendable that the Episcopal conference should come to a common agreement about this program. Special attention should also be devoted to the admission of those with little understanding or a minimal practice of the faith.[149]

Another group that discussed about preparation for marriage was the Latin group led by Cardinal Felici. The first two points of this group underscored the importance of marriage preparation and the maintenance for validity of marriage. Though, they supported the idea that marriage preparation should be promoted, but emphasized that it should not be looked upon as a conditio sine qua non to getting married.[150] There was also an emphasis in some groups on the importance of faith preparation for marriage, with a number of groups calling for a catechumenate-type preparation and a special catechesis for engaged couples.[151]

The Synod second phase was very important in the sense that it gave each person an opportunity to share and discuss his ideas and concerns with other people.[152] It is pertinent to say that a clear knowledge of idea can be obtained of the quality and richness of the small groups discussions which had taken place from the summary presentations of these groups.

146 Cfr. J.Grooters – J.A.Selling, Op.cit; p.110.
147 Cfr. J.Grooters – J.A.Selling, Op.cit; pp.74-75.
148 Cfr. J.Grooters – J.A.Selling, Op.cit; p.116.
149 Cfr. Ibid.
150 Cfr. J.Grooters – J.A.Selling, Op.Cit; p.121.
151 Cfr. G.Caprile, IL Sinodo die Vescovi, pp.358-369. Cfr. F.Gavin, Pastoral Care in Marriage Preparation, p.61.
152 Cfr. J.T.Reese, Reporting on the Synod, America 1980, pp.407-411.

3.3.2.3. Phase Three: Resolutions on Marriage Preparation

The final phase of the Synod was described as the most difficult and secretive phase with the task of drawing up a number of propositions to be presented to Pope John Paul II, and a message to be issued by the Synod to the families of the world. A vote was conducted by the bishops to ascertain how many propositions to be presented to the Pope, and a final text of 43 propositions were approved.[153] From the 43 propositions approved, proposition 35 dealt directly to marriage preparation. This proposition emphasizes the importance of marriage preparation as a way of preventing marital failure and irregular situations. This implies a certain level of faith and maturity to assume the responsibilities of Christian marriage.[154] The proposition invokes the idea of gradualism in the growth of faith. The sacramentality of marriage is something that demands a living and ever deepening faith and the preparatory process is referred to as "a faith journey like the catechumenate"[155].The proposition suggests that proximate preparation should help the couple make their sexual relationship an important aspect of their sacramental union.[156] In this very proposition, positive approach to sexuality is brought to light and it goes beyond Gaudium et Spes in appreciation of the sexual aspect of the human relationship and relates it directly to sacramental union. J.Grooters and J.A.Selling point out that this is the first time the church in its official teaching has valued marital sexuality in such a completely positive way that it can be called sacramental. In other words, they view it as a clear endorsement of the "personalist" reading of Gaudium et Spes.[157]

The Episcopal Conferences and Dioceses are encouraged by the proposition to draw up norms with regard to the minimal requirements, content, methods and duration of marriage preparation programs. These programs should also consider the "aspectus doctrinales sacramenti, pedagogici, iuridici, atque medicinales, while stressing that the preparation of engaged couples should not be completely intellectual but also an experiential one, "sed debet esse vitalis, ita ut ipsi nupturientes inserantur ad modum cuiusdam catechumenatus in communitate ecclesiali in paroeciis"[158]. The proposition ends with an insistence that preparation programs should be planned in such a way that it will not be an obstacle to engaged couples in preparing their marriage.

153 Cfr. J.Grooters – J.A.Selling, Op.Cit; pp.76-80.

154 Cfr. T.J.Groarke, Marriage Preparation in Contemporary Theology and Canon Law, p.43.

155 Synod Secretariat, The Synod Propositions, n.3, p.165. Cfr. F.Gavin,Pastoral Care in Marriage Preparation, p.62. For a fuller understanding of "a faith journey like the catechumenate", Cfr. J.Grooters – J.A.Selling, Op.cit;p.28.

156 Cfr. Synod Secretariat, The Synod Propositions, n.3, p.165.

157 Cfr. J.Grooters – J.A.Selling, The 1980 Synod, p.288.

158 Cfr. Synod Secretariat, The Synod Propositions, n.3, p.165.

3.3.3. Conclusion

The decision of the Second Vatican Council to deal with marriage first among the urgent problems facing the world during that particular time showed a desire on the part of the Council Fathers to address the relationship between the church and the world. The vision of marriage and the family for which the church intends couples to prepare adequately is outlined in a number of paragraphs of the Pastoral Constitution, Gaudium et Spes.[159] In this document the Council Fathers made a clarion call on all people to promote marriage and the family, stressing in particular the need for involvement and collaboration in this task. To be noted is the Council's view that Priests be properly trained for this ministry.

The 1980 Synod of Bishops treated as its central theme, the role of the Christian family in the modern world. The Synod talked about the need for a gradual approach to marriage preparation with different stages, and the basic role that the family and the ecclesial community needed to play. There was emphasis on the importance of a faith preparation for marriage and a special catechesis for engaged couples. The final phase of the Synod drew a list of propositions which was later presented to Pope John Paul II. The proposition among other things stresses the importance of marriage preparation programs, seeing the family and the local community as vital parts of them. At the end of the Synod, a message to Christian families in the modern world was issued. This message sees family ministry as being very important to the church, and part of that family ministry is preparation for marriage.

3.4. Apostolic Exhortation Familiaris Consortio of Pope John Paul II

From the propositions of 1980 Synod of Bishops, Pope John Paul II on 15 December 1981 published his Apostolic Exhortation on the Family, Familiaris Consortio, on the role of the Christian family in the modern world.[160] The Apostolic Exhortation of Pope John Paul II is an extremely long document with the official Latin text comprising of 111 pages and consisting of more than 30,000 words.

159 Cfr. GS, 46-52.

160 The official text, found in AAS 74 (1982) pp.81-191, issues the date for the apostolic exhortation as 22 November, 1981. But the text was not released to the world until 15 December,1981. Cfr. J.Grooters – J.A.Selling, The 1980 Synod of Bishops, p.303. All references to Familiaris Consortio employed here are taken from the English translation: Apostolic Exhortation of John Paul II: The Role of the Christian Family in thr Modern World, Bosten 2007.

The Pope in this very document relied heavily upon the propositions made by the Bishops of the 1980 Synod and very often took over their ideas directly. The ideas he took over point to continuity with the Synod. A study reveals that no less than one half of the text of the propositions appears in Familiaris Consortio in one form or the other.[161]

The document is made up of 86 sections, excluding the introduction (1-3) and the conclusion (86). It is generally divided into four major chapters: Chapter one: Bright sports and shadows for the family today (4-10), chapter two: The plan of God for marriage and the family (11-16), chapter three: The role of the Christian family (17-64), chapter four: Pastoral care of the family (65-85). However, our concern here lies in the final chapter of the document which addresses the pastoral care of the family. This chapter has four sections: stages, structures, agents and finally pastoral care of the family in difficult situations.

Under the stages of pastoral care of the family, the Pope emphasizes that the pastoral intervention of the church in support of the family is a matter of urgency. He goes further to say that every effort should be made to strengthen and develop pastoral care for the family, which as a matter of fact, should be treated as a real matter of priority, in the certainty that future evangelization depends largely on the domestic church.[162] The Pope urges that the church's pastoral action must be progressive so as to follow the family, accompanying it step by step in the different stages of its formation and development.[163]

In preparation for marriage, the Pope contends that what is of utmost importance in our times is preparing young people for marriage and family life. He observes that in some countries it is still the duty of the families themselves in accordance with ancient customs to ensure the passing on to young people of the values concerning married and family life, and they do this through a gradual process of education or initiation.[164] The Pope insists that the changes that have taken place within almost all modern societies demand that the society and the church should take active part in the effort of properly preparing young people for their future responsibilities.[165] John Paul II opines that experience teaches that young people who have been well prepared for the challenges of family life generally succeed better than others. The church in view of this, must therefore promote better and more intensive programs of marriage preparation, so as to eliminate as far as possible the difficulties that many married couples find them-

161 Cfr. J.Grooters – J.A.Selling, The 1980 Synod of Bishops, p.304.

162 Cfr. FC, 65 §3.

163 Cfr. FC, 65 §5.

164 Cfr. FC, 66 §1.

165 Cfr. Ibid.

selves into, and more so in order to favour positively the establishing and maturity of successful marriages.[166]

The Pope views marriage preparation as a gradual and continuous process. It includes three main stages: remote, proximate and immediate.[167] Remote preparation begins in early childhood in the family. It is in that wise family training that children discover themselves as being endowed with a rich and complex psychology and with a particular personality with its own strengths and weaknesses.[168] It is during this period that children learn authentic human values, social relationships, formation of character for the control and right use of one's inclinations, the manner of regarding and meeting people of opposite sex, solid spiritual and catechetical formation that will show that marriage is a true vocation and mission, and so on.[169]

The second stage, proximate preparation, subsequently and gradually builds upon the base of remote preparation, and it is seen as a catechumenate process involving a more specific preparation for the sacraments.[170] The Pope proposes that the renewed catechesis of young people and others preparing for Christian marriage is absolutely necessary so that the sacrament may be celebrated and lived with the right moral and spiritual dispositions.[171] He urges that the religious formation of young people be integrated at the proper time in accordance with the various concrete requirements, including preparation for life as a couple. The preparation will further present marriage as an interpersonal relationship between a man and a woman that has to be continually developed.[172] Other areas which should be taken into consideration at this stage include: the nature of conjugal sexuality, responsible parenthood, essential medical and biological knowledge, well-ordered family life, such as stable work, sufficient financial resources, sensible administration and notions of housekeeping.[173] The Pope stresses finally that preparation for the family apostolate, fraternal solidarity and collaboration with other families, for active membership in groups, associations, movements and undertakings put together for the human and Christian benefit of the family must not be overlooked.[174]

From the on-going, it suffices to say that the proximate preparation for marriage refers to a period in life before there is a serious intention of marriage. Al-

166 Cfr. FC, 66 §1&2.
167 Cfr. FC, 66 §3.
168 Cfr. FC, 66 §4.
169 Cfr. FC, Ibid.
170 Cfr. FC, 66 §5.
171 Cfr. Ibid.
172 Cfr. Ibid.
173 Cfr. Ibid.
174 Cfr. FC, 66 §6.

though not stated specifically, it appears that this stage of preparation is intended to be provided during teenage years.[175]

The immediate preparation which is the third stage of marriage preparation should take place in the Months and Weeks immediately preceding the wedding. The purpose is to give a new meaning, content and form to premarital investigation required by canon law.[176] This preparation in every case is necessary and urgently needed for those engaged couples who show weaknesses and difficulties in Christian doctrine and practice.[177] John Paul refers to this stage as a journey of faith similar to the catechumenate. It is intended to lead the couple to a deeper understanding of the mystery of Christ and the church, as well as the meaning of grace and the responsibility of Christian marriage. It is also meant to assist engaged couples take an active and conscious part in the rites of the marriage liturgy.[178]

The Pope urges the Christian family and the entire ecclesial community to take active part in the different phases of marriage preparation which have been emphasized only in their broad outlines. He goes on to encourage the Episcopal Conferences to take steps to issue a directory for the Pastoral Care of the Family.[179] Stressing further, he says: "In this they should lay down, in the first place,

---

175 Cfr. G.Kelly, Pastoral Care of the Family: Stages, Structures, Agents, and Situations, Art; 65-72, in: M.J.Wrenn, eds; Pope John Paul II and the family, Chicago 1983, p.220. See also, M.Miller, The Post-Synodal Apostolic Exhortations of John Paul II, Huntington 1998, p.131; J.S.Hamlon, A Call to Families: Study Guide and Commentary for Familiaris Consortio, Minnesota 1984, p.68.

176 Cfr. FC, 66 §7.

177 Cfr. Ibid.

178 Cfr. FC, 66 §7-8.

179 The issue of setting up guidelines for preparation programs is also found in proposition number 35 of 1980 Synod of Bishops. However, a thorough and careful look at the two statements shows a clear difference between the two. Examining Familiaris Consortio, we find the statement that "it is to be hoped that the Episcopal Conferences, just as they are concerned with appropriate initiatives to help engaged couples to be more aware of the seriousness of their choice and also to help pastors of souls to make sure of the couples' proper dispositions, so they will also take steps to see that there is issued a Directory for the Pastoral Care of the Family". While proposition number 35 states that "Bishops conferences and dioceses should established the minimal content, duration and methods for these programs." Here, it is to be noted that the Bishops were referring only to immediate marriage preparation. In proposition number 43, the Synod had called for each Episcopal Conference to draw up its own " Pastoral Directory" which should explain church teaching and discipline in a manner suitable for varying circumstances." It is to be observed that the suggestion made by the Synod is here in Familiaris Consortio given only veiled reference by the use of the term " Directory for Pastoral Care" and speaking from context, it is highly restricted to marriage preparation programs. It is not to be seen anywhere, where Familiaris Consortio credits the notion of independent " Directories" dealing with all of " Church Teaching and Discipline". For a fuller understanding of this, see: J.Grooters – J.A.Selling, The 1980 Synod of Bishops, p.321; see also. Synod Secretariat, The Synod Propositions, n.3, p.165; F.Gavin, Pastoral Care in Marriage Preparation, p.68.

the minimal content, duration and method of the "Preparation Courses", balancing the different aspects-doctrinal, pedagogical, legal and medical – concerning marriage, and structuring them in such a way that those preparing for marriage will not only receive an intellectual training, but will also feel a desire to enter actively into the ecclesial community"[180].The Pope, while affirming the importance and obligation of the immediate preparation for marriage if dispensations from it are not easily given, insists that such preparation must always be set forth and practice in such a way that its omission cannot be an impediment to the celebration of marriage.[181]

Speaking in article 67, he turns his attention to the actual celebration of marriage itself. He declares that the "Christian marriage normally requires a liturgical celebration expressing in social and community form the essentially ecclesial and sacramental nature of the conjugal covenant between baptized persons"[182]. The celebration of marriage with its sanctifying power must in its entirety be valid, worthy and fruitful. It should be simple and dignified in accordance with the norms of the competent authorities of the church.[183] Also in conformity with the norms issued by the Apostolic See, elements proper to each culture may be included provided that such elements have nothing that is not in harmony with Christian faith and morality.[184]

The liturgical celebration should include "a proclamation of the word of God and a profession of faith on the part of the community of believers"[185]. John Paul II asserts that pastoral commitment is made known through the intelligent and careful preparation of the liturgy of the word and education to faith of those participating in the celebration, most especially the couple to be married.[186] The liturgical celebration of marriage as a sacramental act of the church should involve the active participation of all the Christian faithful present, including the bride and the bridegroom, the priest, the witnesses, the relatives, the friends and other members of the faithful.[187]

Pope John Paul II shifts his attention to the celebration of marriage of non-believing baptized persons. He opines that the faith of the engaged couples asking the church for marriage can exist in different degrees and as a matter of fact, it is the full responsibility of pastors to bring about a rediscovery of this faith and to

180 FC, 66 §9.
181 Cfr. FC, 66 §10.
182 FC, 67 §1.
183 Cfr. FC, 67 §2.
184 Cfr. Ibid.
185 FC, 67 §3.
186 Cfr. Ibid.
187 Cfr. FC, 67 §4.

nourish it and bring it to maturity.[188] He reminds pastors of souls to be cautious of the reason why the church admits to the celebration of marriage those who are imperfectly disposed.[189] The Pope while admitting that in some places, marriage for some engaged couples are both for religious and social motives asserts that, "marriage, in fact, is not an event that concerns only the persons actually getting married. By its very nature it is also a social matter, committing the couple being married in the eyes of the society. And its celebration has always been an occasion of rejoicing that brings together families and friends. It therefore goes without saying that social as well as personal motives enter into the request to be married in church"[190]. The Pope was not willing to marshal out further criteria that would concern the level of faith of those wanting to marry as it would involve grave risks. He nevertheless, warns that amidst all effort, when engaged couples manifest that they reject explicitly and formally what the church intends to do when the marriage of baptized persons is celebrated, they cannot be admitted to the sacrament. In so doing it is the engaged couple themselves and not the church that is placing the obstacle.[191]

The Pope in article 69 provides words of encouragement for all families to work together and help in pastoral care throughout married life. It is the commitment of all the members of the local ecclesial community to provide assistance and support for all families most especially young married couples to help them to adjust to the responsibilities of their vocation and mission. This is very important in the sense that a sizeable proportion of all divorces take place in the first five years of marriage, or the situations which precipitate divorce later on often have their roots in the early in the early years of marriage.[192] The Pope urges young married couples to learn how to accept willingly and make good use of the discreet, tactful and generous help offered by other couples that already have more experience of married and family life.[193] The ecclesial community must also help the young couple to "harmonize the intimacy of home life with the gener-

188 The question of faith here is a naturalistic idea of a marital sacramentality, which is based on the plan of God. Since it is God's intention for marriage to take place, anyone approaching it has an attitude of profound obedience to the will of God. The only requirement is the decision to commit by their irrevocable conjugal consent their whole lives in indissoluble love and unconditional fidelity. Therefore, any couple who commit themselves to marriage in a lasting way have a valid union because it is de facto in conformity with the will of God. If they are baptized Christians, there is also a valid sacrament. For more detail, see: J.Grooters – J.A.Selling, The 1980 Synod of Bishops, p.322; Familiaris Consortio, 68 §3.

189 Cfr. FC, 68 §2.

190 FC, 68 §4.

191 Cfr. FC, 68 §7.

192 Cfr. J.Dominian, Make or Break, London 1984, pp. 19-20.

193 Cfr. FC, 69 §2.

ous shared work of building up the church and society"[194].The entire community should assist new families to accept their children and love them as a gift from the Lord.[195]

3.5. Conclusion

The Apostolic Exhortation, Familiaris Consortio of Pope John Paul II sees marriage preparation as a gradual and continuous process which includes three stages of remote, proximate and immediate preparations and the need for on-going pastoral care after marriage. It is presented as catechumenate type experience with the faith aspect being emphasized.

4. Conclusion of Chapter One

We can sum up marriage preparation in the Code of 1917 as preparation that was chiefly concerned with ensuring the validity and licitness of marriage celebration. Through this means the institution of marriage was protected from what would have made it to be celebrated invalidly and illicitly[196]. The parish priest responsibility was to instruct the parties adequately about the sanctity of marriage, their mutual obligations, and the duties of parents to their children. His duty was also to admonish the parties in making a remorse confession of their sins prior to the celebration of marriage and to receive the sacrament of the Eucharist[197].

The general instruction and the particular instruction were both concerned that everything was done in ensuring that marriage was not entered into invalidly and illicitly and that the sanctity and dignity of the marriage sacrament were intact.

We examined also marriage preparation in some papal and ecclesial documents of the church prior to the Second Vatican Council. Pope Pius XI's encyclical, Casti Connubii saw marriage preparation as both remote and proximate that endures through a lifetime. He regarded this preparation as a collaborative effort of bishops, priests and the lay people. He made emphasis on the spiritual and moral formation of the persons marrying as well as the removal of material obstacles on the way of those who want to enter into marriage[198].

194 69 §3.
195 Cfr. Ibid.
196 Cfr. J.H. Provost, Marriage Preparation in the New Code, p.174.
197 Cfr. C. 1033 CIC/1917.
198 Cfr. F. Gavin, Pastoral Care in Marriage Preparation, p.42.

Pope Pius XII believed that the success of marriage preparation is based on early preparation. Marriage preparation should begin right from infancy and the responsibility that goes with it. The whole ecclesial community should take active part in the marriage preparation process. He enumerated the functions of parents, priests and those involved in educating the youth as that of active participation in preparing the young people for marriage.

John XXIII spoke about the Christian teaching on the importance of marriage and called for a continuous and persuasive instruction of the faithful to all levels of the society. He stressed very profoundly on reaching the young people who are about entering marriage in order to pay serious attention on religious instruction in preparing for marriage[199].

Gaudium et Spes stressed that the family is the foundation of society, and that all those who exert influence over communities and social groups should at the same time promote marriage and family life[200]. It made mention of the young people being timely and suitably instructed "about the dignity of married love, its role and its exercise; in this way they will be able to engage in honourable courtship and enter upon marriage of their own"[201].

The 1980 Synod of Bishops emphasised on the need for a gradual approach to marriage preparation with various stages. The Synod also stressed the crucial role the family and the ecclesial community are to play with regard to marriage preparation process. Great concern was given to faith preparation for marriage and a special catechesis for prospective couples.

Pope John Paul II's apostolic exhortation, Familiaris Consortio insisted repeatedly on the urgent need for marriage preparation. This was emphasised in the three stages of remote, proximate, and immediate preparation for marriage. The exhortation also laid emphasis on the need for adequate pastoral care for married couples after marriage.

199 Cfr. John XXIII, Address to the Sacred Roman Rota, October 25, 1960, AAS 52 (1969), p.900.
200 Cfr. GS, 52 §2.
201 GS, 49 §3.

Chapter Two: The Canonical Understanding of Marriage

1. The Understanding of Marriage in the Code of 1983

1.1. Introduction

The first chapter of our work has been an attempt at describing and analyzing marriage preparation in the 1917 Code of Canon Law and also in some ecclesial documents and encyclicals of some Popes. The aim of the second chapter is to delve into the 1983 Code of Canon Law which directly concerns marriage, searching for the canonical understanding of marriage, its nature, ends, properties, and matrimonial consent, and the fundamental principles underlying the more important texts.

It is not within the scope of the present study to discuss everything about the nature, ends, essential properties of marriage, and marital consent. We limit ourselves to, and focus our attention to those essential things which bear direct light on the Igbo traditional marriage system and what should be transmitted into it.

1.2. The Nature of Christian Marriage

Canon 1055 §1 of 1983 Code says, "the marriage covenant, by which a man and a woman establish between themselves a partnership of their whole life, and which of its own nature is ordered to the good of the spouses and the procreation and education of offspring, has between the baptized, been raised by Christ the Lord to the dignity of a sacrament"[202].

The 1983 Code, unlike the 1917 Code, which offered no definition of marriage, starts its treatment of marriage with a definition. This definition is taken almost literally from the constitution Gaudium et Spes of the Second Vatican Council: "The intimate partnership of life and the love which constitutes the married state has been established by the Creator and endowed by him with its own proper laws; it is rooted in the contract of partners, ie, in their irrevocable consent....

202 C. 1055 §1 CIC/1983: "Matrimoniale foedus, quo vir et mulier inter se totius vitae consortium constituent, indole sua naturali ad bonum coniugum atque ad prolis generationem et educationem ordinatum, a Christo Domino ad sacramenti dignitatem inter baptizatos evectum est".

By its very nature the institution of marriage and married love is ordered to the procreation and education of offspring, and it is in them that it finds its crowning glory"[203]. The Catechism of the Catholic Church reiterates this teaching of the Council Fathers in its exposition of the sacrament of matrimony[204].

It is to be noted that a union between a man and a woman to be a marriage must correspond to this definition. Thus marriage as a human and natural institution was desired by God with a view both to the mutual help that the spouses must give to one another in love and fidelity, and to the formation and upbringing that must be given to the children born from this union. It is this natural and human institution that Christ the Lord has raised to sacramental dignity for the baptised[205]. It has been unanimously observed that while the identity of marriage was obviously left intact, the Council Fathers showed an express intention of adapting the language, the perspective and the degree of depth and richness of the terminology used to regard the conjugal covenant[206].

This very text of canon 1055 of 1983 Code contains the following canonical-doctrinal principles with regard to marriage: the object of the covenant is a special partnership which comprises the whole life of the partners, marriage between baptized persons is a sacrament, the sign of the sacrament is a covenant of a special nature, and the purpose of this partnership of life is the common good of the spouses who enter into this special companionship for the procreation and education of children[207]. Although the language of ends has disappeared in this definition, but the reality to which those technical terms had always referred remains and is now expressed in the more personalist language of partnership community of life and love, and marital goods.

The complementarity of the sexes is essential to marriage as it is being established between a man and a woman. There is such widespread confusion today about the nature of marriage that some would wish to extend a legal 'right' to marry to two persons of the same sex. The very nature of marriage makes such a proposition impossible. God as the author of marriage inscribed the vocation to

203 GS, 48 §1.

204 Cfr. CCC, no; 1601.

205 J. Listl – et al; Handbuch des katholischen Kirchenrechts, Regensburg 1983, p.730. "Jesus Christus, der die Ehe zum Sakrament erhoben hat verweist ausdrücklich auf die Schöpfungsordnung (Mk 10,6-9; Mt 19,4-6). Die Ehe dient nicht nur dem Wohl der in der Ehe verbundenen Personen, sondern auch der menschlichen Gesellschaft insgesamt. Insofern hat sie auch an der geschichtlichen Existenz menschlicher Gesellschaft teil und ist sie in bestimmten Grenzen rechtlicher Regelung durch menschliche Gesetzgeber zugänglich".

206 Cfr. J.I. Banares, "Commentary on canons 1055-1062", Pastoral Care and the Prerequisites for the Celebration of Marriage", in: A. Marzoa – J. Miras – R. Rodriguez-Ocana, ed; Exegetical Commentary on the Code of Canon Law, Vol.111/2, Montreal 2004, p. 1050.

207 Cfr. I. Gramunt – et al; Canons and Commentaries on Marriage, Minnesota 1987, p. 3.

marriage in our very being by creating them as male and female. Marriage in this sense is governed by his laws, faithfully transmitted by his bride, the Church. For marriage to be what it is, must therefore conform to these laws. Man, therefore, is not free to change the meaning and purposes of marriage. Marriage follows from the very nature of humankind which is divided into two mutually attracting and complementary sexes from whose stable and sexual union of life, the prolongation and education of the human race is assured or achieved[208].

The 1983 Code of Canon Law looks beyond the 1917 Code's contractual notion of marriage[209]. The matrimonial foedus comprises the "consortium totius vitae" which consists of more elements than the procreation and education of offspring. This intimate partnership of the whole life is made up of various goods and ends which we are going to see when dealing with the partnership of the whole life. The hierarchical structure of ends in the 1917 Code is no longer followed, but procreation and education of children remain the crowning glory of marriage[210].

1.2.1. Matrimonium in fieri and Matrimonium in facto esse

Canonists in their discussions on marriage have classically distinguished between marriage at the moment of its celebration (matrimonium in fieri) and marriage as a state of life (matrimonium in facto esse). By matrimonium in fieri is meant the entry into married state through the marriage covenant. The essence of matrimonium in fieri is the marriage consent. By matrimonium in facto esse is meant the married state itself, the essence of which is the marriage bond, precisely, the new relationship which exists between the married partners. This has been described as the source of all their rights and duties as husband and wife[211].

As it was the case in the Code of 1917, canonical doctrine has from its earliest days approximated, by way of analogy, matrimonium in fieri to the juridical concept of "contractus", thus underlying the principle of consensuality upon which it is based[212]. Nevertheless, the use of the term contractus, while offering the obvious advantage of underlining consent, could present some notable disad-

208 Cfr. G. M. Okoye, The Sacredness of Marriage and Family Life, Enugu 1973, p. 11.

209 Cfr. C. 1012 §1 CIC/1917.

210 Cfr. GS, 50 §1: "Marriage and married love are by nature ordered to the procreation and education of children. Indeed children are the supreme gift of marriage and greatly contribute to the good of the parents themselves. God himself said; "It is not good that man should be alone" (Gen.2:18), and "from the beginning he made them male and female" (Mt.19:4); wishing to associate them in a special way with his own creative work, God blessed man and woman with the words: "Be fruitful and multiply" (Gen.1:28)".

211 Cfr. G. Taylor – E. de Bekker, Parish Priests and Marriage Cases, Bangalore 2005, p. 3.

212 Cfr. F. X. Wernz – P. Vidal, Ius Canonicum, Rome 1946, pp. 42-45, in: A. Marzoa – et al; op.cit; p. 1050.

vantages, especially given the loss of the original meaning of contract in canon law, and given the ever more technical and aseptic development of contractualist doctrines in civil systems of law[213]. According to one author, "while the classical theologians acknowledged that conjugal society (matrimonium in facto esse) was the true object of marital consent, by the late nineteenth century, the Western canonical tendency to equate the right to sexual intercourse with the essence of marriage had become firmly established"[214].

However, the term used by the Vatican II Council Fathers in describing the matrimonium in fieri is "foedus": foedus coniugii or foedus coniugale and foedus inter personas indissolubile[215]. The Conciliar document Gaudium et Spes 48 §1 refers to the moment or event which causes marriage as an irrevocabilis consensus personalis and as an actus humanus "quo coniuges sese mutuo tradunt atque accipiunt[216]. The term used also by the Council to describe the matrimoniun in facto esse is "status matrimonialis" and more technically as an institutum ordinatione divina firmum" and "vinculum sacrum"[217]. This underscores the fact that Gaudium et Spes insistently stresses the societal aspect of marriage.

In another development, Canon 1055 §1 follows the lead of Vatican II in identifying matrimonium in fieri as "the marriage covenant" and matrimonium in facto esse as the "partnership of the whole of life which is ordered by its nature to the well-being of the spouses and the procreation and education of children, resulting from the conjugal covenant. This partnership of the whole of life which is ordered

213 Cfr. J.I. Banares, "Commentary on canons 1055-1062", p. 1050.

214 P. Connolly, The Nature of Marriage as Proposed in the Codex Iuris Canonici and in the Codex Canonum Ecclesiarum Orientalium, Ottawa 1995, p.22, in: J. McAreavey, The Canon Law of Marriage and the Family, Dublin 1999, p.20. " The view of that period is reflected in Wernz's statement in Ius Matrimoniale 1, 23-4, as translated by Connolly: "If marriage is considered in fieri; it can be defined: the lawful and undivided contract of man and woman for the generation and education of offspring… if, on the other hand, marriage is taken as the bond or permanent society, as in common speech and even that proper to theologians and canonists, it is defined as the lawful and undivided union of man and wife for the generation and education of offspring, or more briefly: the undivided conjugal or marital society of man and wife".

215 Cfr. GS, 48 §1; 50 §3.

216 Here, the Council Fathers affirms the consensual nature of the initial moment of marriage. The "foedus coniugalis" gives rise to the community of life and love (48 §1); to the "institutum" and "vinculum" (48 §1). Through this conjugal covenant the man and woman are not two but one flesh (as, 48 §1 quoting Mt. 19,6). What is ambiguous is the term "sese". It cannot mean a total surrender of all human faculties annihilating the spouses' sense of autonomy fundamental to human dignity. If on the other hand it means a handing-over of those faculties essentially linked to the nature of marriage, then the term explains only little on its own, and certainly does not refer to the formal object of the irrevocable personal consent which causes marriage between the two spouses. For a fuller understanding of this, see: C.J. Scicluna, The Essential Definition of Marriage According to the 1917 and 1983 Codes of Canon Law, Lanham 1995, p.167.

217 GS 47 §3; 48 §1.

to the good of the spouses and the procreation and upbringing of children is a much richer understanding of matrimonium in facto esse[218] than "the legitimate, perpetual and exclusive union of a man and a woman, arising from their mutual consent, ordered to the procreation and education of offspring"[219] of the Code of 1917. Beal urges that, "greater maturity and interpersonal integration are required to established a partnership of the whole of life than to give and accept the right to the body for acts suitable for the procreation of children"[220].

1.2.2. Marriage as Covenant and Contract

The 1983 Code of Canon Law follows the Conciliar document, Gaudium et Spes in describing marriage as a "covenant" and not as a "contract" according to the 1917 Code. However, the word "covenant" appeared only three times in the revised Code[221], while the word "contract" was used often by the same revised Code[222].

During the period of the revision of the marriage legislation there were suggestions to change the word "contractus" to "foedus" in the canons, but for the fact that marriage covenant can be instituted in no other way for the baptized than through a contract – even though it is a contract of a special kind, the "contractus" was retained[223].

The terminology used by Gaudium et Spes in describing marriage as a "covenant" has led some canonists and theologians to a claim whether there was any substantial difference between "foedus" and "contractus". Kasper, in speaking in favour of covenant, opines that: "The most suitable word, then, would seem to be the biblical term "covenant", which was also used in the documents of the Second

218 Cfr. J.P. Beal, "Commentary on canons 1055-1062", p.1241.

219 F. Capello, De Matrimonio, Rome: Marietti 1961, n. 3; P. Gasparri, De Matrimonio, Vatican city 1932, n. 8; F.X. Wernz – p. Vidal, Ius Canonicum, Rome 1946, 5: n. 21, in: J.P. Beal – et al; op.cit; p. 1241.

220 Ibid.

221 Cfr. Cc. 1055 §1; 1057 §2; and 1063, 4° CIC/1983.

222 Cfr. Cc. 1055 §2; 1058; 1068; 1073; 1085 §2; 1086 §3; 1089; 1094; 1095; 1096 §1; 1097 §2; 1098; 1101 §2; 1102 §1; 1104 §1; 1105 §1, 1° and §4; 1106; 1108 §1 and 2; 1114; 1115; 1117; 1120; 1121 §2 and 3; 1122 §1 and 2; 1125 §3; 1125, 3°; 1127 §1; 1143 §1; 1144 §1; 1146; 1147; 1148 §2; 1149; 1160; 1684 §1; and 1706 CIC/1983. Cfr. J.P. Beal, "Commentary on canons 1055-1062", p. 1241.

223 In reaction to an objection made by a Code Commision member in using both `"covenant" and "contract" in what culminated to canon 1055 of 1983 Code, the Secretariat asserts: "The terms "contract" and "covenant" are used in one and the same sense, indeed deliberately, so that it may be more clearly evident that the matrimonial covenant concerning which Gaudium et Spes speaks can be constituted for the baptized in no other way than through a contract, even if it is sue generis". Cfr. Comm. 15 (1983) p. 222. See also, J.P. Beal, "Commentary on canons 1055-1062", p. 1241; T. Pazhayampallil, Pastoral Guide, Vol. 2, New Delhi 2004, p. 779.

Vatican Council. "Covenant" expresses the personal character of the consensus better than "contract" or "institution". It is also able to express the legitimate intention of marriage, its public character, which is contained in the term "contract". A covenant is both private and public. The covenant of marriage is not simply a personal bond or covenant of love – it is also a public and legal matter concerning the whole community of believers"[224]. Häring supports the use of covenant in his commentary on Gaudium et Spes[225]. Beal and Kaiser accept both terms but lean towards the use of covenant[226]. Örsy does not see any qualitative differ-

224 W. Kasper, Theology of Christian Marriage, New York 1993, p. 41.

225 Cfr. B. Häring, Pastoral Konstitution über die Kirche: Das Zweite Vatikanische Konzil, Dokumente und Kommentare, Freiburg 1968, III, pp. 423-447, here p. 429. „Die von Gott so verfaßte Lebens – und Liebesgemeinschaft wird mit ‚Ehebund' bezeichnet. Er wird begründet durch „das unwiderrufliche Ja – Wort der Personen". Die Einführung des Wortes „contractus" (Vertrag) statt „foedus" (Bund) wurde trotz der wiederholten, zahlreichen Petitionen und gegen 190 modi von der Kommission entschieden abgelehnt. Die Gründe sind viele. Das Verhältnis zwischen Christus und der Kirche ist nicht ein „Vertrag", sondern ein „Bund". Geschichtlich war der „Ehevertrag" oft etwas, das von den beiden Familien ausgehandelt wurde und nicht selten das eigentliche Wesen des Ehebundes, die Liebesgemeinschaft, verdunkelte. Der moderne Mensch versteht unter Vertrag eine Abmachung, deren Inhalt die Vertragsschließenden selbst bestimmen können, wie sie auch bei gegenseitiger Zustimmung später wieder zurücktreten können. Gegenstand eines Vertrages sind Sachen, Leistungen und Rechte, die so oder so von der Person losgelöst werden können".

226 J.P. Beal, "Commentary on canons 1055-1062". "Covenant has at least three advantages over "contract" as the prime analogue for articulating an understanding of marriage. (1) A first advantage of the covenant analogy is that a covenant is a sacred reality, while a contract is essentially secure in nature. Although 'covenant' was also used for ordinary pacts between peoples, it was the term chosen by the Old Testament authors to designate the faithful and loving relationship between Yahweh and his chosen people Israel. Especially in the prophetic books, this covenant was analogized to a marriage between Yahweh and his people, a marriage to which his people were chronically unfaithful. This covenantal analogy was carried forward in the New Testament, especially in Ephesians 5 where the love of husband and wife is called a "great foreshadowing" that refers to Christ and the Church". (2) The covenantal model of marriage, while recognizing that marriage gives rise to mutual rights and obligations, places primary emphasis on the mutual personal commitment of the spouses. Thus, it is an apt vehicle for expressing the personalist dimension of marriage… The contractual model, on the other hand, emphasizes the rights and obligations that are mutually given and accepted to constitute marriage and when these rights and obligations are overemphasized, the personal dimension of marriage can be altogether or at least largely lost from view. (3) As a result of its emphasis on rights and obligations the contractual model has encouraged a narrow focus on matrimonium in fieri, the moment when marriage and its attendant rights and obligations come into being. This primary focus has historically led to a relative neglect of matrimonium in facto esse, the spouses living out of their marital commitment amid the vicissitudes of daily life…. The covenantal model with its emphasis on the personal aspects of marriage can foster more balanced attention to both dimensions of marriage and more effective pastoral support to the married"; M. Kaiser, Grundfragen des kirchlichen Eherechts, Regensburg 1980, p. 537. "Das zweite Vatikanische Konzil hat mit Bedacht den geläufigen Ausdruck "contractus" (Vertrag) durch „foe-

ence between "contractus" and "foedus" but appreciates the biblical nuances of "foedus" when he remarks: "It follows that, as long as we are moving in the world of law, it matters little if the exchange of promises is called contract or covenant, provided it is understood that the word refers to the external sign through which the mystery is identified. If we are moving in the world of theological reflection, either term, contract or covenant, is inadequate to describe the reality. Yet overall, covenant has the advantage of having scriptural roots; hence, it may well become the standard term for marriage in both the world of law and that of theology"[227].

From the foregoing, while marriage involves a legal contract, it should be subordinate to the spousal covenant which provides a stronger, more sacred framework for marriage. A covenant goes beyond the minimum rights and responsibilities guaranteed by a contract. A covenant calls the spouses to share in the free total, faithful, and fruitful love of God. For it, is God who, in the marriage of his own covenant with his people, joins the spouses in a more binding and sacred way than any human contract. The term "foedus" signifies bond, mutual commitment, partnership, communion, love. It deals with people and it is a relationship of mutual trust and fidelity[228].

Marriage is a covenant of love. It is a privilege from which flow many blessings and responsibilities. Vatican II extols this covenantal love in the following words: "Married love is an eminently human love because it is an affection between two persons rooted in the will and it embraces the good of the whole person; it can enrich the sentiments of the spirit and their physical expression with a unique dignity and ennoble them as the special elements and signs of the friendship proper to marriage. The Lord, wishing to bestow special gifts of grace and divine love on it, has restored, perfected, and elevated it. A love like that, bringing together the human and the divine, leads the partners to a free and mutual giving of self, experienced in tenderness and action, and permeates their whole lives…"[229].

The marital covenant of love is considered unique in that it means a union of the spouses on all levels of human activity. Pope John Paul I provided a beautiful picture of this covenant of love when he writes: "I consider that matrimonial love is the gift of oneself to the other partner; but it is so intimate and noble, so loyal and trusting, that on the one hand it claims everything, while on the other hand it

---

dus" (Bund) ersetzt (GS Art. 48 Abs.1) und damit betont, dass die Ehe mehr und etwas anderes ist als ein bloßes Rechtsverhältnis zwichen Mann und Frau. Der Begriff „Bund" läßt die Ehe in einem umfassenden Sinn zwar auch als rechtliche, aber darüber hinaus auch und vor allem als personale und religiöse Wirklichkeit sichtbar werden".

227 L. Örsy, Christian Marriage: Doctrine and Law. Glossae on Canons 1012-1015, The Jurist 40 1980, p. 292.

228 Cfr. T. Pazhayampallil, op.cit; p. 773.

229 GS, 49 §1; See also, Pius XI, Casti Connubii, pp. 547-548; Denz. 2232 (3707).

excludes everything"[230]. The marital love of the Spouses is naturally so exclusive that it can only exist in absolute honesty if both partners give themselves to one another wholly and unconditionally.

Marriage is also a contract because the two persons give consent to the covenant of love. At the heart of the covenant or contract, there is the exchange of consent which is the efficient cause of marriage, for the consent of the party causes marriage. Contract is not a pact like other pacts, the terms of which perhaps can be determined by the contracting parties. It is a pact of a special kind[231]. It is a unique kind of contract because of the nature of marriage, its purpose, its benefits and the means of realizing its ends and purposes. The legal idea of marriage involving the mutual exchange of rights and duties towards each partner is both expanded and enriched, when we view marriage as rooted in the conjugal covenant of irrevocable personal consent[232].

Be that as it may, there is no doubt that the word "foedus" sums up the personalistic view of marriage expressed in the Conciliar document Gaudium et Spes and in the canons of the 1983 Code of Canon Law on marriage. This very word stresses the theological and juridical content of marriage in biblical language and provides a universal basis for doctrine and jurisprudence to channel their research and study on the personalistic, religious, and socio-cultural dimensions of marriage[233]. Hence, the matrimonial covenant calls spouses to share in the free, total, faithful and fruitful love of God.

But the Church's recent claim on marriage as a covenant does not exclude the concept that marriage is also a contract. Though a covenant goes beyond the rights and obligations guaranteed by some contracts and provide a stronger, more sacred framework for marriage, but the canon law of the church still purposely makes use of both terms to describe the nature of marriage[234].

1.2.3. Marriage as a Sacrament

Paragraph one of canon 1055 which we quoted earlier on in this very chapter restates also the teaching of the church, defined as an article of the faith, that marriage covenant of two baptized persons has been raised by Christ to the dignity

230 Art. A Life at the Service of the Church, Gift of Charity and Simplicity, in: 'L' Osservatore Romano', eds. English, 31 August, 1978, p. 2.

231 Cfr. T. Pazhayampallil, op.cit. p.779.

232 Cfr. A.O. Gbuji, The Pastoral Care of Marriage and Family Life in Nigeria, Ibadan 2006, p.30.

233 Cfr. A. Mendonca, art. The Theological and Juridical Aspects of Marriage, in: Studia Canonica, 22 (1988), pp. 283-284.

234 Cfr. C. West, Good News about Sex and Marriage: Answers to Your Honest Questions about Catholic Teaching, Cincinnati 2004, p.47.

of a sacrament. In this way Christ himself determined that matrimonial "foedus" of two Christians should not only be lived in accordance to the pattern of his own union with his church, that is, the unbreakable and unconditional fidelity, but also be an image of it, for which the marriage bond has a natural aptitude, and be a participation in it, in order words, a new realization of Christ's union with and love for his church. Hence, the spouses are in a position to participate in a new way in the flow of grace which animates it and which in this way directs them to find in their marriage their way to union with God[235].

The sacrament of marriage is therefore, the blessing of divine love to spouses which expresses the indissoluble union and love of Christ. Each Christian who enters into this sacrament comes to participate in that love in a very special way. It is this sacramental character[236] of Christian marriage that confirms the properties, which is unity (the purpose of monogamy), and indissolubility (the impossibility of divorce).

It is to be noted that Christ did not institute the sacrament of marriage since it was there before Christianity; Christ rather raised this natural institution of marriage to the dignity of a sacrament. Regardless of the fact that there is no scriptural evidence of direct institution by Christ, the sacramentality of marriage is founded in his saving work of redemption[237]. In the words of Pope Paul VI:

---

235 Cfr. G. Taylor – E. De Bekker, op.cit. p. 3.

236 Cfr. U. Mosiek, Kirchliches Eherecht: Unter Berücksichtigung der nachkonziliaren Rechtslage, Freiburg 1972, p.38. "Durch den Sakramentscharakter erhebt Christus die Ehe in die übernatürliche Ordnung und umkleidet sie – als Abbild der gnadenvollen und fruchtbaren Verbindung Christi mit seiner Kirche – mit einer neuen Würde. Den Gatten werden dauernd neue Gnaden vermittelt, die sie befähigen, ihre schweren Verpfichtungen zu erfüllen, die wegen der Einheit und Unauflöslichkeit der Ehe besondere Anforderungen an sie stellen".

237 D. Hauser, Marriage and Christian Life: A theology of Christian Marriage, Lanham 2005, pp. 84-85, 100. "As a sacrament, and therefore redemptive, marriage does not deal with simply one aspect of life,... rather, marriage is religious in the sense that it is both comprehensive and profound. In the sacrament of marriage, the spouses participate in both the order of redemption and the order of creation that have their origin and purpose in the New Covenant, which is the one flesh union of Christ, the second Adam, with the church, the second Eve.... The marriage bond, as a relationship and participation in the New Covenant, is an action which orders human life at its very foundation. Like all of the sacraments, the event character of marriage is determined by its participation in the redemptive events of the life of Christ. Christ alone saves, and only by participating in those events is one saved.... The unique character of marriage is found in its very structure. In the concrete day-to-day living out of the one sacrifice of Christ by means of the mutual love of man and wife, the married couple enters more deeply into the salvation offered by Christ. Within this sacramental economy, the husband and wife are initiated more deeply into the love of God in all the dimensions of married life. In marriage, the couple partakes of the spousal love of the New Covenant, into the mystery of the nuptial relationship between Christ and His church. The bond, although freely entered into by the couple, is the bond of New Covenant given by Christ. Only in Christ is such redemptive love possible".

“Marriage is not, then, the effect of change or the product of evolution of unconscious natural forces; it is the wise institution of the Creator to realize in mankind his design of love. By means of the reciprocal personal gift of self, proper and exclusive to them, husband and wife tend toward the communion of their beings in view of mutual personal perfection, to collaborate with God in the generation and education of new lives”[238].

Marriage as a sacrament has become a means of encountering Christ in a special way and bringing about the salvation of the spouses. It is Christ who gives the spouses to each other in Christian marriage and with it his love for the church and each individual person in the church. The sacrament of marriage is then the blessing of divine love to the spouses which expresses the indissoluble union and love of Christ. As each Christian who enters into this sacrament comes to participate in that love in a very special way, Christian married life is a way of sanctity.

The sacrament makes a lot of impact to marriage. The principle of the sacramentality of marriage is the new covenant, by which God forms with humankind an exclusive, everlasting and bodily communion. This new covenant is exclusive and everlasting because Jesus, the Incarnate Word, joins God with his people in the unique communion that will become the heavenly kingdom, a communion that will last forever because God is perfectly faithful. It is bodily because those who enter into it not only share in Jesus’ divine life and cooperate with him in human acts, but share in his risen bodily life[239].

A sacrament is an effective sign which imparts grace instituted by Christ. It is a channel between our souls and the graces poured forth by our Lord Jesus Christ on the cross. It infuses the soul with God’s grace. In the sacrament of marriage, not only do spouses receive an abundance of sanctifying grace, but they receive a special sacramental grace which elevates the natural order of marriage and perfects it, giving them the right, as a gift from God, to receive from him whatever actual graces they need throughout their married life to live the sacrament in the way God intended.

The official statement of the Council of Trent is that “sacraments contain and confer grace”[240]. Canon 1134 of the 1983 Code states that: “From a valid marriage there arises between the spouses a bond which of its own nature is permanent and exclusive. Moreover, in Christian marriage the spouses are by a special sacrament strengthened and, as it were, consecrated for the duties and the dignity of their

238 Cfr. Paul VI, HV, 8 §2, in: Enchriridion on the Family: A Compendium of Church Teaching on Family and Life Issues from Vatican II to the Present, Boston 2004, p. 21.

239 Cfr. B.K. Nwakonobi, Igbo System of Kinship and Family: Christian Response, A Study of One of the Important Pastoral Moral Challenges in Africa, Rome 1997, p.246.

240 B. Cooke, Sacraments and Sacramentality, Mystic: Twenty-third Publications, 1983, p. 79.

state"[241]. The grace of the sacrament, which is of course exclusive to Christian marriage or marriage between two baptized persons legally celebrated, strengthens the spouses to take up their responsibilities and assume the dignity of their new state. It is precisely in view of the sacramental grace and its effects that the church claims the exclusive right to regulate the marriages of Catholics, except for the purely civil effects[242].

It is pertinent to note that many Christian married couples are not aware that the sacramental grace is always operative throughout their entire marriage, and not just during the ceremony in the church. It is against this background that John Paul II opines: "The gift of Jesus Christ is not exhausted in the actual celebration of the sacrament of marriage, but rather accompanies the marital couple throughout their lives"[243]. This very fact is explicitly recalled by the Vatican II Council when it asserts: "Just as of old God encountered his people with a covenant of love and fidelity, so our savior, the spouse of the church, now encounters Christian spouses through the sacrament of marriage. He abides with them in order that by their mutual self-giving spouses will love each other with enduring fidelity, as he loved the church and delivered himself for it"[244].

Hence, married Christian couples would make a valuable contribution to the preparation of marriage by teaching others how to appropriate the sacramental grace, not only during the reception of the sacrament of matrimony, but throughout the marriage. In doing so, they would open the way to married Christians in living out a lifetime communion of life and love[245].

John Paul II describes marriage as sacrament of mutual sanctification of the spouses. "The sacrament of marriage is the specific source and original means of sanctification for Christian married couples and families. It takes up again and makes specific the sanctifying grace of baptism. By virtue of the mystery of the death and resurrection of Christ, of which the spouses are made part in a new way by marriage, conjugal love is purified and made holy: "This love the Lord has judged worthy of special gifts, healing, perfecting and exalting gifts of grace and of charity"[246]. Christ is made manifest in and through the sacra-

241 C. 1134 CIC/1983: "Ex valido matrimonio enascitur inter coniuges vinculum natura sua perpetuum et exclusivum; in matrimonio praeterea christiano coniuges ad sui status officia et dignitatem peculiari sacramento roborantur et veluti consecrantur".

242 Cfr. C. 1059 CIC/1983: "The marriage of Catholics, even if only one party is baptized, is governed not only by divine law but also by canon law, without prejudice to the competence of the civil authority in respect of the merely civil effects of the marriage".

243 FC, 56 §2.

244 GS, 48 §2.

245 Cfr. L. Lee, Contribution of Lay People towards Preparation of Marriage: Commentary on Canons 1063 and 1064, Washington 1990, p.53.

246 FC, 56 §1.

ment of marriage. The presence of Christ in the sacrament of marriage heals and transforms the reality of two person's love, faithfulness and commitment into the reflection of God's presence and love. The spouses love for one another in the marriages of Christians becomes the vehicle through which the faithful and irrevocable love of God in Jesus Christ is made concrete and visible. In the words of Kasper: "Marriage, then, is in its own way a form by means of which God's eternal love and faithfulness, revealed in Jesus Christ, are made historically present. The love and faithfulness existing between Christ and his church is therefore not simply an image or example of marriage, nor is the self-giving of man and wife in marriage an image and likeness of Christ's giving of himself to the church. The love that exists between man and wife is rather a sign that makes the reality present, in other words, an epiphany of the love and faithfulness of God that was given once and for all time in Jesus Christ and is made present in the church"[247].

The sacramental nature of marriage[248] is indicated in Ephesians 5:21-33. Here, St. Paul sees the union of husband and wife as a symbol of the union between Christ and the church. He calls on Christian couples to live their marriage relationship in mutual self-sacrifice by following Jesus example. The total self-giving involved in marriage symbolizes the total self-giving of Jesus for his Bride, the church. Hence, the sacramental nature of any marriage is expressed in the love between the spouses; a love which is not just limited to the other partner, but which is the expression of people's desire to meet the ultimate and unlimited reality which is God. In Christian marriage the spouse becomes the sacrament of God who gives himself totally to people and to whom people give themselves totally. God's covenant with his people makes the covenant between husband and wife possible, and in as much as each of the partners tries to express God's love in his

247 W. Kasper, op.cit. p.30.

248 D. Hauser, op.cit. p.95. "In order to understand the sacramental nature of marriage in its relationship to the New Covenant, it is best to see marriage as it affirms and exists in relationship to the economy of salvation, an economy that is essentially Christocentric. As focused on Christ, who is the one true covenant, the economy of salvation is covenantal and nuptial. Within this nuptial order, marriage is understood in terms of the relationship of the Bridegroom and the Bride, the relationship between Christ and his Church, which stands at the heart of this order. This covenantal unity is that of the incarnate Son who acts in history to save His people. In Christ, the creative and redemptive orders find their unity. Again, this is not to say that only an aspect or a dimension of reality finds their meaning in Christ, but all of reality has its origin in the New Covenant. The "one flesh" unity of the second Adam and the second Eve, is the very heart of reality, a reality in which one participates in the sacrament of marriage. What this means is that marriage has a reality that is rooted in the very structure of the way things are, it is rooted in the order of creation. It is not the construct of society, but reflects the truth of existence. It is not only a moral choice, but part of the very ontological order of creation itself".

or her own love for the other, their marriage becomes an effective sign of God's grace, of God's covenant love[249].

God's definitive acceptance of man and woman brings them salvation. Salvation, in other words, is God's 'yes' to humanity. It is God's communication of himself in love to humanity. In Jesus Christ, God has accepted all that is human and affirmed it in its human dignity[250]. The marital love and faithfulness of those who are in Christ through faith and baptism are defined by the Second Vatican Council as: "Authentic married love is caught up into divine love and is directed and enriched by the redemptive power of Christ and the salvific action of the church, with the result that the spouses are effectively led to God and are helped and strengthened in their lofty role as fathers and mothers"[251]. The love and faithfulness Christian couples have for one another are "not simply the sign and symbol of the love of God – they are the effective sign, the fulfilled symbol and the real epiphany of the love of God that has appeared in Jesus Christ"[252].

For the faithful Christians, marriage is not only an effective sign of God's love, it is also a sign of that love as it has been revealed in the life, death and resurrection of Jesus Christ. In the perspective of the incarnation, marriage acquires its deepest significance as an expression of God's irrevocable love for those in Jesus Christ. Kasper complements this statement when he says: "If marriage represents a special form of being human in Christ that is based on baptism, it is also a special form of sharing in the death and resurrection of Christ…. Just as Christ loves the church as a church of sinners, purifies it and makes it holy, so too must married couples accept each other again and again with their conflicts, in all their dissatisfactions and with all their guilt"[253]. As a participation in Christ's love, marital love accepts nothing less than a total service – sacrifice of the spouses[254].

Marriage and family life give a special significance to the building up of the church. And in as much as married couples express in their union the mystery of Christ's love for his church, their family becomes a 'domestic church', having a vocation within, and a responsibility to the church in its entirety. Therefore the marriage of two baptised persons is more than a private affair between themselves, but a sacramental function within the church at large[255].

---

249 Cfr. B. Kisembo – et al; African Christian Marriage, Limuru 1998, p.42.

250 Cfr. W. Kasper, op.cit. pp. 34-35.

251 GS, 48 §2.

252 W. Kasper, op.cit. p. 35.

253 Ibid.

254 Cfr. H. Lacerte, Theological Reflections on Marriage as a Humanizing Experience in a Dehumanizing World, in: Marriage Studies II, Washington 1982, p.63.

255 Cfr. B. Kisembo – et al; op.cit. p.43.

1.2.4. A Partnership of their whole Life

The 1983 Code describes marriage as a partnership, a consortium. In ordinary usage, a partnership implies a joining of efforts among some people who commit themselves to the pursuit of a common good. Banares complements this meaning when he says that the term consortium "makes reference to a reality of a relational nature, and, more concretely, to a relationship with a societal character, to a community. Yet it is itself in keeping with its consensual origin founded in the will of the parties, but at the same time it points to a solid and objective quid, which is already constituted. It includes, moreover, an explicit allusion to a unique life project, to a "common lot". Thus, regarding the past, it refers to the willed origin of the pact; regarding the present, it points out the constitutive character of the pact; and regarding the future, it indicates the pact's capacity to extend itself fully into the future"[256]. The words of their whole life (totius vitae) which in other words, qualify the marital partnership mean that this is a life-long, unbreakable common lot. It consists in the gift of partners themselves which is the acceptance of each other "with all their strengths and weaknesses, their qualities and their faults, through all life's stages and situations; a sharing of one destiny, a coming together under one yoke for a common activity and a common aim – a community of life in which each will find his or her fulfillment"[257]. "The specification of their whole life is included as a particular characteristic of the partnership itself, not only as a condition for stability, as a quid permanes, but also as a requirement of the will of the woman and of the man for founding a relationship as woman and man, in what refers to the sexual dimension of their persons"[258].

This life-long partnership of their whole life embraces every aspect, but in different degrees of the married partners lives. It expresses in juridical terms the bond of marriage in view of its rights and obligations. The important juridical content is found in the ends of marriage as "the good of the spouses and the procreation and education of offspring" as well as in the essential properties of marriage in canon 1056 as "unity and indissolubility". However, these ends and essential properties will be discussed later on this very chapter. It is interesting to observe that when the parties decide and agree to enter into a relationship sanctioned by law, which is also ordered to the ends and qualified by the essential properties, they in turn obtain besides certain moral duties, the right and obligation to the acts ordered to those ends and to the furthering of those properties.

The partnership of their whole life according to Taylor – Bekker "cannot be defined absolutely since it can be achieved in a variety of ways according to the cul-

256 J.I Banares, "Commentary on canons 1055-1062", p.1053.

257 G. Taylor – E. Bekker, op.cit. p.1.

258 J.I. Banares, "Commentary on canons 1055-1062", p.1053.

ture to which the partners belong. It can be described as that relationship between the spouses, which according to the common estimation of the culture to which the partners belong, is considered normal, acceptable and humanly liveable"[259].

God endowed the union of husband and wife with its own benefits and purposes. Its benefits are those values which render the married life worthy of choice; its ends are the obligations to which it is ordered. Hence, the spouses who give themselves in marriage should be capable to a relationship in a human-satisfying manner and should be able to fulfill those obligations inherent in the state of marriage.

1.2.5. Conclusion

From the foregoing, it is to be noted that it was by the will of Christ, as in the case of the other sacraments, that the sacrament of marriage was instituted. In the sacrament of marriage what is elevated is precisely something already existing, a reality in nature itself, which was not converted into a sacrament, rather it was raised and transcended to the plane of the dignity of a sacrament[260].

Canon 1055 §1 calls marriage a "covenant", although it is not consistent in its use of covenant, but for the purpose of the law, marriage is to be understood as a covenant of love with a contractual aspect. This very covenant signifies the relationship of the spouses itself, the bond that exists between them and which constitutes them as husband and wife. Marriage also is to be seen as a contract because the two persons give consent to each other to the covenant of love. It is a glaring fact that a covenant goes beyond the rights and responsibilities guaranteed by some contracts and provides a stronger, more sacred framework for marriage, but canon law still deliberately uses both terms to describe marriage. So the church's recent emphasis on marriage as a covenant does not exclude the idea that marriage is also a contract[261].

Marriage as a sacrament is one of the principal ways in which the mystery of Christ and the church is realised. The secular reality of marriage becomes a sacred mystery by virtue of the sacrament. John Paul II alludes to this when he says: "By virtue of the sacramentality of their marriage, spouses are bound to one another in the most profoundly indissoluble manner. Their belonging to each other is the real representation, by means of the sacramental sign, of the very relationship of Christ with the church"[262].

259 G. Taylor – E. Bekker, op.cit. p.2

260 Cfr. J.I. Banares, "Commentary on canons 1055-1062", p.1052.

261 Cfr. C. West, Good News about Sex and Marriage: Answers to Your Honest Questions about Catholic Teaching, Cincinnati 2004, p.47.

262 FC 13 §7.

Marriage is above all a partnership of the whole life of the partners. But it is not a closed reality. It is normally destined to be fulfilled by the mission of child bearing. "But marriage is not merely for the procreation of children: its nature as an indissoluble compact between two people and the good of the children demand that the mutual love of the partners be properly shown, that it should grow and mature. Even in cases where despite the intense desire of the spouses there are no children, marriage still retains its character of being a whole manner and communion of life and preserves its value and indissolubility"[263].

2. The Ends of Marriage

2.1. Introduction

Speaking from the formulation of the ends of marriage in the Code of 1917 as 'primary' and 'secondary'[264] canonists and theologians drew the conclusion that marriage was primarily defined by "procreation and education of offspring" and that "mutual help" also defined marriage but as end subordinate to the primary end. This of course, brings us to Igbo traditional marriage. The main aim of every marriage in Igboland is procreation. And without prejudice to the other ends of marriage, the Igbo man gives procreation the primacy of value in the ends of marriage. For the traditional Igbo people, any marriage devoid of offspring is regarded as no marriage at all. This will be discussed fully in chapter four of our work. However, in the new revised Code of 1983, the ends to which marriage is ordered of its own nature are formulated as "the good of the spouses and the procreation and education of offspring"[265] by which it is perhaps more clearly expressed that marriage is for the spouses' perfection as persons and for offspring without implying any separation between these two ontological ends. This statement is repeated by Sebott[266].

263 GS 50 §3.

264 Cfr. C.1013 §1 CIC/1917: „Matrimonii finis primarius est procreatio atque educatio prolis: secundarius mutuum adiutorium et remedium concupiscentiae".

265 C.1055 §1 CIC/1983.

266 Cfr. R. Sebott, Das Neue kirchlichen Eherecht, Frankfurt 2005, pp.14-15. "Nach c.1013 §1 CIC/1917 war der primäre Zweck der Ehe die Erzeugung und Erziehung von Nachkommenschaft (procreatio et educatio prolis). Als sekundärer Zweck wurden die gegenseitige Hilfeleistung (mutuum adiutorium) und die geordnete Befriedigung des Geschlechtstriebes (remedium concupiscentiae) gennant. Diese Ehezwecklehre wurde im Laufe der Jahre von den Theologen häufig in Frage gestellt. Sie ist auch heute nicht ausdiskutiert. Auf den vorliegenden Paragraphen hat sicher das Eheverständnis des Zweiten Vatikanums und besonders die Pasto-

The Code of 1983 unlike the 1917 Code does not formulate a hierarchical ordering of the ends of marriage. "Neither the good of the spouses nor the procreation and education of offspring is designated as the primary end of marriage. Instead, both are equally essential to and inseparable in marriage"[267] In the covenant of conjugal love the spouses commit themselves to that total personal self-giving in order to seek the good of each other and the good of the children born from their conjugal love. The total personal self-giving refers to the giving of both body and soul but not to a giving of self of those things not required by the ends of marriage. As John Paul II puts it: "In its most profound reality, love is essentially a gift, and conjugal love, while leading the spouses to the reciprocal "knowledge" which makes them "one flesh", does not end with the couple, because it makes them capable of the greatest possible gift, the gift by which they become cooperators with God for giving life to a new human person. Thus the couple, while giving themselves to one another, give not just themselves but also the reality of children..."[268].

To say, therefore, that marriage is by nature ordered to the good of the spouses and the procreation and education of children, means that the very substance of marriage should be studied not only through its material and formal causes but also through its final cause, that is, its ends or purposes. In view of this, to define the nature of marriage, we should identify the moral good which is the ontological end, or finis operis of marriage. This ontological end is not to be confused with the finis operantis or intention of the spouses, which may or may not coincide with the finis operis. "Since the achievement of the ends of marriage is somewhat beyond the power of the spouses, the failure to attain them does not in itself affect the validity of a marriage. For example, even though marriage is ordered to the procreation and education of offspring, childless marriages are presumed to be valid. However, if one or both parties exclude this essential end of marriage from their consent (i.e; refuse to give and accept the right to these ends) by a positive act of the will, they contract invalidly"[269]. We shall now look at these ends of marriage separately by explaining succinctly what we mean by the good of the spouses and the procreation and education of offspring.

ralkonstitution „Die Kirche in der Welt von heute" eingewirkt. Die Hierarchie der Zwecke, die den alten CIC beherrschte, wurde aufgegeben. Die personale Beziehung der Ehegatten und die Fruchtbarkeit der Ehe durch dringen sich gegenseitig und werden nicht mehr gegen einander ausgespielt".

267 J.P. Beal, "Commentary on canons 1055-1062", p. 1243.

268 FC, 14 §2.

269 J.P. Beal, "Commentary on canons 1055-1062", p.1243.

2.2. The Good of the Spouses

The 1983 Code of Canon Law speaks of the good of the spouses as one of the ends of marriage. This is contrary to the 1917 Code which speaks of "mutual assistance and the remedy of concupiscence" as the secondary end of marriage[270]. The phrase "the good of the spouses" is used to explain why the bond of marriage no longer depends on human decision alone but is of its nature eternal[271].

It is through the marriage covenant that the spouses enter into a partnership of the whole life in which they commit themselves to share the gifts of their own humanity. This involves not only sexual acts but also those spiritual goods unique to their own humanity by which they complement each other. This complementariness is designed by God and is expressed in the book of Genesis 2:18, where it is stated that "it is not good for man to be alone". Thus by their commitment, the spouses pursue the good of each other as desired by God. It is pertinent to underscore here "that the good of the spouses cannot be identified simply as the good to any two persons, but rather that it refers directly to the partnership established between a man and a woman, hence it is clear that it is the partnership which is ordered by its own nature"[272].

It is through this love – the union of heart that the spouses bring their spiritual and material resources and learn how to understand, accept, sustain, forgive each other, and assist each other to achieve their human fulfillment. This type of love embracing the good of the entire person of the spouses prompts their "persevering endeavour to bring each other to the state of perfection"[273].

Conjugal love is an interior force which moves the spouses to desire union with each other and to seek to give themselves to and for the benefit of each other. It is the intimate partnership of a responsible, sincere sharing of life and its promises, and its ups and downs in the married state. Be that as it may, conjugal love is not included as an essential element of marriage. In other words, it is an element which lies outside the juridical order. According to Taylor and de Bekker, "a marriage can be validly contracted without it. Its absence is not in itself a cause of nullity though it might indicate the presence of other causes of nullity e.g; grave fear, simulation, insufficient deliberation.... Hence even if conjugal love is not required for the making of a valid marriage contract it is expected to grow in the course of the married life making the two become one"[274]. Hence, the importance of conjugal love for the success of a marriage indicates that "unless the spouses at

270 Cfr. C.1013 §1 CIC/1917.

271 Cfr. GS, 48 §1.

272 J.I Banares, "Commentary on canons 1055-1062", p.1055.

273 Pius XI, Casti Connubii, p.548.

274 G. Taylor – E. de Bekker, op.cit. pp.2-3.

least intended from the beginning of their union to give and accept the right to a loving relationship, their union were fundamentally flawed"[275].

The good of the spouses is an ontological end of marriage in officium naturae, in other words, a finis operis or end intended by God. In view of this, a person who chooses to marry even when procreation is not physically attainable still chooses a true marriage because the good of the spouses is also an ontological end and as such a good that endows to the particular relationship the character of marriage[276]. The good of the spouses is the good tha is characteristic of the person and fulfils the person. It comprises of the power to communicate to others the gifts of one's own life through self-giving. And in as much as through the self-giving, the person seeks and finds his own fulfillment and perfection, self-giving is "the good of the person" and "the good of the spouses". This good of the spouses is "the sum of all goods which flow from the interpersonal relationship of the spouses"[277] which, "at least as to their substance, bring about and promote the spiritual, intellectual, physical, moral, and social good of the spouses"[278].

2.3. Procreation and Education of Children

Marriage is also by its own nature ordered to the procreation and education of children. The Fathers of Vatican II Council tactfully refrain from speaking of primary and secondary ends of marriage, and by so doing, avoid the suggestion connected with those terminologists, that marriage is instrumental to ends extrinsic to it. The Council Fathers do acknowledge the truth contained in the traditional theology of the primary end of marriage, when they emphasis that: "By its very nature the institution of marriage and married love is ordered to the procreation and education of the offspring and it is in them that it finds its crowning glory"[279]. This statement tries to avoid the risk of seeing marriage and conjugal love as means to the end of offspring, and points instead to the view that having and raising up children naturally belong to marriage and conjugal love themselves[280]. The Igbo traditional marriage system, which we shall entertain later in the fourth chapter, is solely based on this particular end of marriage, but with a different understanding. It is understood as a means of getting children in fulfillment of cultural and religious obligations and the continuation of family

275 J.P. Beal, "Commentary on canons 1055-1062", pp.1244-1245.

276 Cfr. FC, 14 §4..

277 Coram Bruno, July 19, 1991, SRRDec 83 (1991) p.466, in: J.P. Beal, Op.cit; p.1245.

278 Coram Bruno, December 17, 1987, SRRDec 79 (1987) p.765, in: J.P. Beal, Op.cit; p.1245.

279 GS, 48 §1.

280 Cfr. B.K. Nwakonobi, Igbo System of Kinship and Family, p.165.

lineage. Although with the current wave of globalization the Igbo people now try to moderate their family size, yet they do not rule out entirely the possibility of getting children from the union to continue their lineage.

The fundamental task of marriage is to actualize in history the original blessing of God in transmitting by means of procreation the divine image and continually keeping it in being. Thus, human procreation entails more than biological reproduction. It suggests also the education of offspring to human maturity. As John Paul II puts it: "Consequently, sexuality, by means of which man and woman give themselves to each other through the acts which are proper and exclusive to spouses, is by no means something purely biological, but concerns the innermost being of the human person as such.... This fertility is directed to the generation of a human being, and so by its nature it surpasses the purely biological order and involves a whole series of personal values"[281].

While priority has traditionally been given to the procreation of children, their upbringing and education are also of utmost important. The goal of education of children is to impact to the children the person's ability to give and share the good of one's own life with another, which is the good of the person. In this regard, it can be said that the procreation and education of children is the final cause or finis operis of conjugal love and marriage and the moral good ordering and giving meaning to all other acts within the marriage relationship. Thus, the good of the spouses is implied in bearing and upbringing of children and is inseparable from it, for this end requires that the spouses give each other those goods needed to fulfill their role as parents.

Parents have both obligation and the right "to ensure their children's physical, social, cultural, moral, and religious upbringing"[282]. Children are persons who must be looked after and treated in a morally good manner. Parents have the obligation to provide for this. Speaking of the obligation of parents to educate their children, the Council Fathers say: "As it is the parents who have given life to their children, on them lays the gravest obligation of educating their family. They must therefore be recognized as being primarily and principally responsible for their education. The role of parents in education is of such importance that it is almost impossible to provide an adequate substitute. It is therefore the duty of parents to create a family atmosphere inspired by love and devotion to God and their fellow-men which will promote an integrated, personal and social education of their children"[283]. It is to be noted here that the obligation of parents towards the education of their children should with correct judgments through docile respect

281 FC, 11 §5 and §6.

282 C. 1136 CIC/1983: "Parentes officium gravissimum et ius primarium habent prolis educationem tum physicam, socialem et culturalem, tum moralem et religiosam pro viribus curandi".

283 GE, 3 §1.

for God and common reflection and effort correspond to the number of children they will be able to care for. "It is the married couples themselves who must in the last analysis arrive at these judgments before God. Married people should realize that in their behaviour they may not simply follow their own fancy but must be ruled by conscience – and conscience ought to be conformed to the law of God in the light of the teaching authority of the church, which is the authentic interpreter of divine law"[284].

Therefore, the reality of children is for the spouses, "a living reflection of their love, a permanent signs of conjugal unity and a living and inseparable synthesis of their being a father and a mother"[285].

2.4. Conclusion

The church has always emphasized that marriage exists in function of the good of the spouses through their mutual services and procreation and education of children. The human person is inclined by natural reason itself to attain these goods through the existence of marriage and to fulfill an obligation of nature (in officium naturae). The bedrock of this human inclination is made more explicit by the teaching of John Paul II when he affirms that it comprises of human person's vocation to love. Through the creation of human person in love and for love, "God inscribed in the humanity of man and woman the vocation, and thus the capacity and responsibility, of love and communion"[286]. This love between a man and a woman is only true to their human personhood when it takes the form of an exclusive commitment to each other in order to generate the divine image into a new human person through procreation and upbringing[287].

Canon 1055 §1 of 1983 Code becomes clearer in the light of these ends. The "good of the spouses", on the one hand, and the "procreation and education of children", on the other – to both of which "the matrimonial covenant... is by its nature ordered", cannot properly be considered as separable. Both ends are mutually supportive of the other. In rearing of children, spouses not only fulfill the aspirations of mutual love and conjugality, but they also by so doing, obtain a moral duty towards these children, which is a duty to love and care for them and not merely as a perpetuation of their own spousal love or as an outward manifestation of their conjugal union. Thus, since the transmission of the divine image by means of "procreation and education of offspring" requires the personal and

284 GS, 50 §2.
285 FC, 14 §2.
286 FC, 11 §2.
287 Cfr. FC, 28 §3.

mutual self-giving of the spouses, the covenant of conjugal love is ordered to the good of the spouses and of the children[288].

3. The Inseparability of Sacrament and Contract

Paragraph 2[289] of canon 1055 of 1983 Code, like the old Code of 1917, identifies[290] the human marriage contract with the sacrament when both parties are baptised. The sacrament is not something added to the marriage consent, it is the sanctification of the natural consent of the spouses by its participation in the mystery of Christ and the church. Thus, whenever there is a valid marriage between two baptised persons, catholic or non catholic, it has ipso facto a sacramental character[291].

In the 1917 Code, the very fact that marriage is presented not only as a sacrament but also as a contract brings to mind a struggle which the church had been waging with civil governments for many centuries. With the growing secularization of society governments wanted to claim for themselves the right to determine the conditions for bringing marriages into being and for judging their validity. They maintained that since marriage was seen as a "natural" institution as well as a sacrament, that the state should be able to determine the validity of its natural character of marriage being a contract while the church determines its sacramental quality[292]. The church in responding to this claim, withhold its position that for Christian the reality of marriage as contract could not be separated from its reality as sacrament. They maintained that the sacramental and contractual character of marriage were both important to it and therefore inseparable.

Before the new Code, there had been a strong pronouncement of the Sacred Congregation of the Holy Office with respect to the question of the inseparability of contract and sacrament in marriage. "It is heresy… to separate absolutely by means of a law the sacrament of matrimony from the contract of matrimony, just as if the contract did not enter into the essence and substance of the sacrament by the force of divine institution, and the sacrament of marriage would be

288 Cfr. CCC, nos 1652-1654.

289 Cfr. C.1055 §2 CIC/1983: „Quare inter baptizatos nequit matrimonialis contractus validus consistere, quin sit eo ipso sacramentum".

290 This conclusion refers not to the inseparability, but rather to the identity between the conjugal pact and the sacramental reality: there cannot be between the baptized, a merely natural marriage, for if the contract is by law invalid, there is no marriage but an unlawful union. For more details, see: J.I. Banares, "Commentary on canons 1055-1062", p.1052; I. Gramut – et al; op.cit., p.4.

291 Cfr. G.V. Lobo, The New Marriage Law, Bangalore 2005, p.19.

292 Cfr. G.W. Olsen, eds; Christian Marriage: A Historical Study, New York 2001, pp.338-339.

discovered to be nothing other than a quality floating over the contract or a frame decorating a painting to which it is foreign.... Matrimony... is on that account a sacrament because the contract also pertains to the sacrament and enters into the definition of the sacrament. There can be a contract of marriage which may not be a sacrament; nevertheless, there cannot be a sacrament of marriage, in which the contract itself is not a sacrament"[293].

It is to be noted that some attention is here given to the contractual nature of marriage because there are theologians who have written after the Second Vatican Council maintaining that the Council Fathers had not acknowledged the notion of contract in Christian marriage and had substituted it with the idea of covenant. It is to be said that though the Conciliar Pastoral Constitution on the Church in the Modern World, Gaudium et Spes, does not refer to marriage as a contract, there is no evidence that the Council Fathers rejected the contractual character of marriage. It would be impossible to do, from the theological point of view in as much as the Magisterium has emphasized its importance to marriage, and it has been included in the revised Code of Canon Law[294].

The challenge to this strong teaching of the church since the Second Vatican Council arises from pastoral experience. There are many instances where Priests find themselves in officiating at marriages of baptised Catholics who appear no longer to believe in or practice the Christian faith[295]. The church teaches at the same time that the sacraments "not only presuppose faith, but by words and objects they also nourish, strengthen, and express it. That is why they are called sacraments of faith"[296].

There is no difficulty when the baptised persons are also believers. But the questions are: But what if some baptised persons do not have faith? Can a person receive the sacrament of matrimony validly, or can the sacrament take place if one of the baptised partners has no faith, in other words, does not believe that marriage between the baptised is a sacrament, or does not believe that Christian marriage is a sacrament? These questions however, will be taken care of in chapter three when we treat Faith and Marriage Preparation under the sub-heading, "Difficulties in Marriage Preparation". But it is to be emphasized that faith is never mere belief in something but a personal response to God addressing us in this life, it is a personal relationship[297].

There is truth in the church's teaching that a baptised couple cannot contract a marriage validly if the making of their marriage covenant is not at the same time

293 P. Gaspari – G.J. Seredi, eds; Codicis Iuris Canonici Fontes, Rome 1926, 4: pp.137-138, in: G.W. Olsen, op.cit. p.339.
294 Cfr. G.W. Olsen, op.cit. p.339.
295 Cfr. J. McAreavey, op.cit. p.34.
296 SC, 59 §1.
297 Cfr. G. Taylor – E. de Bekker, op.cit. p.4.

a sacrament. If they exclude sacramentality from their marriage pact they contract invalidly. Suffice it to say that the baptism of one party alone does not make due for the full sacramental character of marriage in the Christian sense. If one or both were unbaptised at the time of marriage, this becomes a sacrament when both receive baptism[298] which transforms their natural union by its insertion into the mystery of Christ's union with the church. Thus no new ceremony is needed for the reception of the sacrament of matrimony[299].

4. The Essential Properties of Marriage

4.1. Introduction

Canon 1056 of the New Code, like canon 1013 §2 of the Old Code of 1917, describe the essential properties of marriage as unity and indissolubility, which in Christian marriage obtain a special firmness in virtue of the sacrament[300]. The covenant of conjugal love is endowed with these two essential properties, which further qualify the nature of the covenant and of the relationship emanating from it. They are required by natural law and are present in every valid marriage even that contracted by non-Christians[301]. To support this statement further, Beal remarks: "Unity and indissolubility are considered by the church to be properties of marriage in virtue of the natural law. Thus, they are properties of all marriages and not just those of Christians. However, in the marriages of the baptised, these properties "obtain a special firmness by reason of the sacrament"[302]. Also Prader, in his book entitled "Das kirchliche Eherecht in der Seelsorglichen Praxis", commented on the essential properties of marriage[303].

298 Cfr. J. Listl – et al, op.cit. p.739. "Aus der Identität von Ehebund unter Christen und Ehesakrament ergibt sich zwingend, dass die gültige Ehe nur dann Sakrament ist, wenn beide Partner getauft sind. Wie die Ehe nicht für einen Partner gültig und für den anderen ungültig sein kann, so auch nicht für den einen sakramental und für den anderen nichtsakramental. Wenn zur Zeit der Eheschließung ein oder beide Partner ungetauft sind, wird die gültige Ehe ohne weiteres Zutun Sakrament, sobald beide Partner die Taufe empfangen haben".

299 Cfr. G.V. Lobo, op.cit. p.21.

300 Cfr. C.1056 CIC/1983: „Essentiales matrimonii proprietates sunt unitas et indissolubilitas, quae in matrimonio christiano ratione sacramenti peculiarem obtinent firmitatem".

301 Cfr. I. Gramunt – et al; op.cit. p.4.

302 J.P. Beal, "Commentary on canons 1055-1062", p. 1249.

303 "Die Ehe ist ihrem inneren Wesen nach einpaarig und unauflöslich. Alle christlichen Kirchen stimmen seit jeher darin überein, daß die Einpaarigkeit und die grundsätzliche Dauer bis zum Wesen der christlichen Ehe gehört. Wenn eine dieser Eigenschaften bei der Eheschließung

The integrity of the ends of marriage – "the good of the spouses and the procreation and education of offspring", requires that marriage be one and indissoluble. The Conciliar Pastoral Constitution on the Church in the Modern World, Gaudium et Spes, confirms this when it says: "Thus the man and woman, who "are no longer two but one" (Mt.19.6), help and serve each other by their marriage partnership; they become conscious of their unity and experience it more deeply from day to day. The intimate union of marriage, as a mutual giving of two persons, and the good of the children demand total fidelity from the spouses and require an unbreakable unity between them"[304].

The essential properties of marriage are strengthened by the grace of the sacrament which provides a specific support to the spouses to remain indissolubly faithful to each other. The union of spouses is naturally so exclusive that it can only exist in absolute honesty if the partners give themselves to one another totally and unconditionally[305]. Unity and indissolubility as essential properties of marriage belong to the marriage relationship as it was created by God and confirmed by his own positive law. They are qualities inherent in the institution of marriage itself[306].

4.2. Unity

The unity of marriage refers to the fact that marriage is by its nature an exclusive union between one man and one woman. As Kasper notes: "The act in which the bride and bridegroom give and receive each other has in itself an inner tendency towards definitiveness and exclusiveness"[307]. Some theologians and Canonists have expressed in their various books what is meant by unity as an essential property of marriage[308]. The book of Genesis describes this unity with the profound expression of "they two become one flesh"[309].

---

ausgeschlosen wird, kommt keine gültige Ehe zustande. Der Christ ist nicht frei, zu wählen zwischen einer monogamen oder polygamen, zwischen einer Ehe auf Zeit oder einer Ehe für das ganze Leben". Cfr. J. Prader, Das kirchliche Eherecht in der seelsorglichen Praxis, Würzburg 1983, p.33.

304 GS, 48 §1.

305 Cfr. B. Häring, Marriage in the Modern World, Cork 1965, p.258.

306 Cfr. J.P. Beal, "Commentary on canons 1055-1062", p.1249.

307 W. Kasper, op.cit. p.45.

308 Cfr. H. Zapp, Kanonisches Eherecht, Freiburg 1983, pp.37-38. "Unter der in c.1056 genannten Einheit der Ehe ist die Einpaarigkeit zu verstehen. Die umfassende personale Lebengemeinschaft der Ehegatten schließt jede Einbeziehung eines Dritten in die eheliche Gemeinschaft aus; zu ihrem Wesen gehört die vorbehaltlose eheliche Treue"; J. Listl – et al; op.cit. p.735. „Einheit ist als Einpaarigkeit zu verstehen. Ehe gibt es daher jeweils nur zwischen einem Mann und einer Frau. Beide Partner sind zur unbedingten Treue verpflichtet, die sich daraus ergibt,

Unity excludes the union of one man with several women (polygamy) as contrary to the very nature of marriage, for in such cases the woman is not made an equal partner but is left to raise the children without the full participation of the man, who cannot give the woman an undivided heart as implied in the biblical idea of "one flesh". The Council Fathers affirm this when they say: "The unity of marriage, distinctly recognized by our Lord, is made clear in the equal personal dignity which must be accorded to man and wife in mutual and unreserved affection"[310]. However, the prohibition of polygamy admits of divine dispensation[311] which was granted by God for the increase of his chosen people.

Pope John Paul II in his address to the Bishops of Kenya on May 7, 1980, had this to say: "It is the divine law proclaimed by Christ that gives rise to the Christian ideal of monogamous marriage, which in turn is the basis for the Christian family"[312]. The Pope in condemning polygamy writes, "this, in fact, directly negates the plan of God which was revealed form the beginning, because it is contrary to the equal personal dignity of men and women who in matrimony give themselves with a love that is total and therefore unique and exclusive"[313].

The Igbo traditional marriage system favours and promotes polygamy as an honourable and prestigious form of marriage. But this acceptance is not without a reason. Hence Mbiti opines: "Today, getting married to two or more wives is a custom found all over Africa.... The custom fits into the social structure of the traditional life and into the thinking of the people, serving many useful

---

daß sie zu einer personalen Lebenseinheit zusammengewachsen sind, so dass eine gleichartige Beziehung zu jedem Außenstehenden ausgeschlosen ist"; J. Prader, op.cit. p.34. "Die naturrechtliche Begründung der Einpaarigkeit der Ehe setzt ein Verständnis von Naturrecht voraus, dass erst im Glauben an das Menschenbild, wie Christus es uns gelehrt hat, zu erfassen ist. Die Polygamie leugnet in direkter Weise den Plan Gottes, wie er am Anfang offenbart wurde; denn sie widerspricht der gleichen personalen Würde von Mann und Frau, die sich in der Ehe mit einer Liebe schenken, die total und eben deshalb einzig und ausschließlich ist".

309 Gen.2:24.

310 GS, 49 §2.

311 In the Old Testament polygamy was practiced among the people of Israel. When God undertook to educate his people by giving them his law, the institution of marriage was no longer at the level of the primitive ideal. The ideal of fecundity and the concern to have a powerful family caused the desire for very many children. This naturally led to the practice of polygamy. Some Catholic theologians explain it as a dispensation given by God in a secondary principle of natural law. A better explanation seems to be this. Without the full light of the Revelation of the New Testament, it was very difficult to arrive at the idea that polygamy was opposed to natural law. God, like a wise pedagogue, revealed the full moral truth only gradually. Therefore, God tolerated it in the Old Testament. The practice then was not a positive approval but a juridical toleration. Cfr. A.O. Gbuji, op.cit. p.35.

312 John Paul II, African Addresses, Bologna 1980, p.29.

313 FC, 19 §4.

purposes"[314]. The Igbo people as well as Africans love children and that is the reason why a childless marriage is hardly called a marriage as such. It is based on this that polygamy is considered as a way of helping to satisfy the need and the desire of having a large family comprising of children for the continuation of family lineage. It also caters for the childless union and offers a kinder solution than that of divorce when a wife is barren[315].

In the union of one woman with many men (polyandry), the man is denied equal partnership as well as his lawful paternity and the children are denied their exclusive filiation, for neither father nor children can be certain of their true mutual relationship.

Unity as one of the essential properties of marriage stresses that a man and a woman in equal terms should not share with any third party the promise they made to each other. A marriage cannot be extended to include a third party, in other words, the husband cannot make another marriage Contract by taking a second wife, nor can it be cancelled out by any mere human authority. Thus, unity helps the spouses to maintain and develop a happy communion of life and love which is dynamic, exclusive and perpetual and also in the pursuit of the marital holiness of life by the daily performance of both their Christian and conjugal duties[316].

4.3. Indissolubility

The indissolubility[317] of marriage means that the matrimonial bond is permanent for life. "To say that marriage is indissoluble means that it is a perpetual relationship which not only should not be terminated but cannot be terminated, even if the couple's existential relationship is irretrievably broken"[318]. A valid marriage cannot be dissolved by the will or consent of the parties contracting the marriage or by any mere human authority.

314 J.S. Mbiti, African Religion and Philosophy, Heinemann 1990, p.186.

315 Cfr. B. Kisembo – et al; op.cit. p.86.

316 Cfr. E. Okonkwo, Marriage in the Christian and Igbo Traditional Context: Towards an Inculturation, Frankfurt 2003, p.135.

317 Cfr. J. Listl – et al; op.cit. p.736."Unauflöslichkeit besagt, dass die Ehe nicht aufgelöst werden kann, so dass die Ehegatten dadurch wieder frei würden, eine neue Ehe mit einem anderen Partner zu schließen. Weder die Gatten selber können ihre Ehe auflösen (innere Unauflöslichkeit) noch kann dies eine außerhalb der Ehe stehende Autorität (äußere Unauflöslichkeit). Auch die Unauflöslichkeit ergibt sich daraus, dass die Gatten durch den Ehebund zu einer personalen Lebenseinheit verschmolzen sind, in die sie sich nicht nur selber durch ihre gegenseitige Selbstübereignung hineingegeben haben, sondern zu der sie auch von Gott miteinander verbunden wurden".

318 J.P. Beal, "Commentary on canons 1055-1062", p.1249.

The church has always taught that Christ solemnly confirmed this teaching. This is clear from Mt. 19:4-6 and Mk. 10:6-9: "Have you not read that the Creator from the beginning made them male and female and that he said: This is why a man must leave father and mother, and cling to his wife, and the two become one body? They are no longer two, but one body; what God has joined together, let no man put asunder". The indissolubility of marriage is especially confirmed by the sacramental nature of marriage between Christians, for whom marriage is a sign of that faithful and indivisible bond between Christ and his bride, the church which he loved to the end[319].

The indissoluble union is rooted in the personal and total self-giving of the spouses and in the fact that they are no longer two but one body. Kasper asserts that "this unity and this indissolubility, already an essential part of marriage as a reality of creation, are given an ultimate and unambiguous meaning in the Old Testament by the insertion of the order of creation into God's plan of salvation. God's faithfulness to his people is a constant theme throughout the Old Testament (see, for example, Ex 34:6; Ps 99:5)"[320]. Faithfulness in marriage was seen as an image of God's faithfulness in the covenant. It is in this context that Deuteronomy 24:1-4, which treats about the drawing up of a bill of divorce, must be interpreted. What this text means is not permission for divorce, but a prohibition to remarry a divorced wife. It was not until the later period of Judaism that the idea of permission for divorce was derived from this passage in circumstance where the husband found some "scandal" in his wife[321].

Suffice it to say that in upholding and defending the indissolubility of marriage, the church is safeguarding the well-being of the spouses, the welfare of children and the society. The Second Vatican Council[322] outlines three major reasons which militate against divorce: the good of the spouses, the good of their children and of society. The fourth reason is theological in nature and derived from the sacramental status of Christian marriage[323]. Therefore, for the good of

319 Cfr. FC, 20 §3; CCC, nos. 1614-1617.

320 W. Kasper, op.cit. p.46.

321 Ibid.

322 Cfr. GS, 48 §1.

323 Cfr. K.H. Peschke, Christian Ethics, Bangalore 1992, pp.483-485. "(1) Divorce is opposed to the good of the spouses. It frustrates the end of mutual assistance and completion in love. A husband and wife cannot surrender themselves fully to each other when there lurks in the mind of either one even the possibility that their union might be broken. Already by its psychological structure human love aspires to permanent companionship. The aim of mutual help and protection, precisely when it is most necessary, namely in the more difficult situations of life, is fully granted only in a permanent union of husband and wife.... The certainty that the marriage bond is indissoluble constitutes a powerful incentive to safeguard the good of conjugal fidelity and love. It provides a strong motive for the spouses to bear each other's limitations in patience forbearance and to preserve unity and harmony between each other....

the spouses, their offspring and of society, the conjugal bond cannot depend on the simple decision of the human will.

Marriage dissolution is against marital fidelity and conjugal love. It negates the indissoluble bond of love that unites Christ and his body, the church, of which Christian marriage is both the mirror and the symbol. John Paul II writes: "Being rooted in the personal and total self-giving of the couple, and being required by the good of the children, the indissolubility of marriage finds its ultimate truth in the plan that God has manifested in his revelation: He wills and he communicates the indissolubility of marriage as a fruit, a sign and a requirement of the absolutely faithful love that God has for man and that the Lord Jesus has for the church"[324].

The church views indissolubility as an essential property of marriage by virtue of the natural law. Thus every valid marriage is indissoluble in the sense that it cannot be dissolved by the spouses or by any human power. While the value of a sacramental and consummated marriage bond is so supreme that it can never be dissolved (c.1141)[325], the value of a ratified non-consummated marriage bond can be dissolved for the benefit of only one of the spouses (c.1142)[326]. Canons 1143-1150 outline several other means in which the church can dissolve natural marriages provided the dissolution is for the benefit of faith. In canons 1151-1155 we learn that the marital rights and duties of the spouses of Christian and natural marriages can be permanently suspended and the spouses separated, sometimes for life. The law also enforces permanent celibacy on couples living under the

---

(2) A dissoluble marriage is prejudicial to the Child. Whenever the bond is severed, the children are deprived of either parent or both, and this inevitably affects their confidence, security and education.... Children never undergo the divorce of their parents without problems nor do they experience it as a veritable solution.... The good of the children very rarely demands absolute divorce, on the contrary, it argues for the stability of the marriage. (3) The good of society requires stable families. For only in this way can the healthy education of the young generation be assured and sure dependence and solidarity within the community protected and aided.... Positive measures in support of marriage and family are as much a demand as human divorce laws. The education in all schools ought to give positive images and value parameters for marriage. (4) A last argument is of theological nature. It is founded on the sacramental status of Christian marriages and therefore only holds for Christians. Since Christ has revoked for his followers the concession of divorce granted by Moses to the Israelites and since in 1Cor 7:12-16 Paul allows for a divorce only in the case of a non-Christian marriage (i.e. in favour of the faith), it follows that a sacramental marriage between Christians can never be dissolved".

324 FC, 20 §3.

325 Cfr. C.1141 CIC/1983: "Matrimonium ratum et consummatum nulla humana potestate nullaque causa, praeterquam morte, dissolvi potest".

326 Cfr. C.1142 CIC/1983: "Matrimonium non consummatum inter baptizatos vel inter partem baptizatam et partem non baptizatam a Romano Pontifice dissolvi potest iusta de causa, utraque parte rogante vel alterutra, etsi altera pars sit invita".

same roof. Such couples are advised to live as brother and sister in the same house[327].

The indissolubility of marriage is so intrinsic to marriage that not even the mutual agreement of the spouses can terminate it. In extreme cases, a separation of the couples may probably be necessary, but this separation does not mandate either spouse to enter into another lawful union as long as the other spouse is still alive. An appreciation of recognition is to be given to those spouses who still hold firm to their faith even after their partners have abandoned them. John Paul II writes: "But it is proper to recognize the value of the witness of those spouses who, even when abandoned by their partner, with the strength of faith and of Christian hope have not entered a new union: these spouses too give an authentic witness to fidelity, of which the world today has a great need. For this reason they must be encouraged and helped by the pastors and the faithful of the church"[328].

4.4. Conclusion

The marriage of Christians as has been noted, partakes in a special way in the union of Christ and the church. Thus the essential properties of unity and indissolubility are confirmed by the sacrament of matrimony. These properties acquire a distinctive firmness and yield to no exception since Christian marriage is not only a symbol of but also a participation in Christ's covenant of unconditional fidelity and unbreakable union with his church. To exclude these properties in the marriage contract renders the marriage covenant itself invalid. On the same note, civil divorce cannot dissolve the marital bond, and a divorced person cannot enter into a new valid marriage while the first spouse is still alive.

Therefore, couples are advised from the very beginning to consider it as a serious obligation to support and strengthen this marriage bond. This in fact, lays credence to the encouragement giving by John Paul II to married couples: "To bear witness to the inestimable value of the indissolubility and fidelity of marriage is one of the most precious and most urgent tasks of Christian couples in our time.... I praise and encourage those numerous couples who, though encountering no small difficulty, preserve and develop the value of indissolubility; thus, in a humble and courageous manner, they perform the role committed to them of being in the world a "sign" – a small and precious sign, sometimes also subjected

327 Cfr. E.A. Akpan, "Problems of Christian Marriage and Family Life in the Nigerian Situation", in: B. Etafo – H.O. Okeke, eds; Marriage and the Family in Nigeria, Onitsha 1993, pp.86-87.

328 FC, 20§6.

to temptation, but always renewed of the unfailing fidelity with which God and Jesus Christ love each and every human being"[329].

5. Matrimonial Consent

5.1. Introduction

Having discussed the essential properties of marriage as unity and indissolubility which obtain a special firmness in virtue of the sacrament in Christian marriage, we now focus our attention to what constitutes or makes marriage. In our earlier discussion we made mention of marriage as also a contract of a special kind. Now, a contract can be effected by no other means than by the consent of the parties. Consent is thus necessary to marriage and neither the states nor the church, nor any human power can supply it. Consent lawfully manifested actually brings marriage into being. Our main thrust here is to study this consent, its nature and object, and how it constitutes to the marriage of Christians and that of the Igbo people.

5.2. The Nature of Matrimonial Consent

The first paragraph of canon 1057 textually reiterates §1 of canon 1081 of 1917 Code. It states that: "A marriage is brought into being by the lawfully manifested consent of persons who are legally capable. This consent cannot be supplied by any human power"[330]. Marriage is a lifelong interpersonal relationship between a man and a woman. It is an enduring partnership to which two matured partners give their consent[331]. The matrimonial consent occupies a central position in the canonical doctrine. It is a deep-seated act in the spirit of a human person. Marriage being a specific way of life that requires a total gift of self, demands that the mutual exchange of consent must be given only by the spouses themselves. Beal – et al put it succinctly: "Consent is not only an indispensable element of marriage but the efficient cause that brings marriage into being. As a result, no human power can supply for the absence of consent by one or both parties"[332]. According-

329 Ibid.

330 C.1057 §1 CIC/1983: „Matrimonium facit partium consensus inter personas iure habiles legitime manifestatus, qui nulla humana potestate suppleri valet".

331 Cfr. J. Burke, Marriage and Nullity of Marriage, Ibadan 1993, p.36.

332 J.P. Beal, "Commentary on canons 1055-1062", p.1250.

ing to the Conciliar document of the Second Vatican Council, Gaudium et Spes, matrimonial consent is an irrevocable personal commitment which involves the giving of self and acceptance of the other[333]. This in actual fact, shows that the personal consent of the spouses is the cause of marriage since the contractual marriage is between a man and a woman.

Hence, the quality of the spouses' consent is a matter of utmost importance. Consenting to establish a marriage is certainly one of the most important decisions that most people make in the journey of their whole lives. Its importance endures; it is a lifelong choice and an irrevocable commitment of a highly personal nature. The parties involved must exchange this consent with their eyes wide open, with an informed mind and with adequate Christian maturity[334].

Paragraph One further states that consent must be legitimately manifested in order to achieve its intended juridic effect. The internal act of the will must not only be expressed by external signs such as words or gestures, but it must take place within the context of certain prescribed formalities[335]. Apart from canon 1057, other canons like canons 1108-1123 also prescribe some norms which have to be fulfilled for the valid manifestation of matrimonial consent. The consent must be mutual, external, free, it has to be between persons determined juridically capable and regularly to be expressed by words of the present tense before a competent person, that is, before the local ordinary or the parish priest or those lawfully delegated, and two witnesses (1108)[336].

It is to be noted that in traditional Igbo marriage system, the consent of the parties is also very pertinent in bringing marriage into existence, but there are other things to be fulfilled before a marriage can be contracted by the two parties. Ojemen confirms this when he writes: "The problem in the case of Nigeria is that marriage is much less individualistic than in Europe and America. The extended family plays very dynamic roles. Consent of the parties is important but there are other preliminaries to be fulfilled before a marriage can be said to truly exist. These would include visits to the extended members of the girl's family, the payment of dowry, the presentation of gifts and the handing over of the girl to the man by a group of women and some specially selected men. Christian marriages are valid irrespective of the fulfillment of these preliminaries but the church is not interested in isolating her members from their family roots. Thus, ways must be found by which these cultural values are gradually integrated within the catholic framework of marriage"[337].

333 Cfr. GS, 48 §1.

334 Cfr. A.O. Gbuji, op.cit. p.31.

335 Cfr. E.A. Akpan, The Path to Holy Orders, Owerri 1999, p.280.

336 Cfr. C.A. Ojemen, „Canonical Requirements of Matrimonial Consent in the Nigerian Context", in: B. Etafo – H.O. Okeke, op.cit. p.24.

337 Ibid, p.25.

The canon also stipulates that both parties must be legally capable of contracting marriage. This legal capability of the parties contracting marriage is one of the indispensable elements. For the parties to be legally capable, means that they have to be of right age and free from all diriment impediments[338]. The presence of a diriment impediment or defect in the form or complete absence of it merely renders ineffective the marital consent. To contract marriage also a person "must possess at least the minimal psychological capacity to establish and nurture an intimate partnership of life, sufficient knowledge of the nature of this partnership, and the intention to undertake it (cc. 1095-1107). If these psychological, intellectual, or volitional requirements are lacking, a person's consent is deficient and fails to give rise to a marriage"[339]. However, a defect of consent in itself may be remedied by renewing the consent again but psychic defects may remain and may even be incurable. Also an ineffective consent may be made effective through a dispensation from the diriment impediment or the obligation to observe the required form when the marriage contract is validated[340].

As marriage is effected by the free consent of the parties, this is the central factor which can in no way be supplied by any human authority. Freedom of choice is a very important prerequisite for the integrity and legal validity of matrimonial consent[341]. Zavalloni views freedom of choice in the light of personal autonomy or self-determination. This entails the highest level of consciousness; the only level in which deliberation and free choice can operate. The more freedom one enjoys, the more conscious he is about his decisions, in other words, the more light he has to illuminate his path through life[342].

Matrimonial consent therefore, cannot be given by parents on behalf of their children. But the Igbo traditional marriage consent is contrary to this. Sometimes a person contemplating marriage cannot do so without prior knowledge, due consultation with, and approval by his parents. Mba complements this when he asserts: "Boys and girls in principle could marry without the parents' consent; but in practice, No. The lack of parental consent constituted a diriment impediment of marriage"[343]. Parental consent in Igboland is a synthesis of family consent. The success or failure of many marriages depends solely on it. In Achebe's book, "No longer at Ease", Obi's mother in rejecting to his marriage to an "Osu" (caste) girl, reprimands Obi in these words: "I have nothing to tell you on this matter except one thing. If you want to marry this girl, you must wait until I am no more. If God

338 Cfr. cc. 1073, 1083-1094 CIC/1983.

339 J.P. Beal, "Commentary on canons 1055-1062", p.1250.

340 Cfr. G. Taylor – E. de Bekker, op.cit. p.7.

341 Cfr. C.A. Ojemen, op.cit. p.30.

342 Cfr. R. Zavalloni, Self-Determination: The Psychology of Personal Freedom, Chicago 1962, p.240.

343 C.S. Mba, Matrimonial Consent in Igbo Marriages, Rome 1964, p.93.

hears my prayers, you will not wait long. But if you do the thing while I am alive, you will have my blood on your head, because I shall kill myself"[344].

The influence of parents and the extended family members is of utmost importance in Igbo traditional marriage system. The consent of parents is symbol of the consent of members of the extended family. The parents in receiving the consent of their children, act on behalf of their respective clans on whose behalf the parties contract marriage and effect the perpetuation of both clans. The would-be partners are guaranteed the support and cooperation of their respective clans in receiving the consent of their parents[345].

In view of this one may start to ask the place of the spouses' individual consent, since it cannot be given by any human power. It is worthy to emphasis that the intervention of parents and extended family members does not in actual fact vitiate consent but only acts as guardianship to the welfare of the parties and the protection of the lineage from disintegration through the introduction of bad people into the family circle. Although the extended family members may give their consent which may not be welcomed by the person contracting marriage, there is no force to enter marriage. There is always that room for the prospective partners to do their wish only that sometimes the family blessing may not be given if the elders feel too aggrieved over the stubbornness of the either party to listen to them.

This brings us to canon 1103 which says "a marriage is invalid which was entered into by reason of force or of grave fear imposed from outside, even if not purposely, from which the person has no escape other than by choosing marriage"[346]. When we look at the parents and extended family pressure on the intending spouse alongside the canonical provision to analyse the quality of consent of the spouse, it may be opined that notwithstanding the fact that the pressure is very high based on the social influence of the extended family system among the Igbo people, yet it is not as if the parties have no alternative option on the right to choose his or her prospective partner.

The Igbo traditional idea of choosing a wife for a boy when he is still young is in line with the canonical obligation of parents to minors[347] and may not be taken as unfounded as such. Basden, writing about the Igbos during the period of colonization highlighted the reality of some instances where wives are simply given to the young men for marriage. He acknowledges also the freedom to choose

344 C. Achebe, No Longer at Ease, London 1978, p.123.

345 Cfr. B.K. Nwakonobi, op.cit. p.117.

346 C. 1103 CIC/1983: „Invalidum est matrimonium initum ob vim vel metum gravem ab extrinseco, etiam haud consulto incussum, a quo ut quis se liberet, eligere cogatur matrimonium".

347 Cfr. C. 1071 §1, 6° CIC/1983: „matrimonio filii familias minoris, insciis aut rationabiliter invitis parentibus".

which has always been there. “Parents of the richer class often select a wife (or wives) for a son while he is still quite a boy, irrespective of his wishes or inclinations; he probably is not even told of the transaction until it is an accomplished fact, and the girl is presented to him as his wife. In the majority of cases the young man makes his own choice”[348].

The bond of unity tying villages together in every founded Igbo marriage is so strong that an outright dismissal always hinders the socio-cultural and inter-communitarian peace and harmony. The approval by parents and extended family members for prospective partners is still invoke today in Igboland as well as in other communities in Africa, though the influence of modern city life has effected some changes in making a choice of partner. Young people intending to marry nowadays make their own choice of their would-be partners in accordance with the canonical doctrines without undue influence of and pressure from their parents and extended family members.

5.3. The Object of Matrimonial Consent

The 1917 Code of Canon Law defines matrimonial consent as “an act of the will by which each party gives and accepts perpetual and exclusive rights to the body, for those acts that are of themselves suitable for the generation of children”[349]. Here the object of consent is described as a primodial “ius”, ad actus per se aptos” for generating offspring. The 1983 Code defines consent in apparently different terms with its enrichments from the Magisterium, most especially from Second Vatican Council, from canonical jurisprudence and doctrine, and from other human sciences[350]. According to the New Code, “matrimonial consent is an act of the will by which a man and a woman by an irrevocable covenant mutually give and accept each other for the purpose of establishing a marriage”[351].

This definition is broader that the former definition of the Old Code. It corresponds to the more personalist view of marriage that has been emerging over the years. Pope Pius XI, in his encyclical, Casti Connubii of 1930, teaches that a person enters marriage “through the generous surrender of his or her own person

348 G. Basden, Among the Ibos of Nigeria, Lagos 1921, p.69.

349 C. 1081 §2 CIC/1917: „Consensus matrimonialis est actus voluntatis quo utraque pars tradit et acceptat ius in corpus, perpetuum et exclusivum, in ordine ad actus per se aptos ad prolis generationem“.

350 Cfr. J. Ignacio, “Commentary on canon 1057”, in: A, Marzoa – J. Miras – R. Rodriguez-Ocana, eds; Exegetical Commentary on the Code of Canon Law, Vol.III/2, Montreal 2004, p.1070.

351 C.1057 §2 CIC/1983: „Consensus matrimonialis est actus voluntatis, quo vir et mulier foedere irrevocabili sese mutuo tradunt et accipiunt ad constituendum matrimonium“.

made to another for the whole span of life"[352]. The Conciliar document Gaudium et Spes, accepted and consecrated this concept of "self-giving" as being at the heart of the conjugal union when it teaches that marriage "is an institution confirmed by the divine law and receiving its stability, from the human act by which the partners mutually surrender themselves to each other"[353]. In other words, canon 1057 §2 is simply giving juridical expression to this aspect of the thought of the Council Fathers.

The definition of consent by the New Code "brings out not just the personal dimension and object of the act of consent, but also the place it occupies as an essential piece in the canonical marriage system"[354]. Therefore, the phrase "each party" of canon 1081 §2 of the Code of 1917 is replaced by the phrase "a man and a woman" of canon 1057 §2 of the 1983 Code. Beal complements this when he asserts: "The change was prompted by a desire to underscore the personal dimension of consent. Consent is no longer exchanged by impersonal contractants but between a concrete man and a concrete woman for the purpose of establishing an irrevocable covenant"[355].

The definition of matrimonial consent as "an act of the will" is derived from the Roman contract law. During this period when the church was strategizing its own theory on the formation of marriage, marriage was classified as a contract by canonists[356]. It is pertinent to mention here that Aristotelian categories were implored to describe human acts during this era. "Human persons were described as composed of matter and form, that is of body and soul; the soul as operating through its distinct faculties, the mind and the will, one able to perceive the truth, the other to pursue the good.... Since marriage belonged to the category of 'good', consent to marriage had to be an act of the will. Because marriage would enrich any well-disposed person, no more than some initial cooperation of the mind was required. Thus consent became fully defined as "an act of the will"[357].

Consent as an act of the will implies that it can only originate in the will and must therefore be a concrete and sure expression of a decision, something new

352 Pius XI, Casti Connubii, p.543.

353 GS, 48 §1.

354 J. Ignacio, "Commentary on canon 1057", p.1070. "In addition, the proximity of the texts of cc. 1055 and 1057 point out more clearly the intrinsic reference of each to the other: to substitute the explicit mention of man and woman for the terms "parties", thus immediately showing the relationship of consent and its object with the sexual (conjugal) dimension of a human being; to explain the mutual nature of consent through the expression "give and accept one another"; and to show the relationship between consent, "the covenant", in which they mutually give and accept one another, its irrevocable nature and its proper effect: "for the purpose of establishing a marriage", with an almost explicit reference to the contents of §1 of c. 1055".

355 J.P. Beal, "Commentary on canons 1055-1062", p.1251.

356 Cfr. L. Örsy, Marriage in Canon Law, Delaware: Michael Glazier 1986, p.62.

357 Ibid.

and "original", emanating from a person[358]. Surrendering to another person the right over one's acts entails giving one's will over those acts, and since free will means also possession of self, by giving one's free will over certain acts, the person gives his or herself. In this, McAreavey defines human act when he asserts: "An act is truly human when the person is able to exert or give effect to his or her own will or intention. The human act is the freely willed act. It expresses the inner disposition of the person, not the disposition of another. Both reason and will are involved in it: the reason perceives a proposed course of action as good, makes a judgement (discernment) about it; the will moves freely towards it. An act is voluntary when it follows clear reflection and full consent of the will"[359].

The object of the matrimonial consent is the parties' gift of themselves to and acceptance of each other to form a conjugal union. This means a mutual exchange of rights and obligations to those acts and elements required to establish a marriage. Therefore if either or both partners give a fictitious consent or exclude by a positive act of the will either of the essential properties or any essential element of marriage, they contract invalidly[360].

The Conciliar description of the object of matrimonial consent and its canonical formulation as (sese mutuo tradunt atque accipiunt) has been criticized as inadequately juridical in nature. "It cannot mean a total surrender of all human faculties annihilating the spouses' sense of autonomy fundamental to human dignity. If on the other hand it means a handing-over of the right to those faculties essentially linked to the nature of marriage, then the term explains only little on its own, and certainly does not refer to the formal object of the irrevocable personal consent which causes marriage between the two spouses"[361].

However, the right to common conjugal life is not to be confused with the consortium or partnership which consists of all the matrimonial rights and obligations including the particular right to the convictum coniugale[362] or the right to live together with the mutual services this implies. All marital rights and obligations form the juridical content of marriage, but those essential rights and obligations that express the essential object of consent are necessary and sufficient to establish the marriage partnership. This assertion, in other words, should not lead to any legalistic and reductionist concept of marriage if we admit that when the spouses, knowingly commit those very personal acts implied in the formal object

358 Cfr. J. Ignacio, "Commentary on canon 1057", pp.1070-1071.

359 J. McAreavey, op.cit. p.49.

360 Cfr. c. 1101 §2 CIC/1983: „At si alterutra vel utraque pars positivo voluntatis actu excludat matrimonium ipsum vel matrimonii essentiale aliquod elementum, vel essentialem aliquam proprietatem, invalide contrahit".

361 C.J. Scicluna, op.cit. p.167.

362 Cfr. c. 1151 CIC/1983: „Spouses have the obligation and the right to maintain their common conjugal life, unless a lawful reason excuses them".

of consent as mutual, exclusive, perpetual and irrevocable rights and obligations, they do give and accept each other and form an incipient but true communion personarum in conformity with the laws which the Creator assigned in the humanity of man and woman.

Since matrimonial consent is "an act of the will", the vital question to be asked is, if there is anything particularly Igbo about an "act of the will" or about the object of this "act"? Since an act of the will participates in the whole personality of the person effecting the act, it could be said therefore, that a will-act participates in the socio-cultural reality of the person who performs the act. So the Igbo man who consents to a marriage does so with all the values of the society in which he was raised up. That "act of the will" could have some influence which directly comes from the environmental culture in which he lives and his idea of matrimonial reality could be easily affected by the same socio-cultural reality[363]. Canon Law as the law of the church should endeavour to accommodate and integrate some of these socio-cultural values peculiar to a particular set-up in the interpretation of the canonical requirements of matrimonial consent.

5.4. Conclusion

We have seen that matrimonial consent comes about through an act of will of the contracting parties. This act of the will is absolutely irreplaceable, and no human authority, civil or ecclesiastical, can dispense from it. Marital consent is perpetual and exclusive and must be manifested externally between legally qualified persons in the form established by the church[364].

The spouses consent to give to each other the right to certain acts ordered to the ends of marriage, and through the mutual, exclusive, perpetual and irrevocable right to these very personal acts, they mutually give and accept each other in order to establish a marriage. It is imperative to understand that the ends of marriage (the good of the spouses and the procreation and education of children) cannot be the direct object of a contractual agreement because the attainment of those ends is not always within the spouses' power. A marriage is valid in as much as the spouses' consent to the acts ordered to those ends even if the good of the spouses and the procreation and education of children may not be successfully attained.

363 Cfr. C.A. Ojemen, in: B. Etafo – H.O. Okeke, op.cit. p.24.

364 Cfr. J.M. Estevez, transl; Male and Female He Created Them: On Marriage and the Family, San Francisco 2003, p.38.

6. Conclusion of Chapter Two

From the foregoing marriage as natural and human institution was raised by Christ the Lord to the dignity of a sacrament for the baptized. It was desired by God with a view both to the good of the spouses in love and fidelity and to the good of the children emanating from their union.

The influence which the 1983 Code exerted on the development of the canonical understanding of marriage was indeed considerable. This Code followed the Conciliar document Gaudium et Spes in describing marriage as a covenant and not as a contract. But the word contract was used often by the same Code. Marriage is also a contract because the two parties give and consent to the covenant of love. It is a special kind of contract because of the nature of marriage, its purpose and the way of realizing its ends and purposes.

The sacramental nature of marriage has become a way of encountering Christ in a unique manner and bringing about the salvation of the spouses. It is Christ who in Christian marriage gives the spouses to each other for his love to the church. Thus marriage as a sacrament is the blessing of divine love to the spouses which expresses the indissoluble union and love of Christ.

The 1983 Code unlike the 1917 Code does not give a hierarchical ordering of the ends of marriage. This Code views both ends as equally necessary to and inseparable in marriage. The spouses commit themselves to that total personal self-giving with a view to seeking the good of each other and equally the good of the offspring born from their conjugal bond of love.

The new Code like the old Code emphasizes the church's teaching that a baptized couple cannot contract a marriage validly if the making of their marriage covenant is not at the same time a sacrament. In other words, both sacrament and contract cannot be separated from each other.

The covenant of conjugal love is endowed with the essential properties of marriage – unity and indissolubility which in Christian marriage obtain a special firmness in virtue of the sacrament. To exclude these essential properties of marriage in the marriage contract makes the marriage covenant itself invalid.

Finally, we have also seen that consent as an efficient cause of the marriage covenant consists of an act of the will concerning very personal rights and which cannot be supplied by any human power other than the persons consenting. In the marriage covenant the man gives himself as spouse to the woman, and the woman does the same thing and both give and accept each other as husband and wife.

Chapter Three: Marriage Preparation and Pastoral Care of Marriage in Canon 1063 of 1983 Code

1. Marriage Preparation in the Code of 1983

1.1. Introduction

The views about marriage preparation in the 1983 Code are broader than the parallel section of the Code of 1917 which stressed the assurance of the freedom of the parties to marry, with some concern about their adequate instruction regarding marriage[365]. It is indisputable that the new Code, unlike the old Code shows more concern and interest in regulating marriage preparation when it puts together in a single chapter all the norms concerning marriage preparation that were formerly dispersed, when it offers special attention to the pastoral aspects of marriage preparation and not just to the juridical aspects of 1917 Code, and when it stresses more vividly the correct preparation of the parties for a lawful and fruitful celebration of the sacrament of matrimony[366].

For the purpose of this chapter our study will focus succinctly on the new Code revision and the influence the 1975 Schema exacted on marriage preparation. Our study will also be dependent on those canons which deal more specifically with marriage preparation and pastoral care of marriage preparation. Canon 1063 will be dealt with separately because of the influence it exerted in bringing out the broader implications of marriage preparation and pastoral care regarding the preparation of the parties for marriage and also helping them in their marital union after marriage. The rest of the other canons which deal with marriage preparation will be treated together under the general norms concerning marriage preparation.

1.2. Revision of the New Code

The person who set the revision of the new Code of canon law[367] in motion was Pope John XXIII when, just few months after his election, on January 25, 1959,

365 Cfr. CC. 1019-1034 CIC/1917.

366 Cfr. T. Rincon-Perez, "Commentary on Canons 1063-1072", p. 1112.

367 Cfr. John XXIII, Addr. Primus Concilii Oecumenici nuntius, AAS 51(1959),pp. 65-69.

he announced his vision of a three-way enterprise for his papacy: (a) a synod for the diocese of Rome, (b) an ecumenical council, and (c) a modernization (aggiornamento) of the Code of canon law[368]. Not long after the commencement of the Second Vatican Council and a short time before his own death, he created a Commission for the revision of the Code of canon law in 1963[369]. It was Pope Paul VI who, after the death of Pope John XXIII, set the commission[370] to work before the Council closed in November 1965. It is to be noted that the Commission's assignment was more than the updating of the 1917 Code of canon law. In this way, "they were to reorganize the church's discipline and to accommodate it to the teachings of the Council. They were also to reform the church's canonical style, to give it a "new way of thinking" (novus habitus mentis), responsive to new needs"[371].

However, among the sixteen groups of consultors, composed mostly of canonists saddled with the responsibility of revising the Code, with specific areas of revising the church's legislation[372], two groups were handed the task of the revision of sacramental law. One of these two groups, was given the assignment of revising and drafting the Schema of marriage legislation[373]. In a bid to prepare a combined Schema that would be acceptable by all, the two groups met together on the 8 and 12 January 1974 respectively. The sacramental law Schema containing 361 norms out of which a total of 120 dealing with marriage law was then sent to the Episcopal Conferences of Bishops and other consultative organs in 1975[374]. This sacramental law Schema came to be known as the 1975 Schema[375] on marriage preparation.

368 Cfr. J.A. Coriden, An Introduction to Canon Law, New Jersey 2004, p.38.

369 Cfr. John XXIII, Addr. Diarium Romanae Curiae, AAS 55 (1963), p.363.

370 Cfr. Paul VI, Addr. Singulari cum animi, AAS 57 (1965), pp.985-989.

371 J.A. Coriden, An Introduction, p.38.

372 For more details on how these groups were to execute their assignment, see T.G. Green, The Revision of the Code: the First Decade, The Jurist 36 (1976), pp.353-355; Address of Cardinal P. Felici to the Austrian Society of Ecclesiastical Law, in: Comm.6 (1974), pp.107-108.

373 Cfr. P.K. Amevor, New Approaches to Marriage Preparation in the 1983 Code of Canon Law: Challenges to the Particular Church in Ghana, Regensburg 2009, p.134.

374 Cfr. F. Gavin, Pastoral Care in Marriage Preparation, p.72.

375 Cfr. Communicationes 6 (1974), pp.199-220; T.J. Green, The Revision of Marriage Law: An Exposition and Critique, Studia Canonica 10 (1976), p.363 f; P. Wirth, Das neue kirchliche Eherecht: Kurzer Überblick und kritische Würdigung, Österreichisches Archiv für katholisches Kirchenrecht 26 (1975), p.326.

1.3. The 1975 Schema

To come to terms with the influence and significance which the 1975 Schema exerted on the development of marriage preparation in the Code of 1983, it is important to start with Peter Huizing's proposal to enlarge the law on marriage preparation. He published this proposal in recognition of the need for a broader participation in the preparation for marriage. "It is a fundamental right of church members that the church community and especially their own local church provide them with active support for the realization of Christian marriage. This support will above all be provided through:

- appropriate enlightenment concerning the meaning of Christian marriage in catechesis for children, youth, and young adults and in preaching;
- personal preparation for marriage;
- a pleasing celebration of the wedding;
- pastoral accompaniment of married persons and especially through active and competent help when they experience difficulties in married life"[376].

It is also imperative in the 1975 Schema to begin with the first section of the canons forwarded for reactions to the Episcopal Conferences of Bishops concerning marriage preparation. The canons in this Schema look towards the same direction as they did in the Code of 1917, though with a very slight change. From the outset, the notion was to submit only the general principles concerning this in the new Code, while the rest of the principles would go to particular law. In line with this, pastors of souls, in adhering to local conditions, were advised to take necessary means to avoid all the dangers to the valid and lawful celebration of marriages. In this, specific norms for the parish priest's investigation were to be left to the Episcopal Conferences of Bishops[377].

376 P. Huizing, Alternativentwurf für eine Revision des kanonischen Eherechts, in: Für eine neue kirchliche Eheordnung, eds. P. Huizing, Düsseldorf 1975, p.86. The proposal here is listed as canon 2 of the proposed revision of the canons concerning marriage. "Es ist ein Grundrecht der kirchenmitglieder, das die Kirchengemeinschaft und besonders auch ihre eigenen Ortskirchen der christlichen Verwirklichung der Ehen ihre tatkräftige Unterstützung angedeihen lassen. Diese Unterstützung soll vor allem gegeben werden durch:
- entsprechende Aufklärung über die Bedeutung der christlichen Ehe in Jugend, Jugendlichen-Erwachsenen katechese und in der Verkündigung;
- die persönliche Vorbereitung auf die Ehe;
- die ansprechende Feier der Trauung;
- pastorales Geleit der Eheleute und ganz besonders in der tatkräftigen und sachkundigen Hilfe, wenn sich im Eheleben Schwierigkeiten ergeben".

377 Cfr. P. Huizing, Relator, Opera Consultorum: De Matrimonio, in: Comm. 3 (1971), p.71; J.H. Provost, Marriage Preparation in the New Code, p.179.

The first chapter in the Schema 1975 on what must take place before marriage is treated in canon 249. This canon taken from the original canon 1019 of 1917 Code speaks of the responsibility of the parish priest to see to it that nothing prevents the valid and lawful celebration of marriage (can.249, Schema 1975). This is followed by canon 250, equivalent of canon 1020 of 1917 Code, which deals with the norm concerning the competence of Episcopal Conferences of Bishops to specify certain formalities in order to determine a person's freedom to marry (can.250, Schema 1975).

Prospective couples are urged to receive the sacrament of confirmation before marriage (can.251, Schema 1975; can.1021 of 1917 Code). Canon 252 speaks of the obligation of the people to notify the proper authorities of impediments to marriage. (can.252, Schema 1975; can.1027 of 1917 Code). This is followed by the local ordinary's discretion in dispensing from the Banns of marriage (can.253, Schema 1975; cann.1023-1025 of 1917 Code). In this way, the local ordinary of the parties may for a just cause, dispense from making the publications. If there is more than one ordinary, then it is the ordinary in whose diocese the marriage is to be celebrated who has the right to dispense. If the priest carrying out the investigation into the couple's freedom to marry is not the person authorized to assist at the marriage, he must notify the parish priest responsible about the results of his investigations (can.254, Schema 1975; can.1029 of 1917 Code). Special permission of the local ordinary is required into different cases. It is required before assisting at the marriage of migrants (can.255, Schema 1975). It is also required on those persons committing adultery during a prior marriage and attempting to marry under civil law (can.256, Schema 1975). It is to be noted that before assisting at the marriage of the minors without the knowledge of or against the reasonable opposition of their parents, consultation with the local ordinary is required[378].

However, it is interesting to note that in the Schema 1975, canon 1033 of the previous Code of 1917 was replaced with a canon in two sections: Can.275 (c.1033 CIC/1917) §1: "The pastor is to teach the spouses, in keeping with the condition of various persons, about the sanctity of matrimony, the mutual obligations of spouses, and the obligations of parents toward children". §2: "The pastor is to take care to prepare the celebration of matrimony so that its sacramental dignity will shine forth and the spouses and others present will participate actively in the sacred rite"[379].

378 Cfr. F. Gavin, Pastoral Care in Marriage Preparation. p.74.

379 Can.257 (c.1033 CIC/1917) §1: "Parochus sponsos, secundum diversarum personarum condicionem, doceat sanctitatem matrimonii, mutuas obligationes et obligationes parentum erga prolem". §2: "Parochus curet de paranda celebratione matrimonii, ita ut dignitas sacramentalis eluceat et coniuges ac ceteri adstantes actuose participent ritum sacrum". (1975 Schema),p.74. The English version of this Schema is taken from J.H. Provost, Marriage Preparation in the New Code, p.180; see also F. Gavin, Pastoral Care in Marriage Preparation, p.74.

The canons of the 1975 Schema were at a point restructured so that a general canon on catechesis, an equivalent of canon 1018 of the 1917 Code would surface at the beginning of the chapter on what was to precede marriage[380]. Canon 248 of the Schema reads: "Pastors of souls are bound in virtue of their office to fulfill the function of providing catechetical instruction on the sacrament of matrimony according to norms issued by ecclesiastical authority"[381].

Suffice it to say that it is these last two canons (cann. 257 and 248) of the 1975 Schema that formed the nucleus of canon 1063 of the Code of 1983.

1.4. Evaluation of the Schema and Formulation of canon 1063

The Coetus[382] met so many times to discuss and analyse the 1975 Schema at the wake of the mixed evaluation received from the different Episcopal Conferences of Bishops and various consultative groups. Although the Coetus reported that the 1975 Schema was generally received and accepted, it does not remove the fact that it was greeted with both positive and negative reactions. To some respondents it was quite satisfactory. For others, it concentrated so much with marriage as a contract, thereby lacking in a truly ecclesial dimension for matrimony. Some respondents felt it was too concerned with avoiding dangers and establishing so many avenues for nullity[383]. A small number of respondents thought that it did not include enough innovations and therefore did not really take into consideration the new theology that was emerging, and that it relied solely on the ecclesiastical situation in Europe and North America which was not in consonant with the experience of the church in mission areas[384].

380 Cfr. J.H. Provost, Marriage Preparation in the New Code, p.180.

381 Can.248 (c.1018 CIC/1917): "Pastores animarum vi officii sui tenentur, ut munus impertiendi catecheticam instructionem de matrimonii sacramento adimpleant, secundum normas ab auctoriatate ecclesiastica tradendas". (1975 Schema), p.73.

382 The reorganizing of the canons in this Schema and the reworking of the Schema itself was done by the general Coetus that prepared also the Schema. At the inception of it was a small group who examined and synthesized the various observations of the consultative organs totaling 172 on the whole. This group evaluated the De Sacramentis Schema in such a way that they particularly considered the marriage norms. Then the general body of the Coetus took some reasonable time to reflect on the general comments concerning the Schema before the detailed examination of specific norms. For more details, see T.J. Green, The Revised Schema De Matrimonio, Jurist 40 (1980), pp.60-61; F. Gavin, Pastoral Care in Marriage Preparation, p.75.

383 Cfr. Comm. 9 (1977), p.117; J.H. Provost, Marriage Preparation in the New Code, p.180.

384 Cfr. Comm. 9 (1977), p.117. See also F. Gavin, Pastoral Care in Marriage Preparation, p.75; T.J. Green, The Revision of Marriage Law, pp.373-374.

Some useful insights were given with regard to pastoral care of marriage preparation that it should be treated properly and carefully. Interestingly, the relator, Peter Huizing and another consultor, were asked by the Coetus to formulate a totally new canon which would pull together material from the canon on catechesis and other canons, taking into cognizance the recommendations from so many of the responses[385]. The relator together with the help of another consultor propounded a new title called "Pastoral Care and the Prerequisites for the Celebration of Marriage"[386]. This very title was welcomed and approved by all the respondents and the result of their work was a canon reminiscent of Peter Huizing's published proposal which we discussed in the 1975 Schema:

Can.249. "The Christian faithful have the right that the church and specifically their own ecclesial community provide effective assistance so the matrimonial state might be preserved and progress in a truly Christian spirit. This assistance is to be provided especially:

1) By instruction in the meaning of Christian marriage and the functions of spouses and Christian parents, through preaching, through the use of the media, and through appropriate catechizing of children, youth and adults;
2) By personal preparation for entering marriage, so that the spouses will be disposed for the duties and sanctity of their new state;
3) By a liturgical celebration of their matrimonial covenant in which "the savior of men and women and the spouse of the church comes into the lives of married Christians through the sacrament of matrimony" (GS 48);
4) By pastoral aid to married persons so that "they increasingly advance their own perfection, as well as their mutual sanctification, and hence contribute jointly to the glory of God" (GS 48); and especially by expert and effective matrimonial and familial assistance"[387].

385 Cfr. Comm. 9 (1977), pp.130-132; J.H. Provost, Marriage Preparation in the New Code, p.180; F. Gavin, Pastoral Care in Marriage Preparation, p.75.

386 Cfr. F. Gavin, Pastoral Care in Marriage Preparation, p.75.

387 The English version of this very canon is taken from J.H. Provost, Marriage Preparation in the New Code, pp.180-181. The original Latin version from Comm. 9 (1977), p.137, reads: Can.249. "Christifidelibus ius est, ut Ecclesia et in specie propria communitas ecclesialis efficacem assistentiam praebeant ut status matrimonialis in spiritu vere christiano conservetur et progrediatur. Haec assistentia imprimus praebenda est:

1) institutione de significatione matrimonii christiani ac de munere coniugum ac parentum christianorum in praedicatione, in usu instrumentorum communicationis, in catechesis minoribus, iuvenibus et adultis aptata;
2) praeparatione personali ad matrimonium ineundum, ita ut sponsi ad novi sui status official et sanctitatem disponantur;
3) liturgica foederis matrimonialis celebration in qua "hominum Salvator Ecclesiaeque Sponsus per sacramentum matrimonii christifidelibus coniugibus obviam venit" (GS 48);

There were so many arguments within the Coetus as regards the insertion of the word "right" (ius) of the Christian faithful to marriage preparation. It is against this background that one consultor insisted that if the Christian faithful do have the right to pastoral care, then they could as well go to court to implement this right over against a negligence ecclesial community. In line with this argument which he posited, he was reluctant to admit it. Another consultor who spoke in favour of the notion of right insisted that it should be a right which could be urged against the representatives of the community and not the entire community as such. He continued with his argument that since the church imposes so many laws and burdens on the Christian faithful in matters relating to matrimony, that a corresponding right of the Christian faithful should also be incorporated so that the faithful would be properly and diligently instructed with regard to the obligations. Still on the debate of drafting of the canon, a third consultor envisaged that the canon should be written in favour of the obligations of the pastors instead of the rights of the Christian faithful. He argued further that it would be more suitable and proper to start with the obligations, and from these obligations rights could be deduced. There was no unanimous agreement from this debate within the Coetus, and a vote was cast, and by four to three margins, it was unanimously decided to speak of the obligations of the pastors rather than the rights of the Christian faithful[388].

The revised canon[389] was then submitted to the members of the Code Commission for their inputs. This was followed by a collection of their inputs which was responded to in a report from the secretariat before the 1981 plenary meeting of

---

4) auxilio pastorali pro coniugatis ut "magis ac magis ad propriam suam perfectionem mutuamque santificationem ideoque communiter ad Dei glorificationem accedunt" (GS 48); et maxime assistentia matrimoniali et familiali perita et efficaci".

388 Cfr. Comm. 9 (1977), pp.138-139. See also H. Zapp, Kanonisches Eherecht, 7; neubearbeitete Auflage, Freiburg 1988, pp.76-77. The Coetus decided to use "de obligatione pastorum" in the canon instead of "de iure christifidelium". This vote manifests the seriousness of the obligation placed upon pastors and subsequently upon bishops for their assistance in its proper fulfillment.

389 Cfr. Comm. 9 (1977), p.139. The text of the revised canon reads: "Pastores animarum obligatione tenetur curandi ut propria ecclesialis communitas christifidelibus assistentiam praebeat qua status matrimonialis in spiritu christiano servetur et in perfection progrediatur. Haec assistentia imprimis praebenda est:

1) praedicatione, catechesis minoribus, invenibus et adultis aptata, imo usu instrumentorum communicationis socialis, quibus christifideles de significatione matrimonii christiani deque munere coniugum ac parentum christianorum instituantuur;
2) praeparatione personali ad matrimonium ineundum, qua sponsi ad novi sui status sanctitatem et official disponantur;
3) fructuosa liturgica matrimonii celebratione; qua eluceat coniuges mysterium unitatis et foecundi amoris inter Christum et Ecclesiam significare atque participare;
4) auxilio coniugatis praestito, ut foedus coniugale fideliter servants atque tuentes, ad sanctiorem in dies plenioremque in familia vitam ducendam perveniant".

the Code Commission itself[390]. There were two most important proposals made with regard to the canon. The first proposal demanded that something should be added as regards the obligations or duties proper to couples. Such obligations include the education of children, the assistance to be given to Catholics entering mixed marriages, and that mention be made about Catholics who lack faith when they are to enter marriage. An additional canon was called for on the second proposal which would have mandated pastors to exclude from marriage those who had only mundane or merely social reasons for marrying. The two sets of proposals were rejected by the secretariat on the ground that the first suggestions were already contained in the other canons or belonged to particular law, if there is any law as such[391]. With regard to the text of the proposed canon, only one minor change[392] was made. The minor change was from "communitas ecclesialis" to "communitas ecclesiastica" in the first sentence of the canon. After this minor change and with no other changes to the proposed canon 249 of the earlier formulation, the new canon came to us as canon 1063 of the Code of 1983.

1.5. Conclusion

We have seen so far that the process of revising the 1917 Code of canon law which Pope John XXIII put in motion in 1959 eventually resulted in the 1983 Code. This very process of updating was called a recognitio, a rethinking of the Code. The significance which the 1975 Schema exerted on the formulation of canon 1063 of 1983 Code as a "Novus Habitus Mentis" (new way of thinking) about pastoral care of marriage preparation cannot be over-emphasised. The Coetus unanimous approval of the title as "Pastoral Care and the Prerequisites for the Celebration of Marriage" was indeed essential evidence in this formulation process. It shows the seriousness of the obligations placed upon pastors for their assistance in its proper fulfillment.

The task of the Coetus to inculcate to the various provisions of the canon on catechesis with the other canons that are related to marriage preparation is reflected properly in the proposed new canon 249 on the many dimensions of the pastoral care for marriage, especially in terms of its preparation[393]. Report-

390 Cfr. Pontificia Commissio Codici Iuris Canonici Recognoscendo, Relatio Complectens Synthesim animadversionum, Vatican City 1981.

391 Cfr. PCCICR, Relatio Complectens synthesim animadversionum, p.248. See also Comm.15 (1983), p.225; J.H. Provost, Marriage Preparation in the New Code, pp.181-182; F. Gavin, Pastoral Care in Marriage Preparation, p.79.

392 Cfr. PCCICR, Codex Iuris Canonici. Schema novissimum iuxta placita patrum commissionis emendatum atque summo pontifici praesentatum, Vatican City 1982, p.190.

393 Cfr. T.J. Green, The Revised Schema, p.73; F. Gavin, Pastoral Care in Marriage Preparation, p.77.

ing on this proposed new canon, Morrisey enumerates what is in many ways both its strength and weakness. "It goes without saying that this entire program could be carried out in a minimal fashion, simply observing the prescriptions of the law. On the other hand, with a bit of imagination and pastoral zeal, this program can be but the beginning of a constructive plan to do much to help young couples as they embark on their married life. But it is impossible to legislate for generosity"[394].

On the whole, the proposed new canon has been recognized as an expression of the Conciliar way of thinking which Paul VI called for, at work[395] and something quite new in comparison with the Code of 1917.

2. General Norms Concerning Marriage Preparation in the Code of 1983

2.1. Introduction

Echoing the spirit of Second Vatican Council, the Code of 1983 introduces the notion of "Pastoral care and what must precede the celebration of marriage"[396] into the very title of the section concerning pre-marriage preparation. The norms concerning marriage preparation in this very Code are due to the conviction that marriage of Christians is a path to sanctity, and a special vocation within the church, to achieve which Christian spouses "peculiari sacramento roborantur et veluti consecrantur"[397]. The title of the present Code is a clear indication of the two great sections of the bone of contention. On the one hand, there is the section which refers to pastoral care proper. On the other hand, there is also the section that concerns juridical prerequisites, whose goal is to achieve a valid and lawful celebration of marriage. The requirement of permission from the local ordinary for lawful assistance at different marriages as a precautionary measure to safeguard various values is also included[398].

394 F.G. Morrisey, Revising Church Legislation on Marriage, Origins 9 (1979), p.213.

395 Cfr. V. Fagiolo, In Commento al Codici di Dritto Canonica, eds. Pio V. Pinto, Rome 1985, pp.622-624.

396 It is seen in chapter II of Title VII De matrimonio of book IV – De ecclesiae munere santificandi, under the title of De cura pastorali et de iis quae matrimonii celebrationi praemitti debent.

397 GS, 48. See also T. Rincon-Perez, "Commentary on canons 1063-1072, Pastoral Care and the Prerequisites for the Celebration of Marriage", in A. Marzoa – et al. eds; Exegetical Commentary, p.1112.

398 Cfr. T. Rincon-Perez, "Commentary on canons 1063-1072", p.1112.

Emphasis is thus placed on the pastoral care in the present new Code, whereas in the Code of 1917 emphasis was placed on the necessary things that had to be done before a marriage could actually take place and on the publication of the marriage Banns as reflected in the corresponding title[399]. Speaking on the shift of emphasis, Gavin asserts: "It is important to note that nothing is lost of the church's insistence on and pre-occupation with a valid and lawful celebration, but the emphasis is now broader, with specific reference to pastoral care"[400].

The general norms about marriage preparation in the Code of 1983 contain ten canons that cover four areas that are related but at the same time distinct from one another. Canons 1063-65 deal with pre-marriage preparation. These canons speak of the necessity of the sacrament in the whole life of the spouses and of the community, and stress that the concern about marriage is greater than the concern for the valid exchange of the parties consent. They emphasis on the importance both for the preparation of the formation of children to be responsible Christian adults in future for the purpose of comprehending and appreciating the sacrament in their lives, and also the support to be given to those already married[401]. Canons 1066-70 deal with pre-nuptial enquiry. These canons emphasis that adequate attention is to be given in ensuring that the canonical prerequisites for a valid and lawful marriage celebration, are met before the proper celebration. A number of problem cases where the lawful permission of the Bishop is needed for a valid celebration of marriage to take place are addressed in canon 1071. Canon 1072 deals with the attention that pastors of souls should give to the marriages of the young people who are below the customary age of marriage in different regions. We are now going to look at the rest of the other canons that treated marriage preparation before focusing our attention properly to canon 1063.

2.2. The Norms

The canon which follows canon 1063 directly under the general norms concerning marriage preparation is canon 1064[402]. This canon which is not related to

399 This is found in the Code of 1917, chapter I of title VII in Book III. "De iis quae matrimonii celbrationi praemitti debent et praesertim de publicationibus matrimonialibus". See also B.D. Hajovsky, Marriage Preparation and Pastoral Care: A Comparison Between the 1917 and 1983 Codes of Canon Law, Washington 1984, p.89.

400 F. Gavin, Pastoral Care in Marriage Preparation, p.80.

401 Cfr. L.A. Robitaille, "Commentary on canons 1063-1072, Pastoral Care and what must precede Celebration of Marriage", in: J.P. Beal – J.A. Coriden – T.J. Green, ed; New Commentary on the Code of Canon Law, Bangalore 2004, p.1261.

402 Cfr. C.1064 CIC/1983: "Ordinarii loci est curare ut debite ordinetur eadem assistentia, auditis etiam, si opportunum videatur, viris et mulieribus experientia et peritia probatis".

any canon in the 1917 Code upholds that it is up to the local ordinary to make provisions that such assistance as we are going to see in canon 1063 is duly organized[403], in his diocese of jurisdiction. In keeping with this assistance and with the genuine obligation imposed by canon 1063, its organization is not to be left to chance. In this, appropriate practical arrangements are to be made by the local ordinary whose obligation is not to be confused with that of the ordinary. In canon law the word ordinary means, apart from the Roman Pontiff, diocesan Bishops and all who, even for a time only, are set over a particular church or a community equivalent to it in accordance with canon 368, and those who in these have general ordinary executive power, that is to say, Vicars general and Episcopal Vicars. It also includes the major Superiors of clerical religious institutes of pontifical right and of clerical societies of apostolic life of pontifical right, who have at least ordinary executive power[404]. The term local ordinary means all those enumerated above, except Superiors of religious institutes and of societies of apostolic life[405]. Whatever in the canons, in the context of executive power, is accorded to the diocesan Bishop, is understood to belong only to the diocesan Bishop and to those others in canon 381§2 who are equivalent to him, to the exclusion of the Vicar general and the Episcopal Vicar unless by a special mandate.

The local ordinary is the Bishop of a particular church entrusted to his care and as such he is the first person responsible for all the pastoral action which is to be programmed and implemented[406]. As the pastor of this particular church, it rests on him to ensure that assistance suitable to the situation of the Christian faithful living in that particular territory is provided.

It is to be noted that an earlier draft of this very canon assigned responsibility for marriage preparation to Bishops' Conferences[407]. The Apostolic Exhortation of

403 H. Zapp, Kanonisches Eherecht, p.82. "Besonderes Gewicht erhält diese Verpflichtung der Seelsorger zu einer intensiven Ehevorbereitung und sorgfältigen Familienpastoral schließlich auch durch die an den jeweiligen Ortsoberhirten gerichtete Vorschrift des c.1064, für die Gestaltung und pflichtgemäße Durchführung dieser pastoralen Betreuung zu sorgen".,

404 Cfr. C.134 §1 CIC/1983:"Nomine Ordinarii in iure intelleguntur, praeter Romanum Pontificem, Episcopi diocesani aliique qui, etsi ad interim tantum, praepositi sunt alicui Ecclesiae particulari vel communitati eidem aequi paratae ad normam can.368, necnon qui in iisdem generali gaudent potestate exsectiva ordinaria, nempe Vicarii generals et episcopales; itemque, pro suis sodalibus, Superiores maiores clericalium institutorum religiosorum iuris pontificii et clericalium societatum vitae apostolicae iuris pontificii, qui ordinaria saltem potestate exsecutiva pollent".

405 Cfr. C.134 §2 CIC/1983:"Nomine Ordinarii loci intelleguntur omnes qui in §1 recensentur, exceptis Superioribus institutorum religiosorum et societatum vitae apostolicae".

406 CD, 17§1:"A diocese is a section of the People of God entrusted to a bishop to be guided by him with the assistance of his clergy so that, loyal to its pastor and formed by him into one community in the Holy Spirit through the Gospel and the Eucharist, it constitutes one particular church in which the one, holy, catholic and apostolic church of Christ is truly present and active".

407 Cfr. Comm. 9 (1977), p.138.

John Paul II, Familiaris Consortio also deemed it necessary for the Conferences of the Bishops to assume the responsibility of publishing a directory for pastoral care of the family when he says: "In this they should lay down, in the first place, the minimum content, duration and method of the "Preparation Courses", balancing the different qualified persons in making provisions for marriage preparation. This is absolutely necessary in programs which require the skills of experts[408] or professionally trained personnels such as canon lawyers, doctors, psychiatrists, psychologists and counselors. The local ordinary can learn what is suitable for marriage preparation programs through these professionals whom he is to consult. With regard to these experts who have expertise and experience in this area, Green opines that such experts have assisted in developing contemporary marriage nullity jurisprudence especially in the area of psychic incapacity for marriage. One could reasonably expect such contributions in other areas of pastoral care for marriage preparation[409]. Care should be taken to ensure that such assistance is updated regularly to keep in touch with any changing issues which should be addressed[410].

The consultation of the local ordinary with men and women of proven experience and expertise is a clear indication of the church's desire that the laity would actively participate in its mission of salvation[411]. This is seen in canon 212 §3, which emphasis that the Christ's faithful have the right, indeed at times the duty, in keeping with their knowledge, competence and position, to manifest to the sacred pastors their views on matters which concern the good of the church. It is also addressed in canon 228 §2, where it states that lay people who are outstanding in the requisite knowledge, prudence and integrity, are capable of being experts or advisors, even in councils in accordance with the law, in order to provide assistance to the pastors of the church[412]. This shows that the necessity for obtaining the experience and expertise of the lay faithful in this matter of marriage preparation and counseling seems to be much greater that the words of the canon would suggest.

---

408 H. Heimerl – H. Pree, Kirchenrecht: Allgemeine Normen und Eherecht, Wien 1983, p.190. "Ob und welche Experten der Bischof heranzieht, steht in seinem klugen Ermessen. Er wird sich auch bestehender Institutionen wie Familienseelsorger, Familienverbände oder des Pastoralrates bedienen können".

409 Cfr. T.J. Green, The Church's Sanctifying Mission: Some Aspects of the Normative Role of the Diocesan Bishop, Studia Canonica 25 (1999), p.267. See also P.K. Amevor, New Approaches to Marriage Preparation, p.145.

410 Cfr. L.A. Robitaille, "Commentary on canons 1063-1072", p.1264.

411 Cfr. D. Kelly, "Commentary on Pastoral Care and the Prerequisites for the Celebration of Marriage", in G. Sheehy – et al. eds; The Canon Law Letter and Spirit: A practical Guide to the Code of Canon Law, Dublin 1995, p.580.

412 C.228 §2 CIC/1983: "Laici debita scientia, prudential et honestate praestantes, habiles sunt tamquam periti aut consiliarii, etiam in consiliis ad normam iuris, ad Ecclesiae Pastoribus adiutorium praebendum".

Sebott in his book[413], acknowledges the fact that since the promulgation of this very canon some special forms of marriage preparation[414] have been developed in some Countries like France and Italy. He goes on to mention the popular one being the so-called "Equipes Notre-Dame", which was founded by Abbe'Caffarel in 1938. In addition to this, the General Synod of Bishops, Priests, Deacons and Laity in the Federal Republic of Germany (1971-1975)[415] made also some suggestions with regard to time for preparation of marriage and pastoral work of the family[416].

Thus, it belongs to the local ordinary in the first place to promote and organize this assistance in all its stages. He should seek to involve the entire ecclesial community in this pastoral care, including if appropriate, the assistance of men and women of experience and proven expertise.

In agreement with canon 1021 §2 of the 1917 Code, canon 1065 §1 establishes the requirement of receiving the sacrament of confirmation before being admitted to marriage, if this can be done without grave inconvenience[417]. In line with this paragraph, it is interesting to know that during the work of codification[418] for the proposition of the first norm, some consultors requested two different things. Some spoke on eliminating the confirmation requirement, while others, on the contrary emphasized the absolute importance of it and empowering parish priests to administer the sacrament of confirmation before marriage. In accordance with this, the legislator literally reproduced the norm of the 1917 Code which urged the parties to be confirmed before marriage, but not absolutely. Rincon-Perez admits that: "It is clear that in this way the legislator is showing tactful respect for ius connubii by not imposing a new hurdle to exercising it when there is grave difficulty in being confirmed, such as for lack of a

---

413 Cfr. R. Sebott, Das Neue Kirchliche Eherecht, p.46.

414 Cfr. J. Lehmann, Ehevorbereitung in der Bundesrepublik Deutschland: Möglichkeiten der Verwirklichung anhand des Codex Iuris Canonici und der Adhortatio apostolica, "Familiaris Consortio" Papst Johannes Pauls II; München 1985, pp.4-12.

415 Cfr. H. Hallermann, Gemeinsame Synode, in: A.V. Compenhausen – I. Riedel-Spangenberger – R. Sebott, Hgg; Lexikon für Kirchen – und Staatskirchenrecht II, Paderborn 2002, pp.41-44.

416 GSyn 1: Christlich gelebte Ehe und Familie 3.1.2.1.1, in: R. Sebott, Das Neue Kirchliche Eherecht, pp.46-47. "Eine zeitgerechte Ehe – und Familien pastoral muß Brautleutetage, Brautleutewochenenden, Brautleutewochen oder ähnliche Veranstaltungen anbieten, die in Inhalt und Form genügend Anreiz geben, von dem Angebot Gebrauch zu machen. Es ist sehr zu begrüßen, wenn befreundete und verlobte Paare möglichst früh an einem Brautleutekurs teilnehmen, um aufgeworfen Fragen in Ruhe bedenken und sich gegenseitig prüfen zu können".

417 C.1065 §1 CIC/1983: "Catholici qui sacramentum confirmationis nondum receperint, illud, antequam ad matrimonium admittantur, recipiant, si id fieri possit sine gravi incommodo".

418 Cfr. Comm. 9 (1977), pp.140-141.

minister"[419]. It is to be noted that the norms lay down by canons 882 and 883[420] on administering the sacrament of confirmation must be followed as regards whether the parish priest may confirm the parties in that type of situation of a lack of a minister.

Notwithstanding the fact that the reception of this very sacrament is not an absolute one for the validity of the marriage covenant, it is even more necessary for the faith of the parties and the fruitful celebration of marriage. It is also to be argued from the point that since marriage is a sacrament of adulthood that embodies with it grave obligations both in the daily life of a Christian and in the Christian upbringing of a family, it is imperative that those embarking on it should be confirmed[421]. It is good to bring to mind what the Dogmatic Constitution on the Church, Lumen Gentium says about the proper vocation of married partners as being "witnesses of faith and love of Christ to one another and to their children"[422]. Married couples are also "cooperators of grace and witnesses of the faith. They are the first to pass on the faith to their children and to educate them in it. By word and example they form them to a Christian and apostolic life; they offer them wise guidance in the choice of vocation, and if they discover in them a sacred vocation they encourage it with all care"[423].

The sacraments of the church are closely inter-related with one another. In this Walsh gives insight on the link between the sacrament of confirmation and the sacrament of matrimony: "Confirmation reinforces the witnessing and missionary status of the sacrament of marriage and its own meaning is made more concrete by its relationship with marriage. Marriage can build up a nuclear family, a tribe, a social class, a nation, and can cement loyalties within these groups. By that very fact it can also become (inward-looking and self-centered)…. Confirmation will not allow Christian marriage to be of this sort. The men and women who received the spirit at Pentecost become people for whom human love sealed in marriage could never again lock them into any kind of tribal or linguistic particu-

419 T. Rincon-Perez, "Commentary on Canons 1063-1072", p.1124.

420 C.882 CIC/1983: "The ordinary minister of confirmation is a Bishop. A priest can also validly confer this sacrament if he has the faculty to do so, either from the general law or by way of a special grant from the competent authority".
C.883 CIC/1983: "The following have, by law, the faculty to administer confirmation:
1° within the confines of their jurisdiction, those who in law are equivalent to a diocesan Bishop;
2° in respect of the person to be confirmed, the priest who by virtue of his office or by mandate of the diocesan Bishop baptizes an adult or admits a baptized adult into full communion with the catholic Church;
3° in respect of those in danger of death, the parish priest or indeed any priest".

421 Cfr. D. Kelly, "Commentary on Pastoral Care", pp.580-581.

422 LG, 35§3.

423 AA, 11§2.

larism…. They would rather stand for a human love that reaches across such barriers, that keeps open house and hospitality from which no one is excluded…"[424].

While it is important for those intending to marry to be administered the sacrament of confirmation, from a theological point of view, it is noteworthy to say that the church does not make the reception of this sacrament as an absolute conditio sine qua non for marriage to take place[425]. Be that as it may, those intending to marry who are not yet confirmed should not be rushed into receiving this sacrament without adequate preparation for it. This is the very reason why marriage preparation should start early enough so that the sacrament of confirmation be received before the marriage celebration. The Introduction to the Rite of Confirmation puts the matter clearly: "If it is foreseen that the conditions for a fruitful reception of confirmation cannot be satisfied, the local ordinary will judge whether it is better to defer confirmation until after the marriage"[426].

Paragraph two of this very canon which also corresponds to canon 1033 of the 1917 Code states that in order to receive the sacrament of marriage more fruitfully, spouses are earnestly recommended that they approach the sacraments of penance and that of the blessed Eucharist. It has been and it is still the church's desire that the celebration of the sacrament of matrimony be not only lawful and valid, but at the same time fruitful. "Marriage is a pivotal moment in the life of a couple and it is appropriate for the parties to celebrate this moment by being fully reconciled to God and the church in the sacrament of penance"[427]. Repentance and mutual forgiveness within the circle of the family of Christians which form part of a daily life receive their proper sacrament in the sacrament of penance[428].

Since the sacrament of the Eucharist is the nuptial banquet of those partaking in the covenant between Christ and his body the church, it is pertinent that spouses are called upon to receive it during the nuptial mass and in order to receive it, it is appropriate that they be in a state of grace according to canon 916. In this, the theological and spiritual importance of it is highlighted by Walsh when he discloses that: "The Eucharist provides initiation into Christian marriage in a still more intimate way. It unites the body of a Christian to the body of Christ. It is that same body that becomes one with the body of a marriage partner. It is because the bodies of Christians are seen to be made one with Christ in the Eucharist that their becoming one with one another in the sexual bond of marriage becomes

424 L. Walsh, The Sacrament of Initiation, London 1988, p.55.

425 Cfr. Comm. 15 (1983), p.225.

426 DOL, 2521.

427 J. McAreavey, The Canon Law of Marriage and the Family, p.66.

428 Cfr. FC, 58§2.

Christ-bearing and Christ-revealing, and can be a statement of the human love of Christ for his brothers and sisters who form his church"[429]. So the Eucharist being the very source of Christian marriage represents Christ's covenant of love with his church which is ratified with his blood on the cross. Christian spouses encounter in this sacrifice of the new and eternal covenant, the source through which their own marriage covenant flows. The encounter is interiorly structured and continuously renewed[430].

It is imperative to note that while the reception of the sacraments of penance and Eucharist is strongly recommended to ensure the more fruitful reception of marriage, the obligation to receive them by the intending marriage couples is not absolute. The sacrament of matrimony may not be refused to the spouses because of their unwillingness to receive these two sacraments[431]. However, this does not remove the fact that intending spouses should approach these two sacraments before the celebration of their marriage since marriage is the proper source and authentic means of sanctification for Christian married couples and families.

It is to be noticed that there is a slight difference between the present Code and the old Code with regard to the recommendation of the reception of the sacraments of penance and Eucharist. While the old Code puts the obligation upon parish priests to earnestly exhort the intending couples to carefully confess their sins before their marriage, and to receive with devotion the most blessed Eucharist, the new Code places the recommendation to the spouses themselves. This slight difference does not mean that both parish priests and spouses do not possess the pastoral responsibility to make the parties to be aware of this very recommendation. On the contrary, "they must make the future spouses understand that a valid celebration of marriage is not sufficient, but also that the obstacle of sin must be removed for the sacrament to be fruitful. They must also inform the parties that the Eucharist is "the source and summit of every Christian life" (LG 11) and that therefore the conjugal community should be built thereon from the beginning"[432].

429 L. Walsh, The Sacraments of Initiation, pp.66-67.

430 Cfr. FC, 57§2.

431 D. Kelly, "Commentary on Pastoral Care", p.581. "However, such an unwillingness might well be indicative of a careless practice of the faith, perhaps even of a loss of faith – in which case the diligent priest will see the need for further sensitive pastoral care and evaluation. It is only in the situation where both parties show that they reject explicitly and formally what the church intends to do when the marriage of baptized persons is celebrated that the sacrament has to be refused".

432 T. Rincon-Perez, "Commentary on Canon 1063-1072", p.1124.

Canon 1066[433] in repeating canon 1019 §1 of the Code of 1917 expresses the general principle that before marriage is celebrated; it must be evident that nothing stands in the way of its celebration being valid and lawful. Given the fact that there is a natural right to marry as established in canon 1058 of the present Code, there is no question of intending couples having to prove that they are capable of marrying. But since the right to marry is not absolute, it is subject to the limitations of both divine and ecclesiastical law[434]. In view of the pastoral means to prepare adequately for the fruitful celebration of marriage, the legislation establishes a number of juridical prerequisites designed to investigate if the intending couples are free to marry and that there as such no hindrances to a valid[435] and licit celebration of marriage. It is after this investigation can the parish priest assist and then the marriage will be legitimate[436]. Thus, for a marriage to be decleard valid, the parties marrying must be canonically free to marry, that means no impediment must be found (cc.1083-1094), the parties must marry without force or coercion and true matrimonial consent must be given (cc.1095-1107), and the proper canonical form must be used in celebrating the marriage (c.1108). And in order that a marriage is celebrated lawfully, the prescriptions of canons 1067-1072 and also that of canon 1102 §3 should be adequately followed[437].

Canon 1067 obliges the Episcopal Conferences of Bishops the determination of procedures to acquire the certainty recorded in canon 1066. It stresses three lines of investigation: (a) personal examination of the intending couples, (b) publication of Banns for marriage, and (c) other necessary means of inquiry. The personal examination of the parties here is quite different from that of personal preparation prescribed in canon 1063, 2° which we are going to discuss later in

433 The implication of this canon is that not everyone who intends to marry is necessarily capable of doing so. It is against this background that parish priests have a grave moral obligation to ensure the capacity of the couples to celebrate a valid and lawful marriage. Be that as it may, the level of certainty required here is that of moral in the sense that it is the same level of certainty needed by a tribunal judge to pronounce certain judgments on marriage cases. But while the tribunal judge must arrive to a moral certainty within the ambience of a strict judicial process, the parish priest on the other hand, can have recourse to whatever prudent means that are available to him. Besides, to establish a legal freedom to marry is geared towards a positive proof and not just a matter of guess idea or presumption. In view of this, positive measures should be embarked on to ensure that the intending couples are free to marry one another.

434 Cfr. F. Gavin, Pastoral Care in Marriage Preparation, p.84.

435 H. Heimerl – H. Pree, Kirchenrecht, p.192. "Der Gültigkeit kann ein Ehehindernis, ein Konsensmangel oder ein wesentlicher Formmangel entgegenstehen, Erlaubtheitsvoraussetzungen sind die Einhaltung der nicht zur Gültigkeit vorgeschriebenen Formerfordernisse sowie gegebenenfalls das Vorliegen einer notwendigen Trauungserlaubnis des Ortsordinarius (Trauugsverbote, Mischehen)".

436 T. Rincon-Perez, "Commentary on canons 1063-1072", p.1126.

437 Cfr. L.A. Robitaille, "Commentary on Canons 1063-1072", p.1265.

this very chapter. By personal examination we mean an investigative process about possible obstacles to marriage which should not be omitted or taking for granted. The personal preparation is a pastoral instruction to dispose the couples to the holiness and obligations of marriage and can only be disposed for clear sound pastoral reasons[438].

This very canon replaces the expanded legislation of the Code of 1917 and the Instruction of the Sacred Congregation for the Discipline of the sacraments which was given in 1941[439]. The canon states that the Episcopal Conference is to issue norms concerning the questions to be asked of the parties, the publication of marriage banns, and the other appropriate means of enquiry to be carried out before the celebration of marriage. The parish priest may only assist at a marriage when these norms have been carefully observed. The manner of making this prenuptial enquiry in accordance with local conditions is left to the decision of each Bishops' Conference. The Bishop Conference may decide to leave some discretion to the diocesan bishop. The canon lays emphasis on some kind of examination of the couples. This examination of the couples is usually done separately[440]. The purpose of this investigation is to establish: "(a) that there are no impediments or prohibitions against the marriage; (b) that both parties are entering marriage freely; (c) that both parties understand the nature and obligations of the married state and are able, and actually intend, to accept these obligations"[441].

It is to be observed that in the past, the details of the investigation may be contained in a form to be completed before the wedding ceremony. Some of those forms have also shown steps to be taken in the preparation of the engaged spouses in more recent times. It should be noted that neither the investigation nor the preparation is merely a matter of filling in a form. "Indeed, any such impression would be an abuse of the church's stance in this context: whatever the form or its structure, it can never be more than a record of a preparation and an enquiry already diligently carried out"[442].

The certificate of baptism prescribed in canon 1021 of the 1917 Code is not mentioned in this canon of the present Code. But the non mention of the recent baptismal certificate should not be interpreted as a derogation of this procedural requirement, because for this requirement and other procedural requirements are grouped now under particular legislation of the Episcopal Conference of Bishops and as such require not to be included in the general legislation of the Code. As a matter of fact, a certificate of baptism issued within the last six months stands

438 Cfr. I. Gramunt – et al, Canons and Commentaries, p.11.

439 Cfr. CLD 2, p.253 ff.

440 Cfr. L.A. Robitaille, "Commentary on Canons 1063-1072", p.1265.

441 D. Kelly, "Commentary on Pastoral Care", p.582.

442 Ibid.

as a confirmation of a person's freedom to marry[443]. However, the recent baptismal certificate, notwithstanding that it is not in the present canon, has been also included in the norms prescribed by some Episcopal Conferences of Bishops. A recent baptismal certificate is an important tool for finding out the freedom of the parties to marry, since it consists of other useful information with regard to a person's canonical status. While the injunction of this baptismal certificate was not explicitly prescribed in the canon of the present Code, it does not remove the obvious fact that it still applies at least by reason of the implications of canon 535 §2 which states that in the register of baptisms, a note is to be made of confirmation and of matters pertaining to the canonical status of the faithful by reason of marriage, without prejudice to the provision of canon 1133, and by reason of adoption, the reception of sacred order, the making of perpetual profession in a religious institute, or a change of rite. These annotations are always made to be reproduced on a baptismal certificate[444].

It has to be mentioned that the obligation of making investigation of assuring that no impediments stand in the way of the parties that are marrying falls primarily on the parish priest whose function it is to assist at the marriage (c.530 4°). It could be conducted by others who are entrusted to partake in the exercise of the pastoral care of the parish in accordance with canon 517 §2[445]. The obligation falls also upon the person who, empowered with due delegation, is called to assist at the marriage according to canon 1114[446].

Canon 1067 makes allowance for the possibility of publishing the Banns[447] of marriage (which was prescribed in canon 1022 of the 1917 Code) if the local condition warrants it. In this situation, it rests on the Episcopal Conferences and

443 Cfr. I. Gramunt – et al, Canons and Commentaries, pp.11-12. It is pertinent to state here that the old Code required that the pre-nuptial investigation include a baptismal certificate, of not more than six months from the date of issue, of every catholic party to a marriage.

444 C.535 §2 CIC/1983: "In libro baptizatorum adnotentur quoque cofirmatio, necnon quae pertinent ad statem canonicum christifidelium, ratione matrimonii, salvo quidem praescripto can.1133, ratione adoptionis, itemque ratione suscepti ordnis sacri, professionis perpetuae in instituto religioso emissae necnon mutate ritus; eaeque adnotationes in document accepti baptismi simper referantur".

445 C.517 §2 CIC/1983: "Si ob sacerdotum penuriam Episcopus diocesanus aestimaverit participationem in exercitio curae pastoralis paroeciae concredendam esse diacono alive personae sacredotali character non insignitae aut personarum communitatis, sacerdotem consituat aliquem qui, potestatibus et facultatibus parochi instructus, curam pastoralem moderetur".

446 C.1114 CIC/1983: "Assistens matrimonio illicite agit, nisi ipsi constiterit de libero statu contrahentium ad normam iuris atque, si fieri potest, de licentia parochi, quoties vi delegationis generalis assistit".

447 "Im Bereich der DBK gilt ab dem 1. Jan. 1990 der folgende Beschluß zu c.1067:
1. Form des Aufgebots. Das Aufgebot, d.h. die öffentliche Ankündigung einer beabsichtigten Eheschließung zur Aufdeckung eines etwa bestehenden Hindernisses, erfolgt durch Vermeldungen im Sonntagsgottesdienst oder durch Aushang unter Angabe des Namens, des Vorna-

diocesan bishops to assess local conditions to ascertain whether the publication of Banns would be an effective means of proving that the engaged couples are free to marry[448]. In Igboland just as in Africa, Banns are an effective method of establishing freedom to marry. The publication of Banns in this regard, is the traditional means of making the catholic community to be aware of the coming marriage between the parties and of giving the people the opportunity of bringing reasonable objections if there is any, to the marriage that is to take place and also of intimating the parish priest of any impediment.

Canon 1068 emphasis that in danger of death[449], if other proofs are not available, it suffices, unless there are contrary indications, to have the assertion of the parties, sworn if need be, that they are baptized and free of any impediment[450]. The canon supplies an alternative method for examining the parties when one or both parties are in danger of death, it may not be possible to execute the task of carrying out the pre-nuptial investigation proposed for normal circumstances.

---

mens und des Wohnsitzes der beiden Brautleute. Ob Vermeldung oder Aushang, entscheidet der Pfarrer.

2. Ort des Aufgebots. Das Aufgebot ist in der Pfarrkirche vorzunehmen, in deren Pfarrei der katholische Bräutigam und/oder die katholische Braut zur Zeit Wohnsitz haben. Liegt der Wohnsitz innerhalb einer Filialgemeinde, kann das Aufgebot stattdessen in der Filialkirche erfolgen. Wenn jemand keinen Wohnsitz hat, so dort, wo er zur Zeit tatsächlich wohnt.
   Der für die Vorbereitung der Eheschließung zuständige Pfarrer hat, wenn hiernach das Aufgebot in einer auswärtigen Pfarrei vorzunehmen ist, deren Pfarrer um das Aufgebot zu bitten; dieser ist zur alsbaldigen Antwort nur verpflichtet, falls beim Aufgebot ein Ehehindernis entdeckt wird.
3. Zeit des Aufgebots. Das Aufgebot durch Vermeldung erfolgt an einem einzigen Sonntag durch Ankündigung in allen Messen einschließlich der Vorabendmesse. Das Aufgebot durch Aushang erfolgt vom Samstagnachmittag bis zum folgenden Montagmorgen.
4. Dispens vom Aufgebot. Der für die Vorbereitung der Eheschließung zuständige Geistliche mit allgemeiner Traubefugnis hat, sofern nicht begründete Zweifel hinsichtlich des status liber bestehen, die Befugnis, aus gerechtem Grund vom Aufgebot zu dispensieren. Die so erteilte Dispens vom Aufgebot ist im Ehevorbereitungsprotokoll unter Nr.26a zu vermerken".
   Cfr. R. Sebott, Das Neue kirchliche Eherecht, pp.52-53; H. J.F. Reinhardt, Die kirchliche Trauung. Ehevorbereitung, Trauung und Registrierung der Eheschließung im Bereich der Deutschen Bischofskonferenz: Text und Kommentar, Essen 2006, p.16.

448 Cfr. L.A. Robittaile, "Commentary on Canons 1063-1072", p.1266.

449 H.J.F. Reinhardt, Todesgefahr, in: LKS+KR III (2004), p.690. "Im Unterschied zum unmittelbar bevorstehenden Eintritt des Todes (articulus mortis) steht der Begriff Todesgefahr (periculum mortis) für eine Lage, in der mit dem Ableben eines Menschen ernsthaft gerechnet werden muß, in dem Sinne, daß dies sehr wahrscheinlich oder doch möglich ist (Gründe: schwere Krankheit, Unfall, Katastrophe, drohende Kriegseinwirkungen, insofern diese Situationen im Konkreten Fall für den Einzelnen zum Tode führen können".

450 C.1068 CIC/1983: "In periculo mortis, si aliae probationes haberi nequeant, sufficit, nisi contraria adsint indicia, affirmatio contrahentium, si casus ferat etiam iurata, se baptizatos esse et nullo detineri impedimento".

In this condition, unless there are bases for doubt, the assertion of the parties concerning their baptism and freedom to marry is sufficient to enable the marriage to go on. The new Code unlike canon 1019 §2 of the old Code demands that "this assertion be made under oath only "if need be", i.e. where there is real doubt about the truthfulness of the parties'"[451]. The norms concerning dispensation of impediments in danger of death are prescribed in canon 1079[452], and therefore should be kept in mind.

There are also times when people are motivated to marry in danger of death because of some benefits which may be attached to it. Kelly captures this attitude clearly when he asserts: "The motivation of those who marry in danger of death may be, at least in part, to secure some civil benefit, such as inheritance or a pension for the surviving spouse. In all such cases therefore the priest should be aware of the relevant civil requirements for the valid celebration of this marriage and, in so far as may be possible, ensure that they are complied with'"[453]. What Kelly is saying here is correct but we have to add that it is not only civil benefit as such, in the sense that there may be also situation when one of the parties is in danger of death, but because his or her personal life situation is considered not in order by the church because of the fact that he or she is cohabiting with his or her partner without marriage. So in this situation, he or she wants to make things right by entering marriage before dying. So in this case, he or she is not motivated by civil benefit but by full reconciliation with God.

Since marriage is shaped and also understood as interpersonal relationship, it has a social relevance, among other reasons because the original family structure is based upon marriage, and the family is a pivotal nucleus of society and of the ecclesial community. In view of this social dimension, the main aim of publication of Banns or other means of investigation that may be established by particular law is to publish the marriages that are to be celebrated so that other

451 D. Kelly, "Commentary on Pastoral Care", p.582.

452 C. 1079 CIC/1983 §1: "When danger of death threatens, the local Ordinary can dispense his own subjects, wherever they are residing, and all who are actually present in his territory, both from the form to be observed in the celebration of marriage, and from each and every impediment of ecclesiastical law, whether public or occult, with the exception of the impediment arising from the sacred order of priesthood.
§2: In the same circumstances mentioned in §1, but only for cases in which not even the local Ordinary can be approached, the same faculty of dispensation is possessed by the parish priest, by a properly delegated sacred minister, and by the priest or deacon who assists at the marriage in accordance with can.1116 §2.
§3: In danger of death, the confessor has the power to dispense from occult impediments for the internal forum, whether within the act of sacramental confession or outside it.
§4: In the case mentioned in §2, the local Ordinary is considered unable to be approached if he can be reached only by telegram or by telephone".

453 D. Kelly, "Commentary on Pastoral Care", p.582.

members of the community may be informed and may contribute to ensure that nothing stands in the way of marriage celebration[454]. That is the prescription of the obligation imposed by canon 1069 on all faithful to reveal any impediments they are aware of to the parish priest or to the local ordinary before the celebration of marriage. This very canon is a repetition of canon 1027 of the Code of 1917. It is practically pertinent to comprehend here that the obligation is to furnish the appropriate parish priest not necessarily impediments in the strict sense of it of canons 1083-1094, such as an existing marriage bond, a degree of consanguinity, affinity in a degree of the direct line, sacred orders or antecedent and perpetual impotence, but also other possibly invalidating factors, such as an established history of gross personal immaturity, a serious psychiatric illness, a manifestly serious problem with alcohol or drugs, and an indications that one or other party may be agreeing to marry under duress or only on the established fact that the couple will not have any children or that one or other party would feel less concerned to leave the marriage if eventually things do not augur well between them, and so forth[455].

It is to be noted that not everybody who is aware of particular impediment affecting one or the other party is obliged to reveal that impediment. Those who are aware of the impediment in a sacramental confession can speak to the penitent about it only under the condition of the confessional unless the penitent brings it up again outside the sacramental forum. Those who aware of such information in other confidential relationships such as doctor-patient, lawyer-client relationships and so on may not be free to reveal what they know. Be that as it may, it is not universally enshrined that these latter people are exempted from the obligation of this canon to reveal impediments they know about to the parish priest or local ordinary before the celebration of marriage. While acknowledging the importance of upholding a confidential relationship it must also be emphasized that the good of the person who is probably entering an invalid marriage unknowingly must also be protected[456].

There is a direct link in this canon between the publication of Banns and the obligation. In that respect, it is of particular practical and pastoral importance that in the announcement of marriage the Christian faithful are informed about the necessity to pray for the intending couples and to partake in the happiness of the coming wedding feast. But the main aim of the Banns is to publish the nuptials and by so doing invite the Christian faithful to fulfill their obligation of revealing any impediment that they know about before the celebration of marriage[457].

454 T. Rincon-Perez, "Commentary on canons 1063-1072", p.1129.
455 D. Kelly, "Commentary on Pastoral Care", p.583.
456 Cfr. L.A. Robitaille, "Commentary on canons 1063-1072", p.1267.
457 Cfr. T. Rincon-Perez, "Commentary on canons 1063-1072", p.1129.

When an impediment concerning one or the other party is revealed, then, the task of acting on the information, after having pondered the nature and gravity of what he has learned, who informed him of the impediment, how that person got the information, and whether it can be corroborated, rests on the parish priest or the local ordinary. In such a situation, the parish priest or the local ordinary may consider speaking with the parties or their parents in order to understand the situation more reasonably[458].

For the obligation in this canon to be fulfilled, care must be taken to instruct the Christian faithful properly concerning the nature of marriage, its essential properties, and the laws governing it. This clarion call is even more urgent nowadays when false views about marriage are widespread in our society and have infiltrated into the ecclesial community. Thus, pastors of souls must be solicitous for the general catechesis prescribed in canon 1063, 1°[459], which we are going to discuss later in this very chapter.

Canon 1070 which is an equivalent of canon 1029 of the Code of 1917 states that if someone other than the parish priest whose function it is to assist at the marriage has conducted the investigations, that person is to notify the parish priest of the results as soon as possible through an authentic document[460]. According to canon 530, 4°[461], the duty of assisting at marriages is entrusted to the parish priest of the parish where the marriage takes place. When both parties live in the parish where the celebration of the marriage is to take place, the parish priest or a priest of the parish will carry out the pre-marriage investigation. If on the other hand, one of the parties lives in another parish, the pre-marriage investigation for that party will be conducted by a priest of that parish in his or her parish. In this context, the priest who carries out the pre-marriage investigation will forward to the parish priest of the place of marriage the results of that investigation. This is normally done by means of the pre-marriage investigation form approved in that very region for use[462]. It should be born in mind that this is in no way an attempt to settle any conflict between parish priests, but to return the investigation made by another priest to the parish priest originally responsible for carrying such investigation. The problem only arises when it must be determined who the parish priest to assist at the marriage will be and consequently be responsible for performing such investigation[463].

---

458 Cfr. L.A. Robitaille, "Commentary on Canons 1063-1072", p.1267.

459 Cfr. I. Gramunt – et al, eds; Canons and Commentaries, p.12.

460 C.1070 CIC/1983:"Si aluis quam parochus, cuius est assistere matrimonio, investgationes peregerit, de harum exitu quam primum per authenticum documentum eundem parochum certiorem reddat".

461 C.530, 4° CIC/1983: "assistentia matrimoniis et benedictio nuptiarum".

462 Cfr. J. McAreavey, The Canon Law, pp.68-69.

463 Cfr. T. Rincon-Perez, "Commentary on canons 1063-1072", p.1131.

"Authentic document"[464] here means that the document must be drawn or ordered to be drawn by the priest who has carried out the investigations. The document itself should not be spurious or one that originated from another person all together. Notifying the results of the investigation to the parish priest is not enough without supporting it with the testimony of the priest that investigated it and who in actual fact, should bear the responsibility for it[465].

It has been established beyond reasonable doubt that some intending spouses often live in different parishes, and because they may live in a parish different from the one in which they will be married, it is very imperative to inform the parish priest of the parish when the marriage will be celebrated of any preparations happening outside his parish. By so doing, he will be convinced that adequate preparation and investigations have been made. The parish priest is responsible for ensuring adequate preparation for marriages that are celebrated in his parish, since he is responsible for fostering the spiritual welfare of his parish. He should be well informed that all the prerequisites for a valid and lawful marriage celebration have been accomplished even if he does not personally prepare the intending spouse for marriage[466].

Still on this canon, canon 1115 states that marriages are to be celebrated in the parish in which either of the contracting parties has a domicile or a quasi-domicile or month's residence or, if there is question of vagi, in the parish in which they are actually residing. With permission of the proper ordinary or the proper parish priest, however, they may celebrate their marriage elsewhere. At any rate, assistance by the parish priest at a marriage celebrated in his own parish is always valid even if the parties are not his parishioners (c.1109).

In line with this canon 1070, the Bishop Conferences of Germany, Austria and Switzerland have instructed that when marriage is to take place in another country, the complete marriage transfer documents should be made available with the corresponding documents about the diocesan authority of the parish priest making the transfer[467].

Canon 1071 details a number of cases in which the parish priests, deacon or any other delegate is prohibited from assisting at a marriage without prior authorization from the local ordinary, except in case of necessity. This canon consists of two duties: (a) the parish priest's duty to seek authorization to assist at the marriage, (2) the local ordinary's duty to grant or deny authorization after look-

464 C.535 §3 CIC/1983: "Unicuique paroeciae sit proprium sigillum; testimonia quae de statu canonico christifidelium dantur, sicut et acta omnia quae momentum iuridicum habere possunt, ab ipso parocho eiusve delegato subscribantur et sigillo paroeciali muniantur".

465 Cfr. I. Gramunt – et al, Canons and Commentaries, pp.12-13.

466 Cfr. L.A. Robitaille, "Commentary on canons 1063-1072", p.1267.

467 Cfr. R. Sebott, Das Neue kirchliche Eherecht, p.55.

ing into the case. These delicate cases demand special pastoral care especially during the preparation of couples for marriage. The goal of this canon is to take care of abnormal cases in which, to ease the burden on the local parish priest, it is deemed necessary to have the advice and sanction of the local ordinary[468].

It is pertinent to note that this canon puts a precautionary measure that limits the parish priest's authority to assist lawfully at a marriage celebrated in his area of jurisdiction; the question of validity does not in anyway count here. The case is then forwarded to the local ordinary in order to respond adequately from the local ordinary's jurisdiction to the problems caused by the case so that marriage or other values that might be at risk are protected[469]. The ratio legis behind this canon with recourse to the administrative instrument of authorization is that, with regard to the problems raised by some marriages, the decision should not fall only on the parish priest but also the local ordinary should be intimated about the problems so that all concerned will proceed with more prudence and caution before the celebration of the marriage[470].

The prohibition not to celebrate certain marriages unless with the permission of the local ordinary, does not however affect the validity of the marriages concerned. If certain marriages were celebrated without the permission of the local ordinary, they would still be valid and lawful, the only thing that would be unlawful is assisting at these marriages. Be that as it may, the permission of the local ordinary is important for the lawfulness of the marriage. In this regard, Kelly lists two preliminary points that are to be taken into consideration: "(a) while not affecting the validity of the marriage, this permission is necessary for the lawfulness of its celebration, and the obligation to seek it as a serious one. (b) this permission is not, however, required when there arises "a case of necessity", i.e; not only a danger of death, but any situation in which an undue delay could involve a serious pastoral risk. It will be for the person who is to assist at the marriage to make a prudent judgment in this regard, bearing in mind that the purpose of the rule is to protect both the sacrament and the ultimate well being of the parties'"[471].

Still with regard to area of cases of necessity, a proposal was unanimously rejected, during the work of codification in which only in danger of death could a parish priest lawfully assist at a marriage without prior permission from the local ordinary[472]. This proves to the fact that cases of necessity should not be limited to danger of death, nor even to cases of urgent need, rather an idea of relative necessity should be born in mind, relative to the value being safeguarded through

468 Cfr. D. Kelly, "Commentary on Pastoral Care", p.584.

469 Cfr. T. Rincon-Perez, Commentary on canons 1063-1072", p.1133.

470 Ibid.

471 D. Kelly, "Commentary on Pastoral Care", p.584.

472 Cfr. Comm. 9 (1977), p.143.

recourse to diocesan jurisdiction, and relative to the fundamental right whose exercise is being limited[473]. Thus, the cases that this canon highlights as requiring the prior permission of the local ordinary are:

1°. A marriage of vagi. These are people who have no domicile or quasi-domicile[474]. Those under this category could include migrant workers, immigrants, perpetual wanderers, the homeless, asylum seekers and illegal aliens who may not have fixed addresses[475]. There are two problems facing the people in this category. On the one hand, it is absolutely difficult to find out if a person who has no fixed abode is really free to enter into marriage. On the other hand, depending on the reason established why such a person has no domicile or quasi-domicile, it may affect his or her ability to marry. For instance, some people have no fixed addresses because they are travelers, migrants or because of their way of life. In cases like this, the precautionary measure of soliciting for permission from the local ordinary in order to ensure as well as possible a valid and lawful marriage celebration is recommended[476].

In canon law, domicile is acquired by residence in the territory of a parish, or at least of a diocese, which is either linked to the intention of remaining there permanently if nothing should occasion its withdrawal, or in fact protracted for a full five years (c.102 §1). A quasi-domicile is acquired by residence in the territory of a parish, or at least of a diocese, which is either linked to the intention of remaining there for three months if nothing should occasion its withdrawal, or in fact protracted for three months (c.102 §2). Domicile or quasi-domicile in the territory of a parish is called parochial; in the territory of a diocese, even if not in a parish, it is called diocesan (c.102 §3). Domicile or quasi-domicile is lost by departure from the place with the intention of not returning, without prejudice to the provisions of canon 105.

Thus, all that is required to acquire quasi-domicile with regard to legal effects is the intention of residing, or the fact of having resided, in a given diocese for three months. However, if one of the couples intending to be married has no fixed residence, the case must be referred to the local ordinary who will then decide how to carry out the investigation about the freedom from obstacles to enter a valid and lawful marriage. In this case, the local ordinary would take careful measures that will eventually lead to the capability of such a person to enter marriage.

473 Cfr. T. Rincon-Perez, "Commentary on canons 1063-1072", p.1134.

474 Cfr. CC.100-101.

475 Cfr. T.P. Doyle, Marriage, p.753; B.A. Siegle, Marriage According to the New Code of Canon Law, New York 1986, p.38; F. Gavin, Pastoral Care in Marriage Preparation, p.86; P.K. Amevor, New Approaches to Marriage Preparation, pp.151-152.

476 Cfr. T. Rincon-Perez, "Commentary on canons 1063-1072", p.1135.

2°. A marriage that cannot be recognized or celebrated under civil law. This is a new norm that was introduced into those that need permission from the local ordinary. This particular norm was not included in the Code of 1917. By establishing this norm the legislation wished to stress respect and esteem for civil law and by so doing avoid as much as possible any conflicts between canon law and civil law in a way of great social importance for both the church and the state. Its main purpose is to ascertain to the maximum the civil effects of every marriage that is canonical[477].

A civil obstacle of marriage celebration could be lack of minimum age, if the minimum age needed by civil legislation is higher than the sixteen years of age for the man and fourteen for the woman required by canon legislation[478]. Another obstacle could still arise if the person intending to enter marriage is still bound by a civil marriage, even though the type of marriage may not be considered valid by the canon legislation.

There are various possible conflicts between the canon legislation and civil legislation that hinder full recognition of the civil effects of canonical marriage and as such make it absolutely necessary for the parish priest to request permission from the local ordinary. For instance, an attempt made by a person to enter into canonical marriage with a dispensable civil impediment. In such a situation, before going on with the canonical marriage, a dispensation from the civil impediment must be requested so that the canonical marriage could be recognized, registered and receive all civil effects by the state. Another serious problem exists if there is a non-dispensable civil impediment. An example would be the impediment of a bond not dissolved by divorce[479]. In canonical legislation, a civil marriage of a catholic obligated to canonical form is considered null. If canonically, he shows interest of marrying another person, "the new marriage would be valid in the eyes of the church, but could not be registered civilly, nor would the state recognize it due to the impediment of prior bond. Only after a civil marriage is dissolved by divorce does the problem of assisting at the marriage disappear. If, however, there is no proof of dissolution of the prior bond, the parish priest will have to approach the ordinary, who, on principle, cannot grant authorization, since such a canonical marriage would have no civil effect and cause all the attendant social problems"[480]. That is the reason why this very canon requires that such cases be referred to the local ordinary, who is in the best position to strike a

477 Ibid, p.1136.

478 C.1083 CIC/1983 §1: "Vir ante decimum sextum aetatis annum completum, mulier ante decimum quartum item completum, matrimonium validum inire non possunt".
§2: "Integrum est Episcoporum conferentiae aetatem superiorem ad licitam matrimonii celebrationem statuere".

479 Cfr. T. Rincon-Perez, "Commentary on canons 1063-1072", p.1137.

480 Ibid.

balance on the relationship between the church and the state and make sure such unhealthy conflict does not in the first place arise. And so is the need for this norm to work hand in hand with canon 1059[481] which establishes that marriage of Catholics, even if only one party is baptised, is governed not only by divine law but also by canon law, without prejudice to the competence of the civil authority in respect of the merely civil effects of the marriage. Thus, notwithstanding the avoidance of unnecessary conflicts between the church and the state, there may be situations, for higher reasons that justify the local ordinary granting authorization for marriage to be celebrated notwithstanding the prohibition from the civil legislation.

3°. Marriage of a person bound by natural obligations toward another party or children, arising from a previous union. This norm, which has no direct equivalent in the Code of 1917, underscores a principle of natural law, which establishes that a person, if for any reason, wishes to enter a marital union subsequent to a previous one, must take steps to ensure that the proper provision due to the former partner or children from the previous union is not prejudiced by any subsequent marriage in the church[482]. The objective of this norm is attributed to the desire to avoid any scandal from assuming the obligations specified by marriage without additionally assuming the natural obligations emanating from a previous union[483].

The natural obligations include only those that could render the new marriage invalid and unlawful, or lead to serious legal complications. For example, a widow or widower with offspring has natural obligation towards the children of his or her prior union, but these obligations do not constitute a legal hindrance for the new union, and are not the type of natural obligations being emphasized by the canon. But if one of the parties intending to enter marriage has entered a prior invalid union or had being emphasized by the canon. But if one of the parties intending to enter marriage has entered a prior invalid union or had in fact lived in concubinage, and by so doing, contracted natural obligations toward another party or the children born from the prior union, then it should be ascertained that these obligations do not constitute a legal obstacle to the new union[484].

---

481 D. Kelly, "Commentary on Pastoral Care", p.585. "Two ancillary points may be made:(a) since there is in so many places today a considerable diversity between civil and canonical requirements concerning marriage, it is obviously appropriate "agreements entered into by the Apostolic See with nations or other civil entities"(can.3); (b) in interpreting "the civil law of this canon, account would have to be taken also of cultural and even tribal traditions, which in some communities are, in effect, "the civil law" within which the community has to operate".

482 Cfr. D. Kelly, "Commentary on Pastoral Care", p.585; F. Gavin, Pastoral Care in Marriage Preparation, p.87.

483 Cfr. T. Rincon-Perez, "Commentary on canons 1063-1072", p.1139.

484 Cfr. I. Gramunt – et al, Canons and Commentaries, p.14.

Normally, anyone who wishes to enter canonical marriage may be subject to other natural obligations that must be fulfilled out of justice, charity, or natural fairness, but that does show they are instances of the situation in this norm under which a parish priest must request permission from the local ordinary to assist lawfully at a marriage. In order words, this is a cautionary norm that does not so much affect the marriage itself or the parties involved, rather it directly affects the assistance of the parish priest at a marriage[485].

In accordance with the marriage preparation protocol of Germany[486], despite that the natural obligations correspond to regulations in the decree of divorce and the subsequent civil agreements and decisions, if an important occasion arises, the natural obligations must go beyond the civil laid down regulations. The obligation should take into consideration the children born outside the marriage. Hence, if during the pre-nuptial preparation it is discovered that nothing seems to suggest that the intending marriage would obviously affect the fulfillment of the legal or moral obligations to the partner or the children of a prior union, the marriage authorization expressed in this canon is to be granted, otherwise, the case should be referred to the office of the Vicar General or Bishop's secretariat[487].

There are some cases that must be kept in mind of both the parish priest in his request for permission and the local ordinary in his commitment to grant the request. These cases are natural obligations that may arise from the irregular unions such as trial or experimental marriages, civil marriages of persons obligated to marry canonically, de facto free unions with no juridical relationships, and civil marriages of divorced persons, certainly without prior canonical bonds[488]. With regard to these cases, permission for the canonical marriage celebration should not be given to the person requesting it unless there is every assurance that the person will continue to fulfill the obligations arising from the previous union. It is the local ordinary's right and duty to assess the situation and make sure that all

---

485 Cfr. T. Rincon-Perez, "Commentary on canons 1063-1072", p.1139.

486 H.J.F. Reinhardt, Die kirchliche Trauung, p.27." – Beschluß zu can. 1071 §1 n. 3 CIC. Für die Eheschließung einer Person, die natürliche Verpflichtung gegenüber einem anderen Partner oder gegenüber Kindern aus einer anderen früheren Verbindung hat, gilt die in can. 1071 §1 n.3 CIC geforderte Trauerlaubnis als erteilt, wenn bei der Ehevorbereitung festgestellt wird, daß die Erfüllung der rechtlichen und moralischen Verpflichtungen gegenüber Partnern oder Kindern aus einer früheren Verbindung durch die beabsichtigte Heirat nicht gefährdet wird. Zu beachten ist, daß die natürlichen Verpflichtungen über die Regelung im Scheidungsurteil und über ergänzende zivilrechtliche Entscheidungen und Vereinbarungen hinaus gehen können".

487 Cfr. Ehevorbereitungsprotokoll (Niederschrift zur kirchlichen Ehevorbereitung und Eheschließung, Amtliches Formular der Deutschen Bischofskonferenz), Fulda 2008. Anmerkungstafel, no.9; See also P.K. Amevor, New Approaches to Marriage Preparation, p.153.

488 Cfr. T. Rincon-Perez, "Commentary on canons 1063-1072", p.1139.

who need care and support are being attended to before granting the authorization. If the local ordinary discovers that the person is dodging his obligations to former partner or children, he could as well forbid the proposed marriage, at least for a while[489].

4°. Marriage of a person who has notoriously rejected the Catholic faith. This norm repeats canon 1065 of the Code of 1917 which first made a strong appeal to the faithful to avoid marrying anyone who had notoriously[490] abandoned the faith, and secondly imposed upon the parish priest the duty to consult the ordinary before assisting at a marriage of that type. The two basic reasons justifying both are, even though that of the old law was based on serious impediments, to avoid or forestall the danger of perversion of the Catholic party or believer, and to ensure the education of their children. Hence, the purpose of the new norm is identical to that of the Code of 1917. Neither the validity nor the sacramental nature of the marriage of a person who has notoriously abandoned the faith is prejudiced. However, the norm of requiring permission from the local ordinary does not intend to protect or guarantee validity, rather to ensure with every possible means that the faith of the believer and the children does not suffer any special risk, just as for mixed marriages. Therefore, the local ordinary has the obligation as prescribed in paragraph 2 of canon 1071, not to grant permission unless the provisions of canon 1125 concerning mixed marriages are duly observed[491].

In order to be at home with this particular norm, it is a matter of utmost necessity to clarify once more the term "notorious rejection of Catholic faith". The word "Notoriety" according to Rincon-Perez, means "a situation publically known either because the unbeliever's lack of faith has been made public, positive and explicit, or because it is implicit through the affiliation with or membership in manifestly atheistic or anti-Christian groups"[492]. Proving that a person has notoriously rejected or abandoned the Catholic faith is a serious matter. The rejection in this case, must be publicly known. Also some clarifications have to be made here between a person who notoriously rejects the Catholic faith and the person who no longer practice the faith or who because of certain things done in the church which he is not at home with, has stopped going to the church without necessarily

---

489 C.1077 §1 CIC/1983: "Ordinarius loci propriis subditis ubique commorantibus et omnibus in proprio territorio actu degentibus vetare potest matrimonium in casu peculiari, sed ad tempus tantum, gravi de causa eaque perdurante".

490 A notorious rejection of Catholic faith means more than an ordinary negligence of religious duties. It depicts a person who professes that he is no longer a Catholic, or one who openly refuses obedience, not necessarily to some particular law or decree, but to the church in general. It also designates a person who habitually sneers at or rejects the Catholic doctrine. For more detail on this, see T.L. Bouscaren – A.C. Ellis, Canon Law, p.511.

491 Cfr. T. Rincon-Perez, "Commentary on canons 1063-1072", p.1140.

492 Ibid, p.1141.

rejecting the teachings of the church publicly. In this situation, the two are not the same. It would not be legitimate and appropriate to make the term non-believer equivalent to non-practicer of the faith for the purpose of requesting permission from the local ordinary. The words of Pope John II can lead us in evaluating a notorious rejection of the Catholic faith: "When in spite of all efforts engaged couples show that they reject explicitly and formerly what the church intends to do when the marriage of baptized persons is celebrated, the pastor of souls cannot admit them to the celebration of marriage"[493].

An attention is to be drawn here also that a notorious rejection of the Catholic faith does not include leaving the church by formal act[494]. To be exempted in accordance with the publicity and notoriety of the case of non-belief, there must be formal act of rejection in a written statement addressed to the parish priest or local ordinary of the diocese. In line with this, publicity and notoriety concerning the case are sufficient and they do not mean exemption from the obligation of canonical form, either legally, in accordance with canon 1117 or dispensation according to canon 1127 §2[495], as regards mixed marriages[496].

It has to be mentioned that during the work of the revision of canon law a proposal was made about the marriage of a person who had notoriously rejected the faith to be made a diriment impediment. The proposal did not gain ground because of the rejection of the consultors on the basis that even when a person rejects the catholic faith, the person's right to contract a marriage is not lost be-

493 FC, 68 §7.

494 I. Gramunt – et al, Canons and Commentaries, pp.14-15. "(a) Defection from the Catholic faith is said to be formal when a person baptized in the catholic faith, knowingly and willingly, joins another religion or explicitly and externally rejects the faith or authority of the church. A practical but not formal defection exists when a person does not practice the faith or behaves in a manner that conflicts with Catholic teaching. Defection, whether formal or practical, is notorious if the fact is well known in the community; it cannot be called notorious if it is known only within a limited circle of family and friends. (b) If the defection is formal, whether notorious or not, this constitutes a case of mixed marriage which is forbidden by law; this prohibition, however, can be dispensed by the bishop for "just and reasonable cause"…. If the defection is practical and notorious, the matter must be referred to the bishop; the bishop can grant permission for the celebration of marriage, but in order to do so he must have assurance that the conditions prescribed by C1125 have been fulfilled…. (c) When the defection is practical and not notorious as it may often happen with Catholics who do not practice their faith, or whose behaviour is in conflict with Catholic teaching but wish to be married in the church, the celebration of marriage cannot be forbidden".

495 C.1127 §2 CIC/1983: "Si graves difficultates formae canonicae servandae obstent, Ordinario loci partis catholcae ius est ab eadem in singulis casbus dispensandi, consulto tamen Ordinario loci in quo matrimonium celebratur, et salva ad validitatem aliqua publica forma celebrationis; Episcoporum conferentiae est normas statuere, quibus praedicta dispensation concordi ratione concedatur".

496 Cfr. T. Rincon-Perez, "Commentary on canons 1063-1072", pp.1141-1142.

cause marriage being a sacrament is the only thing possible for a baptised person, when the principle of indivisibility of covenant and that of sacrament is taken into consideration. The proposal also to make the norm a serious impediment was rejected intoto by a great number of consultors[497].

5°. Marriage of a person who is under censure. This very norm stipulates that a person who is under the censure of either excommunication or interdict is prohibited from celebrating the sacraments and receiving any of the sacraments (cann.1331 §1, 2°; 1332). In the old Code, canon 1066 included not only one under censure, who refuses to confess beforehand or to reconcile with the church, but also one who is a public sinner. What has to be said here, is that, with regard to the old and new norms, the parish priest is prohibited from assisting at the marriage unless for grave reasons, in which case he has to consult if possible, with the local ordinary. The aim of the new norm is to balance the effects of the censure, that is, exclusion from the sacraments, and the person's natural right to enter marriage. Rincon-Perez, speaking on the ultimate reason behind consulting the local ordinary asserts: "Since censure, especially excommunication, implies a prohibition against celebrating and receiving the sacraments, it is frequently asserted that the purpose of the precept, of the cautionary measure to which we are referring, is to have the faithful party become reconciled with the church, absolved of the penalty and thus eliminate the prohibition against celebrating and receiving the sacrament of marriage"[498].

In view of referring the case to the local ordinary, he must first see to it whether the censure can in the circumstances be remitted prior to the celebration of marriage and the person reconciled with the church, since the ultimate goal of every canonical norm is the salus animarum. If his effort is possible and yields fruit, the problem may disappear. If this is not possible, then authorization may be granted for the marriage only in the most exceptional circumstances, taking into consideration not only the spiritual status of this censured person but also the danger to the faith of the other person[499].

6°. Marriage of a minor whose parents are either unaware of it or are reasonably opposed to it. This norm speaks only of marriages of minors whose parents are unaware of the marriage proposed or reasonably opposed to it. A minor in this case, is a person who has not completed his or her eighteen years of age[500]. The purpose of this norm is to safeguard the value of the parent-child relationship. There are values of respect, love and obedience among family members in the nucleus of the

497 Cfr. Comm. 9 (1977), p.144; T. Rincon-Perez, "Commentary on canons 1063-1072", p.1140.

498 T. Rincon-Perez, "Commentary on canons 1063-1072", p.1142.

499 Cfr. D. Kelly, "Commentary on Pastoral Care", p.587; F. Gavin, Pastoral Care in Marriage Preparation, p.88.

500 Cfr. C.97 §1.

Christian idea of the family. It is to be taken that these values must be exhibited principally in the request for pieces of advice at the moment of making important decisions like proposing to enter into marriage. Thus, it is against this Christian concept of family if a minor decides to enter marriage without the awareness of the parents or in the sense that they are opposed to the proposed marriage.

It has to be affirmed that over the years, marriages of minors had always been accompanied with various problems because of the danger of their not having enough maturity of judgment to make a reasonable decision of what marriage is all about and the rightful way of entering into it, and the danger of their lack of emotional stability to cope with the reality of married life[501]. Besides, owing to the glaring fact that parents play a pivotal role in the education and upbringing of their children, there is no gain saying that they can assist in the discernment of their children's choice of a state of life, without coercing or forcing them into making such a choice (c.219)[502]. In any giving family, parents are presumed to know their children well and to be able to judge their capability and maturity for marriage. But the opposition of the parents of their children not marrying as proposed must be reasonable in accordance with canonical norm. "Therefore, if the parish priest deems the reason invoked by the parents to be clearly irrational, he has no obligation to approach the ordinary and may assist at the marriage of the minor.... To evaluate rationality it is important to ponder carefully not only the parents' reasons, but also the child's allegations, which may reveal egotistical parental attitudes, hostility towards the family of the other party, and other feelings that cloud the common sense and prudence of decisions"[503]. Hence, if it is to be seen that the minor has a serious and sufficient reason why the parents should not be informed or why the celebration of the marriage should proceed notwithstanding the opposition of the parents, then the local ordinary can authorize the marriage after evaluating the reasons presented by the minor. The local ordinary, in granting permission to any of the cases, must see to it that a special and adequate preparation concerning this particular marriage is made.

7°. A marriage entered by proxy. Proxy marriages are marriages in which either one or both parties are not personally present at the ceremony but represented by a proxy according to canon 1105. In view of the doctrine of inseparability of sacrament and contract, there can be no rejection or objection to validity and lawfulness of a marriage by proxy, or to the sacred nature of such a marriage to the degree that it rests upon the validity of the marriage covenant[504].

501 Cfr. D. Kelly, "Commentary on Pastoral Care", p.587.

502 Cfr. L.A. Robitaille, "Commentary on canons 1063-1072", p1270.

503 T. Rincon-Perez, "Commentary on canons 1063-1072", p.1144; M.L. Alarcon, "El Matrimonio de los menores (cc.1071. 1. 6°, 1072 and 1083. 2)", in: El Matrimonio Cuestiones, p.174.

504 Cfr. T.P. Doyle, Marriage, p.754; P.K. Amevor, New Approaches to Marriage Preparation, p.155.

Canon 1104 §1 of the present Code stipulates that contracting marriage validly it is necessary that the contracting parties be present together, either personally or by proxy. However, the purpose of this very norm is to ensure the validity and lawfulness of marriage. It is rare to see such marriages, but there are cases when those entering into marriage are not personally present at the wedding due to danger of death, military service or when it might be important for immigrants to be present in another place in order to procure a visa[505]. Proxy marriage brings with it serious pastoral problems and difficulties such as doubt about the freedom of the parties or their preparedness for marriage. Thus, authorization for such a marriage will be granted only for very grave reasons.

Canon 1072 is the final canon on the general norms concerning marriage preparation in the 1983 Code. This very canon, in repeating the provision of canon 1067 §2 of the old Code, establishes a serious pastoral concern for the marriages of the young. In canonical marriage legislation, the age for entering into marriage is the object of a special concern. Hence, canon 1083 §1 establishes a certain age for marriage. A man before he has completed his sixteenth year of age and a woman before she has completed her fourteenth year of age cannot enter into a valid marriage. The reason for this cautionary measure is for the parties to enter marriage with sufficient maturity as well as with biological and mental discernment that marriage requires and to safeguard the natural right of marriage.

It is to be born in mind that because of the wide diversity of customs and situations, the common age is still kept very low by canonical legislation. In affirming this, Rincon-Perez opines: "The goal of achieving a balance between the age of puberty and the right to enter marriage is the reason why canon law does not raise the age for entering into a valid marriage. This canon law is universal; its scope includes very different geographical and cultural areas, in some of which the custom is to marry at a very early age"[506]. However, canon 1071 §1, 2°, 6° states that the approval of the local ordinary is required when the marriage cannot be recognized or celebrated in accordance with civil law, or when the parties are minor and the parents are not aware about the marriage or are reasonably opposed to it. One should not regard the legislation of the church as being less-concerned to the request of effective reflective capacity and exhibition of maturity at the time of marriage celebration because of the issue of not raising the age for entering into a valid and lawful marriage. That is why canon 1083 §2 empowers the Episcopal Conference of Bishops to fix a higher age for the lawful celebration of marriage.

Apart from canons 1083 §1 and 1071 §1 6°, which have norms that affect the validity or lawfulness, depending on the situation, canon 1072 recommends pas-

---

505 Cfr. D. Kelly, "Commentary on Pastoral Care", p.588; J. McAreavey, The Canon Law of Marriage, p.71; F. Gavin, Pastoral Care in Marriage Preparation, p.89.

506 T. Rincon-Perez, "Commentary on canons 1063-1072", p.1146.

tors of souls to take account of local customs[507] and to dissuade young people from the celebration of marriage before the age at which a person usually enters marriage according to the accepted practices of the region. It has to be emphasized here that this particular norm does not make explicit which age group is referred as young people, but in law, "marriage of the youth" according to Doyle, would mean minors and marriages entered prior to the customary age of the region. He continues by saying that though in most part of the world the adulthood is attended at the age of eighteen, still local custom or opinion may argue that marriages of those who are a few years older than eighteen are still marriages of the young[508]. However, the prohibition set up by canon 1072 is not an absolute one, but a pastoral directive or guideline based on experience[509].

In Igbo traditional marriage, age is neither considered as a factor nor an impediment. But it is a glaring fact that marriage does not take place before the age of puberty. In the Eastern States of Nigeria (Igboland), the age of marriage under customary law is sixteen for both male and female. Any marriage entered before this age is invalid and unlawful. This is praiseworthy measure, but seems to have been taken in a hurry without much preparation so that a very large number of marriages in Igboland still take place much below this age. And this is the reason why so many marriages of the young fail very often because of lack of maturity and good judgment to handle the obligations of marriage.

2.3. Canon 1063 of 1983 Code

As we already pointed out, the Second Vatican Council does not provide a comprehensive program for marriage preparation rather, it emphasises the need for it and encourages its implementation. In this regard, preparation for marriage was given little attention, instead the support which must be accorded to married couples and the family was emphasised (GS 52). However, the Council recovers through its Conciliar Document, Gaudium et Spes a richer understanding of marriage as an interpersonal covenant. The Council does encourage parents to instruct young people concerning the dignity, duty and the need to express conjugal love (GS 49). The family itself is expected to carry the main responsibility for marriage preparation in its entirety. Equally, priests are to be adequately trained

507 McAreavey noted that local customs in this matter may be reflected in the age at which marriage is permitted in civil law since national legislatures take account of the specific circumstances of time and place. Cfr. J. McAreavey, The Canon Law of Marriage, p.72.

508 Cfr. T.P. Doyle, Marriage, p.756.

509 Cfr. L.A.Robitaille, "Commentary on canons 1063-1072", p.1271.

to deal with family matters and to nurture the vocation of spouses in their married and family life (GS 52)[510].

In the Ordo Celebrandi Matrimonium, promulgated by Paul VI in 1969, renewed emphasis about marriage preparation was given pastoral attention. In this rite, priests are to strengthen and nourish the faith of those preparing to marry, to review with them the fundamentals of Christian doctrine, most importantly the church's teachings about marriage and the family, and the rites to be used in their wedding celebrations[511]. For the celebration of the marriage of the spouses to be fruitful, the priest should stress certain elements in the marriage celebration: "1) the liturgy of the Word which situates Christian marriage within the whole history of salvation and the duties and responsibilities it involves in the sanctification of the couple and their children; 2) the consent of the parties; 3) the special nuptial blessing of the bride and groom by which the priest implores God's blessing on the wedding covenant; 4) the reception of the Eucharist by the couple themselves and by those others present"[512].

It is to be noted that the significance of the instruction of the prospective spouses and of a fruitful celebration of the marriage liturgy discussed in this very rite came to form an important part of canon 1063 of 1983 Code. The relevance and pastoral importance of canon 1063 of 1983 Code echoes the deep concern expressed by the Second Vatican Council Fathers with regard to the pressures and problems inherent in the institution of Christian marriage in our contemporary world. "However, this happy picture of the dignity of these partnerships is not reflected everywhere but is overshadowed by polygamy, the plague of divorce, so-called free love, and similar blemishes; furthermore, married love is too often dishonoured by selfishness, hedonism and unlawful contraceptive practices. Besides the economic, social, psychological and civil climate of today has a severely disturbing effect on family life"[513]. Also the Papal Commission on Marriage and the Family of the United States Catholic Conference in alluding to these serious contemporary problems facing the marriage of the Christians states: "The crises which gravely affects the family in those countries (European and North American) arises directly from the development of a mentality which stresses material success, individualism, efficiency, technology that is becoming more and more refined, and the development of a lifestyle that stresses money, action and power"[514]. Still on this problem militating against the fruitful celebration of

510 Cfr. J.H. Provost, Marriage Preparation in the New Code, p.176.

511 Cfr. SCR; Ordo Celebrandi Matrimonium, Typis Polyglottis Vatican City 1991, nn. 5-7; J.H. Provost, Marriage Preparation in the New Code, p.176.

512 Ordo Celebrandi Matrimonium, 6,8; F. Gavin, Pastoral Care in Marriage Preparation, p.55.

513 GS 47§2.

514 Papal Committee on the Family, "The Family in the Pastoral Activity of the Church", Washington D.C; USCC 1978, p.5. See also T.P. Doyle, Marriage, p.747.

Christian marriage, the Pontifical Council for the Family asserts: "In other areas of the world, situations of underdevelopment including extreme poverty and misery, as well as the simultaneous presence of cultural elements against or outside the Christian vision make both the stability of the family and building up an in-depth education in Christian love difficult and precarious"[515].

In this view, canon 1063 which deals on marriage preparation is an attempt by the church to counteract this malaise facing Christian marriage. In other words, it stresses strongly the important attention to be given to pre-marriage pastoral care, because left to judicial or administrative preparation alone, the purpose and the goal of marriage of Christians will be counter productive and the stability of marriage save by preventing the entering into invalid or unlawful marriage celebration cannot be assured[516].

Canon 1063[517] obliges pastors of souls to ensure that their own proper ecclesial community provides assistance to the Christian faithful such that the married state is preserved in its Christian spirit and continues to progress in its perfection. To preserve the Christian character of married state is to safeguard the fundamental properties of Christian marriage such as unity and indissolubility. They are the essential properties of marriage that give stability to married life. The phrase, "in perfectione progrediatur", echoes the supernatural goal of every Christian marriage. It is a road towards holiness to which married spouses are also called to share and follow.

---

515 PCF, Preparation for the Sacrament of Marriage, n.12. This document consists of guidelines from the Pontifical Council for the Family, which is an administrative body. In other words, the text is not a legislative document. It cannot derogate from universal law. Rather, it seeks to explain the law and give suggestions for practice. For more understanding of this, see L.A. Robitaille, Commentary on Canons 1063-1072, p.1262.

516 Cfr. V.J. Pospishil, Eastern Catholic Marriage Law according to the Code of Canons of the Eastern Churches, Brookyln 1991, p.251; P.K. Amevor, New Approaches to Marriage Preparation, p.158.

517 C.1063 CIC/1983: "Pastors of souls are obliged to see to it that their own ecclesial community furnishes the Christian faithful assistance so that the matrimonial state is maintained in a Christian spirit and makes progress toward perfection. This assistance is especially to be furnished through:
1° preaching, catechesis adapted to minors, youths and adults, and even the use of the media of social communications so that through these means the Christian faithful may be instructed concerning the meaning of Christian marriage and the duty of Christian spouses and parents;
2° personal preparation for entering marriage so that through such preparation the parties may be predisposed toward the holiness and duties of their new state;
3° a fruitful liturgical celebration of marriage clarifying that the spouses signify and share in that mystery of unity and of fruitful love that exists between Christ and the Church;
4° assistance furnished to those already married so that, while faithfully maintaining and protecting the conjugal covenant, they may day by day come to lead holier and fuller lives in their families".

The purpose of this canon is to assist prospective couples preparing for marriage or spouses already married so that "their married lives may be lived out in a Christian spirit and continue to grow in the realization of that mystery which is at the core of each marriage"[518].

The Pontifical Council for the Family, in explaining what is meant by marriage preparation asserts: "What is called preparation in this document includes a broad and thorough process of education for married life which must be considered in totality of its values…. In fact, preparation is educating for the respect and care for life which, in the sanctuary of families, must become a real and proper culture of human life in all its manifestations and stages for those who are part of the people of life and for life"[519]. It should be emphasised that marriage preparation has a broader meaning than dealing only with individual spouses and their care. In this regard, the Council opines that "marriage preparation must be set within the urgent need to evangelise culture – by permeating it to its roots… – in everything that concerns the institution of marriage: making the Christian spirit penetrate minds and behaviour, as well as the laws and structures of the community where Christians live"[520].

Marriage preparation, for the Christian couple is "a journey of faith which does not end with the celebration of marriage but continues throughout family life"[521]. In this view, it is pertinent to bring to light what Gil and Ortega say about the purpose of marriage preparation: "The purpose of this pre-matrimonial preparation or pastoral attention cannot limit itself to a mere negative aspect, or a simple bureaucratic procedure or formality which takes place in the weeks immediately proceeding the wedding: rather it is necessary to have a catechesis which is oriented towards the actualization of faith, a conscious preparation for marriage… in summary, it refers to a preparation that stimulates a growth or spiritual and human development on which, to a large extent, depends on the possibility that the new family can responsibly achieve its task in society and in the ecclesiastical community"[522].

518 J.H. Provost, Marriage Preparation in the New Code, p.186.

519 PCF, n.10.

520 PCF, n.20.

521 PCF, n.16.

522 F.R. Aznar Gil – M.E. Olmos Ortega, La Preparacion Celebracion e Inscripcion del Matrimonio en Espana, Salmanca 1996, pp.133-134, in F. Gavin, Pastoral Care in Marriage Preparation, p.92.

2.3.1. Pastors of Souls

The phrase, "pastores animarum" in canon 1063 refers to all who are entrusted with the pastoral and spiritual care of the Christian faithful, namely the diocesan bishops according to canon 375, and their equivalents (c.376), parish priests (c.515) in relation to their parish communities, and chaplains according to canon 564[523]. In carrying out the function of a pastor, a bishop is to be concerned for all the faithful entrusted into his care[524]. Besides, the diocesan bishop is to offer special pastoral care to those unable to make reasonable use of ordinary pastoral care because of the unhealthy condition they found themselves and those who have ceased religious practice[525]. As a matter of fact, the diocesan bishop is saddled with the responsibility of co-ordinating the various initiatives of pastoral and spiritual activities within his jurisdiction. In speaking about the responsibility of the diocesan bishop the decree on the Pastoral Office of Bishops in the Church, Christus Dominus declares that: "The various forms of the apostolate should be encouraged. Close collaboration and the co-ordination of all the apostolic works under the direction of the bishop should be promoted in the diocese as a whole or in parts of it. Thus, all the undertakings and organisations, whether their object be catechetical, missionary, charitable, social,familial, educational, or any other pastoral purpose, will act together in harmony, and the unity of the diocese will be more clearly evident"[526]. In view of this, the bishop has the primary obligation of providing for the various forms of pre-marriage and post-marriage assistance mentioned in canon 1063. The bishop's responsibility in his diocese is clearly summarized by John Paul II when he proclaims: "The person principally responsible in the diocese for the pastoral care of the family is the Bishop. As father and pastor, he must exercise particular solicitude in this clearly priority sector of pastoral care. He must devote to it personal interest, care, time, personnel and resources, but above all personal support for the families and for all those who, in the various diocesan structures, assist him in the pastoral care of the family. It will be his particular care to make the diocese ever more truly a "diocesan fam-

523 C.564 CIC/1983: "A chaplain is a priest to whom is entrusted in a stable manner the pastoral care, at least in part, of some community or special group of Christ's faithful, to be exercised in accordance with universal and particular law".

524 Cfr. C.383 §1 CIC/1983: "In exercendo munere pastoris, Episcopus dioecesanus sollicitum se praebeat erga omnes christifideles qui suae curae committuntur, cuiusvis sint aetatis, condicionis vel nationis, tum in territorio habitantes tum in eodem ad tempus versantes, animum intendens apostolicum ad eos etiam qui ob vitae suae condicionem ordinaria cura pastorali non satis frui valeant necnon ad eos qui a religionis praxi defecerint".

525 Cfr. CCEO, 192§1.

526 CD, 17 §1.

ily", a model and source of hope for the many families that belong to it"[527]. In line with canon 1064 of 1983 Code which we have already discussed, the bishop is advised to formulate programs for pastoral care of the family with the assistance of qualified lay people, if opportune to do so, in those areas outlined in canon 1063. In this regard, Gavin cautions that: "While this should allow for the creativity of particular parish groups, associations and movements involved in the pastoral care of the family, it should also ensure that broad uniform guidelines will be provided to assist each local community to fulfil its obligation with regard to marriage preparation"[528].

The parish priest according to canon 519[529] is responsible for providing this pastoral care in his parish community under the auspices of the diocesan bishop in whose ministry of Christ he has been called to partake[530]. The parish priest by fulfilling the functions of teaching, sanctifying and governing, he extends this pastoral care to his parishioners.

Canon 1063, 1° outlines the various means by which pastors of souls are obliged to take care of the church community entrusted into their care. They are to do this through preaching, catechetical instruction adapted to children, young people and adults, and by the use of social communications so as to explain the real meaning of Christian marriage and the obligation of Christian couples and parents. The parish priest with the help of other priests in proclaiming the word of God must be more accurate and exact in their preaching about the sacramentality and purposes of marriage[531]. In preaching about marriage to prospective couples, they should present the sacrament of marriage as something outstanding among all human relationships, because it is the privileged, exclusive, and definitive covenant between a man and a woman[532].

The canon does not suggest or propose the means of making this preaching fruitful to the prospective couples. It suffices to say that the manner of carrying out this preaching rests on the shoulder of those entrusted with the pastoral ac-

527 FC, 73 §1.

528 F. Gavin, Pastoral Care in Marriage Preparation, p.94.

529 C.519 CIC/1983: "The parish priest is the proper pastor of the parish entrusted to him. He exercises the pastoral care of the community entrusted to him under the authority of the diocesan bishop, whose ministry of Christ he is called to share, so that for this community he may carry out the offices of teaching, sanctifying and ruling with the cooperation of other priests or deacons and with the assistance of lay members of Christ's faithful, in accordance with the law".

530 Cfr. J.A. Renken, Commentary on Canons 515-544, "Parishes, Pastors, and Parochial Vicars", in J.P. Beal – J.A. Coriden – T.J. Green, eds; New Commentary on the Code of Canon Law, New York 2000, p.690.

531 Cfr. B.D. Hajovsky, Marriage Preparation and Pastoral Care, p.48.

532 Cfr. NCCB, The Role of the Christian Family in the Modern World, Washington 1979, p.16.

tivities of a particular ecclesial community[533]. The prescriptions of this particular canon are not satisfied by an occasional preaching on marriage, because preaching alone will not be adequate for a fruitful marriage preparation. In this sense, Amevor suggests that: "More acceptable means and techniques must be applied to proclaim the word competently. In such a proclamation the primary focus should be on scriptural sources, sound theological reflections and the cultural values of marriage"[534]. Also other means of enlighten prospective couples on what they are about to enter are encouraged in this canon as preaching need only not be sermon which in other words, is reserved to ordained pastors[535] and may not be sufficient to prepare young adults adequately for marriage. In this regard, lay faithful can be admitted to faction other means of preaching in order to prepare couples well for marriage, since according to canon 767 §1, the homily, which is part of the Eucharistic liturgy, is reserved to priests and deacons. Provost captures this argument when he asserts: "It is not unknown for married persons to be invited to preach about the experience of Christian marriage at various occasions within a church building; this is now permitted provided the appropriate limitations are observed (c.766). It is an example of how the church community can work toward fulfilling its obligation"[536]. Still on this issue of preaching, Coriden suggests that pastors or rectors who are in charge of the churches and oratories can authorize lay persons to preach as they have the obligation of providing for the proclamation of the word of God to the people (c.528 §1)[537].

Hence, the general catechesis of all prospective couples should not as a matter of fact, focus only on occasional sermon preached during liturgical celebrations "but should be an integral part of catechetical and adult education programs, catholic school curricula, and other forms parish and diocesan programs"[538]. There is a serious duty on the part of pastors of souls to provide proper catechesis to children, young people and adults. This obligation is outlined in canons 773, 776, and 777 of 1983 Code[539].

533 Cfr. L. Örsy, Marriage in Canon Law, Texts and Comments: Reflections and Questions, Washington, Delaware 1988, p.76.

534 P.K. Amevor, New Approaches to Marriage Preparation, p.159.

535 Cfr. C.767 §1 CIC/1983: "Inter praedicationis formas eminet homilia, quae est pars ipsius liturgiae et sacerdoti aut diacono reservatur; in eadem per anni liturgici cursum ex textu sacro fidei mysteria et normae vitae christianae exponantur".

536 J.H. Provost, Marriage Preparation in the New Code, p.188.

537 Cfr. J.A. Coriden, "Commentary on canons 747-833", "The Teaching Office of the Church", in J.A. Coriden – T.J. Green – D.E. Heintschel, eds; The Code of Canon Law, A Text and Commentary, New York, Mahway 1985, p.552.

538 T.P. Doyle, Marriage, p.747.

539 C.773 CIC/1983: "There is a proper and serious duty, especially on the part of pastors of souls, to provide for the catechesis of the Christian people so that the faith of the faithful becomes living, explicit and productive through formation in doctrine and the experience of Christian living".

The decree on the Pastoral Office of Bishops in the Church, Christus Dominus, states that the function of catechetical instruction is to develop in men a living, explicit and active faith, enlightened by doctrine[540]. In defining the meaning and the aim of catechesis, Coriden says: "Catechesis is that form of the ministry of the word directed toward those who have been evangelised, who have heard the gospel, and who have responded in faith. The aim of catechetical instruction is to render that faith lively, conscious, and effective ("viva... explicita atque operosa"); in other words, to help faith develop and grow so that it can be real guiding force in the believer's life"[541]. In his Apostolic Exhortation, Catechesi Tradendae, John Paul II emphasises the importance of catechesis, especially of adolescents. "A catechesis capable of leading the adolescent to re-examine his or her life and to engage in dialogue, a catechesis that does not ignore the adolescent's great questions – self-giving, belief, love and the means of expressing it constituted by sexuality – such a catechesis can be decisive"[542]. Doyle considers that "education and catechesis are more effective than law to bring about an acceptance of Christian values"[543]. Thus, in order to teach young people and engaged couples the real meaning of Christian marriage, catechetical instruction must be applied in its fullness.

C.776 CIC/1983: "In virtue of his office the pastor is bound to provide for the catechetical formation of adults, young people and children, to which end he is to employ the services of the clerics attached to the parish, members of institutes of consecrated life and of societies of apostolic life, with due regard for the character of each institute, and lay members of the christian faithful, above all catechists; all of these are not to refuse to furnish their services willingly unless they are legitimately impeded. The pastor is to promote and foster the role of parents in the family catechesis mentioned in can.774 §2".

C.777 CIC/1983: "In accord with the norms established by the diocesan bishop, the pastor is to make particular provision:

1° that suitable catechesis is given for the celebration of the sacraments;

2° that children are properly prepared for the first reception of the sacraments of penance and most Holy Eucharist and the sacrament of confirmation by means of a catechetical formation given over an appropriate period of time;

3° that children are more fruitfully and deeply instructed through catechetical formation after the reception of First Communion;

4° that catechetical formation also be given to those handicapped in body or mind insofar as their condition permits;

5° that the faith of young people and adults be fortified, enlightened and developed through various means and endeavours".

540 CD, 14 §1.

541 J.A. Coriden, The Teaching Office of the Church, p.555.

542 CT, 38. "Immo partes decretorias explere poterit catechesis, quae adulescentem ducere valebit ad recognoscendam propriam vitam et ad dialogum faciendum quaeque minime vitabit graves ipsius quaetiones: donationem sui, fiduciam, amorem euisque communicationem, quae sexualitas est".

543 T.P. Doyle, "The Canonical Foundations for Pre-marriage Preparation Guidelines", Marriage Studies, Vol. 1 (Toledo: Canon Law Society of America), 1980, p.71.

Canon 1063, 1° also urges the full use of modern mass media so as to achieve the broad objective of educating people of all ages and leading them to an appreciation of the real meaning of marriage and the pertinent role that married couples and parents must fulfil in the church and community. The decree on the Means of Social Communication, Inter Mirifica, in affirming the authority of the church to have and make use of the media states that: "Pastors of souls have the task of instructing and directing the faithful how to use these media in a way that will ensure their own salvation and perfection and that of all mankind"[544]. Canon 822 of the 1983 Code echoes Inter Mirifica and calls the attention of the pastors of souls "to make use of the instruments of social communication"[545] and to make sure that "the faithful are taught that they are bound in duty to cooperate so that the use of the instruments of social communication is animated with a human and Christian spirit"[546].

Paul VI calls the attention of educators and those who perform functions of responsibility with regard to the common good of society to the need for respect and action for moral order in the use of modern media. In emphasising this respect for moral order he asserts: "Everything in the modern media of social communications which leads to sense excitation and unbridled customs, as well as every form of pornography and licentious performances, must arouse the frank and unanimous reaction of all those who are solicitous for the progress of civilisation and the defence of the common good of the human spirit"[547].

John Paul II in outlining the importance and dangers of this media of social communication has this to say: "They can thus exercise a beneficial influence on the life and habits of the family and on the education of children, but at the same time they also conceal "snares and dangers that cannot be ignored"[548]. Also in using the means of social communication to preach the gospel to all nations and safeguard revealed truth, canon 747 §1 of 1983 Code declares: "The church, to whom Christ the Lord entrusted the deposit of faith so that, assisted by the

544 IM, 3§2.

545 C.822 §1CIC/1983: "Ecclesiae pastores in suo munere explendo iure Ecclesiae proprio utentes, instrumenta communicationis socialis adhibere satagant".

546 C.822 §2 CIC/1983: "Iisdem pastoribus curae sit fideles edocere se officio teneri cooperandi ut instrumentorum communicationis socialis usus humano christianoque spiritu vivificetur". The local ordinaries are encouraged in this paragraph to outline the assistance of the faithful in making social communications media true instruments of human development and the salvation of souls. It is a glaring fact that members of the ecclesia community have more influence over the media of social communications and at the same time probably more affected by them than the pastors of souls. That is the reason why reflecting the decree on the Means of Social Communication, Inter Mirifica 3, this very paragraph recalls this unique obligation of lay persons. For more details, see J.A. Coriden, The Teaching Office of the Church, p.579.

547 HV, 22 §2.

548 FC, 76 §1.

Holy Spirit, it might reverently safeguard revealed truth, more closely examine it and faithfully proclaim and expound it, has the innate duty and right to preach the gospel to all nations, independent of any human power whatever, using the means of social communication proper to it"[549].

It is important to say that canon 1063, 1° did not enumerate the tools to be used in imparting this communication, but the press, cinema, radio, television, internet, telephone, newspapers, post and other forms of publications are to be used in instructing the Christian faithful concerning the meaning of Christian marriage and the obligation of married couples and parents in the family. Therefore, married couples are in a position to use these means of social communications to relate the sacramental dimension of marriage and family life with day to day realities. This is because the instruments of social communications are powerful and effective means for teaching and evangelisation[550] and most especially, for marriage preparation programs.

Canon 1063, 2° declares that it is the personal preparation of the parties that will dispose them to the holiness and obligation of their new state. This particular norm requires more than a mere theoretical presentation of the duties and holiness of marriage as was the case in the Code of 1917[551]. In this case, the preparation should follow a pastoral manner which truly helps the spouses in their understanding and appreciation of the married state and family life. The most important thing is for the spouses to be disposed[552] to the holiness and obligations of their new state, and not just hear about them in passive[553].

Canon 1063, 3° refers to the importance of a fruitful celebration of the marriage liturgy which clarifies that the spouses signify and participate in the mystery of the unity and fruitful love between Christ and the church. To this, Doyle argues that the fact that this liturgical celebration is emphasised on canon 1063, 3° indicates that it is not only a means of sanctifying spouses, but it is equally a source of instruction for all present on the theological importance of the Christian marriage[554]. A fruitful celebration of the marriage liturgy requires a greater interaction between the priest and the spouses. The legalistic approach to marriage

549 C.747 §1 CIC/1983: "Ecclesiae, cui Christus Dominus fidei depositum concredidit ut ipsa, Spiritu Sancto assistente, veritatem revelatam sancte custodiret, intimius perscrutaretur, fideliter annuntiaret atque exponeret, officium est et ius nativum, etiam mediis communicationis socialis sibi propriis adhibitis, a qualibet humana potestate independens, omnibus gentibus Evangelium praedicandi".

550 Cfr. L. Lee, Contribution of Lay People Towards Preparation of Marriage, p.44.

551 Cfr. C.1033 CIC/1917.

552 Cfr. C.843 §1 CIC/1983: "Ministri sacri denegare non possunt sacramenta iis qui opportune eadem petant, rite sint dispositi, nec iure ab iis recipiendis prohibeantur".

553 Cfr. B.D. Hajovsky, Marriage Preparation and Pastoral Care, p.49.

554 Cfr. T.P. Doyle, Marriage, p.748.

in the Code of 1917 did not encourage a more personal relationship between the priest and the spouses. Because of this very fact, the understanding of marriage was given an abstract dimension with little connection to the practical reality[555].

Canon 1063, 4° recognises the necessity for ongoing support and formation of those already married. This norm is stressing that the priest is responsible for the ongoing support of those already married by developing in his ecclesia community means of, and helping married couples to grow in their special vocation[556] so that by observing and safeguarding their conjugal bond they may come to lead a holier and fuller family life. It stresses the necessity for a deeper and more mature relationship in the development of pastoral care programs for married couples and prospective couples preparing for marriage.

2.3.1.1. The Nature and Object of Obligation for Pastors of Souls

It is to be mentioned here that both pastors of souls and the ecclesia community are to take part in discharging this obligation. On the one hand, there is a direct obligation for pastors of souls, and on the other hand, there is also an indirect obligation for ecclesia communities under the pastors' charge, to implement and ensure this pastoral care[557]. Fagiolo stresses that this type of obligation is one that is in solidum, which is jointly by pastors of souls and the ecclesia communities but the special responsibility is on the pastors to exhibit leadership in executing it[558].

"Obligatione tenentur" is the technical term used in analysing this obligation. The phrase is applicable to making the profession of faith (c.833), in keeping oaths (c.1200 §1), and obeying constitutions and decrees of the pope (c.754). It is also used to express some basic precepts of the church such as Masses on Sundays and holy days of obligation (c.1247), annual confession (c.989), annual communion (c.920 §1), assistance to the church (c.222 §1). It continues to express the obligation of clergy to obey the pope and the ordinary (c.273), to say the liturgy of the hours (c.276 §2, 3°), and to observe perfect and perpetual continence (c.277 §1)[559].

By way of analysing the technical term "obligatione tenentur", we have found out that pastors of souls are not only being shouldered with this obligation but they have also a more serious one for the implementation of pastoral care for perspective couples and those already married in different families. According to Provost, "to say that "pastors of souls are obliged to see to it..." is saying

555 Cfr. B.D. Hajovsky, Marriage Preparation and Pastoral Care, p.50.

556 Cfr. J.A. Alesandro, Marriage Legislation in the New Code: Preparation for Marriage, Washington 1980, p.84.

557 Cfr. J.H. Provost, Marriage Preparation in the New Code, p.183; F. Gavin. Pastoral Care in Marriage Preparation,p.95.

558 Cfr. V. Fagiolo, "La Preparazione al Matrimonio", pp.10-11, in V. Fagiolo, Commentary, p.631.

559 Cfr. J.H. Provost, Marriage Preparation in the New Code, p.184.

something quite serious, essential to what is expected of parish pastors (c.528 §1), and therefore not something optional or secondary"[560]. Gavin on his own part says, "By examining how this phrase obligatione tenentur is used elsewhere in the Code it becomes clear that we are dealing with a most serious obligation, one which the church expects to be observed"[561]. Because of the seriousness of these obligations pastors of souls are to work harder to adhere to them and carry them out because failure to observe them can result to a penalty being imposed in some cases[562].

The problem with this phrase "obligatione tenentur" from a practical point of view, is that there is no way of ensuring its implementation by pastors of souls. Alluding to this, Amevor opines: "Unlike the civil society, the bishop or the church has no law enforcement agencies to enforce or monitor the pastors that the obligation is executed. This means that the church cannot do much if it comes to probity and accountability of pastors"[563]. Notwithstanding this difficulty arising from the implementation of the obligation by pastors, there is a clarion call for all and sundry for an effective and diligent means of accountability so as to ensure how serious these obligations stipulated in canon 1063 are for the entire ecclesia community[564]

The canon broadly emphasises furnishing assistance to "the Christian faithful" concerning marriage. In this regard, the beneficiaries are not only couples who are about to marry, although the canon recognises them in a special way (2, 3°) but to the community as a whole. The ecclesia community has a right to anticipate maturity and real Christian commitment from engaged couples. In other words, marriage preparation is not something confined to a special interest group or something meant to last for a short period of time, rather it is a life-long journey comprising of various stages[565]. So the assistance to be furnished is addressed to so many groups that form the ecclesial community. "So the assistance to be furnished is addressed to families themselves, for it is here that children

560 Ibid.

561 F. Gavin, Pastoral Care in Marriage Preparation, p.96.

562 Cfr. C.1389 §1 CIC/1983: "Ecclesiastica potestate vel munere abutens pro actus vel omissionis gravitate puniatur, non exclusa officii privatione, nisi in eum abusum iam poena sit lege vel praecepto constituta".

563 P.K. Amevor, New Approaches to Marriage Preparation, p.162.

564 Cfr. H.D. Skillin, "Marriage in the Year 2000: Canonical Pastoral Considerations", in CLSA Proceedings 52 (1990), p.38; F. Gavin, Pastoral Care in Marriage Preparation, p.97; J.H. Provost, Marriage Preparation in the New Code, p.184. Although theoretically the bishop's visitation should assure that the obligations in canon 1063 are being fulfilled, and his own periodic accountability to the Apostolic See should assure the same for the diocesan church, in practice there seems to be little attention paid in accountability structures to marriage preparation as a priority for pastoral activity. Cfr. J.H. Provost, Marriage Preparation in the New Code, p.191.

565 Cfr. J.H. Provost, Marriage Preparation in the New Code, p.187.

first learn the patterns of relationship which influence their own married lives. It is addressed to various educational groups, such as children, youth and young adults, who are not yet married. It is addressed to those who are already married, and whose married lives set an example and standard for others. It is addressed to older people whose wisdom needs to be brought to a younger generation, to unmarried persons whose lives affect those who marry, to the community at large which has such an influence on how values are lived out even in families. In other words, marriage preparation is an integral dimension of evangelization, catechesis, and pastoral action"[566].

So, in order to respond to this clarion call of furnishing assistance to the Christian faithful, pastors of souls and the ecclesial community are to collaborate so as to work for prospective couples and those already married "in order that their married lives may be lived out in a Christian spirit and continue to grow in the realization of that mystery which is at the core of each marriage"[567].

2.3.2. The Role of the Ecclesial Community

The ecclesial community has also a responsibility to furnish this assistance to the Christian faithful in solidarity with the pastors of souls. This is the reason why the Code emphasises that pastors should draw on the resources of the entire ecclesial community. It is imperative to know that marriage as a sacrament is not only a private bond between two persons, rather it is a commitment before God and the ecclesial community, and as such, it comprises the good of the community. This, marriage should be elevated and cared for by the ecclesial community[568]. Taping from the Conciliar Document, Gaudium et Spes, Fagiolo argues that all "ecclesial components" should be subjected to this pastoral care with the obligation subordinate to that of the bishop and the parish priest, whose duty is to guide the whole particular church and the local church respectively[569].

The inclusion of the ecclesial community in this obligation is not something baseless because by virtue of being baptised they have the fundamental call to participate in the church's mission by exercising the threefold functions of teaching, sanctifying, and above all, ruling through which the people of God, the ecclesial community continue the mission of Christ (c.204 §1), and which is further specified in view of promoting the growth of the church and its continual sanctification (c.210), working so that the divine message of salvation may increasingly

566 Ibid.

567 J.H. Provost, Marriage Preparation in the New Code, p.186.

568 Cfr. L.A. Robitaille, "Commentary on canons 1063-1072", p.1262.

569 Cfr. V. Fagiolo, "La Preparazione al Matrimonio", pp.10-11; F. Gavin, Pastoral Care in Marriage Preparation, p.97.

reach the whole of humankind in every age and in every land (c.211), to sustain or promote apostolic activities by their own undertakings in accord with each one's state and conditions (c.216), to develop the maturity of a human person and at the same time come to know and live the mystery of salvation (c.217) and to take account of the common good of the church and of the rights of others as well as their own duties toward others (c.223)[570].

Another reason for the involvement of the ecclesial community as regards this obligation has to do with the obvious fact that only through other members of the ecclesial community may it be possible for the full import of the gospel to become manifest. It is also based on the duty of the whole ecclesial community, laity as well as clergy, to bear witness to the gospel especially in those circumstances in which people can hear the gospel and know Christ only through the lay faithful (c.225 §1)[571]. Provost declares that the ecclesial community's obligation is a very serious moral one and remains problematic today and unless the ecclesial community assumes this responsibility, its own future will be at risk[572].

2.3.3. The Role of the Religious

Since the ecclesial community is to take part in this obligation of preparing those intending to marry for marriage and also furnishing assistance to those already married, the religious who are part of this community are not left out in this task. "By exposing young people preparing for the married vocation to various aspects of the religious vocation, their understanding of the complementarities of the two vocations can be deepened"[573]. The contribution to be made by religious to marriage preparation finds its original meaning in their consecration to God. "By reason of this consecration, "for all Christ's faithful religious recall that wonderful marriage made by God, which will be fully manifested in the future age, and in which the church has Christ for her only spouse"[574].

Speaking on how the religious can assist prospective couples in their marriage preparation programs and those already married to become responsible parents,

570 Cfr. J.H. Provost, Marriage Preparation in the New Code, p.185.

571 Cfr. C.225 §1 CIC/1983: "Laici, quipped qui uti omnes chritifideles ad apostolatum a Deo per baptismum et confirmationem deputentur, generali obligatione tenentur et iure gaudent, sivi singuli sive in consociationibus coniuncti, allaborandi ut divinum salutis nuntium ab universes hominibus ubique terrarium cognoscatur et accipiatur; quae obligatio eo vel magis urget iis in adiunctis, in quibus nonnisi per ipsos Evangelium audire et Christum cognoscere hominess possunt".

572 Cfr. J.H. Provost, Marriage Preparation in the New Code, p.186.

573 F. Gavin, Pastoral Care in Marriage Preparation, p.99.

574 FC, 74 §1.

John Paul II opines that "they can offer their own work of teaching and counselling in the preparation of young people for marriage, and in helping couples towards truly responsible parenthood"[575].

2.3.4. The Role of Married Couples

The role of married couples in exercising this obligation of furnishing assistance and preparing couples for marriage cannot be over-emphasised since all Christians are called in virtue of their baptism to work with their pastors in solidum to achieve these objectives.

With regard to their status as married spouses, they are to be fully included with primary responsibility in the pastoral care of marriage[576]. It is pertinent to bring to light the importance of the witness value of married spouses and parents outlined by the Dogmatic Constitution on the Church, Lumen Gentium: "Christian married couples and parents, following their own way, should support one another in grace all through life with faithful love and should train their children (lovingly received from God) in Christian doctrine and evangelical virtues. Because in this way they present to all an example of unfailing and generous love, they build up the brotherhood of charity, and they stand as witnesses and co operators of the fruitfulness of mother church, as a sign of, and a share in that love with which Christ loved his bride and gave himself for her"[577].

One should not narrow down the significance of those spouses particularly trained for the pastoral care of marriage preparation in different dioceses and parishes or the worth and importance of different groups and organisations directly involved for the promotion of marriage and family because of the involvement of married couples through the witness of their own marriage, to assist in this obligation[578]. It is also not to be confused with the work of the lay specialists such as doctors, lawyers, psychologists, social workers, consultants etc, addressed in canon 1064, who John Paul II described their contribution as "commitment that well deserves the title of mission, so noble are the aims that it pursues, and so determining, for the good of society and the Christian community itself, are the results that derive from it"[579]. Taking cognisance of this, the responsibility of married couples in the pastoral care of marriage preparation and their witness are fundamental and cannot be substituted by anybody else[580].

575 FC, 74 §2.
576 Cfr. V. Fagiolo, "La Preparazione al Matrimonio", pp.13-17.
577 LG, 41 §5.
578 Cfr. F. Gavin, Pastoral Care in Marriage Preparation, p.99.
579 FC, 75 §1.
580 Cfr. G. Campanini – P. Scabini, "Nuove Prospettive della Pastorale Prematrimoniale", p.83.

2.4. Conclusion

We have seen so far that the general norms about marriage preparation in the Code of 1983 are due to the conviction that Christian marriage is a path to sanctity, a special vocation within the church, to realize which Christian spouses are fortified and consecrated for the duties and dignity of their state of life (GS 48 §2)[581]. The norms covered three great areas of subject matter about marriage preparation. These areas are: norms with regard to pre-marriage pastoral care, juridical prerequisites for ensuring the validity and lawfulness of marriage celebration, and the requirement of obtaining permission from the local ordinary to assist at certain marriages[582].

The significance and pastoral importance of canon 1063, an entirely new formulation in the Code cannot be over-emphasised. It brings out the broader implications of pastoral care concerning the preparation of prospective couples for marriage and also giving them pastoral care after marriage. This goes contrary to the rather narrow preoccupation of the 1917 Code with only the juridical requirements for marriage. Canon 1063 places a serious obligation on pastors of souls to see that the local ecclesial community provides suitable and adequate assistance to safeguarding and developing the Christian character of marriage. Although the direct obligation is on the pastors of souls, the ecclesial community is also involved in giving this support.

2.5. Stages of Marriage Preparation

2.5.1. Introduction

Canon 1063 points to four principal ways in which all concerned, both pastors of souls and the ecclesial community, are obliged to cooperate in this supportive assistance giving to the Christian faithful in ensuring that the matrimonial state is preserved and advanced in a Christian spirit. The four principal ways[583] are:

581 Cfr. T. Rincon-Perez, "Commentary on canons 1063-1072", p.1112.

582 Cfr. Ibid.

583 Cfr. H. Heimerl – H. Pree, Kirchenrecht, p.189. "Als pastorale Hilfe soll vor allem geboten werden:

1) Entferntere Ehevorbereitung in Predigt, Katechese für Kinder, Jugendliche und Erwachsene, sowie auch durch Gebrauch der Massenmedien. Durch diese Mittel sollen die Gläubigen über die Bedeutung der christlichen Ehe und über die Aufgaben der christlichen Gatten und Eltern unterwiesen werden.
2) Unmittelbare Ehevorbereitung in persönlicher Vorbereitung auf die Eheschließung; dadurch sollen die Brautleute für die Heiligkeit und die Pflichten ihres neuen Standes disponiert werden.

general education and catechesis with a special focus on the meaning of Christian marriage and on the obligation of married couples and parents (c.1063, 1°), personal preparation of those who are about marrying with a particular focus on the sanctification and the obligations of their new state (c.1063, 2°), fruitful liturgical celebration with a special focus on the community aspect of marriage in ensuring a fruitful marriage celebration (c.1063, 3°), and the ongoing support after marriage with a particular focus on the sanctity of family life as a sign of God's grace, given to the spouses by virtue of the sacrament they received and as a witness to the entire ecclesial community (c.1063, 4°). It is interesting to note that in listing these four principal ways, the canon characterizes them as "especially" (imprimis) meaning that it is not exclusive, rather open to other forms and means to ensure that the obligation of furnishing this assistance is carried out in a fruitful manner[584].

The four principal ways presented in canon 1063 in ensuring that the matrimonial state of the Christian faithful is maintained and progresses in a Christian spirit could be studied in terms of the stages for marriage preparation described in the Apostolic Exhortation of John Paul II, Familiaris Consortio[585], and which was further developed by the Pontifical Council for the Family in the instruction they issued out on May 13, 1996[586]. The Pope described marriage preparation as a gradual and continuous process with three principal stages: a) remote, b) proximate, c) and immediate preparations. In addition to these three stages, the Pope referred to a fourth stage, pastoral care after marriage, the equivalent of permanent formation of the couples and parents[587]. We shall now take a detail look on these four principal stages outlined in canon 1063 and in the Pontifical Council for the Family document.

2.5.2. Remote Preparation

In accordance with canon 1063, 1°, the means to carry out the remote preparation program is by preaching, catechesis adopted to minors, young people and adults

3) Fruchtbare liturgische Feier der Eheschließung selbst, in der aufleuchten soll, dass die Gatten das Geheimnis der Einheit und der fruchtbaren Liebe zwischen Christus und der Kirche darstellen und daran teilnehmen;
4) Eheseelsorge, nämlich Beistand, damit die Gatten ihren Ehebund treulich bewahren und so zu immer heiligerer und vollkommenerer Lebensführung in der Familie gelangen".

584 Cfr. J.H. Provost, Marriage Preparation in the New Code, pp.187-188; H. Heimerl – H. Pree, Kirchenrecht, p.189; R. Sebott – C. Marucci, Il Nuovo Diritto Matrimonialle della Chiesa, Napoli 1984, p.64.

585 Cfr. FC, 66,67,69.

586 Cfr. PCF, Preparation for the Sacrament of Marriage, nn.21-59.

587 Cfr. FC, 69; T. Rincon-Perez, "Commentary on canons 1063-1072", p.1117.

and also the use of instruments of social communication. The paragraph concerning the means is phrased in order to stress the necessity to use whatever means that are available to enhance a better comprehension of Christian marriages and the obligations of Christian couples and parents. Provost concludes by saying that the three stages enumerated indicate the great range of possibilities without rejecting other means of furnishing assistance to the Christian faithful[588].

The Pontifical Council for the Family in defining what remote preparation is says: "Remote preparation includes infancy, childhood and adolescence and takes place first of all in the family and also in the school and formation groups, as a valid assistance to the family. This is the period in which respect for all authentic human values both in interpersonal and social relations is transmitted and instilled, with all this implies for the formation of character, self-control and self-esteem, the proper use of one's inclinations, and respect for persons of the other sex. Moreover, especially for Christians, a solid spiritual and catechetical formation is also required"[589]. It is in the home that this process of remote preparation must begin, based upon the influence and examples which the Christian parents impart on the children to acquire the Christian and moral values as future parents in the making. Hence, adequate marriage preparation must start in childhood so that by so doing, children and young people in the process of learning the responsibilities involved in marriage and the appreciation of the importance of the sacrament of marriage, will be better positioned to apply those teachings to their own moral way of life when they get married[590].

There are certain goals to be achieved in this period of remote preparation. The Council suggests that this very preparation should "attain the goal whereby every member of the faithful called to marriage will understand completely that, in the light of God's love, human love takes on a central role in Christian ethics"[591]. On the other hand, the necessity of obtaining more and more the parameters of a right judgment concerning the hierarchy of values demanded in selecting the best that society has to offer and instil on children and young people is to be encouraged[592]. During this stage, pastoral assistance should be the motive of bringing moral behaviour aligned with faith. The example which parents exhibit as real witness for those intending to marry in the future will provide consistency, assistance and stimulus to the Christian lifestyle[593]. Another goal of this remote preparation is to assist young people obtain "a critical ability with regard to their surroundings,

588 Cfr. J.H. Provost, Marriage Preparation in the New Code, p.188.
589 PCF, Preparation, n.22.
590 Cfr. L.A. Robitaille, "Commentary oncCanons 1063-1072", p.1263.
591 PCF, Preparation, n.25.
592 Cfr. PCF, Preparation, n.26.
593 Cfr. Ibid.

and the Christian courage of those who know how to be in the world without belonging to it"[594].

The presentation of the parents' educational mission is another goal of this remote preparation because "a Christian lifestyle, witnessed to by Christian families, is in itself a form a form of evangelization and the very foundation of remote preparation"[595]. In this regard, the Council stresses that parents should be equipped with proper and adequate assistance since they are the foremost witness and educators of their children with regard to the growth of "faith, hope and charity", and in the process of each child finding his or her own vocation in life[596].

The Conciliar Schema on marriage, De Matrimonio, emphasises that parental obligations on their children include "instilling in their children a good value system, sex education, and instruction about the real meaning of love. Their obligation further includes teaching their sons and daughters the difference between a union which is entered into by blind instinct and marriage which has been established by God"[597].

Canon 226 §2 of the 1983 Code says that parents have the primary right and duty to educate their children and as Christians to see that their children receive a Christian education in accordance with the teaching handed on by the church[598]. With regard to catechetical instruction, parents have a primary responsibility for the growth in faith and Christian moral living of their children as stated in canon 774 §2[599]. Also concerning this parental role in the education of their children, they are to work for the sanctification of their children through a Christian upbringing[600], and have the duty and right to see to the "physical, social, cultural,

594 PCF, Preparation, n.27.

595 PCF, Preparation, n.28.

596 Cfr. Ibid.

597 "De Matrimonio", Acta Synodalia, vol.3, period 3, part 8, pp.471-473. "Pastores animarum frequenter in memoriam parentum revocent obligationem curandi filiorum educationem, ut in ipsis informent ur virtutes et humane et Christianae. Ad parentes imprimus pertinent tum prudenter et gradatim et tempestive filios instituere quoad mysterium vitae propagandae; tum curare ut filii discant in quo verus amor consistat, eum experiendo exercendoque erga familiars sodalesque studiorum ac laboris. Doceant etiam iuvenes coniugem eligendum esse non caeco instinctu, sed vero ac recto et sincero affectu, eos fines in matrimonio prosequendo propter quod illud esta a Deo constitutum".

598 Cfr. C.226 §2 CIC/1983: "Parentes, cum vitam filiis contulerint, gravissima obligatione tenentur et iure gaudent eos educandi; ideo parentum christianorum imprimis est Christianam filiorum educationem secundum doctrinam ab Ecclesia traditam curare".

599 C.774 §2 CIC/1983: "Before all others, parents are bound to form their children, by word and example, in faith and in Christian living. The same obligation binds godparents and those who take the place of parents".

600 Cfr. C.835 §4 CIC/1983: "In munere sanctificandi propriam sibi partem habent ceteri quoque christifideles actuose liturgicas celebrationes, eucharisticam praesertim, suo modo partici-

moral and religious upbringing of their children"[601]. They have an important duty to display in preparing their children for the sacrament of matrimony[602].

In order to achieve and carry out this task of educating their children, the Council recommended that parents need to be assisted adequately. In this, Gavin suggested that: "One very practical way the parish or, on a large scale, the deanery or diocese, can help parents in this task is by organising meetings, information sessions or support groups for parents to enable them to confront and respond to difficulties they encounter in their task as the primary educators of their children"[603]. Corti adds that if the task of assisting the parents is systematically well organised so as to last for a period of time, the various dangers encountered in childhood or adulthood could be resolved in their religious, moral, psychological, pedagogical and medical aspects[604].

In giving suitable and adequate assistance to parents recourse should be made to parish as it is the first place of Christian ecclesial formation and plays a vital role in this stage of preparing young people for marriage. It is also in the parish that a way of staying and living together as ecclesial community is learned[605]. The Council further contends that it is also in the parish that the "educational process must also be taken to heart by Catechists, animators of the pastoral care of youth and vocations and, above all, pastors who will take advantage of homilies during liturgical celebrations and other forms of evangelization, personal meetings, and ways of Christian commitment, in order to stress and highlight the points that contribute to a preparation directed toward possible marriage"[606].

The parish catechists[607] assist in spreading the gospel and organising liturgical celebrations and works of charity. Apart from this, their role in the remote preparation of young people for marriage cannot be over-emphasised as they take active part in preparation for marriage and family life. In exercising their function as catechists, they deal with some of the difficulties involved with young people

---

pando; peculiari modo idem munus participant parentes vitam coniugalem spiritu christiano ducendo et educationem christianam filiorum procurando".

601 Cfr. C.1136 CIC/1983: "Parentes officium gravissimum et ius primarium habent prolis educationem tum physicam, socialem et culturalem, tum moralem et religiosam pro viribus curandi".

602 Cfr. CC.1063, 1071 §1, n.6.

603 F. Gavin, Pastoral Care in Marriage Preparation, p.105.

604 Cfr. A. Corti, "Chiesa locale e preparazione al matrimonio", 41 (1971), p.63.

605 Cfr. PCF ,Preparation, n.29.

606 PCF, Preparation, n.30.

607 Cfr. C.785 CIC/1983 §1: "Catechists are to be employed in carrying out missionary work; catechists are those lay members of the Christian faithful who have been duly instructed, who stand out by reason of their Christian manner of life, and who devote themselves to expounding the gospel teaching and organizing liturgical functions and works of charity under the supervision of a missionary". §2: "Catechists are to be educated in schools destined for this purpose or, where such schools are lacking, under the supervision of missionaries".

living in today's culture, especially those intending to marry, and thereby offer some concrete and helpful solutions that will help these prospective couples when they finally marry.

The Council also made a clarion call that school and other institutions of higher learning, as well as movements, groups, catholic associations and, of course, associations of Christian families must not be left out in this assistance as they play a fundamental role in the education of young people for marriage[608]. In this regard, canon 796[609] outlines the preponderance of schools among all the different means of imparting education to children and young people and encourages the Christian faithful to value them as they serve as principal aid to parents in the education of their children. It also urges parents and teachers to work as partners in the educational process. This will no doubt help the children in the pursuit of good moral values. The Christian faithful are also admonished to strive for educational laws which would provide for religious and moral formation in the schools[610].

Therefore, for these goals enumerated in this particular stage to be successful, all hands must be on deck to impart the Christian moral values to children and young people in their early stage of remote preparation for marriage. In this view, the Council concludes: "Therefore, the ways and means must be "invented" for the on-going formation of adolescents in the period preceding engagement which follows the stages of Christian initiation.... Families joined together in the parishes, institutions and different forms of association; help create a social atmosphere in which responsible love will be healthy"[611].

2.5.3. Proximate Preparation

Canon 1063, 2° refers to personal preparation for entering marriage which disposes the parties to the sanctity and duties of their new state as a means of carrying out the proximate preparation for marriage. This form of preparation "takes place during the period of engagement. It consists of specific courses and must be dis-

608 Cfr. PCF, Preparation, n.29.

609 C.796 CIC/1983 §1: "Inter media ad excolendam educationem christifideles magni faciant scholas, quae, quidem parentibus, in munere educationis implendo, praecipuo auxilio sunt". §2: "Cum magistris schlarum, quibus filios educandos concredant, parentes arcte cooperentur oporti; magistri vero in officio suo persolvendo intime collaborent cum parentibus, qui quidem libenter audiendi sunt eorumque consociationes vel conventus instaurentur atque magni existinientur".

610 Cfr. C.799 CIC/1983: "Christifideles enitantur ut in societate civili leges quae iuvenum formationem ordinant, educationi eorum religiosae et morali quoque, iuxta parentum conscientiam, in ipsis scholis prospiciant".

611 PCF, Preparation, n.31.

tinguished from immediate preparation which is usually concentrated during the last meetings between the engaged and pastoral workers before the celebration of the sacrament"[612]. But how these specific courses are to take place may vary according to local circumstances and cultures. During this stage, maturation of the human values with regard to the bond of friendship and dialogue that characterize the engagement period should be verified[613].

The proximate preparation period should as a matter of fact, determine the readiness of the parties to marry. Notwithstanding the requirements for canonical validity, a certain level of psychological and emotional maturity is needed for the success of this period. And since marriage is a dynamic process, what is required is some evidence of a basic level of maturity and the potential for further growth in accordance with the ability to cope with the stress and strain involved in a developing marriage relationship[614]. It should also determine the parties' comprehension of the commitment involved in the sacrament of marriage and their eagerness to live out its implications. This period should also explore the interpersonal dimension of marriage. Some basic questions to be asked include: personal motives in marriage; their acceptance of each other's mistakes and idiosyncracies; their capacity to enunciate and evaluate their reasons for getting married, knowing fully well that the motive is for the capacity not only to make a gift of themselves to each other but also the ability to accept the gift of other's self[615].

This stage, the Council affirms, coincides generally with the period of youth which comprises everything that concerns the pastoral care of the youth with regard to the integral growth of the faithful[616]. The Council makes it clear that "the pastoral care of youth cannot be separated from the framework of the family as if young people make up a kind of separate and independent "social class". It should reinforce the young people's social sense, first with regard to the members of their own family, and orient their values toward the future family they will have. The young people should have already been helped to discern their vocation through their own personal efforts and with the aid of the community, and above all the pastors. This discernment must take place before any commitment is made to get engaged. When the vocation to marriage is clear, it will be sustained first by grace and then by adequate preparation. The pastoral care of youth should also keep in mind that, because of various kinds of difficulties – such as a "prolonged

612 PCF, Preparation, n.32.
613 PCF, Preparation, n.32.
614 Cfr. T.P. Doyle, Marriage, p.748.
615 Cfr. Ibid; T.J. Groarke, Marriage Preparation, p.61; L.G. Wren, "Refining the Essence of Marriage", The Jurist 46 (1986), pp.541-543.
616 Cfr. PCF,Preparation, n.33.

adolescence" and remaining longer in one's family (a relatively new and troubling phenomenon), young people today tend to put off the commitment to get married for too long"[617].

In other words, within this period preparation should encompass biological, psychological, sociological, economical exigencies, conjugal sexuality and responsible parenthood and not just being isolated only to the biblical understanding of marriage. It should make the individual to be aware of the basic requirement for a well-ordered family life such as sensible administration, sufficient financial resources, stability at domestic work, and ideas of housekeeping[618].

The Council points out the direction of this pre-matrimonial catechism. At this stage, preparation should focus first and foremost on a catechesis that is based on listening to the word of God, interpreted with the guidance of the church's Magisterium in the light of a well comprehension of the faith and giving witness to it in real life. Instruction on this should be given in the realm of a community of faith among families, most especially in the parish, who take part and work in the forming of young people in accordance with their roles and charismas, and by so doing widen their influence to other social groups in the area[619]. The Council continues that engaged spouses should receive instruction concerning the natural needs of the interpersonal bond between a man and a woman in God's plan for marriage and the family life. Such requirements include: "awareness regarding freedom of consent as the foundation of their union, the unity and indissolubility of marriage, the correct concept of responsible parenthood, the human aspects of conjugal sexuality, the conjugal act with its requirements and ends, and the proper education of children"[620]

The Council insists that young people need help during this stage to become conscious of any psychological and emotional weaknesses they may have, especially with regard to the inability to open up to others, and any forms of selfishness that can take away from the total commitment of their self-giving. This, as a matter of fact, will help in discovering the potential and the need for human and Christian growth in their life. For this motive, the persons in charge of preparation for marriage should also be concerned with giving solid formation to the moral conscience of the engaged couples so that they will be adequately prepared for the free and definitive choice of marriage that is expressed in the mutually exchanged consent in the marriage covenant in the presence of the ecclesial community[621].

---

617 Ibid.

618 Cfr. P.K. Amevor, New Approaches to Marriage Preparation, p.168.

619 Cfr. PCF,Preparatio, n.34.

620 PCF, Preparation, n.35.

621 Cfr. PCF, Preparation, n.36.

In accordance with the sound educational principles of a gradual and comprehensive personal growth, this period must not take for granted formation for the social and ecclesial tasks proper to those who will have new homes arising from their marriage. Family intimacy should not be seen as something closed in on itself, but as an ability to interiorize the human and Christian riches inherent in married life as it concerns giving to others. Therefore, the couples should recognize themselves as people having rights and also responsibilities towards the church and the society[622]. This period also should make the young people preparing for marriage understand that the commitment they are going to take before the church through the exchange of their consent makes it important for them to start a road of mutual fidelity in the period of engagement. The human commitment will be advanced by the specific gifts which the Holy Spirit bequeaths to the engaged couples who call upon him[623].

For this type of proximate preparation, the Council recommends that the people who will be at the helm of affairs will have to be known and giving proper formation. It goes on to suggest creating a group, on various levels, of pastoral workers who are aware of being sent by the church. They should be composed of Christian married spouses in particular which will involve experts possibly in law, medicine, psychology, and with a priest who is there to prepare them for their various functions[624]. In this regard, Doyle asserts: "Proximate preparation involves diocesan-wide programs utilizing the talents of priests, deacons (especially married deacons), lay married couples, religious and professionally trained Counsellors. It involves the necessary dynamic of guided interpersonal communication with the parties as well as group presentations and discussions"[625].

There are criteria in choosing these pastoral workers and persons for the proximate preparation programs. To these criteria the Council insists that the persons and the pastoral workers at the helm of affairs must have a sound doctrinal preparation and unconditional fidelity to the church's Magisterium as to be able to transmit the truths of the faith and the duties connected with marriage with enough in-depth knowledge and life experience. It is quite certain that these persons, as educators will have the ability to welcome the engaged couples, no matter their social and cultural extraction, intellectual formation and concrete abilities. More also, their faithful life experience and joyful giving are indispensable tools for executing their task in a systematic manner[626].

622 Cfr. PCF, Preparation, n.38.
623 Cfr. PCF, Preparation, n.39.
624 Cfr. PCF, Preparation, n.42.
625 T.P. Doyle, Marriage, p.748.
626 Cfr. PCF, Preparation, n.43.

The Council assures that the final result of this proximate preparation should be a clear knowledge of the essential qualities of Christian marriage, such as "unity, fidelity, indissolubility, fruitfulness; the conscience of faith regarding the priority of the sacramental Grace which associates the spouses, as subjects and ministers of the sacrament, to the love of Christ, the Bridegroom of the Church; the willingness to carry out the mission proper to families in the educational, social and ecclesial areas"[627].

The Pontifical Council recalls what John Paul II said in his Apostolic Exhortation, Familiaris Consortio about what are involved in the formative journey of young engaged people as deepening of personal faith and rediscovering the value of the sacraments and the experience of prayer. Also the engaged couples should be assisted from the outset to learn how to preserve and cultivate married love, interpersonal marital communication, the virtues and dangers of conjugal life and how to deal with the unavoidable problems that are associated with it[628]. While echoing Familiaris Consortio's description of proximate preparation in terms of a catechumenal process, the Council insists the "the centre of this preparation must be a reflection in the faith on the sacrament of marriage through the Word of God and the guidance of the Magisterium. The engaged should be made aware that to become "una caro" (Mt 19:6) in Christ, through the Spirit in Christian marriage, means imprinting a new form of baptismal life on their existence. Through the sacrament, their love will become a concrete expression of Christ's love for his church"[629].

In this stage of preparation, PCF insists that engaged spouses should also be given formation and strengthened in the values regarding the defence of human life so as to contribute meaningfully "towards creating and developing the culture of life by respecting and welcoming new lives in their love, as the testimony and expression of the proclamation, celebration and service to every life"[630].

The courses during this period should not only stress what patterns to the maturity and vigilant freedom of those who want to enter marriage, but also their own duty as parents and as the first educators and first evangelizers of their children. The courses as a matter of fact, should not be so concise as to reduce them to a mere formality; rather they should provide adequate time for good, clear presentation of the fundamental subjects[631]. In other words, these specific courses should not be degraded to a series of information meetings in which spouses are merely asked what they must do so as to get married in the church, it should rather

627 PCF, Preparation, n.45.

628 Cfr. PCF, Preparation, n.46.

629 PCF, Preparation, n.47.

630 PCF, Preparation, n.49.

631 Cfr. PCF, Preparation, n.48.

go beyond this in order to enable the couples discover the depth and richness of the Christian vocation to marriage, which is celebrated on the day of their wedding and then lived out for their entire married life[632]. The proximate preparation for marriage is not isolated to completion of some needed forms. It is a much more complex reality and therefore, should start some time prior to the date planned for the wedding itself. This will definitely add to the assurance that the engagement period is truly a proximate preparation period for marriage and not simply only for wedding[633].

2.5.4. Immediate Preparation

The immediate preparation period for marriage is the final stage before the wedding itself takes place. During this stage, the provisions prescribed in canon 1063, 2° continue and it is also here that the provisions of canon 1063, 3° which refer to the importance of a fruitful liturgical celebration of marriage are fulfilled. The Pontifical Council for the Family outlines the goals of this period as: "a) A synthesis of the previous preparation, especially its doctrinal, moral and spiritual content, thus filling in eventual gaps in basic formation; b) Experiences of prayer (retreats, spiritual exercises for the engaged) in which the encounter with the Lord can make them discover the depth and beauty of the supernatural life; c) A suitable liturgical preparation which also envisages the active participation of the engaged, with special attention to the sacrament of Reconciliation; d) Good use of the canonical talks that are envisaged with the parish priest, so that everyone can get to know one another better"[634].

For the mere fact that the fruitful liturgical celebration of marriage is mentioned in canon 1063, 3° suggests that it is not only a means of sanctification of the couples, as well as the celebration of their consent but is also a source of instruction for all present in the theological significance of marriage bond. In this liturgical celebration, the couples are undertaking a special vocation in the Christian community, because like the sacrament of Holy Orders, marriage is a specification of the general Christian vocation entered into at the time of baptism. The celebration of marriage itself at this stage, is not a private affair where the parties express their love and commitment by means of words or gestures which have a special importance only for them or for a selected few among the congregation. In other words, the whole liturgy must reflect the fact that the spouses consider

632 Cfr. L. Galli, Fidanzamento, tempo di Dialogo e di Discernimento, Esperienza di Communione Nello Spirito, pp 60/9 (1990), p.50; F. Gavin, Pastoral Care in Marriage Preparation, p.109.

633 Cfr. T.P. Doyle, "The Individual's Right to Marry in the Context of the Common Good", Stud Can 13 (1979), pp.246-301.

634 PCF, Preparation, n.50.

their love to be sacred and that they make their commitment to each other in line with the church's understanding of marriage. Since the spouses are the ministers and recipients of the matrimonial sacrament, their exchange of consent should express their commitment not only to each other, but also to their ecclesial community[635].

The Pontifical document urges that this period of preparation should look for suitable occasions to introduce the rite of marriage to engaged couples "as well as deepening the Christian doctrine on marriage and the family with particular attention to moral duties"[636]. During this period, the engaged couples should be led to take active participation in the marriage celebration, and to understand the meaning of the liturgical activities and the texts of the marriage celebration[637]. In view of this, the Council opines that it is pertinent that prospective spouses avail themselves for the celebration of marriage by first of all receiving the sacrament of penance for the validity, worthiness and fruitfulness of this celebration. The elements of ritual that are at disposal should be used for this liturgical preparation. This is the reason why marriage celebration normally takes place within the Eucharistic celebration so as to indicate a clear link between the sacrament of marriage and the paschal mystery[638].

The Council insists that for the church to be visible in the diocese and be expressed in the parishes, it is well deserved and recommended that all the canonical – pastoral and liturgical preparations be made in the parish and the diocese. This is owing to the fact that it conforms with the church's understanding of the sacrament for the marriage to take place in the church of the parish community to which the couples belong[639]. The Council goes on to recommend the entire parish community to be involved in this celebration that is within the families and friends of the engaged couple, but provisions for this should be prescribed in different dioceses, taking into account local situations but at the same time favouring vehemently truly ecclesial pastoral action[640].

It is important here to add that this type of preparation should focus on the community aspect of marriage in order to ensure a fruitful liturgical celebration of marriage. The liturgy has an important teaching role for both the couples and the entire community in addition to its sanctifying function. The marriage

635 Cfr. T.P. Doyle, Marriage, pp.748-749; T.J. Groarke, Marriage Preparation, pp.62-63.

636 PCF, Preparation, n.52.

637 Cfr. Ibid.

638 Cfr. PCF, Preparation, n.53.

639 Cfr. C.1115 CIC/1983: "Marriages are to be celebrated in the parish where either of the contractants has a domicile, quasi-domicile or month-long residence; the marriages of transients are to be celebrated in the parish where they actually reside; marriages can be celebrated elsewhere with the permission of the proper ordinary or pastor".

640 Cfr. PCF, Preparation, n.54.

liturgical celebration is by a way of definition a community event in that, as liturgy, it is not a private action but the action of the church itself[641]. In this sense, it consists of the whole body of the church, thereby making it to manifest and affect it. Therefore, in this regard, it should be celebrated in a possible way in the presence and active participation of the Christian faithful[642]. Provost continues that the liturgical celebration of marriage as a liturgical action comprising the full participation of the entire community, helps to build up the marriage state in a Christian spirit and also help rekindle the awareness of their own commitment with regard to those already married and assisting those yet to marry to come to understand more richly the mystery of God's love present and fully active in that sacramental event[643].

All those who will take active part in this liturgical celebration are urged to prepare themselves properly for the sacrament of Reconciliation and the Eucharist. The witness should be reminded that they are not only the guarantors of a juridical act, but also representing the entire Christian community and by so doing they take active part in a sacramental act important to it[644] .

The Pontifical Council outlines the importance of this liturgical celebration of marriage when it declares that "preparation for marriage leads to married life, through the celebration of the sacrament, which is the culmination of the journey of preparation which the spouses have made and the source and origin of their married life"[645]. The priest who presides at the liturgical celebration has to involve the spouses as well as their relatives and the witnesses on the goings-on in the church so that they can understand the proper structure of the rite being celebrated[646].

The preparation of this period should be carried out so as to assist the engaged spouses to discover their mission in the church and to continue to carry it out. This serves as a way of linking immediate preparation period with the ongoing pastoral care of marriage and the family. The couples could be assisted by involving "the richness offered by specific family movements, so as to cultivate a

641 Cfr. J.H. Provost, Marriage Preparation in the New Code, p.189.

642 Cfr. C.837 CIC/1983 §1: "Liturgical actions are not private actions but celebrations of the church itself which is "the sacrament of unity", namely, a holy people assembled and ordered under the bishops; therefore liturgical actions pertain to the whole body of the church and manifest and affect it, but they affect the individual members of the church in different ways according to the diversity of orders, functions and actual participation". §2: "Liturgical actions, to the extent that by their proper nature they involve a common celebration, are to be celebrated where possible with the presence and active participation of the Christian faithful".

643 Cfr. J.H. Provost, Marriage Preparation in the New Code, p.189.

644 Cfr. PCF, Preparation, n.55.

645 PCF, Preparation, n.60.

646 Cfr. PCF, Preparation, n.66.

spirituality of marriage and the family and the way they fulfil their tasks within the family, the church and society"[647]. Through this way, the couples are helped to comprehend the mysterious significance of Christian marriage and to participate as couples in this mystery.

2.5.5. On- going Pastoral Care after Marriage

Canon 1063, 4°[648] recognises the assistance to be given to those couples already married, as an assistance which must focus on the sanctity of family life symbolizing God's grace, given to the spouses by virtue of the matrimonial sacrament which they have received as a witness to the whole community[649]. John Paul II describes this post-marital assistance as "the commitment of all the members of the local ecclesial community to helping the couple to discover and live their new vocation and mission"[650]. This support to be given to those married is absolutely necessary during the first five years of their married life as the spouses are adjusting to their new responsibilities as those married and possibly as parents[651].

During the conclusions of the 15th Plenary Assembly in October 2002, the Pontifical Council for the Family insists vehemently on an on-going pastoral care after marriage for the newly married couples. It contends that it is recommended that the married spouses who accompany the engaged spouses in their immediate preparation program will continue to accompany them in the first years of their union in order to assist them cope with the challenges and difficulties encounter in married state before the metamorphous into serious crisis. The Council continues that spouses who are beneficiaries from this assistance will in turn be able to guide and assist others. This guidance should be in form of encounters with other families, organised retreats, recollections and other meetings[652].

The many challenges and problems facing married couples today require not only encouragement from the ecclesial community but also resources from which these couples may get support and assistance to live a holy and exemplary life. "This is especially true for couples and families in crisis. Many troubled marriag-

---

647 PCF, Preparation, n.57.

648 Cfr. C.1063, 4° CIC/1983: "auxilio coniugatis praestito, ut ipsi foedus coniugale fideliter servantes atque tuentes, ad sanctiorem in dies plenioremque in familia vitam ducendam perveniant".

649 Cfr. D. Kelly, "Commentary on Pastoral Care", p.580.

650 FC, 69,§1.

651 Cfr. PCF, Preparation, n.73; L.A. Robitaille, "Commentary on canons 1063-1072", p.1264; P.K. Amevor, New Approaches to Marriage Preparation, p.173.

652 Cfr. PCF, Conclusions of the 15th Plenary Assembly, Rome, 17-19 October, 2002; P.K. Amevor, New Approaches to Marriage Preparation, p.173.

es can be saved with competent intervention before the relationship has totally disintegrated. This intervention can be offered in the form of counselling agencies, support groups, and referral services"[653]. It should be emphasised here that while the need for special support and assistance is virtually evident with regard to problematic marriages, it is also pertinent for marriages that are not in crisis[654].

The on-going pastoral care after marriage has been termed as the most difficult part of canon 1063 to implement. The first difficulty one encounters is attempting to reach the spouses themselves. They often move from the parish where they married to a different parish or city after the marriage. Many a time their not being able to maintain contacts with the church during the first few years of their married life is also common[655]. Gavin suggests that in trying to help them come out of this difficulty, the priest who celebrates the wedding should endeavour to get their new addresses and make sure that the new parish priest gets the new address. The parish visitation team or those coordinating the on-going support could take up in getting these contacts from the newly-wedded couples[656].

The ecclesial community has also an obligation to fulfil in this support given to the married couples, just as their obligations do not cease only on the wedding day but go through the whole married life. This type of support from the ecclesial community, Kelly opines, "will be of special importance in the early years of marriage, particularly in the case of those whose faith is weak or who have difficulty in adjusting to their new state"[657]. Also the support to be given to those newly married could come from such groups as the Christian Family Movement, Teams of our Lady, and Marriage Encounter. Other groups and movements in Igbo dioceses of Nigeria include: Marriage Advisory Council, Marriage Tribunal Council, Natural Family Planning and Catholic Men and Women Organizations. It is pertinent to mention here that many married couples in Igbo dioceses have through these groups and movements got over their challenges and problems they encountered in their married life.

Also in an effort to find a solution to the challenges and difficulties encountered by married couples, Gavin proposes a celebration of important anniversaries in the parishes. These anniversaries could be done in the form of a Sunday liturgy which will equally include a social gathering in terms of having supper together. The parish will be saying something as regards how it values and cherishes the witness and experience of these married spouses in that ecclesial community. The homily on this occasion could equally provide an ample opportunity for a general

653 T.P. Doyle, Marriage, p.749.

654 Cfr. Ibid.

655 Cfr. J.H. Provost, Marriage Preparation in the New Code, p.190.

656 Cfr. F. Gavin, Pastoral Care in Marriage Preparation, p.116.

657 D. Kelly, "Commentary on Pastoral Care", p.580.

catechesis on marriage, while at the same time respecting the norms stipulated in canon 766. In doing this, married spouses would want to share their personal experience of living the sacrament by giving their testimony. A particular Sunday could be designated in the diocese during the liturgical year for this purpose[658].

Another important way of organizing assistance and rendering support to married couples, especially in Igbo dioceses of Nigeria is inviting these couples to wedding ceremonies, Mothering and Fathering Sundays (Uka ndi Nne na Uka ndi Nna). In such occasions, preaching could be used to admonish and exhort married spouses. The occasion could also be used in highlighting and bringing out the real meaning of Christian marriage and family life and by so doing help them to renew their marriage vows to each other. Such occasions could also be a forum for spiritual enrichment of the spouses and help them to rediscover proper values and meaning in their lives and above all, assist them to continue to fulfil their marital responsibilities they owe to each other as husband and wife.

2.5.6. Conclusion

Canon 1063 talks about the most serious obligation of pastors in giving various forms assistance to prospective couples and those already married. In giving this support, the canon lists four principal ways in which all concerned are obliged to carry them out. In the first place, the canon points to remote preparation period with particular emphasis on the meaning of Christian marriage and on the role of couples and parents. The personal preparation or proximate preparation period is focused on the sanctity and the obligation of the prospective couples' new state of life.

The Liturgical marriage celebration is focused on the community aspect of marriage in establishing a fruitful celebration of the marriage liturgy to those preparing to marry. And lastly, the canon speaks of on-going support after marriage which concentrates on the holiness of family life given to the spouses by virtue of the sacrament they received[659].

The four principal ways proposed by canon 1063 correspond closely with stages of marriage preparation proposed by Familiaris Consortio of John Paul II and further developed by the Pontifical Council for the Family.

658 Cfr. F. Gavin, Pastoral Care in Marriage Preparation, p.118.

659 Cfr. D. Kelly, "Commentary on Pastoral Care", p.580.

3. Difficult Cases in Marriage Preparation Program

3.1. Introduction

We have seen that reflecting the spirit of the Second Vatican Council the 1983 Code introduced the notion of pastoral care for marriage preparation into the very title of the section regarding pre-marriage preparation[660]. Thus, emphasis was placed on the pastoral responsibilities and pastoral nature of marriage preparation. We now focus our attention to some of the difficult juridical and pastoral cases that emanate in applying these legislative norms of marriage preparation.

3.2. The Right to Marry and Marriage Preparation

We have seen that the appropriateness and usefulness of marriage preparation cannot be questioned and how the legislative norms concerning pastoral care of prospective couples proposed suitable and adequate marriage preparation. We also saw that immediate preparation period is all the more important in those situations where the spouses did not take part in a marriage preparation programs. However, the question arises about those spouses who refuse to participate in the marriage preparation courses. Is marriage preparation program a must for those intending to marry? Or is it only a pastoral option? Can the local ordinary impose such preparation on his Christian faithful as an obligation, as a condition sine qua non before contracting marriage? What should be the attitude of the parish priest to such spouses? In answering these questions many authors and theologians have outlined the tension existing between the right to marry (ius connubii) and the need for a proper and adequate preparation for marriage with regard to those proposing to marry[661].

It has to be borne in mind that it is not all that easy to distinguish ius connubii and preparation for marriage, but an effort must be made to strike a

660 Cfr. C.1063 CIC/1983.

661 Cfr. T.P. Doyle, Marriage, p.748; L.A. Robitaille, "Commentary on canons 1063-1072", p.1263;L. Chiappetta, Il Matrimonio, pp.66-67; J. Fornes, Derecho Matrimonial Canonico, pp.142-143; M. Lopez Martinez, "Cursillos Prematrimoniales, pp.574-575; F. Bersini, Il Diritto Canonico, p.30; J.M. Huels, "Preparation for the Sacraments", pp.53-54; G. Putrino, "La Cura Pastorale", p.86; F.R. Aznar Gil – M.E. Olmos Ortega, La Preparacion, celebracion e inscripcion, pp.140-142; T. Rincon-Perez, Commentary on Canons 1063-1064, pp.1119-1122; H. Franceschi – Franceschi, "La Preparacion para el Sacramento". Pp.55-61; T. Rincon-Perez, "Preparacion para el Matrimonio-sacramento", pp.37-79; F. Gavin, Pastoral Care in Marriage Preparation, pp.123-127; T. J. Groarke, Marriage Preparation, pp.57-59.

balance between the right to marry of all Christian faithful (c.1058) and the necessary preparation for the faithful to receive fruitfully the sacrament of marriage (c.1065 §2)[662]. This explains why John Paul II writes: "Although one must not underestimate the necessity and obligation of the immediate preparation for marriage in which would happen if dispensations from it were easily given – nevertheless such preparation must always be set forth and put into practice in such a way that omitting it is not an impediment to the celebration of marriage"[663]. In supporting this argument posed by the Pope, the Pontifical Council for the Family asserts that the usefulness of pastoral and positive witness of marriage preparation programs depict that they can be dispensed in matters of proportional serious reasons. It goes on to say that if spouses showcase themselves with the seriousness of celebrating their marriage soon and without proximate preparation, the parish priest and his assistants will have the responsibility of allowing them some opportunities of making up an adequate awareness of the doctrinal, sacramental and moral aspects laid out in the proximate preparation period for marriage and finally inculcate them in the immediate preparation period[664].

In analysing John Paul II comments and that of the Council, Fornes opines that this entails that the means of pastoral action cannot be impediments or quasi-impediments to marriage. The establishment of impediments, he continues belongs only to the supreme authority of the church (c.1075) and not to the local ordinary (c.1077). Also new impediments cannot through custom be introduced (c.1076)[665]. Lopez Martinez in his own contribution advices parish priests to keep in mind that carried away by a comprehensible but erroneous pastoral zeal, by no means should they deny marriage to any couple who cannot or does not wish to participate in the marriage preparation courses as doing that would amount to doing grave harm to the inalienable ius connubii of the Christian faithful[666].

Still on the question of the couples refusing to participate in the marriage preparation programs, Bersini remarks that whereas the preparation of couples for marriage constitutes a grave obligation on the part of the parish priest and the ecclesial community, yet the lack of preparation does not constitute an impediment to marriage[667]. For Cerulli, an interpretation of canon 1063 must strike a balance between two opposite excesses: on the one hand, that which excludes the

662 Cfr. J. Fornes, "El Sacramento del Matrimonio" (Derecho Matrimonial), p.664; T. Rincon-Perez, "Commentary on canons 1063-1072", pp.1120-1121.

663 FC, 66 §10.

664 Cfr. PCF, Preparation, n.51.

665 Cfr. J. Fornes, El Sacramento del Matrimonio, p.664.

666 Cfr. M. Lopez Martinez, "Cursillos Prematrimoniales, pp.565-575. See also O. Fumagalli, in La Normatira del nuoro Codice, Brescia 1983, p.215.

667 Cfr. F. Bersini, Il Nuovo diritto canonico matrimonialle, p.27.

possibility of contracting marriage validly to those who do not wish, or are not able to avail of such pastoral care[668].

The church is fully aware of the importance of adequate preparation for marriage and the need to follow it up. The responsibility of providing this preparation rests on the shoulder of the parish priest and those assisting him, but prospective couples' non participation of these marriage preparation programs are not an impediment and therefore, cannot be denied the sacrament of matrimony. In this, Doyle points out that marriage preparation courses which are compulsory[669] but not optional, neither infringe upon nor violate the ius connubii. Although they are compulsory on some occasions, such courses cannot be made a prerequisite for the validity of marriage. Yet participation in them may be a necessary requirement for authorization to marry in the Catholic Church. The compulsory nature of such courses echoes the church's knowledge of the serious challenges facing marriage in our contemporary age. They are at the same time a response to the right of the couples to receive adequate guidelines and preparation to their marriage. To exercise as such the right to marry is relative to the ability and willingness to carry out the obligations of the sacrament of matrimony[670].

In his annual address to the Roman Rota on Juridical Aspect of Marriage Pope Benedict XVI affirms that the right of a man and woman to marry each other is contingent upon their juridical ability to do so. Regarding the place of "canonical questions" in marriage preparation courses, he noted a common misconception that in admitting couples to marriage, pastors must proceed with generosity since the natural right of the persons to marry is in play. The right to marriage or "ius connubii" presupposes that one can marry, and one intends to authentically celebrate marriage and to do so in the truth of its essence as it is taught by the church. The Pope insists that no can boast of a right to a nuptial ceremony

668 Cfr. O. Cerulli, "La disciplina del matrimonio e il magistero Concilliare", in E. Cappellini, eds. La normative del nuovo codice, Brescia 1983, p.215.

669 While I tend to agree with Doyle on the mandatory nature of marriage preparation in the light of the contemporary situation, he leaves unanswered a crucial question. The very first canon of the 1983 Code dealing with marriage, canon 1055 §2, states: "Therefore, between baptised persons no valid matrimonial contract can exist that is not, by that fact a sacrament". According to canonical legislation the only valid marriage that a baptised person can contract is a sacramental marriage. If a particular couple, who are judged to lack the minimum requisites demanded by the law for a valid celebration of marriage, refuse to participate in marriage preparation and are, consequently, denied permission to marry in the Catholic church, then are they being deprived of their natural right to marry? If they attempt a civil marriage, it will be invalid in the eyes of the church because it lacks the canonical form. So what are they to do? The dilemma created by this situation is, I suspect, the main reason for the ambiguity of the 1980 Synod, Familiaris Consortio and the new Code on the obligatory nature of marriage preparation. Cfr. T.J. Groarke, Marriage Preparation, pp.58-59.

670 Cfr. T.P. Doyle, Marriage, p.748.

because the "ius connubii" also refers to the right to celebrate a real marriage. According to him the right to marry, therefore, is not being denied where it is evident that the premises for its exercise are not present, that is, if the requested capacity to wed is manifestly lacking, or an objective is sought that is contrary to the natural reality of marriage. He concludes that marriage preparation is also a key tool in stopping the "vicious circle", of the granting admission to marriage without adequate preparation or requirements, on the opposing end, the granting of a juridical declaration that sometimes just as easily, but of an opposite nature, makes marriage invalid[671].

The seriousness of the marriage preparation programs made Aznar Gil to suggest that those who do not comply in any form of the preparation should be subject to canon 1077 §1 for as long as they refuse to comply with the preparation programs. He continues that it would be an action tantamount to that prescribed by canon 868 §1, 2[672] which points to the deferring of baptism for those infants whose hope of being brought up in the catholic religion is lacking by making the necessary amendments for the case of marriage. It could only be the case if it is in consonance with the legislative norms established by the local ordinary as regards the obligation of marriage preparation in his diocese of jurisdiction. It is never an establishment of a new impediment reserved only to Supreme Authority, but it is a development of the norms established in canons 1063 and 1064[673].

671 Cfr. Benedict XVI, Address to the Roman Rota on Juridical Aspect of Marriage, Rome, Vatican City, January 22, 2011: http://www.zenit.org/article-31544.(Accessed: 23. 1. 2011).

672 Cfr. C.868 CIC/1983 §1:"Ut infans licite baptizetur, oportet:
1° parentes, saltem eorum unus aut qui legitime eorundem locum tenet, consentient;
2° spes habeatur fundata eum in religione catholica educatum iri; quae si prorsus deficiat, baptismus secundum praescripta iuris particularis differatur, monitis de ratione parentibus".
§2: "Infans parentum catholicorum, immo et non catholicorum, in periculo mortis licite baptizatur, etiam invitis parentibus".

673 Cfr. F.R. Aznar Gil, Derecho Matrimonial Canonico, p.238. Huels also points out that canon 1077 §1 could be used to delay a marriage temporarily until the couple are considered ready. Cfr. J. Huels, "Preparation for the Sacraments: Faith, Rights, Law", Stud Can 28 (1994), pp.56-57. Robitaille in her own argument says that it is difficult to refuse the celebration of a marriage only because of a couple's failure to participate in a specific marriage preparation course. One distinction that should be made is between concrete marriage preparation courses and preparation for marriage. What is important is that the couple be prepared for marriage. How that preparation takes place might not be the same for every couple. Whether a couple is prepared for marriage must be assessed individually and objectively. If the couple is not prepared, then canon 1077, §1 could be invoked and the marriage temporarily delayed. However, the basic human right to marry (c.1058) must also be taken into account in making such a decision and in evaluating such courses. Cfr. L.A. Robitaille, Commentary on canons 1063-1072", pp.1263-1264. Lopez , commenting on canon 1077 stresses that the bishop's prohibition can only be temporary and for a very grave reason. He argues that the refusal to take part in a marriage preparation program does not fit into this category and that this prohibition would not invali-

Based on these arguments, bishops, parish priests and their assistants should endeavour to be sensitive to the right to marriage prescribed in canon 1058, and should also have the principle knowledge that only the Supreme Authority can establish impediments to marriage according to canon 1075[674] and that neither the local ordinary nor local custom have such power to establish impediment. Hence, the parish priest should strike a prudent balance between the need for adequate personal instruction before marriage and the ius connubii which he has absolutely no power to refuse in real practice.

3.3. Faith of the Couple and Marriage Preparation

The faith of those intending to marry is another difficult situation that arises in the pastoral care of marriage preparation. The questions are: Can couples receive the sacrament of matrimony validly or, put in another way, can the sacrament of matrimony take place if one of the baptised couples has no faith, in other words, if one of the partners does not believe that marriage between the baptised is a sacrament, or does not believe that Christian marriage is a sacrament? In considering these questions, it will be pertinent to recall that faith is never mere belief in something but a personal response to God addressing us in this life, a personal relationship[675]. The church teaches that the sacraments "not only presuppose faith, but by words and objects they also nourish, strengthen, and express it"[676].

The challenge to this very teaching since the Second Vatican Council emanates from pastoral experience. Many a time priests find themselves participating at marriages of baptised Catholics who appear no longer to believe in or practice the faith[677]. It is important to know that the law in particular, does not address the

date a marriage if it goes ahead. Cfr. M. Lopez Martinez, "Cursillos Prematrimoniales", p.575. Gavin insists that the refusal of a couple to participate in some sort of preparation cannot become an impediment. Any restriction on the part of the parish priest or the local ordinary can only be temporary and carried out with the utmost sensitivity, with the intention of helping the couple to prepare for marriage so that they can celebrate it fruitfully. Cfr. F. Gavin, Pastoral Care in Marriage Preparation, p.126.

674 Cfr. C.1075 CIC/1983 §1: "Supremae tantum Ecclesiae auctoritatis est authentice declarare quandonam ius divinum matrimonium prohibeat vel dirimat".
§2: "Uni quoque supremae autoritati ius est alia impedimenta pro baptizatis constituere".

675 Cfr. G. Taylor – E. de Bekker, Parish Priests and Marriage Cases, p.4.

676 FC, 59 §1.

677 Cfr. J.A. Allesandro, eds; "Faith and the Sacrament of Marriage, in Marriage Studies IV, p.56. Pompedda comments that the meaning of this phrase is not precise: According to him, "it does not have a univocal meaning, but refers to a datum of fact that is by its nature markedly complex: that is, behind the expression "baptised non-believer" there are situations that run the gamut from the ignorant baptised person to the non-practising baptised person; from the bap-

difficult situation of marriages where the couples, although baptised, are to one degree or another lacking in Christian faith. Taking cognisance of the inseparability of the sacrament and contract, if the partners have sufficient faith to receive the sacrament of matrimony validly, even if the faith they have is weak or careless and considering that the fruits of the sacrament are for less than ideal, they can nevertheless enter marriage validly[678].

On its own contribution, the International Theological Commision declares that: "The intention of carrying on what Christ and the Church desire is the minimum condition required before consent is considered to be a "real human act" on the sacramental plane. The problem of the intention and that of the personal faith of the contracting parties must not be confused, but they must not be totally separated either. In the last analysis the real intention is born from and feeds on living faith. Where there is no trace of faith (in the sense of "belief" – being disposed to believe), and no desire for grace or salvation is found, then a real doubt arises as to whether there is the above-mentioned general and truly sacramental intention and whether the contracted marriage is validly contracted or not. As was noted, the personal faith of the contracting parties does not constitute the sacramentality of matrimony, but the absence of personal faith comprises the validity of the sacrament"[679].

On the question of the relationship that exists between sacramental intention and faith, Lane differentiates between the personal act of faith and the content of faith: "It must be pointed out that the non-practice of faith cannot be taken automatically to imply complete absence of personal faith"[680].

Familiaris Consortio addresses this problem by emphasising that marriage is rooted in the economy of creation. "Therefore the decision of a man and a woman to marry in accordance with the divine plan, that is to say, the decision to commit by their irrevocable conjugal consent their whole lives in indissoluble love and unconditional fidelity, really involves, even if not in a fully conscious way, an attitude of profound obedience to the will of God, an attitude which cannot exist without God's grace. They have thus already begun what is in a true and proper sense a journey towards salvation, a journey which the celebration of the sacra-

tised person who has not the faith but who hold on to a basic religiosity, to the baptised person who has lost the faith altogether; from the baptised person who does not accept the Christian plan of marriage in some of its aspects to the baptised person who contests the sacramentality, and any religious institutionalisation of marriage". For more understanding of this, see J. McAreavey, The Canon Law, p.34.

678 Cfr. O' Callaghan, "Faith and the Sacrament of Marriage" in Irish Theological Quarterly 52 (1986) pp.161-179; D. Kelly, Commentary on Marriage, p.573.

679 ITC, Propositions on the Doctrine of Christian Marriage, p.237.

680 Lane, Unpublished Paper given to the Annual Conference of the Canon Law Society of Great Britain and Ireland in 1990, in J. McAreavey, The Canon Law, p.35.

ment and the immediate preparation for it can complement and bring to completion, given the uprightness of their intention"[681].

The Pope goes on to say that since these spouses are baptised and show by their "right intention" that they have accepted God's plan for marriage, the church is satisfied that the couples "at least implicitly consent to what the church intends to do when she celebrates marriage"[682]. He warns against setting criteria other than baptism and "right intention", especially any criterion that touches on the level of faith demanded from those couples to be married. In this regard, he says: "In the first place, the risk of making unfounded and discriminating judgments; secondly, the risk of causing doubts about the validity of marriages already celebrated, with grave harm to Christian communities, and new and unjustified anxieties to the consciences of couples; one would also fall into the danger of calling into question the sacramental nature of many marriages of brethren separated from full communion with the Catholic Church, thus contradicting ecclesial tradition"[683]. The Pope is trying to say that the germinal faith of those couples intending to marry has to be fostered if their intention to receive the sacrament of matrimony is implicit.

The Pope, however, concludes that "when in spite of all efforts, engaged couples show that they reject explicitly and formally what the church intends to do when the marriage of baptised persons is celebrated, the pastor of souls cannot admit them to the celebration of marriage"[684].

Be that as it may, it is imperative that all hands must be on deck, from the pastoral point of view, to ensure that the celebration of every marriage be recognised as an opportunity of expressing and quickening the level of faith of the spouses participating in this marriage. Since marriage, like every other sacrament, is a sign and a means by which faith is expressed and strengthened (c.840), and that of the fact that it must proceed from and rest upon faith, and by so doing, the sacred

---

681 FC, 68 §3.

682 FC, 68 §5. It has to be pointed out that many theologians are unwilling to presume that such implicit consent is present. For instance, Lawler opines that the faith situation of baptised persons today is anything but clear, and the church and her theologians recognise two types of baptised, believers and non-believers. He says that the two are differentiated theologically on the grounds of the presence of absence of active personal faith. They ought never, therefore, to be equated in law as easily as the Code of canon law equates them. Cfr. M.G. Lawler, "Faith, Contract and Sacrament in Christian Marriage: A Theological Approach", in Theological Studies 52 (1991), pp.720-721. Örsy on his own part, writes that "it is the personal act of faith, however minimal, and always under the grace of God, that transforms the human being from one who can be a believer into one who is a believer… and it is that act of faith that is required for right sacramental intention". L. Örsy, Faith, Sacrament, Contract and Christian Marriage, in Theological Studies 43 (1982), p.383.

683 FC, 68 §6.

684 FC, 68 §7.

ministers strive to arouse and enlighten this faith (c.836). Kelly, in supporting this statement asserts that: "This admonition of the Code is all the more pertinent today when marriage, subject as it is to so many economic, social and even family pressures, is under a distinct threat of being invited to overlook that which is its distinct and essential character in the church, namely that it is a sacrament instituted by Christ"[685].

3.4. Cohabiting Couples and Marriage Preparation

Another problem which militates against couples to prepare adequately for marriage is cohabitation. This problem which, although, not canonical but pastoral needs to be discussed briefly. Today almost half of the spouses who come for marriage preparation in the Catholic Church are in a cohabiting relationship[686]. Cohabitation in an ordinary sense of it means living together in a sexual relationship without marriage[687].

It is a well-known fact that cohabitation is a pervasive and growing phenomenon with a negative impact on the role of marriage as the foundation of life. The state of cohabitation is much greater than it is indicated by the number of cohabiting spouses presenting themselves for marriage. More than half of spouses in first-time cohabitations ever marry. The overall percentage of those who marry is much lower when it includes those who cohabit more than once. Cohabitation being termed as a permanent or temporary alternative to marriage is a major factor in the declining centrality of marriage in family structure[688].

The church condemns cohabitation emphasising that such a relationship is seen as a false sign, contradicting the meaning of a sexual relationship. It violates at the same time the true meaning of the church's teaching about sexual love and marriage. It is condemned under the rubric of "free union" and is considered a grave offence against the dignity of marriage. However, there is an awareness of the pastoral difficulty in treating this issue. There are two extremes that are to be avoided. The first one is immediately confronting the couple and condemning

685 D. Kelly, Commentary on Marriage, p.573.

686 In 1995 a national study of Catholic-sponsored marriage preparation found that 43.6 percent of couples were living together at the time of their marriage preparation. The average length of cohabitation had been 15.6 months. Cfr. Marriage Preparation in the Catholic Church: Getting it Right", CUCMF, 1995, p.43. It is pertinent to know that similar trends have been found in other countries of the world, even though the exact figures are not available.

687 Cfr. NCCB, MFLC, Marriage Preparation, p.1.

688 Cfr. K. Scoth – M. Warren, eds; "Marriage Preparation and Cohabiting Couples", in Perspectives on Marriage, New York 2007, p.104.

their behaviour, and the second one, is that of ignoring the cohabitation aspect of their relationship. A middle way is suggested as a balanced approach to integrate general correction with understanding and compassion; to use it as a "teachable moment" in such a way as to smooth the path for them to regularize their situation[689].

The instruction issued by the Pontifical Council for the family in 2000[690] describes cohabitating unions as a widespread phenomenon and defines them as "heterogeneous human realities… (of a sexual kind) that… ignore, postpone, or even reject the conjugal commitment"[691]. It notes that children are increasingly a part of cohabiting households and contends that while not all de facto unions have the same social status or the same motivations, they all have common elements[692].

Canon 1066 establishes that "before marriage is celebrated, it must be evident that nothing stands in the way of its valid and licit celebration". Cohabitation is a sign that something actually does stand in the way of the valid and lawful celebration of the marriage. That something is the "grave lack of discretion of judgment" that we are warned about in canon 1095 §2. Still on this canon, Doyle acknowledges that "the ability to form an adequate will act at the time of marriage is not sufficient in itself for a valid marriage. It must be preceded by sufficient deliberation or critical judgment about the implications of the act of consent for the person at that particular time. The person does not only consent to a wedding but makes a decision about his or her life and the life of the marriage partner. If there is a serious inability to evaluate critically the decision to marry in light of the consequent obligations and responsibilities, then the consent may be invalid. A person must be able to evaluate his or her motivation for the wedding, personal strengths and weaknesses, as well as those of the other party, and his or her ability to live up to the demands of the marriage"[693]. It is this lack of critical faculty, that is, the ability to relate marriage as an abstract reality to his or her concrete situation that is demonstrated by the decision, in whatever innocently it is arrived at, to cohabit before marriage[694].

Familiaris Consortio acknowledges that there are various reasons that make couples live together before marriage. Each of these factors presents "arduous pastoral problems… and social consequences"[695]. It continues by naming social consequences as "the destruction of the concept of family; the weakening of the

689 Cfr. NCCB, MFLC, "Marriage Preparation", p.11.

690 Cfr. PCF, Family, Marriage and "De facto Unions", nn. 1-50.

691 PCF, Family, Marriage and "De facto Unions", n.2.

692 Cfr. PCF, Family, Marriage and "De factor Unions", n.4.

693 T.P. Doyle, Marriage, p.776.

694 Cfr. D. Konderia, Unpublished Article on Marriage Preparation with Co-habiting Couples, Ignatius Press 2011, p.2.

695 FC, 81 §3.

sense of fidelity... possible psychological damage to the children; the strengthening of selfishness"[696]. It suggests that pastors should make "tactful and respectful contact with the couples concerned and enlighten them patiently, correct them charitably and show them the witness of Christian family life... to regularize their situation... above all there must be a campaign of prevention"[697].

The American Bishops' Committee on Marriage and the Family suggested seven questions that might be used to assist the cohabiting couples reflect on their daily experience of living together and its implications in terms of sacramental marriage: "1) Why did you originally choose to live together? How does the commitment you wish to make now differ from the commitment you made when you decided to cohabit? 2) How do your family and community feel about your living together? How do these feelings affect you? 3) What are your reasons for wanting to marry at this time? Is there any reluctance to marry? Is pressure from family or children a major reason for marriage now? 4) What have you learned from your experience of living together? How do you expect your relationship to grow and change in the future? Does either of you expect marriage to be free from times of discontent? How well do you deal with conflict? Have you agreed on any changes in the way you will handle money after you are married? 5) Why do you want to marry in the Catholic Church at this time? Do you understand the concerns the church has had about your cohabiting situation? 6) What does marriage as a sacrament mean to you? 7) What do you think will be the largest barriers to a life long marriage for you? How do you think you will be especially challenged by the vow of faithfulness?"[698].

Above all, cohabiting couples should be assisted to arrive at that spirited maturity that will enable them to comprehend the richness and supernatural reality of the sacrament of marriage. Therefore, pastors of souls should by way of helping these couples living together, take the marriage preparation programs seriously as a means and opportunity for growth, maturity and conversion.

3.5. Conclusion

We have analysed so far some of the difficult cases that hinder the adequate preparation for marriage. But these problems, when they are handled carefully, do not stop those intending to marry of their right to marry in accordance with canon 1058. The urgency and importance of marriage preparation for a fruitful liturgi-

696 Ibid.

697 FC, 81 §4.

698 NCCB, MFLC, "Marriage Preparation", p.12.

cal celebration and the marital life after cannot be over-emphasised. The obligation of providing this necessity rests on the parish priest and his assistants, but the failure of those intending to marry to comply with the marriage preparation courses is not an impediment.

Also the making of the marriage covenant is an act of the man and woman which is according to the intention of God in creating them. Therefore, if, when entering marriage the couple have the intention of contracting marriage as God created it, then in this act there is submission to God and hence a germinal faith and an implicit intention to receive the sacrament of matrimony. It is only when the couple formally and explicitly reject the sacramentality of marriage according to John Paul II; that the church cannot go further to celebrate that marriage.

The notion of marriage preparation and those couples living together before marriage presents a new challenge to the church in our world today. Its response is still maturing to a reality that cannot be ignored. This response should take cognisance of the tension between accepting these spouses with the gospel values of love, acceptance, understanding, and the need to challenge them with the message of the gospel in terms of faithfulness and commitment[699].

4. Conclusion of Chapter Three

Chapter three was primarily concerned with marriage preparation and pastoral care of marriage in canon 1063 of the Code of 1983. The role played by the Schema of 1975 on the formulation of canon 1063 cannot be over-stressed. The Coatus' general approval of the title as pastoral care and the prerequisites for the celebration of marriage showed the seriousness of the obligations placed upon pastors of souls for their assistance in its effective fulfilment. The proposed new canon 249 reflected the task of the Coatus in imparting into the various provisions of the canon on catechesis with the other canons that are connected to marriage preparation.

We turned our attention also to the general norms about marriage preparation in the Code of 1983. These canons (1064-1072) lay emphasis on how marriage preparation should be carried out, what is to be done before marriage takes place, those responsible for the marriage preparation, and marriages that need the permission of the local ordinary.

Canon 1063 brings out the broader implications of pastoral care about the preparation of engaged couples for marriage and the pastoral care they need after marriage. In doing so, it shoulders the responsibility on the pastors of souls in see-

699 Cfr. NCCB, MFLC, "Marriage Preparation", p.11.

ing to it that the local ecclesial community gives suitable and effective assistance to protecting and developing the Christian charater of marriage. The ecclesial community is not left out in this obligation of giving support to those who are intending marriage and those already married.

The canon lists four major ways in which all involved in this pastoral care are obliged to carry out the task of preparing young people and those engaged for marriage. It points to remote, proximate, immediate, and on going support after marriage. These four ways of preparation corresponded to the stages of marriage preparation given by Pope John Paul II in his encyclical, Familiaris Consortio.

We later turned our eyes to some of the difficult cases involved in marriage preparation. These cases are: the right to marry and marriage preparation, faith of the engaged couple and marriage preparation, and cohabiting couples and marriage preparation. These cases hinder the proper preparation for marriage if not handled carefully. But they do not stop the engaged couples from marrying. The pastors of souls have to see to it that such cases are handled carefully and prudently and they should follow such engaged couples with such cases with maturity and reasonable judgement.

Chapter Four: The Understanding of Marriage and Marriage Preparation in Igbo Tradition

In the preceding chapter we studied canon 1063 of the Code of 1983 by trying to unravel the influence this very canon exerted in bringing out the deeper implications of marriage preparation and pastoral care concerning the preparation of the prospective couples for marriage and the assistance they get after marriage. In other words, the chapter served as a foundation to understanding the meaning of marriage preparation in anticipation of how adequate pastoral care of marriage preparation can be achieved in Igbo dioceses.

In this very chapter then, we shall take a look at the notion and understanding of marriage in Igbo traditional world view, how the Igbo people traditionally prepare their children and youth for marriage, and some of the urgent pastoral problems surrounding it. We shall equally explore the essential qualities of Igbo traditional marriage, what constitutes its impediments to the normal celebration of marriage, and the essential requirements for a valid customary marriage celebration. Our deliberation will focus more on traditional marriage from the Igbo perspective but references shall be made in between to include the whole African society most especially West African region since the essential elements in the traditional African marriages are almost the same thing. What sometimes differs from one country to the other or from one ethnic group to the other is the mode of celebrating this customary marriage.

For a proper work therefore, we shall begin with an exposition of who the Igbo people are, their origin, and what constitutes their political structure and socio-cultural dimension.

We shall equally examine in this particular chapter the Association of Episcopal Conferences of Anglophone West Africa's statement of policy and guidelines regarding pastoral preparation for marriage in West Africa and its significance and implications with regard to marriage preparation in the West African region.

1. The Igbo People of Nigeria: Who are they?

1.1. Introduction

The Igbo people are a group of dynamic, proud, hardworking and resilient people. In the very words of Carlston: "The Igbo people are a viable, resilient, industrious, tenacious, achieving people, and experienced in the way of a group of life"[700]. The present population of the Igbo people of Nigeria is estimated at around thirty million and the greater number of them is found in the cities. In many places the density of population exceeds 1000 per square mile[701]. The Igbo people are not hidden in the midst of millions as they are found almost everywhere in the world. They are at home wherever they settle, very itinerant, industrious and sociable.

The Igbo people have a common language called "Igbo" which they understand among themselves, though with little variations of dialectical differences. The Igbo language being one of the three accredited Nigeria National languages[702], could be departmentalised into four major dialect groups, namely: Onitsha, Owerri, Nsukka, and Abakiliki Igbo. These four groups are further compressed into two major groups, namely: Onitsha and Owerri Igbo. Testifying to this, Arinze says: "It will cause no surprise that there are many Ibo dialects in view of the great political decentralization in the past. Nevertheless… the highly-developed communications of modern times have helped to reduce dialectical differences. The chief dialects today are Onitsha and Owerri"[703]. The main distinctive features of Igbo language are its accents and tonality used to differentiate words and their meanings[704]. There is a more fundamental feature of Igbo language called "Proverbs"[705]. For the Igbo people, if an individual is not able to communicate

700 L. S. Carlston, Social Theory and African Tribal Organisation, Chicago 1968, p.210.

701 V.C. Uchendu, The Igbo of Southeast Nigeria, New York 1965, p.2.

702 With approximately 75% of Nigeria's populace in the rural areas, the major languages of communication in Nigeria are tribal languages, with the most widely spoken being Igbo, Hausa and Yoruba. The number of languages currently estimated and catalogued in Nigeria is over 250. In some areas of Nigeria, ethnic groups speak more than one language. However, the official language of Nigeria is English, the former colonial language, was selected to facilitate and enhance the cultural and linguistic unity of the country. Even though most ethnic groups prefer to communicate in their own languages, English, being the official language, is widely used for education, business transactions and for official purposes.

703 F.A. Arinze, Sacrifice in Igbo Religion, Ibadan 1970, p.2.

704 Cfr. V.C. Uchendu, The Igbo of Southeast Nigeria, p.3.

705 Proverbs are the philosophical and moral expositions shrunk to few words, and they form a mnemonic device in societies in which everything worth knowing and relevant to day-to-day life has to be committed to memory. Of their nature, they perform an ideological function by making available the ideas and values encapsulated in these memorable and easily reproduced forms. For a more detail on this see, E. Obiechina, Culture, Tradition, and Society in the West African Novel, London 1975, p.156.

with the native language, the individual, ideologically, puts himself outside the community. Speaking a language according to Onwubiko, does not, in the Igbo sense, depend on the peripheral knowledge of the language; but on the ability to express oneself adequately in the proverbs and idioms of the language community[706].

Proverbs for the Igbo people can be viewed as a symbolic language in which the discovery of the meaning of the words and phrases demands a penetration of the mind of the speaker[707]. The usefulness of proverbs is represented in a popular saying of the Igbo people: "Ilu bu mmanu eji eri okwu" (proverbs are the palm oil with which words are eaten).

The Igbo people have a common four-day market of "Eke, Orie, Nkwo, and Afo". They are predominantly farmers and business people. While the chief crop is yam[708], the Igbo people cultivate other crops like Cocoyam, Beans, Cassava, Rice, Maize, and other fruits like Mangoes, Banana, Oranges, Pineapple, Pea, Avogadro-pea, Kola nuts, Pumpkins and Cocoa-nuts. A great number of Igbo people are also craftsmen and women, fishermen and traders. Basden captures this when he says: "For the Ibo man the necessities of life are very few. After securing his hut he has need only to make sure of his implements for tilling the soil, fishing, or for practising his trade"[709]. That procreation is high in Igboland account to the fact of having enough manpower for farming while bearing in mind that the more the family is in number, the more input it will make on the farm work.

706 Cfr. O.A. Onwubiko, African Thought, Religion and Culture, Enugu 1991, p.30.

707 Cfr. Ibid; p.31.

708 Yam is a large tuber that grows in tropical and sub-tropical climates; it has starchy, black and pale-yellow flesh. It is a primary agricultural commodity in Nigeria and a tuber of primary importance in Igbo traditional diet and economy. It is regarded as sacred because of the place it assumes in the cultural heritage of the Igbo people. It is a God-given prerogative of the Igbo personality and its abundance and significant possession could only be attained through hard labour guaranteed only by divine favours and providence. A man attains fame and honour which may eventually culminate in title-taking as "Eze ji" (king of Yam) in Igboland through its cultivation in a large quantities. Emphasising on the essence of and high regard for yam, Achebe, a renowned Igbo prolific writer and accomplished author in his famous book, "Things Fall Apart", says: "Yam stood for manliness, and he who could feed his family on yams from one harvest to another was a very great man indeed". Cfr. C. Achebe, Things Fall Apart, London 1978, p.23.

709 G.T. Basden. Among the Ibos of Nigeria, Lagos 1982, p.84.

1.2. Origin

It has to be noted that it has not been easy to definitely state the origin of the Igbo people because of the many different myths surrounding the origin. Many Igbo authors attested this obvious fact that it is difficult to trace the original Igbo settlement[710]. It is because of the intricacies on the origin of the Igbo people that Leonard calls it "a very maze within a maze"[711]. A renowned Igbo writer and anthropologist, V.C. Uchendu has this to say about this enigmatic originality of the Igbo people: "When and from where the Igbos come into their present territory is not known. The origin is a subject of much speculation. The people have no common tradition of origin. It is only rather recently that some Igbo-speaking communities have ceased to claim that they are not Igbo. What local traditions the Igbos have do not provide clues to their origin"[712].

Where the Igbo people came from and when, will remain for a long time a matter of conjecture because of the absence of helpful records or archaeological findings by which we can determine the date of settlement or place of origin[713]. However, some contemporary writers give some insights about finding a solution to it. The history of the Igbo[714] and their forebears according to Isichei, goes back four thousand years or more. But unfortunately most of this history is shrouded in obscurity, and is likely to remain so. We have three main sources of information about the Igbo past before the nineteenth century – the findings of archaeology, the oral traditions of Igbo people themselves, and the observations of the European visitors to the Delta. Each of these deals with a different time scale, and provides different kinds of information, so that it is difficult to combine them in a satisfactory synthesis[715]. The certainty from these statements come from the fact that all the sources before us, at one point or the other agree that Igboland has a history, and therefore began at some unknown date still yet to be discovered

---

710 Cfr. E. Edeh, Towards an Igbo Metaphysics, Chicago 1985, pp.10-14; E. Isichei, A History of the Igbo People, London 1976, pp. 1-16; E. Ilogu, Christianity and Igbo Culture, New York 1974, pp. 1-9; N. Ndiokwere, Search for Greener Pastures: Igbo and African Experience, Nebraska 1998, pp. 13-17.

711 A.G. Leonard, The Lower Niger and its Tribes, London 1958, p.31.

712 V.C. Uchendu, The Igbo of Southeast Nigeria, p.2.

713 Cfr. E. Ilogu, Christianity and Igbo Culture, p.1.

714 The words "Igbo" and "Ibo" have the same meaning. "Ibo" is largely adopted by foreigners to eliminate the difficulty in pronouncing the Igbo double consonant "gb". The word "Igbo" is more widespread among the Igbos themselves. But today, not only foreigners but also many Nigerians from other tribes other than the Igbo people infected by this foreigners' defect, use the term "Ibo" to designate "Igbo". The form "Igbos" is equally used to mean the Igbo people. We shall be using the forms "Igbo people" and "Igbos" all through this work except when quoting authors who use "Ibo" form.

715 Cfr. E. Isichei, The Igbo People and the Europeans, London 1973, p.18.

and put into pen. Some authors posit that the origin of the Igbos is from North Africa or some where in the East. A British Historian and Anthropologist, Talbot, who travelled widely in Africa, posited an account of the migration that started in Egypt in 1870 B.C. He opined that the similarities between the Igbos and the Egyptians call for common origin[716].

Some historical writers maintain that the Igbo people of Nigeria originated from the Jews. This is owing to the fact of many similarities which the Igbo people and the Jews share in common. George Basden[717] even illustrated point of their similarities in language, custom and worship, when he says: "There are certain customs which rather point to Levi tic influence at a more or less remote period. This is suggested in the underlying ideas concerning sacrifice and the practice of circumcision. The language also bears several interesting parallels with the Hebrew idiom"[718].

In addition to this, naming and circumcision ceremonies to mention but a few are as important to the Igbos as they were to the Jews of old. One has only to read the Old Testament to note the similarities between the Igbo people and the Jews. The religion of the ancestors (Judaism and the Igbo Traditional Religion) is a part of the customs and traditions of the two groups wherever they settle. The synagogue is both the religious and cultural centre of the Jews. For the Igbo people, although there is no such physical structure as the synagogue or the temple, the Igbo union is the unifying force, moral centre of the religious, social, cultural and political activities of the Igbo people[719].

In line with the origin of the Igbo people, some writers assert that Onitsha and Oguta Igbos descended from the North precisely from Benin and the Awka and Nri Igbos migrated from the kingdom of Igala. "The tradition of the Umuleri clan which includes the ancient state of Nri states that both they and the Igala are descendant from are still more ancient communities…. We all descended from Eri, but I went one way…. This separating of the Igala from us happened so long ago that now we do not hear Igala nor can they hear our language"[720]. Also some oral traditions have it that Onitsha and Oguta Igbos migrated from Isreal while Awka and Nri Igbos descended from Egypt. And so the problem of the origin and settlement[721] of the Igbo people remain yet to be solved because of the many conflicting

716 Cfr. P.A. Talbot, The People of Southern Nigeria, Vol; 1, London 1926, p.19.

717 George Basden was a member of the Church Missionary Society. He worked in his days in Igboland as a missionary for twenty years in the early 1900s.

718 G.T. Basden, Among the Ibos of Nigeria, p.31.

719 Cfr. N. Ndiokwere, Search for Greener Pastures: Igbo and African Experience, p.17.

720 E. Isichei, A History of the Igbo People, p.4.

721 However, early hypotheses or conjectures on the origin and settlement of the Igbo people would demand a review or be considered superseded by a change in events. Thus, Talbot's theory of an 1870 B.C. migration and the theory of cultural similarities between Egypt and the Igbo

accounts from different authorities, the issue of the missing link in the history of the Igbos remains unresolved. Still, the question of their origin continues to arouse great interest among the Igbos themselves and many historians. However, one thing is to be borne in mind; that no race of mankind is possible without migration and emigration of people from one location to the other.

1.3. The Geographical Location

The Igbos are those who have as their natural home, the Igboland which is located in the south-eastern part of Nigeria in the tropical region of West Africa. The Igboland is divided into two unequal parts by the River Niger with the overwhelming part lying in what was formerly called Eastern Region of Nigeria, while a smaller triangular portion, west of the Niger part of Nigeria's fourth Region – the former Midwestern Region now referred to as Delta state. Nzimiro characterises the anthropological geographical location of Igboland as he writes: "The Igbos are those persons who have been grouped into the kwa linguistic stock but with variations of dialect… Their territorial divisions cover the whole area stretching from the coastlines of the Bright of Benin, and continue to the outskirts of Ibibio and Efik territories in the east with its eastern boundary being formed by the Cross-river. On the Southern and Western sides, it stretches to the borders of Ijaw, Jekiri, Igado and other Ethnic groups and spreads across the Niger to the confines of Benin… its utmost Northern limits reach the boundary between Southern and Northern Nigeria where the Akpoto and Mushins are the nearest neighbours"[722].

Today, in view of the present political structures in the Nigerian political evolution, the Igboland is made up of Anambra, Imo, Enugu, Abia, Ebonyi States and parts[723] of Delta, Rivers, Cross Rivers and Akwa Ibom States of Nigeria. They share common boundaries with other ethnic groups: northwards with the Igala, the Idomas and the Tivs; eastwards with the Ekoi; westwards with the Edoh und Urhobo; southwards with the Binis and the Isokos[724].

---

people, for instance, would now be questionable, since these theories have been systematically disproved by archaeological findings and serious research in cultural anthropology. A British Methodist Missionary in Africa, Geoffrey Parrinder, had to rewrite his first edition of West African Religion in view of many changed circumstances. For more elaboration on this, see G.M. Okorie, The Integral Salvation of the Human Person in Ecclesia in Africa: A Case Study of the theological Implications among the Igbo in Nigeria, Frankfurt 2008, p.311.

722 I. Nzimiro, A Study of Mobility Among the Igbos of Southern Nigeria, Kinship and Geographical Mobility, 1965, pp. 117-118.

723 Like most colonial territories in Africa, State boundaries in Nigeria often cut across lines and put one nation or people into separate States.

724 Cfr. G.M. Okorie, The Integral Salvation of the Human Person, p.309.

Igboland occupies an area of about 15,800sq miles[725]. It lies geographically between latitude 5 to 7 degrees North and longitude 6 to 8 degrees East. It has a tropical climate with annual temperature of about 80 degree F. and an annual range between 5 and 10 degrees. The rainfall is heavy in some areas, sometimes reaching 105 inches. This however decreases as one move northwards[726].

1.4. Political Structure

Politically, the Igbos make up a community, which is democratically life-oriented with a complex culture traditionally reputed to be based on kinships. The ethnic group of the Igbo people is divided into clans, and each clan comprises towns or villages and villages consist of kindred[727]. The Igbo people recognize authority arising from the council of elders and chiefs who make laws and its implementation. They believe in diffused democracy and community life with power and authority in the hands of the male lineage elders[728].

The patrilineal kinship structure called "Umunna"[729] encourages political dialogue, equality, communalism and egalitarianism at all levels of the lineage segment[730]. This extended family system otherwise known as "Umunna" is practised widely and it has been perfected by the Igbo people for community development. Solidarity urges the members of this extended family to seek physical and social, as well as the moral and general well-being of all her members. Members of this extended family system traced their origin to a common ancestral lineage over four to six generations[731]. Uchendu captures this idea very well when he expresses: "It has been stressed that every Igbo man belongs to an agnatic group, a lineage with an unbroken continuity of descent in the male line. This agnatic group (patrilineage), as well as all its members, or agnates is called by the same term "Umunna". Umunna is one form of reference, and exogamic unit (of custom of marrying only outside ones own tribe or group). All its female members who must leave the lineage at marriage are called "Umuokpu". In another frame of reference it is a term for agnates, meaning "children of father", its singular being

725 Cfr. V.C. Uchendu, The Igbo of Southern Nigeria, pp.1-2.

726 Cfr. I.A.C. Maduh, Christianizing the Igbo Traditional Love and Morality Rites, Enugu 2005, p.2.

727 Cfr. G. Ekwuru, The Pangs of an African Culture in Travail, Owerri 1999, p.64.

728 Cfr. E. Azorji, Some Recurrent Problems of Christian Inculturation in Nigeria with Special Reference to the Igbo People, Rome 1988, p.155.

729 Umunna represents children of a number of families claiming descent from a common ancestor.

730 Cfr. M.A. Onwuejeogwu, An Outline of the Dawn of Igbo Civilization, Journal of the Odinani Museum Nri, Vol. 1, March 1972, p.20.

731 Cfr. G. Ekwuru, The Pangs of an African Culture in Travail, p.65.

"Nwanna". It does not distinguish between sex and generation but can be made to do so by the addition of more descriptive phrase"[732].

The Igbo people lay great emphasis on traditional family structure. The family otherwise called "Ezi na ulo" in Igbo language is the bedrock of all community life and events in Igboland. It is a strong tie not just for the individual but also for the community at large and the bond is too strong since it regulates the relation of one person with the other in the large community circle. In the family one finds dialogue in place of monologue. The husband is the head of the household, and the well-being of the family is the man's utmost priority and responsibility not only to his family but also to the larger community. The most important thing here is that problems militating against the welfare of the family are solved within the ambient of the family circle[733].

The nuclear family as one of the layers of the family structure is made of man, wife or wives and the children. The extended family which is also another layer of the family structure is made up of closer kinship relation and comprises a man with his nuclear family, his immediate brothers and their families. In other words, there are more than one nuclear families within an extended family. Thus, Igbo family evokes not only blood communal membership of few living members, but also the themes of clan, tribe, affinity, maternity, priesthood and ancestors[734]. Arinze maintains that family in Igbo African idea is not made up of only those who are still living. The ancestors and those yet to be born are part of the family and are very interested in it[735]. Mbiti affirms this union between the living, the ancestors, and those yet to be born when he asserts: "The family also includes the unborn members who are still in the loins of the living. They are the buds of hope and expectation and each family makes sure that its existence is not extinguished"[736]. Hence, the family in Igboland connotes community of life and togetherness. It is the pivotal point that harnesses the Igbo people to a common bond. The political structure of each community is in the hands of the elders whose permanent members are the family heads. In day to day activities the council of elders' rules by decrees but in matters of crucial moment, the whole village or community had to be consulted[737]. Thus, Igbo institutions, according to Smith, are highly democratic, and business of common concern in a clan, a village or even a family, is regularly transacted by councils and committees[738].

---

732 V.C. Uchendu, The Igbo of Southeast Nigeria, p.68.

733 Cfr. G.M. Okorie, The Integral Salvation of the Human Person, p.326.

734 Cfr. Ibid.

735 Cfr. F.A. Arinze, Sacrifice in Ibo Religion, p.19.

736 J.S. Mbiti, African Religions and Philosophy, p.105.

737 Cfr. D.R. Smock – A.C. Smock, Cultural and Political Aspects of Rural Transformation: A Case Study of Eastern Nigeria, New York 1972, p.44.

738 Cfr. S.S. Smith, The Church in Nigeria: Catholic Life Among the Ibos, "Tablet" 76, 1957, p.53.

1.5. Socio-cultural Dimension

Culture as the specific patterns of behaviour which distinguishes one society from all others, involves the cumulative deposit of knowledge, experience, beliefs, attitudes, meanings, hierarchies, religion, notions of time, roles, concepts of the universe, ways of life, social relationship, norms and values, habits and customs acquired by a group of people from one generation to the other[739]. This is the idea that Edward B. Tylor[740] has in mind when he socially defines culture as "that complex whole which includes knowledge, belief, art, morals, law, customs, and any other capabilities and habits acquired by man as a member of a society"[741]. It is in view of this that the Igbo people define culture as "Omenala"[742], the total way of life of the people. It depicts that culture embraces everything which helps man to survive and solve his human, spiritual, physical, biological, psychological and social wants. Every culture on earth has certain dynamics and key values on which it hinges, and so it is with Igbo culture. It is these aspects and dynamic that give each culture its unique character. Hence, Igbo culture has certain principal values and tenets, which distinguish it from other cultures of the world. Those characteristic dynamics range from religious, social and moral values. Some of these values are to be examined briefly here.

739 Cfr. E.E. Dike, Christian Marriage and Family in Igboland: A Study of the Conflict between Igbo Culture and Christianity, Münster 2001, p.13.

740 Edward Burnett Tylor, is a British anthropologist born on the 2nd of October 1832 in London. He died on the 2nd of January 1917.

741 Cfr. E.B. Tylor, Primitive Culture, London 1871, p.1.

742 Omenala embraces a whole acceptable pattern of living of the Igbo society passing from one generation to another and having its origin from the revered departed ancestors. See, M. Ojike, My Africa, New York 1946, p.182. Broadly speaking, Omenala is the Igbo word for culture. It stands for the totality of the realities and ideals – explicit and implicit – manifested as a mode of life charisteristic of an Igbo community; such that the acquisition of material and spiritual values according to the belief systems cherished by the community becomes the norm of authentic pattern of life of the entire community.... It impels individual to imbibe this pattern and allow themselves to be identified with it as members who are protected by, through and in the community that solves their problems through socially and ritually accepted processes. Omenala is not just the Igbo word for culture, it is the culture itself. See, O. Onwubiko, The Church and the Culture in an African Community, Madrid 1987, p.41. Thus, Eboh writes: "In the traditional Igbo society "Omenani" (which is a generic term for the body of Igbo socio-religious laws, customs and traditions passing from generation to generation and having its origin as far back as the time of the ancestors is believed to have been handed down to the people's ancestors from God (CHUKWU), through the Earth-Spirit (ANA)". Cfr. B.O. Eboh, The Concept of the Human Soul in Igbo Traditional Philosophy, Rome 1972, pp.46-47.

1.5.1. Religious Values

That man is a religious being is true in the case of the Igbo people of Nigeria. The traditional life of the Igbo people, like other African people[743] is imbedded in religious participation that starts before birth and continues even after death. Religion and religious beliefs form the background of the Igbos and the world around them. For them, to live is to be caught up in a religious drama. In other words, man lives in religious universe. No wonder Mbiti asserts: "It is religion more than anything else, which colours their (African) understanding of the universe and their empirical participation in that universe, making life a profoundly religious phenomenon. To be is to be religious in a religious universe"[744]. That is the general conception behind Igbo customs, beliefs, myths, traditions, morals, actions, and social relationships. Hence, the Igbo religious beliefs are deeply implanted in their minds and lives that one can correctly say, their beliefs are "blindly" accepted and made part and parcel of life itself so that full allegiance and loyalty are given to them[745].

There is this existence of integral relationship between religion and culture. The sacred cannot be distinguished from the secular and there is no formal distinction between the spiritual and the material aspect of life. There is religion wherever the Igboman is. Emphasising this religious character of the Igbos, Leonard has this to say: "The Igbo people are in the strict sense of the word a truly and deeply religious people of whom it can be said, that they eat religiously, drink religiously, bathe religiously, dress religiously, and sin religiously. In a few words, the religion of these natives is their existence, and their existence is their

743 A careful look through actual observation and comparative discussions with Africans from various parts of the continent, will show first and foremost, that there is a common factor, which the coined word negritude will aptly express. There is a common Africaness about the total culture and religious belief and practices of Africa. This common factor may be due either to the act of diffusion of the fact that most Africans have common origins with regard to race , customs and religious practices. One could in some cases trace specific cultural or religious elements, which are common over side areas, which lie proximate to one another; and often there are elements which jump over some territories to re-appear in several other scattered areas on the continent. We can thus speak of the religion of African in the singular based on this identical concept. For a more clarifications on this , see, B.E. Idowu, African Traditional Religion – A Definition, London 1973, p.103. Hence, Igbo Traditional Religion is not distinct from the rest of African Religion. Generally, one of the most characteristic features of African traditional religion is its "absorbing character" where the whole of life is wrapped up in religion. See, J.O. Lucas, Religions in West Africa and Ancient Egypt, Nigeria 1970, p.40; K. Okpoku, West African Traditional Religion, Accra 1978, p.11.

744 J.S. Mbiti, African Religion and Philosophy, p.262.

745 Cfr. G.T. Basden, Niger Ibos, London 1966, pp.35-36.

religion"[746]. This implies that the Igbos are deeply religious and they organize their cultural life around their religion in the sense that all aspects of their life and culture have religious undertone.

Their religious beliefs, however, have not been systematised or formulated into a body of dogmas which the citizens have to or are expected to accept. People simply assimilated whatever religious ideas and practices are held or observed in their families and communities. Though these are traditions handed down from their forefathers[747]. Nevertheless, Igbo religion remains the religion that embraces the totality of life of the Igbo people. Thus, Igbo religion and culture is a system of signs and symbols whereby one speaks from the point of view of Igbo civilization as one of the signs and symbols in which the Igbos live and through which the relationship of man to man and man to nature is manifested.

1.5.1.1. Belief in the Supreme Being

The idea of a creator of all things is a focal point in the Igbo traditional religion. The Igbo people believe in a supreme high God who is all good and all powerful[748]. They believe that he rules and controls the universe absolutely in his almightiness. They have two principal names for God – Chukwu and Chineke. Chukwu has two elements: Chi which is the source of being, and Ukwu, meaning "great", "immense", or "superlative". Chukwu then means "the great source of being". Chineke another name of God has three elements: Chi which means "source of being", Ne meaning "who" or "which"; and Ke which means "Creator" or "to create". Chineke, therefore, means, "The source being who creates all things". Edeh testifies to this when he writes: "The Igbo have two different names for the Creator – Chukwu, Chineke. These two names, Chukwu and Chineke, are composed of the word Chi, and a qualifying attribute – Ukwu,(great) and na eke (that creates)"[749]. Among the Igbos, the name of God – Chukwu is commonly found in the proper names given to children when they are born. Such names are: Kenechukwu (thank God), Ngozichukwu (blessing of God), Chukwudi (God lives), Chukwuemeka (God has been very kind), Chukwunyelu (God gave), Chinenyenwa (God gives child), Chukwuma (God knows), Chukwuka (God is greater).

It is also pertinent to note that the concept of the Supreme Being in Igbo religion is found not only in the names and attributes of God, but also in the songs, proverbs, sayings, recitals and liturgies of the people. Maduh succinctly but-

746 A.G. Leonard, The Lower Niger and its Tribes, p.429.

747 Cfr. I.A.C. Maduh, Christianizing the Igbo Traditional Love and Morality Rites, p.9.

748 Cfr. V.C. Uchendu, The Igbo of Southeastern Nigeria, p.94.

749 E. Edeh, Towards an Igbo Metaphysics, p.124.

tresses this when he says: "The Igboman often expresses his knowledge of God in proverbs, short statements, songs, prayers, names, stories and religious ceremonies. All these are very easy to remember and can be easily passed down the generation line…."[750].

Thus, in Igbo religion, God, the Supreme Being occupies the most essential and highest place in religious beliefs and cultural practices. Prayers for guidance and general prosperity are then addressed to God. God is for the Igbo people a Being who is present among them and whose presence means life for them. He is not to be conceived as a vast, inert, static being, but a being that is actively present in all that He creates, continues to create and by so doing manifests Himself in all activities of the daily life[751].

There is also this conception by the Igbo people that each person has a personal Chi. The ordinary Igbo man takes his Chi as his guardian Angel, given to him by God at conception, and which accompanies him wherever he goes. For them, Chi is therefore strictly personal. To one's Chi are ascribed one's successes and failures. Thus, if the individual is in danger, he often exclaims: "Chi m ekwena!" or simply "Chi mu-o!" (My God, do not permit this!). When adversities visit an individual, he blames his Chi[752].

With regard to sacrifices and offerings, there are no shrines or cult symbols for Chukwu, he rarely receives direct sacrifices but he is generally regarded as the ultimate recipient of the offerings to lesser gods[753], who are regarded as intermediaries. Arinze is however of the opinion that God himself is the final recipient of all sacrifices in Igbo religion, even when they are sometimes made specifically to some spirits, in so far as they are regarded as hypostases representations or refractions of God[754]. The reality of sacrifice is therefore evident in African Traditional Religion as a whole and Igbo Traditions in particular. Indeed, Mbiti gives an extensive list of various African peoples and cultures, their types of sacrifices and the reasons for these sacrifices. These reasons range from thanksgiving for harvest, birth, rain, peace, good health and security to pleas for protection, favour, forgiveness and revenge[755]. Thus, the Igbo people are a profoundly religious people who believe in a benevolent Creator known as Chukwu, who created the visible universe (uwa).

It suffices to say that it is this strong sense of God that gives the Igbo worldview its characteristic Theocentric and religious consciousness. Hence, the traditional

---

750 I.A.C. Maduh, Christianizing the Igbo Traditional Love and Morality Rites, p.10.

751 Cfr. E. Edeh, Towards an Igbo Metaphysics, p.130.

752 Cfr. B.K. Nwakanobi, Igbo System of Kinship and Family: Christian Response, A Study of One of the Important Pastoral Moral Challenges in Africa, Rome 1997, pp.31-32.

753 Cfr. F. Daryll – G.I. Jones, Ibo and Ibibio-Speaking Peoples of S.E. Nigeria, W.A. Religion, Vol.XVI. p35.

754 Cfr. F.A. Arinze, Sacrifice in Igbo Religion, p.184.

755 Cfr. J.S. Mbiti, Concepts of God in Africa, London 1970, pp.179-193.

Igbo person is God-conscious and oriented. He respects God and devotes himself to him and seeks to do his will in his daily life. Little wonder then an Igboman begins his day with prayers of thanksgiving, examination of conscience, praise and petition to God. Other spiritual beings are subject to control of the Supreme Being. They function as custodians of various aspects of creation and moral values. Through their activities, the Supreme Being becomes immanent and actively involved in daily concrete affairs of humanity.

Igbo religiosity is very practical. The Igbo pray and see God acts through the mediation of either the divinities or the ancestors. Religions are inseparable with morality for the customs and ethos of daily living is giving by God and guarded by ancestors and elders.

1.5.1.2. Belief in the Divinities

Igbo Traditional Religion is not polytheistic, rather monotheistic. However, other divine beings are made manifest within the structure of the religion. These divine beings as such have no absolute existence. For the Igbo people, the divinities are brought into beings as intermediaries in the theocratic government of the universe. They are in fact ministers in the Supreme Being's monarchical head of department. They are channels through which man believes that he should normally approach the Supreme Being.

1.5.1.3. Belief in Spirit

The Igbo people believe in Spirits and refer to them as those operational entities which form separate category of beings from those described as divinities or even ancestors. Though divinities are grouped under the nomenclature of Spirits but it is pertinent to know that not all spirits are considered as divinities[756]. Spirits are not clearly defined. In other words, they may be anthropomorphically conceived, but they are more often than not thought of as powers, which are almost abstract, as shades or vapours that take on human shape, they are immaterial and incorporeal beings[757]. There exist some categories of spirits and the Igbos have such spirits as guardian spirit which is a spiritual counterpart. It is responsible for one's destiny on earth. It guards one's step and brings prosperity. There is also the Mother Earth (Ala) which is the guardian and supervisor of morality. The spirit is the custodian of law and custom in Igboland. The spirit brings fertility in the Land. There are also other spirits like Ghost Spirit-people, Witches, Sadistic born

756 Cfr. O. Onwubiko, African Thought, Religion and Culture, p.83.

757 Cfr. A. Igwe, An Inquiry into African Traditional Religion and its Theological Status for Inculturation, in Nacaths Journal of African Theology, Vol.12, Nigeria 2002, p.29.

to die spirits, etc. These Spirits sometimes are responsible for one's misfortune in life. Thus, Spirits according to the Igbo belief are everywhere. There is no area or objects which cannot be inhabited by a spirit.

1.5.1.4. Belief in the Ancestors

Ancestorship in Igboland means that death does not in anyway bring to an end the tie between the deceased and his family on earth. In the traditional Igbo society, there is a firm belief in life after death. There are situations whereby the forebears who have lived good lives on earth now share a fellowship with their kins and relatives. Hence, Pope John Paul II vividly acknowledged the positive values in African ancestral cult when in his homily at the opening Mass of the 1994 African Synod he says: "The Church of Rome salutes these (African) peoples, especially their religious traditions, in which is expressed the ardent quest for the one God through veneration of ancestors. These traditions are still the heritage of the majority of the inhabitants of Africa. They are traditions which are open to the gospel, open to the truth…. They believe instinctively that the dead continue to live and remain in communion with them"[758]. Even earlier than the 1994 Synod, Pope Paul VI spoke also in favour of some African traditional values which include the sense of family evidenced by "the bond with ancestors, with whom the African is united so as to have "his continuity beyond earthly life"[759].

Generally, the Igbos believe that death on its on cannot qualify one as an ancestor. There are criteria for ancestorship such as old age (relatively speaking), married life together with offspring, and exemplary life of conduct, proper burial, dying a good death (i.e, not by accident or from deadly disease. It is only on these bases that one can become an ancestor and join other ancestors as guardians of community ethics, traditions and customs[760]. Hence, the dead in question has to be recognised by the entire community as their ancestors.

The ancestors show favour to their kins by good health, numerous progeny, healthy cattle, goat, sheep, and abundant crops. All these are seen as signs of ancestral blessings. They are in invoked both in formal and informal prayers. They are invoked spontaneously to come to the rescue when things go wrong[761]. The ancestors are therefore, venerated, invoked at prayers to intercede for the living. When their living relatives forget them, they are said to be angry with them and

758 John Paul II, Homily at the Opening Mass of Synod of Bishops of Africa, in L'Osservatore Romano 15, 1336.

759 Paul VI, Africae Terrarum, Message to the Peoples of Africa, AAS 59, 1967, p.74.

760 Cfr. A.U. Asiegbu, A Crises of Faith and a quest for Spirituality, Pearls Functions, Enugu 2000, p.258.

761 Cfr. C. Asoqua – N.T. Akpanessien, "African Ancestors in the Christian Communion of Saints, in Nacaths Journal of African Theology, Nigeria 2002, p.19.

to send them misfortunes as punishment. Their anger is usually appeased through prayers and rituals in the form of food and drink.

1.5.2. Moral Values

In Igbo culture there are moral values. The Igbos have a firm belief in a good world created by an All-good God, who requires good conduct from people. For them, traditional moral values are embodied in the "omenala" (moral laws and customs) sanctioned by Chukwu (the Supreme God) and Ala (the mother earth). One important aspect of Igbo morality is that it has direct link with ontological order set up by God. Any infringement on the moral values distorts the ontological order thus incurring the anger of the ancestors, who are the custodians of the customs and morals of the community[762]. These moral values are preserved and taught today through proverbs, folk tales, festivals, etc. Through such proverbs and sayings the Igbos praise virtue and condemn vice, they predict blessings for goodness and warn of evil consequences of bad behaviour. The moral values impose on the various members of the community some moral responsibilities toward one another. We shall examine some of them briefly.

1.5.2.1 Sense of Community

In the traditional Igbo society no one lives on its own. Right from childhood one is brought into communion with others. The individual lives because the community is and he realises his being and life in the complex network of the living and the spiritual members of the community. It is this orientation that makes Igboland a vibrant community. The community is the custodian of the individual, hence, the individual must and always has to be and go where the community goes. This is why it is not surprising that individualism, as an ideology and principle of life, has no place in Igboland even though it is not destroyed. Steve Biko in buttressing this view says: "We regard our living together not as an unfortunate mishap warranting endless competition among us but as a deliberate act of God to make us a community of brothers and sisters jointly involved in the quest for a composite answer to the varied problems of life. Hence, in all we do we always place man first and hence all our action is usually joint community orientated action rather than individualism"[763].

Therefore, the Igbo people emphasise community life and communalism as a living principle of which the basic ideology is community-identity. A person is

762 Cfr. I. Obi, "African Traditional Values in Dialogue with Christianity", in Nacaths Journal of African Theology, p.48.
763 S. Biko, I Write What I Like, New York 1978, p.42.

recognised first and foremost as a member of a particular community. It is the community that defines who he is and he can become. Ikenga Metuh, a Nigerian theologian, succinctly stresses this point when he writes: "An Igbo man is not asked "who are you"? But "whose son are you"? And "what lineage or clan do you belong"? So, from birth, the Igbo like other Africans learn to believe that "I am, because I belong"[764]. It is the community, therefore, in Igboland that fashions and moulds the individual's ideas and censors the execution of such ideas through the family.

1.5.2.2. Human Relations and Hospitality

The Igbo people see life here on earth as something that is not lived alone but lived with others in a given community. People usually depend on and cooperate with one another. The Igbo adage which says "Egbe bere Ugo bere, nke si ibe ya ebena nku kwakwa ya" (let the Kite perch and let the Eagle perch, whichever blocks the other's perching, let its wing break off), testifies to this Igbo philosophy of live-and-let-live. Thus, relationship between individuals recognises their worth as human beings and not only what they possess or what can they do for each other, even though these can come as later or secondary considerations, in terms of reciprocity and in terms of inter-personal relationship. People help one another without demanding immediate or an exact equivalent remuneration[765]. This relational and social attitude involves hospitality, which is a characteristic trait of the Igbos.

Visitors in Igboland are highly regarded in high esteem and warmly treated. Hospitality to visitors and foreigners take different forms. The most important form of receiving visitors in Igboland is the presentation of "Oji" (Kola nuts)[766], which symbolizes life. Such a gesture as this is intended to show the guest that he/she is welcome and safe. Among the Igbo people, the basis of hospitality is the generally accepted principle that a guest must not harm his host and that when

764 E.I. Metuh, African Religions in Western Conceptual Schemes, The Problem of Interpretation, Jos 1991, p.113; E.I. Metuh, Comparative Studies of African Traditional Religions, Onitsha 1987, p.193.

765 Cfr. O. Onwubiko, African Thought, Religion and Culture, p.19.

766 Oji is a tree that is cultivated in Igboland and some parts of West Africa. The nuts grow in pods and vary in sizes from to two inches in diameter. It has both red and white colours. There is a popular but cheap etymology of the Kolanut in Igboland. Oji: O= Omenala (custom); J= Jikotara (that units); I= Igbo. Hence, Oji means "Omenala jikotara Igbo" (customs that units the Igbos). It is a symbol of life and communion. This gave rise to the Igbo proverb, "Onye wetara Oji, wetara ndu" (he who brings Kolanut brings life). Oji is the first thing served in every function or ceremony, personal or communal agreements and welcoming of a visitor to an Igbo home. It symbolises life, friendship, truthfulness and open-heartedness.

he departs, he should not develop a hunch back on the way home[767]. This sense of hospitality is also demonstrated at meal times when all present including a visitor whose coming was not anticipated can join hand to partake in the meal.

1.5.2.3. Sense of the Sacredness of Life

The Igbo people price life above every other thing. Human life is held sacred in Igboland. They see life as the sacred sanctuary of man which by that simple fact belongs to God. This is why the Igbo proverbs, folklores, ritual festivals and other customs are highly loaded with appreciation of life. Life as such is appreciated as the primordial ground for all human endeavour and aspirations. Many names they bear are self-evident: Ndubuisi (life is first), Nduka (life is greater), Chinwendu (God owns life), Chikwendu (If God allows life), Ndukaku (life is greater as wealth), etc.

Any abuse of human life is an abomination just as shedding of human blood is generally detested. Amadi observe that: "In many African tribes the killing of a kinsman, the antithesis of caring for him, was not only a crime but also an abomination. After the murderer had been executed, his family would have to perform sacrifice and rites to remove the stain of evil and ward off the anger of the gods"[768]. Thus, such beliefs and customs make for respect and preservation of life in practical terms.

It should be noted that this type of reverence given to human life is also extended to all other sources of life whether corporal or spiritual. This testifies to the strict moral regulations surrounding the use of the generic organs. It is agreed that human reproductive faculties desire some sanctity from the sacredness of human reproduction[769]. Life, therefore, is at the centre of existence and every other thing finds meaning in life. Hence, the sacredness of life is of paramount importance to the Igbo people.

1.5.2.4. Sense of Authority and Respect for Elders

In Igbo traditional society one recognises the place of authority, respect for elders and wisdom conferred by experience and old age. Respect for constituted authority and elders are cherished values in Igboland. This is because elders are believed to be teachers and directors of the young[770]. The Igbos say: "He who listens to an elder is like one who consults an oracle". The oracles are believed to give the infallible truths, thus the elders are also believed to say the truth and their words

767 Cfr. O. Onwubiko, African Thought, Religion and Culture, p.23.
768 E. Amadi, Ethics in Nigerian Culture, Ibadan 1982, p.58.
769 Cfr. J.S. Mbiti, African Religion and Philosophy, p.14.
770 Cfr. O. Onwubiko, African Thought, Religion and Culture, p.28.

and instructions are heeded to for the promotion of good behaviour among the young[771]. This precious cultural attitude has been generally appreciated. In the words of William Conton: "Africans generally have deep and ingrained respect for the old age, and even when we can find nothing to admire, in an old man, we will not easily forget that his grey hairs have earned him right to courtesy and politeness"[772].

The elders in Igboland are taken to embody communal wisdom and held to be close to the ancestors. Thus, they are given leadership roles and position to direct community affairs. They in turn respect such offices knowing fully well that those legitimate offices were established by the ancestors and therefore stands to lose their respect and obedience as soon as they abuse their office[773]. The elders in discharging their political duties strive always to maintain and preserve the community's customs and tradition. The aged in Igboland are cared[774] for within their families where they enjoy the fruit of their labours as having born and raised up their children to become personalities in the society in which they find themselves.

1.6. Conclusion

We have seen from the brief exposition of the Igbo people that they are those who have as their natural home the Igboland which is located in the South eastern part of Nigeria in West Africa. We examined their political structure to be based on Kinship and such a patrilineal kinship encourages political dialogue, equality, and communalism at all levels. The family plays an important institutional role in Igboland. It serves as a community of persons whose proper way of existing and living as a group is communion. The family comes into being whenever marriage as a conjugal bond that unites a man and a woman comes into being[775]. The Igbos have two layers of family – the nuclear family and the extended family.

We also examined their socio-cultural dimension as having certain principal values and tenets that separates it from other cultures of the world. Religion is

771 Cfr. Ibid.

772 W. Conton, The African, London 1966, p.29.

773 Cfr. B. Daidson, The African Genius, Boston 1969, p.20.

774 The care of the aged, as an African institution, is situated within the family. It is so cherished and so organised that there is no need, in the African setting, for the cheerless nursing homes for the aged as they exist today in Europe and America. The idea of old people's home and its introduction into Africa would lead to the abuse of the African sense of and respect for old age. See, O. Onwubiko, African Thought, Religion and Culture, p.29.

775 Cfr. E. Okonkwo, Marriage in the Christian and Igbo Traditional Context, p.11.

imbedded in the life of every Igbo such that he sleeps and wakes up with religion. The religious and moral values of the Igbo people make them to praise virtue and condemn vice. We shall now focus our attention to the Igbo traditional marriage system, its essential qualities, the essential requirements and how they traditionally prepare their children and youth for marriage.

2. The Igbo Traditional Marriage System

2.1. The Nature of Igbo Traditional Marriage

The institution of marriage has always existed since the creation of the world. Marriage is a great social institution which occupies an outstanding position in the general scheme of things in Igboland. It is one of the most essential events in the life of every Igbo. His birth and his death are pertinent events but he plays no active part in them. Title taking advances his prestige and gives him a high social position – but he is free to take it or not. Marriage for him, on the other hand, is importantly necessary for his life. It is not only that human nature demands it, but it is a duty he owes to his family and his society at large[776].

Marriage for the Igbo people has been described as "the culturally permitted, the lawfully living together of man and woman of different kinships for the purpose of procreation after the native rites of marriage have been performed"[777]. Marriage in Igboland has meaning with the presence of offspring and especially the male ones. It is regarded as the natural fulfilment of the purpose for which human being falls into two mutually attracting and complementary sexes and by which they can perpetuate their existence in the world. A person, who is not married, except for special cases like taking to priesthood or religious life, is regarded as a curse to the community. Such a person is made an object of derision most especially when he or she has overgrown, in the community's view, the normal age of marriage. The unmarried adult of marriageable age is many a time cajoled with the title of Okokpolo (male woman). This depicts a useless man and a societal nuisance. The high esteem of marriage by the Igbo people is seen in their effort to encourage and pressurize the unmarried to get married. In the words of Basden: "Marriage is the most important event in the Igbo's life. From the time boys and girls are capable of thinking for themselves marriage is set before them

776 Cfr. C.I. Akalonu, Procreation in Igbo Marriage: Inculturation of the Christian Ideal, Madrid 1987, p.9.

777 B.N. Oparaugo, Igbo Traditional Marriage Rite and the Roman "Ordo Celebrandi Matrimonium" of 1991, pm, Rome 1994, p.29.

as the one objective to be attained. During the earlier years it does not assume a serious aspect, but question any boy or girl, and the answer is certain to be that, in due course they must marry. Unmarried persons of either sex except in special cases are objects of derision, and to be childless is the greatest calamity that can befall a woman. Hence a very high value is set upon marriage"[778].

It is pertinent, therefore, to point out that in traditional Igbo society, the Igbos have child bearing as the consummation of marriage. This is the reason why the place of a wife in her husband's home remains unstable and as such not welcomed until she finally gives birth to a child. She is fully admitted into the household after the birth of a male child and given a place of honour from then onwards[779]. The centrality and place of marriage in the life of the traditional Igbo people can be underscored from the type of names they give to their children. Such names as "Ahamefula" (let my name not lost), "Nkemdirim" (let my own be for me), "Omumuagwuike" (child bearing does not know tiredness), "Nwakaego" (child is greater than wealth). These names portray how the Igbo people consider marriage.

Igbo traditional marriage entails a traditional marriage that is authentically Igbo. Here marriage is not only an alliance, or a covenant between two individuals, that is, between a man and a woman, but also an alliance between two family groups, kindred or communities. This process contributes immensely in holding the nuclear and extended families together and ensuring the stability of marriage even when and where the partners were ill-suited or ill-disposed for a stable enduring and lasting union. Traditional marriage among the Igbo people according to Atado, "transcends the notion of marriage as a bilateral contract or as a "contract of convenience". It is seen as a covenant between two "Umunna"

778 B.T. Basden, Among the Ibos of Nigeria, in A.E. Onyeocha, Family Apostolate in Igboland, Rome 1983, p.36.

779 G. Hasenhüttl, Schwarz bin Ich und Schön. Der theologische Aufbruch Schwarzafrikas, Wissenschaftliche Buchgesellschaft, Darmstadt 1991, pp.66-67. He asserts:" Was der CIC 1983 aufgegeben hat, nämlich die Lehre des Katholischen Eherechts, dass der finis primarius, das Grundziel der Ehe die Zeugung von Kindern sei, ist in afrikanischer Auffassung der Ehe noch lebendig, ja überhaupt der zentrale Punkt, eine Ehe verstehen zu können. Das bedeutet, obwohl die Hochzeitsfeier ein zentrales Ereignis ist, ist damit die Ehe nicht vollendet. So wie es möglich ist dass das Paar vor der Hochzeit bereits Kinder hat, so ist die Ehe erst wirklich endgültig, wenn ein Kind geboren wird. Ehe ist nicht ein einmaliger Akt, der durch die Feier, und das Jawort besiegelt ist, sondern Ehe ist ein Prozess, ist ein Geschehen, die sich Rest im Vollzug bewahrheitet. So können eben die Brautleute in der ‚Verlobungszeit' bereits zusammenleben, und oft gehen sie, wenn kein Kind kommt, wieder auseinander. Von den meisten Stämmen wird dies als richtig und gut angesehen. Aber auch wenn sich nach der Hochzeit eigen sollte, dass keine Kinder kommen, wird sie rückgängig gemacht. Eine kinderlose Ehe ist keine Ehe. Wo die kinderlose Frau jedoch beim Mann bleibt, ist es auch ihr Wunsch, dass er eine zweite Frau nimmt, damit sie durch diese Kinder bekommt".

(extended families) concretised in the spouses and binding ex iustitia. Neither the man nor the woman may derogate from or abrogate the sealed covenant without the knowledge of the two clans. The philosophy underlying this legal bond is, "I am because we are, and since we are therefore I am". In other words, the individual exists in and for the community: he plans and executes major decisions in consultation with the members of his own extended family"[780].

Extended family system was the dominant system in traditional Igbo society. Thus, there was corporate responsibility in the marriage of every member of the extended family. Also marriage stability was very dependent on the corporate or extended family system and the mode of social and economic life of the people. This process affords every member of the group to feel concerned about the success or failure of any member of the group[781].

2.2. The Essential Qualities of Igbo Traditional Marriage

Igbo traditional marriage is a ceremony recognized as binding by the customs of any particular group of people or entire civilization as a means of bringing about a stable union between a man and a woman. It is family or community oriented, since the supports of both families and communities are vital for all married people. The two families make the union. A wife is married to the husband's family, meaning that she has to identify completely with all her relatives, look after them, care for them and go out of her way to make them happy[782]. Children, as I said earlier, are determined factors for the continuity of this union. Let us now take a cursory look at these essential qualities of Igbo traditional marriage system.

2.2.1. Customary

The Igbo traditional marriage system is customary in the sense that it is dependent on standardized customs and traditional norms. It is a body of standardized patterns of behaviour which have been established by the usage and observance of the people, and having by this gained the force of law. They may or may not

780 J.C. Atado, African Marriage Customs and Church Law, Kano 1988, p.7; J.S. Mbiti, African Religions and Philosophy, pp.108-109.

781 Cfr. B. Etafo – H. Okeke, Marriage and the Family in Nigeria, Onitsha 1993, p.10; A. Echema, Corporate Personality in Traditional Igbo Society and the Sacrament of Reconciliation, Frankfurt am Main 1995, p.19.

782 Cfr. J. Burke, "Is it Advisable to join together in one Ceremony Traditional and Catholic Church Marriage Rites"? In Shalom Proclaim Peace, A Spiritual Pastoral Journal, Vol. XVI, No. 1, 2001, pp.39-40.

be specifically promulgated, but they are established by popular practice and by long usage[783]. Most often these traditional norms are unwritten. It is not regulated by civil or church laws. In Igbo traditional marriage, it serves as the generally accepted process leading to the solemnization of Christian marriage. The Igbo marriage norms are very crucial to the celebration of marriage and they are traditionally followed strictly for their adherence.

2.2.2. Community-Oriented

The Igbo marriage as well as the African marriage is not a private contract between two individuals but an alliance between two families or communities that their children are entering into marriage. Marriage is not a matter for the man and woman alone; rather it concerns the close kin and community of both. Marriage arrangements are negotiated between the two families of the prospective bride and groom. That is why during the marriage preparations the two people involved in the marriage are informed that they are not marrying to an individual rather to a family. This lays credence to the fact that preparation for marriage and its celebration involve not only the two individuals but also the two families and communities of the prospective couple in question. This communal attitude is an offshoot of the Igbo notion of human existence which places man always "in and within" his community. The Igbo man exists because others exist, and to lose this existential paradigm is a leap into annihiliation.

In Igboland as in Africa, "marriage involves not only interpersonal relations but also intercommunity relations. It implies that the survival of Kinship in the social structure depends on marriage between man and woman; such that marriage always establishes very strong bonds between the individuals belonging to different families and clans. Therefore it is the recognised social institution, not only for establishing and maintaining the family, but also for creating and sustaining the ties of kinship. Marriage is thus essential to the development and enlargement of kinship ties, which are a characteristic feature of African society"[784].

It is to be noted that this aspect of community-oriented culture of the Igbos is also identified in reference to the ancestors forming part of the living community. They are being remembered on numerous social occasions such as on the occasion of marriage. Mbiti captures this when he opines: "For African people, marriage is the focus of existence. It is the point where all the members of a giving community meet: the departed, the living and those yet to be born. All the dimen-

783 Cfr. E. Iwuji, Customary Law Marriage in Nigeria, Gottingen 1982, p.6.

784 P.K. Amevor, New Approaches to Marriage Preparation, p.68; K. Gyekye, African Cultural Values: An Introduction, Accra 2003, p.76.

sions of time meet here, and the whole drama of history is repeated, renewed and revitalised. Marriage is a drama in which everyone becomes an actor or actress and not just a spectator. Therefore, marriage is a duty, a requirement from the corporate society, and a rhythm of life in which everyone must participate. Otherwise, he who does not participate in it is a curse to the community, he is a rebel and a law-breaker, and he is not only abnormal but under-human"[785].

The Igbo marriage as community-oriented carries everybody along during the marriage ceremony and after the celebration. It is an intense spirit of solidarity and the man and woman involve in such a marriage can count on the moral and material support of their community. On such an occasion, the two communities act together as a unit in their principles of cooperation and co-responsibility to see to the success of that marriage and in their on-going supportive role after the marriage. "Besides, within the framework of the familial type of marriage arrangement in which the success of the marriage becomes a concern for the other members of the two lineage groups, there are always at hand men and women of goodwill ready to counsel the couple, to help them to sort out their marriage problems, or patch up quarrels, and so help to bring harmony back into the marriage. These men and women serve as marriage or family counsellors offering advice, admonition, and giving encouragement based on their experiences in the practice of marriage"[786].

Hence, as a unifying process, marriage in Igboland creates a lasting pact between families of both parties marrying. It is to be stressed here that in as much as marriage in Igbo view involves not only the two opposite individuals marrying but also their families and communities, it is not to be taken that in doing so the privacy of these man and woman is caged. The involvement of the two families and communities is a matter of support and encouragement.

2.2.3. Igbo Marriage as Sacred

In Igboland it is commonly believed that marriage (ilu nwanyi) is natural and divinely instituted. It is generally conceived as a gift from God and which by that very fact is sacred. It is because of its sacred nature that many religious sacrifices are included in its preparation and ceremonies, and these ceremonies serve as a means in guarding and protecting its sacredness[787]. Until recently, every normal person is expected to marry and get offspring. Hence, to remain unmarried was

785 J.S. Mbiti, African Religions and Philosophy, p.130.

786 P.K. Amevor, New Approaches to Marriage Preparation, p.75.

787 Cfr. A.C. Idigo, Towards Making the Igbo Traditional Marriage a Christian Marriage, Rome 2001, p.18.

taken as a curse and hence an abomination. If a person who has reached the age of marriage fails to marry, it becomes quickly the concerns of the whole family members. The family members of the person in question could resort to pooling their resources together in order to get a wife for that person if it is found out that not having money was the cause of him not getting married. "Therefore marriage is looked upon as a sacred duty which every normal person must perform. Failure to do so means in effect, stopping the flow of life through the individual and hence the diminishing of mankind upon the earth.... Therefore anybody who, under normal condition refuses to get married is committing a major offence in the eyes of the society and people will be against him. In all African societies, everything possible is done to prepare people for marriage and to make them think in terms of marriage"[788]. This in actual fact demonstrates the primacy of marriage in Igboland, its pivotal role in Igbo culture, and the tremendous respect it confers on those who enter it.

It is to be observed that in Igbo culture as also in African culture, society is not limited only to those living in the present, the community, through prayers and sacrifices, lives on in the son that is, through male children the man is then remembered from generation to generation. This gives credence to the fact that the approval and blessing of the elders or the ancestors are important before the customary marriage. This consolidates the relationship between the living and the dead members of the family[789].

2.2.4. Polygamous

Another aspect of Igbo traditional marriage is polygamy. By this word we refer to the union of a husband with two or more wives, the type of union called polygyny. It is quite different from the type of union called polyandry, which refers to the union of one woman with several men. This type of union is conspicuously rare in Africa[790].

Within the Igbo as well as the African traditional context, getting married to several wives is a custom found in it, though in some communities it is less common than in others. This form of marriage is an indication of social status, a sign of affluence and it is regarded in those days as a sound economic and social investment. Commenting on this form of marriage, Mbiti asserts: "Getting married to two or more wives is a custom found all over Africa.... The custom fits

788 J.S. Mbiti, An Introduction to African Religion, Heinemann, London 1975, p.98.

789 Cfr. J.U. Gangwari, Civil Marriage in Nigeria, Portharcourt 1993, p.41; B. Bujo, "Poligamy in Africa: A Pastoral Approach", in Theology Digest 32 (1985), p.231.

790 Cfr. B. Kisembo – L. Magesa – A. Shorter, African Christian Marriage, Nairobi 1998, p.85.

well into the social structure of traditional life and into the thinking of the people, serving many useful purposes"[791]. Basden, in his own emotional exaggeration in equating the lives of the Igbo people with polygamy, opines: "Polygamy is intimately bound up with the lives of the Ibo people.... To the pagan Ibo, a plurality of wives is a laudable ambition.... A man who is able to multiply his wives rises automatically to the social scale"[792].

The conception by most Westerners that African traditional marriage is potentially polygamous gives room to the impression that all African marriages are necessarily polygamous and therefore, monogamy as a form of marriage whereby a man marries only one wife is not tenable in Africa. It has to be said that in Igboland as also in Africa, monogamy is the preferred and acceptable form of marriage. Commenting on this conception, Dike says: "Monogamy was not brought in by Christianity in Igboland but was there from time unknown to the present generation. The majority of the Igbo are monogamous. About 95% are monogamous. It is only about 5% that are polygamous. The majority of women prefer monogamy to polygamy and feel happy being married in a monogamous marriage in order to start off a new family. The wish of every married couple is to enjoy a healthy relationship in peace and love. They wish to bring up their children in this form of peaceful and loving family"[793]. Thus, monogamy is most widely practised in Igboland. Marriage traditionally is characterized in Igboland as "Alum Di na Nwanyi", (the union between a man and a woman) is considered solely as a union of a man and a woman for the sole purpose of companionship, mutual support and procreation.

While not denying the fact that polygamy is recognised as one of the forms of Igbo traditional marriage, yet in real life one wife is specifically recognised. Traditionally, the first wife alone is accorded the position and right of a legal wife. Moreover, the economic obligations entailed by taking several wives could operate to checkmate the level to which polygamy was actually practised during that period. The structural conditions in support of large scale polygamy broke down during the period of colonization. The bringing in of a monetary economy, commerce and trade made polygamy less economically viable and expensive. This form of customary marriage is now relatively infrequent and scarcely involves more than two wives married to one man. Nowadays, large scale polygamy has disappeared completely and women are no longer transacted as primary valuable goods. Thus, many kinds of kinship ideology and traditional practices have been retained, reworked and validated by local courts as the foundation for family laws in general and inheritance rights in particular.

791 J.S. Mbiti, African Religions and Philosophy, pp.138-139.

792 G.T. Basden, Niger Ibos,p.228.

793 E.E. Dike, Christian Marriage and Family in Igboland, Münster 2001, pp.192-193.

A polygamous marriage is referred as a nuclear type of family in its most simple form as it consists of a man, his women and children. In this sense, it is viewed as a micro nuclear unit but not a micro nuclear family, as micro-focal units are not families in themselves[794]. This form of marriage is imbibed with a number of well-defined social functions and benefits and it helps in stabilizing the customary marriage institution and to relate the family with the society[795].

There are so many factors which motivate the practice of polygamy. One of the important reasons for the practice of polygamy is childlessness. A childless marriage in Igboland is scarcely called a marriage in the real sense of it. Children are considered as great asset and because of that marriage in Igboland has procreation as its point of departure. When a marriage proves fruitless, then the next option is to get another wife who will beget children for the continuation of the family lineage. Any other means employed to get children without the method of marrying another wife is not always satisfactory to the ordinary Igbo man, as he would see it as someone else' child or children. "It was necessary to transmit life oneself to another human being, and this was regarded as an essential aspect of being alive. It was a share in the divine prerogative of giving life, and it was insurance that one's memory would be cherished after death. The death of a childless man or woman was final, but the death of a person with a numerous progeny was less feared.... Without the alternative of polygamy, divorce would be practically inevitable, and it was divorce that the practice of the sorarate[796] was designed to forestall"[797].

The desire to have a large family is catered by this form of marriage called polygamy. In Igbo traditional society, it was the desire of every family to have many children because of the important role they played in the house. According to Onibere: "Apart from deriving socio-economic advantages from numerous progeny there is that unshakeable belief that children mean wealth, prestige and a system of blessing from the Deity and the ancestors. Children enjoy the patronage of not only the nuclear family but also that of the extended family. The procurement of children is insurance that one's memory will be cherished after one's demise. It is believed that there is continuing fellowship between the living – dead and their

794 Cfr. A.C. Idigo, Towards Making the Igbo Traditional Marriage a Christian Marriage, p.35.

795 Cfr. E. Okonkwo, Marriage in the Christian and Igbo Traditional Context, p.17.

796 By Sorarate marriage we mean the type of marriage whereby a man engages in marriage or sexual relations with the sister of his wife, most often after the death of his wife or in many cases, when the wife is unable to have a child of her own as a result of one problem or the other. She could on her own will, and with the consent of her husband decides to bring her sister who will in turn beget children on her behalf. This type of marriage strengthens the existing ties between the two families and preserves the contract between the two groups to raise and care for the children and to continue the alliance.

797 B. Kisembo – L. Magesa – A. Shorter, African Christian Marriage, p.96.

children"[798]. Children did not only belong to the nuclear family alone, but also to entire extended family, and as such there was considerable extended family cooperation in the upbringing of children and that made it easier for these children to be raised up from various households within the extended family community[799]. Bareness, therefore, is one of the major motives for polygamous type of marriage in Igboland.

Another factor that motivates polygamy is socio-economic value. In those days, it was the normal ambition of every man to continue to add to the number of wives he had so as to ensure capable hands in the farm work, and women themselves are considered very well at farm work. Hence, having many wives and children means increase in productivity. Therefore, the man who had many wives and children could easily decide to extend his working capability in the farm so as to have increase in productivity. As a result of this, the men were motivated to have several wives and numerous children to cater for cheap labour and as a means to increase ownership of farmland. The number of wives a man had was a sign of social standing and affluence. Thus, "polygamy becomes more of an asset than liability. It increases the labour force and assists food production. A large family community renders all the operations of rural life more efficient: clearing land, building, making artefacts and utensils, guarding the fields against marauding birds and animals, and so forth. It also makes co operation in communal work less demanding, since there are more representatives of the family available to participation"[800].

Polygamy has also the vital role of catering for the sexual needs of the man most especially during the period of lactation and it helps to reduce the chances of prostitution and promiscuity. This is evident in this modern era when men live their wives and children to go to cities and towns where they are employed to work. If on the other hand, the man has so many wives, he may decide to take one with him as to avoid having the temptation of looking for other women or girls to satisfy him. He has a better opportunity of always having one of his wives around him to make him happy and help him avoid sexual scandals.

Another determining factor about polygamy is that of social prestige. Many men in Igboland especially the chiefs marry for social prestige and recognition. The importance of marriage in Igboland is so pronounced that attainment of honourable socio-political roles is often determined by a number of wives one married. The more a person excelled in the acquisition of wives in polygamy the higher status he achieved for himself in the Igbo traditional society. The commu-

798 S.G.A. Onibere, "The Contribution of African Religion to Marital Harmony – the Nigeria Example": CRA 22 (1988) pp. 83-99, p.90.

799 Cfr. B. Kisembo – L. Magesa – A. Shorter, African Christian Marriage, p.95.

800 Ibid; p.90.

nity looked at him in high esteem because of the many children he is bequeathing to the community, something that is highly esteemed by the whole community. In this view, Uchendu asserts that: "Among the Igbo married life is the normal condition for both men and women; polygamy, a symbol of high social status, is the ideal"[801].

A situation also arises when the wife, besides having children of her own, is not content to be the only wife of her husband owing to the domestic burdens of the family. Sometimes the burdens are too worrisome that she could not cope with them. Hence, for the sake of a helper to secure relief in these burdens, she willingly seeks that her husband marries another wife. Mbiti captures this when he argues: "When a family is made up of several wives with their households, it means that in time of need there will always be someone around to help. This is corporate existence.... In cases of sickness, other wives will fetch water from the river, cut firewood, cook and do other jobs for the family"[802].

We must however agree also that there are problems associated with this form of marriage called polygamy. Such polygamous families are sometimes ravaged by quarrels and fights among the wives and also among their children. There are also hatred, envy and jealousy among the husband's wives. It is also a great burden to feed, cloth, and educate these children in a proper way, unless the man is adequately rich. Also problem arises to cope with the indiscipline of the children. Besides, tensions are bound to surface in a polygamous family whether the co-wives are living together or they are separated from one another. The wives in a polygamous family go all out to procure special favours from their husband as to win his heart. There is also the tendency of making many women widows at the death of their husband. Polygamy also encourages men to believe that they have the sole right of getting as many wives as they want irrespective of the wishes of their wives.

It is against this backdrop that many have come to condemn polygamy as being primitive, uncultured, a sin comparable to adultery, and an indication that the sexual morality of those who practice it is low, and a disrespect to the feelings of women. It has to be made clear that in the traditional Igbo society as well as in Africa polygamy is an acceptable form of marriage and it is valid and official when it is properly contracted in accordance with customary law. It is hard to say whether polygamy today is on the increase or decrease, but there is a change of attitude on the part of women because of the stress on higher education and the impact of Christianity.

801 V.C. Uchendu, The Igbo of Southeast Nigeria, p.49.
802 J.S. Mbiti, African Religions and Philosophy, p.139.

2.2.5. Procreation-Oriented

The yearning to have children is the basis of the Igbo man's reason of entering into marriage. It is his primary objective. Through this way he raises a household which nurtures life and keeps the race in existence and at the same time assures him of the continuation of his lineage when he finally departs from this world. Hence, to die without getting offspring especially male ones, depicts being totally cut off from human society without any successor to continue the lineage and therefore losing all links with mankind after one's death[803].

Suffice it to say that in Igboland as well as in Africa any marriage without procreation is totally incomplete. "It is a religious obligation by means of which the individual contributes the seeds of life towards man's struggle against the loss of original immortality. Biologically both husband and wife are reproduced in their children, thus perpetuating the chain of humanity.... A person who, therefore, has no descendants in effect quenches the fire of life, and becomes forever dead since his line of physical continuation is blocked if he does not get married and bear children"[804].

In view of the traditional understanding of marriage as a way of begetting children in fulfilment of cultural and religious obligations and for the continuation of the family lineage, procreation becomes an indispensable value in every Igbo customary marriage. No marriage is contracted in Igboland with the intention to exclude procreation, although people now tend to do family planning because of the current wave of globalization, still the brain behind their marriage is to have children. The Igbos strongly believes that the biological fecundity must be placed in its appropriate place in marriage. "Generally speaking, the biological fecundity of woman had to be used to the full because of the high rate of infant mortality and the frequent epidemics that decimated the population. To live out old age with dignity, there was no other hope than to have enough offspring. Further, in a culture of sustenance farmers, children were important helpers for they returned to the family, in material help, all that they received. Within this context a great love for children could and did frequently develop which, in turn, could strengthen the affection between the spouses. They honoured each other gratefully as father or mother of their children"[805].

The first considerable thing about marriage is the fertility of the spouses. A newly married woman is expected to show signs of pregnancy few months after marriage. When this fails to happen, her own mother and her mother in-law will

803 Cfr. E. Iwuji, Customary Law Marriage in Nigeria, p.23.

804 J.S. Mbiti, African Religions and Philosophy, p.130.

805 B. Häring, Free and Faithful in Christ, Moral Theology for Priests and Laity, Vol.2, Middlegreen 1979, p.518.

be very concern to find out the reason for the delay in conceiving a child. So any marriage without pregnancy resulting to child bearing has not achieved its purpose and end. A marriage is successful when it is accompanied with children. The main purpose of contracting marriage for the Igbo people is to beget children and ensure the continuation of the lineage. There are some Igbo sayings that allude to this claim: "Ihe eji alu nwanyi bu maka imu nwa" (the end of marriage is procreation), "Nwanyi dim ma maka nwa" (a woman is good for begetting children), "Ka m luo nwanyi muta umu" (let me marry and have children). The desire to beget children is for the Igbo people the way of life and the aim of existence. Commenting on what marriage is for the Africans, Contran and Rubin say: "The African does not think of marriage as a union based on romantic love although beauty as well as character and health are sought in the choice of a wife. The strong affection that normally exists after some years of successful marriage is the product of the marriage itself conceived as a process, resulting from living together and co-operating in many activities and particularly in the rearing of children"[806].

In Igboland, a wife's primary function in marriage is to beget children for her husband. The stand of a wife in her husband's household is shaky and cannot be predicted until she bears a child for her husband. She establishes a base after the birth of a child most especially a male child. Then, at this point in time she is recognised as a responsible woman in her husband's nuclear and extended families. More so, the birth of a child automatically elevates her to the status of a wife, and before this stage she is a wife only in anticipation of a child.

The fate of a barren woman as such cannot be overemphasised. It is common in Igboland to see such a woman being made the object of conversation and mockery by some of her women counterparts. Many a time they call her all sorts of names to ridicule her status of bareness. In those old days, women in this category of childlessness frequent the houses of native doctors (Dibias) in search of solution to the problems. Such cases today are better handled in hospitals and maternity clinics in different parts of Igboland[807].

The names giving to children in Igboland are self-evident proof of the love the Igbo people have for children. Such names are: Nwabueze (a child is king), Nwabuisi (a child is the first and foremost), Nwamaka (a child is good), Nwakaego (a child is greater than wealth), Nwakamma (a child is better off). Also when a child is born to a couple after long years of waiting in anguish, such a child is named: Ifeanyichukwu (nothing is impossible to God), Chukwuemeka (God has been very generous), Obiajulu (the heart is relieved at last). Sometimes the birth

806 E. Contra – N.N. Rubin, Readings in African Law II, London 1970, p.93.

807 Cfr. C. Obi, "Marriage Among the Igbo of Nigeria", http:// codewit.com/Igbomarriage.php. (Accessed: 18.06.2011).

of such a child is announced with the shooting of Dane guns (Nkpo na-ala). This testifies to the fact that Igbo people hold children in high esteem because they are blessing from God. A couple who begets up to ten children is rewarded with a ceremony called "Ewu Ukwu"[808] in Igboland. This ceremony no doubt elevates the status of the couple in such a way that they are respected in their community and village.

It is pertinent to underscore the main reasons why the Igbo people as well as Africans attach much importance to children. The quest for children in any marriage in Igboland is because of the values that children give to their parents and the community from where they come from. It is a well known fact that children strengthen the goodness of the bond of marriage. Commenting on the values of having children, Pope John Paul II addressed the Christian families during his Papal visit to Nigeria as follows: "... your families have so many positive and praiseworthy values; based on your traditions... children are regarded as blessings and are desired as the crown of marriage"[809]. Also talking about the fundamental importance of children to the family the Pope made reference to his earlier discourse to the General Assembly of the United Nations on October 2, 1979, in the following words: "I wish to express the joy that we all find in children, the springtime of life, the anticipation of the future history of each of our present earthly homelands. No country on earth, no political system can think of its own future otherwise than through the image of these new generations that will receive from their parents the manifold heritage of values, duties and aspirations

808 C. Akalonu, Procreation in Igbo Marriage: Inculturation of the Christian Ideal, Madrid 1987, pp.46-47. "Ewu Ukwu" is one of the institutions by which the Igbo manifest the importance and value of procreation. "Ewu Ukwu", so called because a great (Ewu) is killed as an essential part of the ceremony to compliment the hip-loins, pelvis – (Ukwu) that has given birth to so many children. The naming of the ceremony after this part of the body is logical for its function in the birth of a child. A woman has a special duty to safeguard the life of a developing human being in the womb for the period of nine months. Therefore when a woman has done this function successfully for ten consecutive times, Igbo custom demands that some respect be paid to this particular woman. It is an honour to have bred ten children. A she goat is killed for this celebration, in appreciation for the work successfully done. This rite is essentially one of thanksgiving to God and of paying homage to a couple that celebrated at least ten childbirths. Husband and wife participate in the ceremony, but attention is very much centred on the wife who had born the ten pregnancies and the ordeals of childbirth. Ewu Ukwu is a ceremony which many Igbo couples desire to celebrate, but not many attain this desire. Some are not able due to death, while others are not able to reach the required number of childbirths. In this ceremony parenthood and in particular motherhood is honoured. To live to celebrate "Ewu Ukwu" with all the children around them is regarded by the Igbo couple as a sign of great blessing from God.

809 John Paul II, Address to the Bishops of Nigeria, in Papal Message to Nigeria (PMN): A Collection of Speeches delivered by Pope John Paul II on the occasion of his visit to Nigeria (12th-17th February 1982), Lagos 1982, p.11.

of the nation to which they belong and of the whole human family"[810]. In view of this, economic, social, psychological, stability, and religious values are the main reasons why the Igbo people attach such importance to children.

Economic Value: Since agriculture serves as the main occupation of the Igbo people in supplying food for its citizen and which is the cultivation of the land for the purpose of producing food for humanity, feed for animals and raw materials for the industry, children serve as great value in cultivating this land and producing this food for mankind. Cultivation of land in large quantity cannot be performed if the number of children in a household is very small. Hence, a high number of children are needed to ensure a large labour force in agricultural work[811]. Children assist at farm work and other domestic activities in the family. They play a supportive role to their parents when they are at their old age. Many a time the skills and styles of trade based on traditional occupations are passed on from parents to their children as a continuation of such trade in the family lineage.

Social Value: Children in Igboland are source of respect and prestige both for their parents and their community. Parents consider it a very big honour to have many children so that their household name and image will not be relegated to the background. They take adequate care of their parents at old age and ensure that appropriate and befitting burials are accorded to their parents when they die. The general practice in Igboland is for children to build their houses near the house of their parents if they cannot live in the same house with them due to lack of space. This as a matter of fact accords them the opportunity to take adequate care of their parents when they are old as to put a smile on their faces everyday and provide them security. The question of dumping them at old people's home as the Westerners do does not arise at all. This is because the children believe strongly that their aged parents are still part of them and that it is their rightful turn to feed, clothe and give them comfort. The aged in Igboland are surrounded by the warmth presence of their children, grand children, great grand children and their relatives. This ever-presence of their children accompanies them to the great beyond[812]. Also when they die they are being buried in their respective compounds to show that they are still part of the family and to take proper care of their grave yards.

Psychological: Children in Igboland are major source of psychological relief and value to their various parents and families. The shame of childlessness and the stigma of bareness are being removed when children are born into a particular

810 FC, 26 §3.

811 Cfr. D. Kayongo-Male – P. Onyango, The Sociology of the African Family, London 1984, p.9; E. Okonkwo, Marriage in the Christian and Igbo Traditional Context, p.172.

812 Cfr. B.K. Nwakonobi, Igbo System of Kinship and Family, p.89.

family. Such children are a practical vindication of their father's manhood and mother's womanhood respectively. Such names as Ekwutosi (cease your criticism), Chidera (what God has written), Akolamuonu (do not insult me), serve as answers to the husband and wife critics. The status of fatherhood and that of motherhood crowns the life of a man and a woman psychologically and accords them prestige and respect among their people. One is not considered a complete human being until after begetting children. Thus, you hear such complementary greetings when a couple beget a child as "unu buzikwa nwoke na nwanyi ugbua, unu abughikwa osisi na-anaghi ami kpuru (you are now real man and woman, and no longer a tree that does not bear fruit).

Stability: The union of a man and a woman is meant to be a permanent one, but when this union is not equipped with children in the Igbo society, the permanency sometimes goes in shambles. Children are source of happiness to their parents. They help in bringing their parents together especially when quarrels ensued between them. They are also bond that keeps the nuclear and extended family together. A woman who finds it hard to live together with her husband because of his bad behaviour may decide to stay put in such a union because of the presence of her children. Such stability is strengthened and encouraged more when a male child is born into that household, the woman will consider herself a strong bona fide member of the family with all the honour and prestige accorded to a woman who has given birth to a male child[813]. Hence, stability is one of the most pertinent values of children in Igboland and in Africa as a whole.

Religious: In Igbo traditional society, rearing up children helps to perpetuate the family name and continue the link between the living and the ancestors. The children's duty is to remember their dead ones, look after the family shrines and cater for other responsibilities[814]. It is an important factor in Igbo society to remember those who have died. They are kept for a very long time in personal memory after they have died. "To lack someone close who keeps the departed in their personal immortality is the worst misfortune and punishment that any person could suffer. To die without getting married and without children is to be completely cut off from the human society, to become disconnected, to become an outcast and to lose all links with mankind"[815].

813 Cfr. Ibid; pp.91-92.

814 Cfr. D. Kayongo-Male – P. Onyango, The Sociology of the African Family, p.7; E. Okonkwo, Marriage in the Christian and Igbo Traditional Context, p.173.

815 J.S. Mbiti, African Religions and Philosophy, p.131.

2.3. Conclusion

Marriage as we have seen, in Igbo traditional society, is considered an indispensable factor for the continuation of the family lineage. It is a natural institution that is patriarchal in nature. Marriage for the Igbos is understood as a natural and ordinary means of a husband and wife to beget children, increase and multiply in order to fill the earth for the continuation of human race. For the Igbo people, marriage has meaning with the presence of children. It is regarded as the natural fulfilment of the purpose for which human beings are created. Hence, failure to get married in Igboland is considered a serious issue that needs urgent attention. Marriage is not only an affair between two individuals but also between the two families and their extended families. It is more than a contract or a covenant between two individuals of the opposite sex in the sense that it comprises an alliance between two families as between the couples themselves[816].

We also saw the essential qualities that make up the Igbo traditional marriage system. We equally found out that the reasons why children are considered paramount in Igbo traditional marriage range from economic, social, psychological, and religious values, as well as stability. Hence, the more children one begets, the greater the guarantee for security and comfort. In an agrarian culture where mechanized method of farming is not available, children assist at farm work and other domestic activities in the family.

3. Impediments in Igbo Traditional Marriage

3.1. Introduction

An impediment is broadly defined "as a circumstance which renders a marriage either illicit or invalid"[817]. It is seen as a circumstance or condition that directly concerns a person which renders that person's marriage invalid. The 1917 Code establishes two types of marriage impediments[818] and they are: impediment, that rendered a marriage illicit but not invalid; and diriment, that prohibited a mar-

816 Cfr. C.S. Mba, Trial Marriage in Nigeria, in Lucerna, Vol.8, no.1, Enugu, p.34.

817 T.L. Bouscaren – A.C. Ellis, Canon Law: A Text and Commentary, p.473.

818 C.1036 CIC/1917 §1: "An impediment impediment contains a grave prohibition against contracting marriage; which, however, is not rendered invalid if it is contracted notwithstanding". §2: "A diriment impediment both gravely prohibits the marriage and prevents it from being contracted validly".

riage and prevented it from being entered validly. The new Code of 1983 contains only diriment impediments which render a person incapable of entering marriage validly[819].

In the Igbo traditional marriage system, an impediment is regarded as anything that obstructs or hinders the normal marriage celebration. These impediments to traditional marriage law differ from ethnic regions and localities. They could be permanent or temporal and as such, one cannot strike a balance between the meaning of impediment and its obstacle. The impediments in Igbo traditional marriage are provable in the external forum. "When it is traced, it does not automatically render marriage already celebrated as null and void. The Igbo have their way to right a wrong and then the marriage is regarded as rectified.... Therefore, for the Igbo, there is no occult impediment. Once the celebration of the marriage is completed, it is assumed to be valid. In order to reverse it, ceremonies of the reversal have to be performed"[820].

Having established this, we are now going to take a cursory look at some of the impediments that constitute obstacle to the celebration of marriage in Igboland.

3.2. Lack of Age

The minimum age for marriage according to the 1917 Code is sixteen for men and fourteen for women. The Code establishes that any marriage entered into before these minimum ages notwithstanding the level of physical and psychological maturity attained by the parties is considered invalid[821]. The 1983 Code follows these minimum ages prescribed by the Old Code[822]. However, the Episcopal Conferences of Bishops can establish a legislation which requires an age higher than the ones mentioned in the canons, but this can be done only by obtaining permission from the local ordinary.

The Igbo traditional marriage does not as such establish any age for entering into marriage. But it does not remove the fact that marriage does not take place before both partners reached the age of puberty. Whereas for the male, the age of adulthood is determined by the performance of some public functions such as initiation rites into adulthood and some form of heroic acts; the commencement of the menstrual cycle is considered always as a determining factor of attaining puberty for a female[823]. So age is neither a factor nor an impediment

819 Cfr. T.P. Doyle, Marriage, p.757.

820 A.C. Idigo, Towards Making the Igbo Traditional Marriage a Christian Marriage, p.47.

821 Cfr. C.1067 §1 CIC/1917.

822 Cfr. C.1083 CIC/1983.

823 Cfr. J.U. Gangwari, Civil Marriage in Nigeria, p.43.

to marriage, in the Igbo traditional marriage. However, the government of the Eastern States of Nigeria (Igbo region) has established a definite age of marriage under the customary law which is governed by the Age of Marriage Law of 1956[824]. Under this law, a man before he has completed his sixteen years of age, and likewise a woman before she has completed her sixteen years of age cannot enter a valid marriage.

3.3. Consanguinity

The impediment of consanguinity is understood as the blood relationship between two persons. It is focused on the descent from one person to another through direct line, or on the descent of various persons that are related to a common ancestor in the collateral line."This relationship is based on a true blood relationship and, therefore, does not depend on the material status of the common ancestor. Consequently, it exists between a person and all of his or her direct descendants even though he or she may not have been married to the natural parent"[825].

In Igbo traditional marriage, consanguinity is regarded as a very serious impediment. The Igbo native law and custom prohibit a man from marrying his daughter or a woman from marrying her brother. That is the more reason why a strict and careful investigation is carried out before the courtship proposal. Any marriage between members of the same lineage is rendered null and void. But if the two persons involved refuse to stop the marriage, it is considered as an abomination (aru) and they are thereby ostracised from their community or village until an expiation rite (ikwa-ala) is performed so as to placate the gods of the land and the ancestors because a great relationship damage has been done between the living members of their families and their ancestors. After this ritual, they are now free to return back to the community or village not as husband and wife again but as separated parties of the same lineage.

It has to be pointed out that the way in which impediment of consanguinity is taken in Igbo culture varies remarkably with that of the Western culture. In this view, Elias explains that: "The degree of consanguinity under customary law is certainly wider than it is in English law. For instance, a family usually consists of the man, his wife (or wives) and his children and a large number of collaterals claiming blood or kinship with him"[826]. Therefore, any sexual intercourse be-

---

824 Cfr. Cap.6 of Laws of Eastern Nigeria, 1963. Section 3(1) of the Law provides that "a marriage... between or in respect of persons either of whom is under the age of sixteen shall be void".

825 T.P. Doyle, Marriage, pp.771-772; see also C.1091 CIC/1983.

826 T.O. Elias, Groundwork of Nigerian Law, London 1964, pp.287-288.

tween related persons of the same lineage is termed as incest. There are four principles that constitute the family in Africa according to Shorter. These principles are: "Prohibition of incest, descent, residence and domination. Incest prohibition means, at least, that primary kin do not meet with one another. Primary kin are parents, children, brothers, sisters, uncles, nieces, aunts, and nephews. In every society in the world, there are prohibitions against sexual intercourse between such categories. The prohibition usually also extends to other categories as well, especially in Africa where a very large kin-group is affected"[827].

The extension of the impediment of consanguinity in Igboland cannot be overemphasised in the sense that no two members of the same extended family are authorised to date each other not to talk of entering into marriage. Atado alludes to this when he asserts: "Whereas the revised Code requires the dispensation before first cousins can marry, Igbo customary law does not even permit the marriage of second cousins. In short, the issue of consanguinity is more protected in Igbo society than (what) the Canon Law prescribes"[828].

Therefore, the impediment of consanguinity is hardly heard of in Igboland as well as in Africa because it constitutes a very dangerous omen within the nuclear and extended families system and may result to loss of family ties and extinction of such families.

3.4. Affinity

The relationship that arises between a spouse and the blood relatives of the other spouse (in-law) is regarded as affinity[829]. Canon 1092 of the 1983 Code states that, "affinity in the direct line in any degree invalidates a marriage"[830].

The Igbo traditional law on the other hand, prohibits the marriage of a spouse with persons whom he is related through marriage. It is considered as "aru" (abomination) for a man to marry his wife's daughter, wife's mother, wife's granddaughter or wife's son's daughter. The impediment of affinity exists only in the direct line and not in the collateral line as regards Igbo marriage.

Hence, there are exceptions to the impediment of affinity. It is permissible and possible for twins to marry another twin of the same blood relation. It is also possible for two brothers to decide to marry to sisters of the same blood. It is

827 A. Shorter, African Culture and the Christian Church, London 1073, p.159.

828 J. Atado, Marriage Custom and Church Law, Kano 1988, p.130.

829 Cfr. C.109 §1 CIC/1983: "Affinitas oritur ex matrimonio valido, etsi non consummato, atque viget inter virum et mulieris consanguineous, itemque mulierem inter et viri consanguineous".

830 C.1092 CIC/1983.

sometimes allowed also for a man to marry his wife's sister after the death of his wife or because of the obvious fact that his wife cannot conceive and get a child or children for him.

3.5. Impotence

Impotence is defined as the incapacity for the marital act or for normal sexual intercourse. This may be as a result of organic problems like an injury to a genital organ that is seen as indispensable for normal intercourse. Also as a result of serious malformation of either the male or female organ which makes the completion of intercourse not possible might also be the cause. Impotence could also be due to a functional disorder such as incapacity to complete the physical act, caused by a psychological or nervous condition notwithstanding the intact of the genital organs[831].

The impediment of impotence is considered a major obstacle and hindrance to Igbo traditional marriage. As we mentioned earlier, procreation is the main goal of marriage in Igboland and it is taken seriously. This is because a childless marriage is seen as a great omen. On this Basden opines: "A childless marriage is a source of grievous disappointment and, sooner or later, leads to serious trouble between man and wife.... Should the wife feel that the husband is to be blamed for her non-conception, she is at liberty to cohabit with another man to prove her contention"[832].

An impotent man in Igboland cannot sustain marriage. And when impotence is discovered in a man who is already married, the wife has a free choice to say goodbye to the marriage but after her family must have paid back the bride wealth and then made some traditional ceremonies attached to it. The wife in question can then return to her parents' home. On account of this, Basden contends that: "If a husband proves to be impotent, the woman is free to live him. In such a case, if the couple be fond of each other and choose to continue together, a meeting of relatives is called, and the situation is stated in their presence. Arrangements are thereupon, made whereby a male friend acts as sponsor for the defaulting husband"[833].

It has to be mentioned that impotence as an impediment to marriage also affects a woman who is considered impotence on account of not having uterus, ovaries, and fallopian tube. In Igboland, when a man notices that his wife is impotent, he could decide to take another wife on his own free decision or through the

831 Cfr. T.P. Doyle, Marriage, p.765.
832 G.T. Basden, Niger Ibos, p.228.
833 Ibid; p.240.

recommendation of his wife and this is another reason why the traditional Igbo people take on polygamy. So impotence generally in Igbo tradition does not invalidate marriage already celebrated as there are different ways of coping with it.

3.6. Public Criminality

One of the notable and conspicuous characters of the Igbo people is that the value prestige, respect, and reputation. Any body who engages in activities inimical to the well being of the community or who has a questionable character, or who is a suspect on such crimes as robbery, murder, theft, to mention but a few can never be allowed or considered worthy to marry from that community. That is why marriage enquiries (iju ese) is very important in Igbo traditional marriage. Why this is pertinent is because if it is finally discovered that the man coming to marry a girl is a public notorious criminal, he will be shown the back door even if he is a millionaire. If the person resists he will be publicly humiliated by the community from where this girl comes from. That is why public incorrigible criminality is a serious obstacle to Igbo traditional marriage.

3.7. Status Bar (Osu Caste System)

In Igbo traditional society, there are two classes of people, the so-called "Nwadiala" (free born) and the "Osu" (a caste person). The Nwadialas are the free-born and they are literally considered as the "sons of the soil". The Osu on the other hand, are known as the slaves, unclean people, strangers, outcastes and the untouchables. The Osu people are seen as people sacrificed to the gods in Igboland. Chinua Achebe defines well what is meant by Osu: "He was a person dedicated to a god, a thing set apart – a taboo forever, and his children after him. He could neither marry nor be married by the free-born. He was in fact an outcast, living in a special area of the village, close to the Great shrine. Wherever he went he carried with him the mark of his forbidden caste – long, tangled and dirty hair. A razor was taboo to him. An Osu could not attend an assembly of the free born, and they, in turn, could not shelter under his roof. He could not take any of the four titles of the clan, and when he died, he was buried by his kind in the Evil forest"[834].

The Osu Caste System could be traced back to hundreds of years ago when slaves, war prisoners and criminals were dedicated to deities, for them to serve and worship them in their shrines. During this period the deity gods' worshipers

834 C. Achebe, Things Fall Apart, London 1958, p.111.

married one another and had children and their children had their own children and it continues till today. The descendants of these deity gods worshipers are made to suffer today from the deeds of their ancestors and forefathers.

The Osu people are treated as inferior human beings. They are socially degraded and suffer an international deprivation of the higher cultural values in Igboland. They are subjected to various forms of abuse and discrimination. They are made to live separately from the so-called free born. They live very close to market places and shrines in most cases.

In the area of marriage is this discrimination very pronounced and conspicuous. There is this belief that if a free born marries an Osu, the whole family is cursed and contaminated. Such a free born defiles the family in which he or she comes from or belongs to. Hence, free born families are always up in arms against any member of their families who wishes to enter into marriage with an Osu. They could go to any length to scuttle the plan. In those olden days "it was scandalous that in the middle of the twentieth century a man could be barred from marrying a girl simply because her great-great-great-grandfather had been dedicated to serve a god, thereby setting himself apart and turning his descendants into a forbidden caste to the end of time. Quite unbelievable"[835].

It is because of this fact that marriages in Igboland are preceded by serious enquiries and investigations. During this inquiry the elders of the community on both sides travel to native villages to find out the social status of the either party. And if it is discovered that one of them is an Osu, the plan of entering into marriage with such a party would be immediately abandoned. Many marriage plans have been terminated, and some married spouses have in essence been forced to divorce because of the Osu factor.

The Osu people go along with this social stigma as those being sacrifised to gods. Some Igbo people who are Christians take part in differentiating the free born and the Osus. They are not favoured to marrying an Osu. In Achebe's "No Longer at Ease", Obi's father, a church Catechist disfavoured the idea of Obi entering into marriage with an Osu. Thus, he says: "Osu is like leprosy in the mind of our people. I beg you, my son, not to bring the mark of shame and leprosy into your family. If you do, your children and your children's children into the third and fourth generations will curse your memory. It is not for myself I speak; my days are few. You will bring sorrow on your head and on the heads of your children. Who will marry your daughters? Whose daughters will your sons marry? Think of that, my son. We are Christians, but we cannot marry our own daughters"[836].

That being the case, there has been several frantic efforts and initiatives to eradicate this harmful tradition and practice. Some communities in Igboland

835 C. Achebe, No Longe rat Ease, London 1960, p65.
836 C. Achebe, No Longe rat Ease, p.121.

where this obnoxious practice is still common should start to envision a new community where people can live peacefully in unity, at the same time marry and be married without discrimination, division, disparity or distinction on the basis of Nwadiala and Osu.

3.8. Chronic Disease

In Igboland there are certain chronic diseases which are generally presumed to be contagious and as such people with such diseases or those who are infected with such dreaded diseases are not allowed to marry other persons who are free from such diseases. Such dreaded diseases or infirmities like HIV/AIDS (oria obere na-aja ocha), madness (ara), leprosy (oria ocha), epilepsy (akwukwu), small-pox (oria oko), and tuberculosis (ukwaranta), are seriously dreaded upon in Igboland. That is the reason why enquiries to marriage are seriously intensified before the proposal as to be certain that both parties are free from these chronic diseases and that such diseases or infirmities are not hereditary in the family lineage of either of them. There is nobody in Igboland who would give out his or her daughter in marriage to a man who has any form of dreaded disease, and no man would seek a hand of a girl in marriage who has any form of chronic disease venereal or mental.

3.9. Conclusion

We have seen that impediment as a circumstance or condition that prohibits a person from marrying is also applicable in Igbo traditional marriage system. In as much as these impediments exist in Igbo customary marriage, there are some of them that are very rare such as consanguinity and affinity, in that a careful inquiry is carried out before any meaningful proposal is made. There are also other possible impediments that act as obstacles to the normal celebration of marriage. These impediments have nothing to do with canon or civil law legislation but they are so powerful in themselves. Such impediments are parental consent, bride wealth, and inter-ethnic marriage, to mention but a few. But one thing that is certain is that such impediments do not render automatically marriage already celebrated as null and void, because of the fact that these impediments are encountered with regard to status, relationship and through the reactions of people to some customs and traditions that guide the people's ways of behaviour.

4. Marriage Preparation in Igbo Tradition

It has to be emphasised that marriage preparation in Igbo tradition is taken seriously because of the high value placed on it. The Igbo people do not enter into marriage without adequate preparation for it. Such a preparation consists of community training and initiations into adulthood which prelude the passage from childhood to adulthood and show that one has grown to having a family of his or her own. During this preparation great attention is paid to parental role, community role, and the processes of initiation into manhood and womanhood.

Traditionally, Igbo marriage preparation consists of remote and proximate preparations and it takes a very long process. What the Igbo people do for such a preparation and how they do it? In other words, what constitutes such a preparation? What training does a boy or a girl who wants to enter into marriage acquire as a preparation for his or her marital life? What should be their behaviour to ensure that they have grown up to take up the challenge of marriage and what is involved in it? These are the things we are going to look at in this very section of marriage preparation in Igbo tradition.

4.1. Parental Role

The role of parents in the marriage of their children is a development of their structure in the household where these children are brought up. In Igboland, parents start to educate their children in matters concerning marriage from their infancy period. The motive of this child education is to inculcate a strong character building in the child. The parents try to aim at the child's behavioural formation while preparing the child for marriage. The child learns to live with others, identify with others and adapt self to the behaviour and yearnings of others[837]. The parents have also the responsibility of teaching their children the community's cultural values, morality and good behavioural traits which manifest themselves in being chaste before marriage and being faithful to the marriage bond, generous, hospitable, kind, just, truthful and rectitude and at the same time trying to avoid stealing, being faithful to a covenant and rejecting falsehood, advocating for the poor and the weak, most especially the women, according honour and respect to older people and at the same time eschewing hypocrisy[838].

During this period of training, parents educate their children on values and

837 Cfr. A.E. Onyeocha, Family Apostolate in Igboland, Rome 1983, pp.140-141; E. Okonkwo, Marriage in the Christian and Igbo Traditional Context, p.21.

838 Cfr. E.B. Idowu, Olodumare: God in Yoruba Belief, Ikeja 1982, pp.157-164.

morality which are pivotal to marriage and the stability in marriage. This is remote preparation. The parents try to teach the male children how to go to the farm for cultivation of the land, looking after cattle, goat and sheep, and going for fishing, taping palm trees for wine, how to conduct oneself before the elderly people and in-laws, how to become a responsible family leader and to learn how to defend the integrity and security of the family that will be entrusted to him finally after he has grown up and married. The girls on the other hand, are taught the code of social and marital behaviour, how to prepare food and keep the compound clean, how to take care of the children, how to behave towards men and how to pay respect to the elders and mothers-in-laws, how to receive and welcome guests and how to respect and look after the husband.

In those days, a girl was meant to learn from her would-be mother- in-law on the manner in which she should behave before her would-be husband and her prospective husband's people. Speaking about her duties, Okonkwo says: "The new wife on the other hand must observe proper decorum and treat her mother-in-law with utmost difference and reverence. This will enhance her love by all the family members. Household management is her first duty. She fulfils this in parley with her husband. She makes a proper annual budget and adjusts the daily expenditures according to it.... She must be openhearted to her husband, respectful to his brothers and sisters, devoted to his mother, affectionate towards his relations, polite to her husband's friends, and hateful to his enemies. She does all these duties and wins the love of all in the family"[839].

But nowadays, the authority of mother-in-laws is no longer what it used to be as in those days. Daughters-in-law no longer rely on their mothers-in-law to assume their positions and do their duties in their various new homes. Igbo women today are independent and enjoy a high level of autonomy in their husbands' homes without mothers-in-law policing them around. Hence, parents in Igboland take active part and role in preparing their children for marriage and family life.

4.2. Community Role

The participation of the community in preparing those wishing to marry in Igbo traditional society cannot be over-emphasised. The community plays a vital role in directing the would-be couple on the necessary things to be done in order to prepare themselves well for their marriage. In this regard, Anameze says: "Marriage as a social institution cannot exist in isolation of the people. Rather it is the people who give it its meaning. Marriage is instituted to satisfy some needs in a

839 E. Okonkwo, Marriage in the Christian and Igbo Traditional Context, pp. 22-23.

manner prescribed by the society. Such needs may be affected by some circumstances to produce forms of marriage. Therefore the study of a people's marriage pattern must take account of their social structure, their marriage system and its forms, as well as its prerequisites…. Igboland is stratified into three main social units: the family, the Umunna unit, and the village. These segments function in such a manner that they foster a harmonious social life and a communitarian spirit. Their influence on marriage is enormous"[840]. The committee of elders in such a community see it as their duty to help prepare adequately and to direct the procedure of marriage of their children because they believe that marriage is for life and once there is no problem arising from any of the marriages of their children it certainly brings progress and prosperity to their community. This alludes to the Igbo saying that "Okenye anaghi ano n'ulo ewu amuo n'obu (an elder does not watch the goat struggle to give birth while still tied to a stake). In other words, an elder does not neglect his duty to make things right. It is this role that the community exhibits in preparing people for marriage.

In those days there were certain things done to make sure that those heading for marriage did not lack. The male counterpart was given farm equipment as to show he was now free to plan for his family and what his would-be household would do to get means of livelihood. In some parts of Igboland, the man was given a gun as a symbol of defending the integrity and security of his family and assuming full responsibility of all that happened in the family. The woman, on the other hand, received cooking utensils as signs and symbols of her future responsibilities to her future husband, children, and her in-laws in the family. Sometimes, marriage lessons were organised by some elderly women in the community on the functions and responsibilities of a married woman for the bride. In this view, Basden comments that "the bride-elect must appear before one or more women, specially appointed, whose function it is to instruct her, and impress upon her the rules governing marriage and the married life of a woman, according to the etiquette of the town"[841].

Hence, the girl leaned on her mother and other elderly kinswomen of the community for learning the code of social and marital behaviour and how to go about her new married life. In the same way, the boy depended on his father and the elders of the community in learning many aspects of adult and married life and how to assume family responsibility. This aspect of preparation is both remote and proximate.

840 L. Anameze, Marriage Among Igbos, Enugu 1996, p.15.
841 G.T. Basden, Among the Ibos, p.75.

4.3. Initiation Rites

No Igbo man who has value for native socio-cultural and religious customs lives and dies without undergoing significant ritual ceremonies in his life. These rituals are celebrated at significant turning points in the life of the individual. The Igbo people recognize that life span of a person has some distant phases whose nature, challenges and responsibilities differ from those of the others. Therefore, each stage requires a maturity or development, a vital force, as it were, for meaningful survivals in it. So the individual would need specific rituals to guide him for the challenges of each phase[842].

The Igbo traditional rites are many and they vary according to different communities and how they go about them. Some of these rites are birth rites, puberty rites, initiation rites, thanksgiving rites, purification rites and funeral rites. Here, we are concentrating on initiation rite/puberty rite as it concerns rite of passage from childhood to adulthood. This rite prepares the young people for marriage and procreation as means for the implementation of the sacred duty of perpetuating and strengthening the life force of the clan[843]. Some of these rites include circumcision or clitoridectomy, wearing cloth ceremony and initiation into age-grade, fattening seclusion and some other rites which are no longer invoke because of civilization and Christianity.

4.3.1. Circumcision/Clitoridectomy

Puberty rite is termed as the rite that ushers one from childhood to adulthood. Among the Igbo people of Nigeria, puberty rite is done by a lot of rites like the male circumcision[844] (ibe-ugwu) and the female clitoridectomy (icho-mma). Cir-

842 Cfr. A. Ngbede – A. Agbaru – F. Asen, "The African Traditional Rites of Passage Vis-à-vis The Christian Rites of Initiation, in NACATHS Journal of African Theology, Vol.12, Enugu 2002, p.55.

843 Cfr. E.I. Metuh, Comparative Studies of African Traditional Religions, Enugu 1999, p.194.

844 Cfr. E. Okonkwo, Marriage in the Christian and Igbo Traditional Context, pp.24-25. In African culture and tradition, circumcision is taken as an important phase and ritual in the life of any new-born child. The Africans believe that sex is something sacred and special, for this simple reason it is hard to find people mentioning it in the open. They also believe that an uncircumcised girl is prone to regular sex orgies and desires. These unnecessary feelings could lead the girl to an unwanted pregnancy, thereby bringing shame to the family. Therefore, the cutting of the clitoris or the over-lapping flesh in the female genital organ reduces or eradicates the child's sexual tendencies, thereby reducing the temptation of indulging in indiscriminate sexual activities. It is also the belief that non-circumcision of a female child hinders and obstructs the safe birth of a child when she gets married. Hence, they see circumcision not as a deformation of the sexual organ of the child but as a precaution to avoid future problems that might harm the

cumcision of a male child is the rounding up and pulling off of the foreskin that extends over the head of the penis in a double layer. The foreskin is cut and pulled off. In this case, there is no other mutilation of the organs. The female clitoridectomy is the cutting of some portions or the removal of the clitoris especially when it is very conspicuous and looks untidy as a means of moderating inordinate sexual indulgence or urge. This ritual takes place in the child's early age normally eight days after the birth of the child.

It has to be recalled that in those days, circumcision is postponed till puberty in order to make it coincide with the puberty rites before the proper marriage ceremony[845]. This is because, in the Igbo traditional society, circumcision among other things ushers a male child into a real adult. It makes him a full man and introduces him into the sexual and marital life. This type of preparation is proximate. Also in those days, because of the significance of circumcision, a lot of rites usually precede it in the Igbo socio-cultural setting. "Boys are usually initiated into some secret societies where they undergo special rites and learn the secrets of the societies. They have to be tested of bravery, which will initiate them into manhood. One of such societies is Mmuo"[846].

In those days also, the removal of the girl's clitoris was done before, during or after the fattening seclusion at puberty which normally takes place when one had finally secured a would-be husband. This was as a result of a common belief that an uncircumcised person is incapacitated of performing a marital sexual act. And if a girl conceived before the rite of clitoridectomy, she would be punished by banishment[847].

Nowadays, the process of circumcising shortly before marriage is no longer obtainable as the rite of circumcision or clitoridectomy is normally performed eight days after the birth of the child on both boys and girls respectively in the maternity homes or hospitals depending on when the umbilical cord falls[848].

4.3.2. Fattening Ceremony (Iru Mgbede)

In those olden days in Igboland, a girl must undergo some ritual ceremonies in preparation for marriage before she finally leaved her home or maternal home.

---

child in future. Circumcision in the case of a male child presents little problem as in the case of a female clitoridectomy. In this case, they do not believe that the cutting of the outer skin on the genital area could prevent sexual activities of the child. It is done only for the decency of the male organ.

845 Cfr. I.A.C. Maduh, Christianizing the Igbo Traditional Love and Morality Rites, p.71.

846 J.O. Awolalu, West African Traditional Religions, Ibadan 1912, p.186.

847 Cfr. I.A.C. Maduh, Christianizing the Igbo Traditional Love and Morality Rites, p.71.

848 Ibid.

One of these rituals is called "Fattening Seclusion" (Iru Mgbede). The name differs from one community to the other. The Mgbidi people call it "Ikwe-ezi", Uli people call it "Igba-orima", while it is called "Ighuahu" by Oguta people. One thing that is obvious is that the importance and meaning of it are similar to these communities and towns. This ritual ceremony is performed for young virgins to prepare them adequately for marriage. It is performed by girls already engaged to be married and those who are not yet being betrothed. The "Iru Mgbede" ceremony usually takes place during a period of confinement which could extend between six months to a year depending on the stipulated period of time for different communities. The girl must be a virgin to qualify for this rite of passage. Many a time, a physical cross-examination is organised to ascertain whether the girl is a virgin or not. Those who go contrary to this qualification are punished severely, sometimes purification rites are organised to atone for the offence committed by defaulters.

During this period of confinement in a fattening hut, she is not allowed to do any work or touch anything. She would be provided with kinswomen who would serve her and instruct her on the lessons of motherhood, her duties and responsibilities in the family, how to love her husband and take care of the family, how to prepare food in the house, how to greet and address people and how to be a good wife. This is also proximate preparation as it is focused exclusively on the betrothed. The work of the maids of honour comprises fattening her, decorating her body with special lotion and ointment. During this period, she is fed with different kinds of food and drinks. She is often entertained with different fascinating stories that keep her busy by the hired kinswomen.

The fattening seclusion is a rite of separation from her former status of girlhood. She is pampered and groomed to become a full woman in order to assume her position in her husband's house[849].

At the end of the seclusion the girl became robust, beautiful and fattened. Many people are invited for the outing ceremony. On this outing day the girl would be dressed in costly attire and with those maids of honour who were with her during the fattening period would parade themselves with dance in the market square to the cheering of the guests and spectators. She would be presented with various kinds of gifts from people while she danced her way through the market square. After this dance, she is now well-qualified to marry and suitors would start coming to seek her hand in marriage if she was not already betrothed. Normally the fattening seclusion is performed on those already betrothed. It has to be noted that the sole aim of this fattening seclusion was to prepare the girl adequately for marriage and what marriage entails.

849 Cfr. E.I. Metuh, Comparative Studies of African Traditional Religious, p.198.

4.3.3. Wearing Cloth Ceremony (Iwa Akwa)

Wearing cloth ceremony is the ceremony into men's age-grade usually performed by boys to show that they have reached the age of adulthood and that they are now ready for marriage. The ceremony takes place every three years and members of one age-group are age-mates of the span of three years. The gap of three years is given in order to allow the boys who would take part in this ceremony to be matured enough as to take full responsibility of adult life after the rite of passage and the ceremony that goes with it. The Iwa Akwa ceremony is common among the Igbo people of Mbano, Obowo, and some parts of Mbaise.

The initiates are usually presented to the community at the beginning of the year marking this puberty ceremony The significance of the presentation is for every member of the village see actually that they have reached the age of manhood and are matured enough to assume the responsibility of a married family man capable of paying levies and contributing to the development of the community. This in the real sense of it is proximate preparation.

The preparation for this rite of passage slightly differs in these communities that participate in it. In this part of Mbaise where it is performed, the ceremony is preceded with cooking of food for the community (Isi Nri Oha) in four different times by those for the initiation. When this is satisfactorily done, it is then accompanied by visitation (Ntughe) to maternal homes of those to be initiated. On this very day of visitation, those to be initiated prepare in their group to visit the maternal home of one of them whose turn it is to visit his maternal home. Food is prepared in the maternal home of that person to serve as a form of welcome to members of his entourage. They usually go to their various maternal homes on foot and with guns which they shoot sporadically as they march along to herald their coming. On reaching there they will dance and then be entertained by the elders of their maternal homes before they will tell them their mission of visiting them. It is normally to tell them that they have reached the age of marrying and to invite them to the ceremony that will really usher them into adult and married life. This ceremony takes place normally in December and January periods as the case may be. After explaining their mission they will dance round the market square of their maternal homes while shooting their guns and Dane guns, and then return back to their various paternal homes.

After the general visitations to different maternal homes a date is now fixed for the wearing cloth ceremony. On the eve of that great day, those to be initiated and their families, relatives, friends and well-wishers keep a dusk to dawn vigil; playing music, dancing, entertaining guests, singing and parading the entire village.

In the morning of the d-day, their predecessors go round the families of each of the candidates to hang the long wrapper meant for the ceremony in front of the candidate's compound. Before they do this, they are presented with some food items and drinks as a sign of welcome, appreciation and gratitude. After hanging of the long wrapper in each of the candidate's compound, the candidates as a group will entertain their predecessors with kola-nuts, food and drinks. At the end of the entertainment, the candidates will choose their age-group name which will be conferred on then by their predecessors.

In the afternoon period, when all the guests and friends must have arrived the candidates will dress up in their uniform with the long wrappers left hanging on their waists and sweeping the ground. They will queue up for the parade-dance in the market square with Dane guns on their hands to show that they are now capable of handling guns. They will dance round the market square with jubilation in the presence of their parents, siblings, relatives, friends, well-wishers and spectators who will be throwing money on them as the case may be. After the parade dance at the market square, they all return to their respective homes to continue merry making and entertaining their guests. After the wearing cloth ceremony, the initiates will now start making plans for marriage.

4.4. Conclusion

This particular section has shown us how the Igbo people prepare traditionally for marriage. The different roles play by parents and the community to see that their children and wards receive adequate preparation for marriage cannot be over exaggerated. The parents take it upon themselves to educate their children on values and morals necessary for marriage and family life. The community on the other hand, teach them also the code of social and marital behaviour and how to handle situations when they arise in the family.

The initiation rites also help prepare young people for the right use of their sexuality, to enter into marriage and raise a family. Wearing cloth ceremony and fattening seclusion have for their objectives the preparation of boys and girls for adulthood, initiation into manhood and womanhood, and the moral preservation of the integrity of the girls and the courageous empowerment of the boys before marriage. Today, because of Christianity and civilization such initiation into adulthood as circumcision or clitoridectomy is regarded as primitive and out of place. The practice of female circumcision is now seen as harmful and unnecessary and therefore, should be stopped. But the wearing cloth ceremony is still practiced today as it ushers in the young people into adulthood and marriage life.

5. Igbo Traditional Marriage Procedures

In the Igbo traditional marriage procedures there are some indispensable elements and requirements that must be put in place properly before a marriage is entered into. These indispensable elements are the essential and formal requirements for the celebration of valid traditional law marriage. Notwithstanding the fact that the details of such requirements vary with people and locality but there is as a matter of fact, a set of basic constituent elements very common to all Igbo traditional law marriages. These essential elements include: consent, choice of a partner, capacity, pre-nuptial inquiries, reciprocal inquiries, betrothal, bride wealth and formal handover of the bride. These essential requirements are what we are going to examine in this section.

5.1. Consent in Igbo Traditional Marriage

One of the essential requirements for a valid traditional Igbo marriage is the consent. The consent of the partners constitutes a marriage. The validity and essence of marriage involve the love and consent of the partners to live together as husband and wife, and in the celebration of marriage in accordance with the accepted rites[850]. Establishing consent for marriage in the Igbo traditional society is arranged in two ways: the consent of the parties themselves and the consent of the parents. The consent of the parties is generally required before the celebration of any marriage in Igboland. The major custom in Igbo traditional society, "is one in which the marriage candidates themselves make the choice of a partner and then inform their parents and relatives who now start making betrothal and marriage negotiations or arrangements"[851]. So the choice of choosing a partner rests in the hands of the candidates themselves, but it still goes to the parents for onward approval. Mbiti explains further: "Even when the choice of marriage is left to the individual concerned the practical working out of their decision is the concern of their social units.... The parents of the boy or girl can still veto the decision, or may not cooperate in the procedures required for the marriage to materialise. This is an ideal custom as far as the two individuals are concerned, since the choice is initially their own. But, in the traditional context this choice is limited by social factors which make marriage subject to the feelings, customs and judgements of the social group from which the individuals come"[852].

850 Cfr. B.N. Oparaugo, Igbo Traditional Marriage Rite and the Roman "Ordo Celebrandi Matrimonium" of 1999, Roma 1994, p.70.

851 J.S. Mbiti, Love and Marriage in Africa, London 1973, p.52.

852 Ibid.

The choice of choosing a partner could also be made by both the young man seeking for a partner and his parents. This is made manifest when the young man sees a girl that attracts his interest and then informs his parents about this girl, and the parents will now begin to negotiate with the parents of the girl. The parents could also spot a good behaved girl of another family and then inform their son about this girl, if he is interested in seeing the girl. Sometimes the success of this search depends so much on the understanding between the parents and their son who is searching for a partner in life, and also if the young man is willing to accept the assistance and pieces of advice of his parents[853].

All said and done, the consent of parents in the Igbo traditional marriage is very important in that their consent is an absolute condition in solemnizing the Igbo customary marriage. By parents here, we mean the father and the mother, the guardian who act in "loco parentis" to the prospective couple[854]. Although the partners are the one who are going to live together as husband and wife, still the family members and their extended counterparts view and regard themselves as having such a high stake in the marriage of their son or daughter, that their consent for such a marriage is still regarded as fundamental[855].

Since nobody in Igboland lives for himself alone and everybody depends on another person for success and survival, the young man who wants to marry will not ignore the suggestions of his parents, family members and the "umunna" regarding marriage. The Igbo traditional marriage is not an individual affair but an alliance between two families or kindred. "It is not uncommon that whenever parents do not sanction the marriage of their sons and daughters, the prospective in-laws normally withdraw"[856].

The Igbo traditional society is made up of the living and the living dead and to bring a girl into the family as a wife, the approval of the parents and family elders of the would-be bridegroom must be sought. This led credence to the significance of the consent of the parents and that of the extended family members. Uchendu confirms this when he writes: "The consent to marriage has been built into an elaborate ritual and is conducted through public channels. The middleman and other relatives of the prospective spouses exert their pressure. The diviner's opinion is sought as to the auspiciousness of the marriage.... If both families are satisfied with their inquiries, the courtship begins and ends with the payment of the bride wealth"[857].

Parental consent in Igboland is given either by the parents of the partners or the guardians who act in "loco parentis", especially of the would-be bride. Before

853 Cfr. L. Policarpo, Customary Marriage in Zambia in the Light of Canon Law, Rome 1986, p.45.

854 Cfr. E. Iwuji, Marriage Form in Nigeria, Rome 1983, p.19.

855 Cfr. T.O. Elias, African Indigenous Laws of Worship, Enugu 1975, p.98.

856 I. Nwogugu, Studies in Igbo Political System, Los Angeles 1972, p.43.

857 V.C. Uchendu, The Igbo Southeast Nigeria, New York 1965, p.52.

this consent is given, there must be widespread consultations of the elders of both families and kindred for their approval and blessing on the prospective couple. Inquiries are also conducted seriously into the family background of both parties. It is only after the consultations and investigations are successfully carried out and both families are satisfied with the outcome that consent is given for marriage to be entered into[858].

In terms of the bride, the procurement of parental consent is very important for the validity of her marriage, notwithstanding the attainment of her maturity and age. This is because, in the absence of parental consent, there will be no one to receive the bride wealth, and there will be no official transfer of the bride to the bridegroom. The marriage as such will be declared void traditionally. Any children born to a woman for whom no consent is given by the parents or no bride wealth is received; belong to the family of the woman's parents and not to that of the begetter traditionally, even if she is still living with the man as if they are married[859].

Whereas in those olden days no marriage could take place without parental approval and involvement but nowadays young people are now free to marry any girl or boy of their choice. They take decisions of their own as regards who to marry. The parents nowadays respect the will of their children in choosing a partner. Amevor captures this well when he asserts: "It has to be noted that although families have great responsibilities in the marriage it does not mean that there is going to be constant invasion of the privacy or the interpersonal relationship of the married couple by the members of the two families. The brain behind the family influence in the marriage could be argued from the responsibilities the couple has towards the family. In simple terms, this responsibility means that the man should – and is expected to show interest in the affairs of his wife's family, and the woman in those of her husband's family, to the extent possible. This is because if the couple becomes cocooned in, or consumed with, their own affairs and the affairs of their nuclear family or household they would be branded as selfish"[860]. Also the involvement of parents and extended family members in the marriage of their children helps to checkmate the problems that arise in the marriages of men and women. Whenever there is a problem between the spouses, the two families come together to ascertain what the problem is all about and find ways of solving it so that it will not repeat itself. This without any doubt promotes and enhances the stability of marital union between a man and a woman, and also helps in reducing the number of divorce cases in Igboland.

858 Cfr. J.U. Gangwari, Civil Marriage in Nigeria, p.45.

859 Cfr. M.O.C. Kalu, Evaluation of the Canonical Form of Marriage in Canon 1108 in the Light of Igbo Traditional Marriage, Port Harcourt 1993, p.23.

860 P.K. Amevor, New Approaches to Marriage Preparation, p.74. The couple could, by their egoistic conduct, not only invite the moral and social disdain of their families, but also cause a denial of the goodwill and needed assistance that could have come to them from their families.

It has to be said also that when the prospective couple does not agree with the input of the parents and that of the relatives with regard to who to marry, they are often given free hand to go ahead with their plan. Many a time the disposition is that of allowing time to take its course to prove right the wisdom of the parents and that of the extended family members as why they are refusing to endorse such a union. They always express their caution to such a disobedient young man with such wise sayings as: "Onye nwere nti ya nuru" (he who has ears let him hear), "Mgbe nkita na – anwu o naghi anu ushi nsi" (a dog does not hear the smell of faeces when it is dying), "Onye mara asu ya suo na ikwe, onye na-amaghi asu ya suo n' ala (he pounds in a mortar who pounds well, but he pounds on the ground who pounds not well). Once such sayings have been said by them, the young man or the young woman is left to follow his or her wish and desire and then face the consequences alone once they arise.

Thus, the parental and extended family approval is imperative in Igbo traditional marriage because on it lays the success or the failure of many marriages in Igboland. Besides, these parental and extended family's consent and approval would have been stopped for certain if the level of failure of such marriages in Igboland was greater than the level of success recorded[861].

5.2. Choice of a Partner

Marriage in Igboland involves not only interpersonal relations as we have earlier seen but also intercommunity relations in that the communities taking part in this very marriage share their existence. The union of marriage in Igboland is generally designed to widen family relations in a culture that is at home with human fraternity and extensive numerical strength of the family. Hence, the Igbo adage "Otu onye adighi alu nwanyi" (one person does not marry a wife) expresses the involvement of the whole community in the choice of a partner and in the process of entering a valid marriage. The Igbo people strongly believe that "gidigidi bu ugwu eze" (great human solidarity graces a king).

Based on this understanding, the choice of a partner is not left to the two parties involved but it is the whole responsibility of the entire community. This is not only limited to the Igbo people alone but it cuts across the African society and even the Western society. Little wonder then Spitzer contends that: "Free selection of mates has become the norm in western society. In part, this is a result of the acceptance of the idea of romantic love. Otherwise, in no area are the cultural norms regulating marriage more specific than with respect to mate selection. No

861 Cfr. J.S. Mbiti, Love and Marriage in Africa, p.50.

society leaves this to chance, all lay down definite rules to govern choice. The groups from which mates can be selected are indicated, and there are prohibitions against consideration of those outside the preferred group"[862]. So marriage in Igboland is priced as a unique opportunity of expanding the human resources of the family relations.

The search for an ideal partner begins when a young man sees a girl of his choice, he intimates his parents who in turn inform other members of their family and extended family about this girl. As we said earlier on when we were discussing about consent in Igboland the opinion of the parents and that of the extended family members matters a lot and must be sought because their approval initiates the procedures to be taken. Confirming this Ogbalu says: "The choice of a wife is not just the concern of the man; it is that of the whole family whose approval must be obtained. A person who sees a girl he desires to marry must inform all relatives, grand parents, uncles, nephews, cousins and nieces distant and near for their 'inspiration' (ka ha le'leere ya nwanyi). Their individual and collective opinion matters a great deal. The umunna of both parties should also endorse the proposal and participate as a right and duty in a number of complicated ceremonies associated with the institution"[863]. When approval is made, the young man will go further to seek the hand of the girl in marriage. But if on the contrary no approval is made, he will not continue with the quest to marry the girl. But once they all agree, they will go to make their intention known to the other members of the extended family before embarking on the enquiry stage.

Another method of searching for a partner is through the recommendation of "Onye aka ebe" (the middle man). His function is to find a suitable girl with good character and when he finds her he recommends it to the young man who is searching for a marriage partner. Normally, the "Onye aka ebe" is one who knows the families of both the young man and the girl very well. He is to investigate all about the girl and report to the young man's family. He equally intimates the girl's family everything he knows about the young man and his family. Once families are satisfied about the outcome of his investigations, the process begins. It behoves on the "Onye aka ebe" to witness all the things that are involved during these procedures leading to marriage. He oversees the monetary and ritual activities of the bride wealth payment and the marriage celebration proper. The middle man "generally serves as liaison between the parties, and even when the marriage had taken place, he settles or assists in settling disputes between the wife and the husband or their parents and relatives. He takes record of the expenses incurred (except entertainment items like food and drinks) on the wife so that in the event

862 A. Spitzer, "Marriage": New Catholic Encyclopaedia Vol.IX, 1967, p.259.
863 F.C. Ogbalu, Igbo Institutions and Customs, Onitsha, p.13.

of the dissolution of the marriage they could be refunded to the husband"[864]. It is pertinent to know that the hand over of the bride wealth is made through the middle man, because it is also through him that the bride wealth will be recovered if there is problem along the line[865].

5.3. Pre-nuptial Inquiries

The pre-nuptial inquiries begin after the young man must have seen an ideal partner of his choice, his parents and other members of the family will now make initial inquiries about the background of the girl – whether the girl is from a decent and peaceful family, whether there is any traceable dreaded diseases like tuberculosis, leprosy, HIV/Aids, epilepsy or an infirmity like madness in her lineage or not. They will also inquire whether her family has cases of mysterious or premature death. Inquiry is also made on the family about bad conduct like theft, fighting and lying, immoral acts, for instance if the father or the mother is known to have been involved in any sexual scandals, if the family is the type that gossips or cast aspersions on other people, a family with high cases of broken marriages.

In addition to these, special inquiry will also be conducted as regards the character of the girl, the way she comports herself, the way she relates to people, if she has a cordial relationship with her parents, siblings and relatives, the way she respects her elders, her ability to work hard, whether she is intelligent and has a good reputation in her village and community. In analysing what this pre-nuptial inquiry is all about, Ogbalu remarks: "Initial inquiry by the man's parents or relatives about the girl, her moral character, ability to work hard, intelligence, good behaviour and home-making ability, her lineage whether her forebears had hereditary diseases such as leprosy, insanity; or bad conduct like theft, lying, fighting, etc"[866].

It is important to say that this initial inquiry is taken seriously and it is conducted secretly without the family of the girl's knowledge. The issue of blood relationship and Osu Caste system is not taken for granted in that if it is found out that such things exist and they will cause obstacle to the normal marriage celebration, the procedures leading to the marriage proper will be stopped from taking place. But if the investigation is satisfactory and nothing poses an obstacle on the side of the girl, then a formal intention is made to the parents of the girl and her family members, who will in turn conduct a similar inquiry concerning the young man and his family.

864 Ibid; p.14.
865 Cfr. E. Okonkwo, Marriage in the Christian and Igbo Traditional Context, p.37.
866 F.C. Ogbalu, Igbo Institutions and Customs, p.14.

5.4. Reciprocal Inquiry

In line with the declaration by the young man's people concerning their intention to seek the hand of the girl in marriage after the successful initial inquiry about the girl in question, some words are now sent across to the parents of the girl who will now inform the members of their clan about the intention of the groom's people. They would request to be given some period of time to assimilate the intention of the bride groom's people to seek the hand of their daughter in marriage.

During this period of assimilation it will be their turn to make reciprocal inquiries about the young man and his family background, whether the young man is responsible and will be able to cater for and take care of their daughter or not, his ability to maintain and control the family especially when things go wrong and whether his family is free from those impediments mentioned earlier on so as to enter into marriage freely with the girl.

In explaining this reciprocal inquiry Nwakonobi opines: "That explains why when the news of the girl's proposed marriage is announced, a massive pre-nuptial inquiry, parallel to the church's legislation in canons 1066-1067 also goes into operation with regard to the character and suitability of the groom-to-be, impediments of consanguinity, whether there was ever any abomination committed in the groom's family which may adversely affect procreation in the prospective family, whether the man's family has a good reputation in the town, whether there have been any historical instances of premature or mysterious deaths in the family…."[867]. When all the investigations are successfully carried out and the bride's people are satisfied with what they have seen and heard on the part of the groom and his family background, they will now arrange for a date of the groom's people visitation to them and send them words in preparation for the visit.

5.5. Visit to the Bride's Family

With their satisfaction on the inquiries made and the discovery that there is no obstacle or impediment that will prevent them from entering into marriage, the bride groom together with his parents, some relatives and the middle man will now embark on their introductory visit (Iju ese nwanyi, Ihe ajuju). This visit to the bride's family is done in two stages before the final celebration of marriage according to locality. The first visit is accompanied with a big jar of palm wine and kola nuts. It is marked with a formal introduction and discussion about the marriage and it provides an opportunity for the girl to make her prelimi-

867 B.K. Nwakonobi, Igbo System of Kinship and Family, pp.79-80.

nary consent on the proposed marriage. It is this preliminary consent that will determine whether the proposed marriage negotiations are to continue or be discontinued.

On arrival at the house of the parents of the girl, the young man and his family entourage will be offered sit and presented with kola nuts as a sign of welcome which will be followed with the traditional method of breaking kola nuts in Igboland. When this is done, the parents of the young man proposing to marry the girl will present the jar of palm wine and the kola nuts and then declare their intention. During this period of declaration the girl will not be present. Normally in some communities in Igboland the girl stays at the backyard with her siblings and other relatives. The girl only comes in after the declaration of intention to seek her hand in marriage by the young man and his family and before the sharing of palm wine brought by the would-be in-laws.

On her emergence in the sitting room her father will ask her some relevant questions concerning the young man seeking her hand in marriage, whether she is aware of his mission. If she answers positively then her father will give her a cup of palm wine from the palm wine brought by the would-be in-laws to drink. If she refuses to drink or sips the wine and hand over the cup of wine to her father, then it is a pure sign that she is not a party to the marriage negotiations and therefore, the negotiations should no longer continue because it is of no use. But if on the other hand, she accepts the cup of wine from her father kneels down and sips the wine and hands the remaining content of the wine to her prospective husband, it becomes symbol of acceptance for the proposal made to her by the young man and that means that the negotiations should go on. Nwakonobi in analysing the symbolic nature of this acceptance remarks: "For the girl to share the drink with a member of her suitor's party is a sign that she has, meanwhile, tentatively given consent to marry into that group"[868]. So the girl in question has given her preliminary consent without fear, favour or force and this will now usher in the betrothal period.

5.6. Betrothal

The betrothal period in Igboland begins immediately after the approval of the proposal to marry by the two parties and it could last for some months or even years. The reason is for both parties to study and know each other very well, whether they will be able to live peacefully together as husband and wife as marriage is a permanent union and is for life.

868 Ibid; p.78.

There is always a second visit during this period of betrothal where the bride groom's people will pay another visit to the bride's family with jars of palm wine and several other items and gifts as a sign of surveying the future in-laws home. This second visit to the bride's family consists of a brief ceremony to discuss very well the line of action to follow for the successful conduct of the traditional marriage procedures.

At the end of the ceremony the girl will be asked by her father to accompany the groom to be and his relatives to their home to return the containers for the wine used during the ceremony. This will serve as an opportunity for both of them to know each other more. The would-be bride will be there for some days or weeks as the case may be under the close observation of her would-be mother-in-law and other members of her groom to be family as marriage in Igboland is not just an affair between the two parties, but it involves the parents, members of the extended family and villages of each of the parties.

The purpose of this very visit to the groom's home is simple. The girl is sent by her family to survey the new home and acclimatise herself with the environment and also acquaint herself with her future husband's people. The family of the prospective groom will use this period to also observe in detail the behaviour of the girl, her ability to work in the art of home management. She will be tested in different aspects of life whether she is humble, obedient, careful, honest and intelligent. Alluding to this Basden says: "The girl is to become a member of the household and, naturally, the relatives are curious and want to have some assurance that in their judgement, she is up to standard and likely to prove a worthy addition to the clan"[869]. The girl will also observe the attitude of her would-be mother-in-law and other members of the family towards her as to know certainly if the family will be suitable for her and also accommodates her when she finally becomes the wife of their son.

One important thing to know is that during the girl's stay in the house of her prospective husband, she is not expected to pass the night on the same room with her would-be husband since they have not finally married and since the girl can decide after her stay not to marry him again depending on what she discovers during her visit. In this case, she can live with her suitor's mother or sisters till the period elapses.

At the end of her short stay she will go back to her parents' house with a lot of gifts raging from money, cloths, jewelleries, pairs of shoes, food items, etc. Her parents on her return will ask her again what her observations are and whether she is still interested in marrying the young man. If she answers yes and the bride groom's people are also on the affirmative side after their observations, then she is considered as finally betrothed and no suitor outside her prospective husband

869 G.T. Basden, Niger Ibos, p.138.

will be allowed to ask her hand in marriage. From that particular time onwards arrangement will be made for the payment of dowry.

Another pertinent thing during this period of betrothal[870] is, there is often an exchange of visits between the two prospective parties. These visits are often more at certain seasons and occasions most especially during the farming season. Many a time the prospective groom pays visit to his prospective bride's family. He assists his would-be parents-in-law in farming and also in the reconstruction of their buildings if they are not in order. He can as well visits with his age mates to assist in cultivating the land for his prospective parents-in-law. This is also applicable to the girl as she is expected to assist her prospective husband's family in farm work. It is at this period that the behaviour of the girl and her ability to work at the farmland and at home are put to scrutiny and if she is a hardworking girl, she endears herself to the heart of her would-be husband's family.

5.7. Bride wealth Ceremony and Formal Consent

The institution of marriage in Igboland as well as in African societies comprises the exchange of some gifts and goods by the two families their children are proposing to marry. Bride wealth ceremony is one of the last ceremonies that cement marriage in Igbo traditional marriage procedures. It assumes an important function in the distribution of family property and the arrangement of exchanges and alliances among families in Igboland.

Bride wealth is a gift or payment paid by the groom or his family to the parents of a girl upon the marriage of their daughter to the bridegroom. From this definition the following characteristics are discernable: it is a gift or payment, it may be in money, natural produce or any other type of property; it must be paid to the parent or guardian of the bride-to-be; it must be paid on account of a marriage of a female person and it must be paid for a marriage which is intended or has taken

870 Cfr. B.K. Nwakonobi, Igbo System of Kinship and Family, pp.80-81. During the period of betrothal which may last for several months or even years, the suitor is obliged to perform specific services for his prospective bride and her parents, as well as make them gifts occasionally. Such bridal labour services include bringing his age mates, sometimes his matrikins and patrikins, to assist in any considerable tasks that the father-in-law undertakes. Such tasks can be: cultivating the farm, lifting and tying of harvested yams, building or repaying house, et cetera. Such services offer the girl's parents a good opportunity to assess the suitor's capability and potentiality of surviving as a husband, and of sustaining a family. Reciprocally too, the girl is asked to render certain services to the suitor's family as occasions demand, offering the groom's people an opportunity also to closely study the girl. The reason behind the prolonged negotiations and betrothal is to impress upon the young people the notion of gravity, dignity and sacredness of matrimonial union. It is a type of "matrimonial catechumenate".

place[871]. Bride wealth could also mean spousal reciprocity. This is because it involves a man's giving of his wealth or property to the family of a girl he desires to enter into marriage with and the girl in turn reciprocates the gesture by giving herself totally to the man. In other words, it is a token of appreciation on the part of the bridegroom's people to the bride's people for their care over her and for giving also their consent with regard to their son marrying their daughter. It is the most concrete symbol of the marriage covenant and security. In this view, it is not only the groom and his people that give; the bride's people also make gifts in return, even if their own gifts are not to be measured with that of the bridegroom's gifts[872].

Although this very practice is not only inherent in African societies as it is found among many customs of the world with some variations, its meaning and importance in the Igbo content as well as in African view have been misunderstood and hence misinterpreted by some Western authors. More still, there has been some confusion among Igbo and African writers on the best name to express the gifts, payment or property that a groom gives before marrying a wife. Some authors use "bride price", others prefer "bride wealth", while other writers make use of "dowry". But the more proper term is "bride wealth". It is important to note that no actual amount or price is fixed for the bride wealth ceremony as that would imply or give negative impression that women are sold as property in Igboland. This is why Parrinder tries to correct the misinterpretation of bride wealth as a selling and buying of a woman in Western and European circles. He contends that the payment made in African forms of customary marriage has often been misunderstood by Europeans and thus has been regarded as selling the woman. The bridegroom and his family transfer gifts, goods or money to the bride's family, but the words used are quite different from buying and selling of a woman[873].

In Chinua Achebe's "Things Fall Apart", the guests of Obierika are amazed at the customs of some areas (Abame and Aninta) which are "upside down". This is because, "they do not decide bride-price as we do, with sticks. They haggle and bargain as if they were buying a goat or coin in the market"[874]. Nzekwu on his own part observes that: "Bride-price is a misnomer. It is applied to the present the suitor makes to the girl and her parents. It consisted at first, of samples of products from his farm"[875]. Mbiti in denying this allegation of wife-selling by the Europeans opines that on no account is this custom a form of payment as outsiders have often so mistakenly said. African words for the practice of giv-

871 Cfr. E.I. Nwogugu, Family Law in Nigeria, Ibadan 1966, pp.184-185.

872 Cfr. J.S. Mbiti, African Religions and Philosophy, pp.184-185.

873 Cfr. E.G. Parrinder, African Traditional Religion, London 1976, pp.97-98.

874 C. Achebe, Things Fall Apart, p.67.

875 O. Nzekwu, Wand of Noble Wood, Ibadan 1971, p.38.

ing the marriage gift are, in some cases, distinct from words used in buying and selling something in the market place[876]. It is crystal clear that there is no commercial undertone or intention in determining the bride wealth, but it is a system established by our customs with regard to the legality and validity of traditional marriage in Igboland.

The necessity and importance of bride wealth in Igbo traditional marriage system cannot be over-emphasised. It gives status to a woman not because of its material worth but it leads to a new marriage within her own family lineage. Her other siblings are now free to marry and be married and this gives her dignity and respect from her brother-in-laws and sister-in-laws. A woman who joins a man without the payment of bride wealth loses her credibility and prestige among her people and she will be subjected to ridicule anytime quarrels ensued between her and other women in her community or village. She will be made to know that no bride wealth was paid for her hand in marriage[877].

The bride wealth ceremony symbolises the marriage covenant and so seals the sacred relationship. It is the legal instrument which authorizes the spouse to cohabit and give birth to children and which constantly reminds them of the permanence of their union. More so, in the event of irretrievable marital breakdown, the gifts and payment are returned to the bridegroom's family as a sign of failure[878]. Still on bride wealth as a means of legalising the marriage, Ottenberg remarks: "A marriage is legalised by the husband-to-be's payment of the bride-price to the bride-to-be's father or guardian…."[879]. He observes further that the payment of bride wealth makes the groom the legal father of any children born to the wife thereafter, regardless of who the genitor maybe[880]. Uchendu on his part asserts that bride wealth not only legalises marriage but at the same time it transfers certain rights in the bride-to-be from her father or guardian to the bridegroom-to-be and his lineage[881].

In Igboland, the bride wealth affirms the legality of the union of the bridegroom and the bride. The bride wealth paid to the bride's family helps to stabilize that marriage and prevents it from breaking down. "Then the practice has served as a stabilizing factor in marriage by giving at once a reasonable guarantee of good treatment of the wife by her husband and of dutiful regard for the husband by his wife. For the wealth stands as a sign that the husband wanted the wife, and

876 Cfr. J.S. Mbiti, African Religions and Philosophy, p.185.

877 Cfr.E. Okonkwo, Marriage in the Christian and Igbo Traditional Context, p.61.

878 Cfr. J.S. Mbiti, Introduction to African Religion, London 1975, p.101.

879 P. Ottenberg, The Afikpo – Ibo of Eastern Nigeria: "Peoples of Africa", J.L. Gibbs, eds; New York 1960, pp.17-18.

880 Cfr. Ibid; p.20.

881 Cfr. V.C. Uchendu, "Concubinage Among Ngwa Igbo of Southern Nigeria", in Afer 35 (1965), p.189.

that she did not run after him offering herself for nothing or being thrust at the man for nothing by her parents. In any case it is a well known fact verified by long experience that the Igbo people do not value at all anything they have not paid dearly for"[882].

The significance of bride wealth in Igbo traditional marriage is far-reaching. Its payment in kind or in cash solidifies and sanctions marriage in the eyes of both families that their children are marrying. No man gives away his daughter in marriage without the payment of bride wealth. For Mba, the bride wealth stands for "the efficacy, the geniuses and seriousness of the marriage. It also stands for the conjugal relationship (that is, a marital one) between the husband, and the wife, and the legal bond between the two families of the parties; it also demonstrates the legitimacy of filiations, the permanence of marital union and the cordial relationship between the man and the woman and their respective peoples. It shows also the bridegroom's financial ability to maintain a home, and gives the wife a good standing and a good image in the new home, otherwise she may be taken for a paramour or one who has run after the husband"[883].

Hence, bride wealth in Igboland cements and confirms the status of marriage. Once the payment has been concluded, the bride-to-be now feels that she is on a safe hand, she no longer feels as someone being stolen but a person given out in mutual accordance and agreement by the two families involved. It raises her value both as a person and a wife and makes her feel belonged to the women folk[884]. Hasting puts it in this way: "It provides a guarantee of the sincerity of the bridegroom's symbol of friendship to the family of the bride, and some impediment to divorce. It proves to a young bride that her marriage is something of real importance and her presence in her husband's home much valued. To omit it may in the eyes of outsiders be progress but to the girl concerned it may appear as an indication that she is little valued"[885].

The bride wealth ceremony provides the bridegroom the ample opportunity to prove and showcase to his bride's people that their daughter they are giving to him will be adequately taken care of and properly looked after when she finally becomes his wife. It strengthens the capability of the groom improving that he is equal to the task in assuming the responsibility of a family man. It also gives the man the right of ownership to the children born from the marriage. "It guarantees that the husband shall have the custody of any children born; for in the absence of a bride price a woman's children are claimed by her family. And it also guarantees

882 C.S. Mba, The Significance of Dowry or Bride Price in the Igbo Traditional Marriage and its Implications for Christianity in Africa Today, in Lucerna 2 1981, p.15.

883 C.S. Mba, Evolving an Igbo Christian Rite of Marriage, Enugu 1994, pp.12-13.

884 Cfr. E. Okonkwo, Marriage in the Christian and Igbo traditional Context, p.65.

885 A. Hastings, Christian Marriage in Africa, London 1973, pp.108-109.

that the husband shall have the continuous services of a wife for himself and of a mother for his children; and that a wife and her offspring shall be provided with a permanent home, and supported by her husband. It prevents wives from leaving their husband's for some trivial cause"[886].

The system of determining the bride wealth varies from place to place. Generally, traditional law does not fix the amount of bride wealth for marriage. In some cases, there are even some variations within the same locality. This is comprehensible because it is believed in Igboland that all girls are not equally endowed. Many a time, bride wealth is negotiated according to the nobility of the family, academic excellence, physical beauty of the girl and the like. Sometimes the amount of the bride wealth will be the subject of negotiation between the two families. Often it is done with a bundle of small sticks or broomsticks without uttering a word. It can be done by asking the groom's people to pay merely what they consider fit and proper for a daughter-in-law. Sometimes it also reflects the wealth of the groom or his family. This is to make sure of avoiding the impression that there is commercial intention in the determination of the bride wealth or that the girl in question is being sold out like a property.

It is pertinent to say that many Igbo authors have written extensible on bride wealth but none of them has succeeded in fixing a price that is greeted with universal acceptance in Igboland. Although the Limitation of Dowry Law of 1956[887] regulates the amount of bride wealth in the Eastern States of Nigeria, which fixes the amount of value of bride wealth in respect of customary law marriage at sixty naira where no incidental expenses[888] of marriage are paid[889]. The Law continues by saying where there are incidental expenses, the amount of bride wealth must not exceed fifty naira and the incidental expenses itself should not exceed ten naira in amount or value[890]. Since this legislation, any family which receives as bride wealth any amount in excess of the maximum prescribed by the law, has committed an offence. "Any person who asks, receives, or obtains, or agrees or attempts to receive or obtain for himself or any other person any dowry in excess of the maximum prescribed in section 3, … and anyone who gives, or pays or promises or offers to give or pays any person dowry in excess of the maximum prescribed in section 3, shall be guilty of an offence, … or term of imprisonment of six months"[891]. That having been said, this particular law enacted since 1956

886 C.K. Meek, Law and Authority in a Nigerian Tribe, London 1937, p.267.

887 Cfr. Cap.16, Laws of Eastern Nigeria, 1963.

888 Incidental expenses are customary gifts or payments other than the dowry, made or incurred, on account of a marriage before, at the time of, or after marriage. Cfr. Cap.16, Laws of Eastern Nigeria, section 2.

889 Cfr. Ibid; section 3a.

890 Cfr. Ibid; section 3b.

891 Ibid; section 4a, b, and c.

has no "Bride Wealth Control Board" and thus is open to all sorts of abuses. The Igbo people consider these laws as not binding and therefore, have no effect. They still transact their bride wealth as a negotiation between the two families.

Normally, the right person to receive the bride wealth is the father of the girl to be married. But the right goes to the head of his immediate family if he is no longer alive. But in the absence of both the father of the girl and the head of his immediate family, the beneficiary becomes the guardian or the person in "loco parentis" to the girl's family[892].

The actual ceremony for the negotiation and acceptance of the bride wealth by the bride-to-be people from the groom's people and also the declaration of the formal consent of the bride to marry the young man seeking her hand in marriage is very unique. Before the ceremony takes place, the bridegroom through the "Onye aka ebe" (the middle man) collects from his bride-to-be family the requirements for the ceremony. It consists usually of jars of palm wine, hot drinks and other drinks, tubers of yam in large numbers, tobacco heads and tins of snuff, packets of cigarettes, the things to be given to the prospective mother-in-law and the sisters of the bride and other valuable items, et cetera. When all these things are gathered, the groom will sent words to the family of the bride through the middle man concerning the date for the ceremony, which will be agreed to by the two families and which will be convenient for them, their kinsmen and women, and the guests.

On that very date normally in the afternoon period or evening period as the case may be, the groom-to-be with his people will be warmly received by the bride-to-be people on their arrival and then offered seats. It follows by exchange of greetings and pleasantries and other issues not bothering on the main issue of the day. The next thing is the presentation of kola nuts to the would-be-in-laws as a symbol of welcome.

Afterwards, the head of the groom's family calls for the attention of all and sundry, using proverbs and metaphors he expresses their mission and thanks and praises the bride's family for accepting and considering them worthy to be their in-laws and for the precious gift of their daughter in whose name they come together for the bride wealth ceremony. After this short preamble by the head of the family of the groom, the formal presentation of the items enumerated above will begin. During this presentation any item found to be missing or that is incomplete is made good in cash by the groom's people through their leader.

Before the actual bride wealth is negotiated and paid, the father of the girl calls the attention of his daughter to ascertain from her before the public her opinion. Her consent as a matter of fact should once more be sought and obtained as marital consent among the Igbo people nowadays is no longer supplied by the parents

892 Cfr. J.U. Gangwari, Civil Marriage in Nigeria, p.56.

or relatives of the girl or any other person other than the girl herself. On her arrival her father will posit some certain questions on her. He will inquire from her whether she is aware of the visitors' mission in their house. If her answer is on the affirmative, her father will continue by asking her whether she knows the suitor looking for her hand in marriage. If the reply is favourable her father will ask her if she wants them to ahead and collect the items they presented, which she will also affirms. Then the ceremony will now continue.

The formal consent starts with the father of the girl pouring some wine into a cup, pouring libation on the wine and blessing his daughter and his prospective son-in-law and then giving the cup of wine to his daughter. The daughter will sip the wine and then gives the cup of wine to her prospective husband who will in turn finish the remaining part of the wine in the cup.

The negotiation over the bride wealth is the second to the last ceremony that seals the marriage. Normally, the bride wealth is settled by the elders of both kindred. The negotiation is done with sticks or other countable materials. Each stick represents the value of money in accordance with the people's custom in their locality. The elders of the bride's family will count on a number of sticks and give them to the elders of the bridegroom's kindred. The groom's kinsmen will remove some sticks on their own part and hand them over again to the bride's kinsmen. The bride's people will continue to add while the bridegroom's people will equally continue to subtract until they reach at a compromise. This in actual fact is done to fulfil the customs and traditions of the people as bride wealth is never paid in full as the girl in question is not being sold or bought like a property. Nwakonobi confirms this when he writes: "At least a very small amount is owed in order to show that the girl is not being sold and no full price can actually be paid on her head. The girl's father continues to have right of fatherhood over her till death. In other words, marriage is not a pay-cash-and-collect business. No matter the bride wealth the parents receive on their daughter, they never sever their parental relationship with her. By marriage the girl is not torn apart or jettisoned from her maternal home, because she is still part of it; she remains her parents' daughter, her children become her parents' grand children, and her husband her parents' son-in-law"[893]. This lays credence to the common Igbo adage which says, "anaghi azucha ahia nwanyi azucha" (the bride wealth can never be completely paid).

Finally, having arrived at a consensus in accordance with the custom, the bride wealth is then handed over to the father of the girl or if the father is dead, to the head of the family or the guardian of the girl privately. After this payment, the people from both families and kindred refer to themselves from henceforth as

---

893 B.K. Nwakonobi, Igbo System of Kinship and Family, p.83; B.K. Nwakonobi, Consent in Igbo Christian Marriage, Port Harcourt 1989, p.36.

"Ogo" (in-laws) according to the tradition and custom of the land. It will be followed with merrymakings, entertainment, jubilations and dance, and with this, the ceremony comes to an end.

5.8. Formal Handover of the Bride (Igba Nkwu Nwanyi)

"Igba Nkwu Nwanyi", the formal handover of the bride by her people to the bridegroom or traditional wedding is the last ceremony that seals marriage in Igbo traditional marriage and it marks the consummation of the long-drawn-out traditional marriage negotiations and procedures. It serves as the last essential and formal requirement for a valid Igbo traditional marriage. It is formalised in the "knotting of the marital tie" before the witnesses who are present, and the escorting of the bride to the home of the bridegroom where she takes her position in the bridegroom's family with the assumption of her marital rights and duties and the enjoyment of the social, economic and political life of the bridegroom's family group[894]. Its importance and significance cannot be overemphasised as the marriage itself is not contracted until the formal handover of the bride take place. Speaking on the legality of this ceremony and the payment of dowry to the bride's family, Ugorji asserts: "The Igba Nkwu ceremony and the payment of dowry serve as a legal instruments which authorises a man and a woman to live together as husband and wife and bear children. They are symbols of the marriage bond between a man and his wife. They are also a demonstration of how much a man cherishes and appreciates the care lavished on his spouse by her parents in her upbringing and training. The Igba Nkwu ceremony and the payment of dowry add to the dignity of a wife as a marriage partner. When these are successfully completed, they are seen as a guarantee that a man can cater for his wife"[895].

Normally the handover of the bride to the bridegroom is accompanied by much festivity. It is an important day keenly looked forward to by the families, relatives and friends of the spouse to be because of its uniqueness. The celebration itself takes place in the family compound of the girl and it is normally done in the afternoon period. Before the date of the ceremony the bride and the bridegroom would have made for themselves a special uniform for the ceremony. There are also different displays of traditional outfits by the bride and her friends, her mother and kinswomen as well as the bridegroom and his family. The whole compound is adorned with colourful objects. Many a time the bride and the bridegroom decide

894 Cfr. C.S. Mba, "Trial Marriage in Nigeria, A Fact or Fiction: A Customary Law Appraisal", pp.299-319, in M.O.C. Kalu, Evaluation of the Canonical Form of Marriage in Canon 1108, p.30.

895 L.I. Ugorji, The Service of the Word, On the Practice of Faith, Enugu 2000, p.99.

on a colour trend for their occasion and guests are expected sometimes to dress in outfits of the same colour pattern as chosen by the would-be couple.

It is pertinent to point out here that invitation cards are printed and shared to those whom the two families would want to invite for the occasion. But it is not always the case that invitation cards will be shared for the occasion, it only depends on the pocket of the would-be couple, if they are well-to do enough then they can embark on it, but if they are not, they will only send words across to those they want to grace their traditional marriage ceremony. Worthy of note here is that everybody is allowed to grace the occasion both those invited and those not invited and this marks out the sense of hospitality of the Igbo people in particular and the African society as a whole. Both families make adequate and proper preparations for this occasion as it is done once in a life's time.

On that very day, when everything must have been arranged and organised, the bridegroom sets out to the bride's family with a large entourage comprising his family members, kindred people, friends and well-wishers. They are welcomed into the family compound of the bride by the bride's family and kindred. They are expected to come along with jars of palm wine, cartons of beer, malt, soft drinks and juice. They also come with wrappers and blouses, jewelleries (gold plated earrings, necklaces), head ties and shoes of different kinds and colours, hand bags and wrist watches, tobacco heads, cigarettes, brandy, schnapps, toiletries, body creams, bathing soaps, washing detergents, food items and other things. Also on this very day, assorted drinks and dishes of food are provided by the bride's family to the bridegroom's people and other guests as a sort of entertainment and refreshments and to tell them that they are happy of their visit and the mission that brought them to their family.

The ceremony is officially declared open with a prayer normally said by the head of the family. The opening prayer is then followed by the traditional presentation of Kola nuts by the father of the bride. "The prayer focuses on life and prosperity and so takes into consideration the man who has now become a husband, the woman who also has become a wife, and the families to which they belong, giving accent to desired fertility of the marriage union. In the event of the girl's "pater familias" being the eldest surviving man in the lineage, he represents the family ancestors, says those prayers, and has the privilege of handing the girl over to the lad's family, normally through a middle man"[896].

It is during this ceremony that the parents of the girl will perform their traditional function of "Idu Ulo" (family property so as to equip the girl in her new home), that is, giving the girl all the essential things she needs to establish herself in her new home. These things will make her to adjust herself and start a new life in her husband's house. The provision of these necessary things normally

896 B.K. Nwakonobi, Igbo System of Kinship and Family, p.85.

household furnishings by the bride's family puts a negation to the misguided and misinformed reasoning by the Westerners that the girl is sold at marriage to her groom like a commodity. This is what is referred to as bridal reciprocity in the Igbo traditional marriage system. Although not all parents can perform this "Idu Ulo" ceremony, most especially the poor ones among them, but still there are certain basic functions that behove on the parents to do to their daughter who is being married to assist her in her new married life, no matter how small.

During this ceremony the bride is called upon by her father or somebody who is acting on his behalf, if the father is no longer alive, and giving a cup of palm wine to sip and offer it to her prospective husband. She then walks around the crowd with dance accompanied by the maids of honour in their traditional uniform attire in search of her intended husband hidden in the midst of the guests. When she finally finds him she will hand him the wine to finish the remaining content of the wine and then they both dance to the admiration of all and sundry towards the direction of the elders and the father of the bride for their blessings. On reaching where the elders of the bride's kindred are they will be bless sometimes with these words by the elders: "May all be well with you; be fruitful and bear us as many children as possible; may evil not come your way and may good come, and may you live long to enjoy your children"[897]. After this blessing from the elders as the case may be, since the elders blessing is not all that common to all Igbo communities, they will knee before the father of the bride for his own blessing on them which sometimes goes this way: "My daughter, this is your husband, go with him and be obedient to him. You shall conceive and bear many children both males and females; live in peace with your husband; do not overlook your brothers or relatives and do not forget your parents. Obey and respect your husband's family members"[898]. The father of the bride now turns to the bridegroom and says: "My son-in-law, here is our daughter. We give her to you, as your wife. She shall bear for you many children. That is our desire. Let no sickness or hunger touch her. Be aware that a wife is very precious. Patience is needed in married life, because a woman is like a flower that must be tenderly looked after. Remember that your bride's family is now your family; and reciprocal assistance is the ideal. A hen never forgets the person who removed her feathers in raining season. In nine months time we hope to be together again just like today to welcome your first child"[899]. Although there are variations in the pattern of prayers and admonitions by the father of the bride according to locality and cultures, the prayers are indispensable in the formal handover of the bride to the bridegroom in Igbo traditional marriage system.

897 E. Iwuji, Customary Law Marriage in Nigeria, p.61.

898 Ibid; p.62.

899 Ibid.

Worthy of note also is that during the dancing period, the mothers of the bride and bridegroom dance to the tune of the traditional music and to the admiration of all guests. It is also customary to the Igbo culture that when the bride and bridegroom dance, the people present will spray money on them to show appreciation and love. The two mothers obtain their own share of the money spray from their respective husbands if they are still alive, their family members, future in-laws and other guests present.

After the blessings from the father of the bride the bride is publicly handed over to the bridegroom's family by her own family to the joyful applause of those present and they are declared as husband and wife traditionally and the traditional marriage is solemnised. The hand over of the bride to the bridegroom by the father of the girl or guardian is always an emotional period for the bride, her parents, siblings and relatives, who may not control the tears flowing out from their eyes as they remember all the years they have been together with her in their family.

When the whole ceremony is over the bride is accompanied to the bridegroom's home which is now her new home by her mother and other kinswomen along with the girls and boys of the bride's extended family and kindred. Okorobia confirms this when he writes: "At the end of the ceremony, the bride is accompanied by her mother, many girls of her own age grade, and some women from her village, to her new home. The women carry the items which were given to her by her parents and relatives.... In the bridegroom's home there is singing and dancing. At the end, her mother and all the protecting company from her village set out for home again leaving her behind, fully handed over as a married girl"[900]. So the women and the girls carrying the bride's items sing as they march along to the bride's new home. This is done to attract the attention of the passers-by to the items they are carrying and to prove to them that the bride is not sold out to her husband but handed over to him with these household furnishings as a sort of reciprocity of paying her bride wealth by the bridegroom.

On arrival at the bridegroom's house, she is welcomed by the groom's family and giving some words of advice and encouragement with regard to her acclimatising herself to the new home and to the operations and etiquettes of the family. The kinswomen and the girls that escorted her to her husband's home are then entertained before their return to their village. Normally the celebration continues for some days in the bridegroom's house as many people especially those who did not grace or attend the traditional marriage ceremony because of one thing or the other continue to troop to the house to congratulate them on their marriage. It is always a thing of pride for a girl to be married this way, and at times the ceremony could be more elaborate than the white wedding itself because of its traditional

900 G. Okorobia, Igbo Marriage and Family Life, Pamplona 1990, p.475.

imports. After this the couple will now start preparing for the solemnization of their white wedding in the church. It could be within a short period of time or longer period of time depending on the financial capacity of the couple at that point in time.

5.9. Conclusion

The discussion so far is based on the stages in the Igbo traditional marriage procedures. They are the essential and formal requirements for the celebration of valid traditional law marriage. These elements are indispensable in the sense that without them no marriage is guaranteed traditionally.

For valid marriage consent, it is imperative that the contracting parties know and understand themselves very well. While it cannot be denied that young people now choose on whom to marry without their parents consent, yet the importance of parental consent cannot be undermined. We do not insist that parents and members of the extended family choose a partner for their son or daughter as it were the case in the past, but we strongly believe that parental approval is still vital for a successful marriage in the Igbo society. Such approval with genuine intention helps in guaranteeing support in times of adversity[901].

6. AECAWA Overview on Marriage Preparation in West Africa

In this particular section we are going to look at the document which the Association of Episcopal Conferences of Anglophone West Africa (AECAWA) has introduced into the topic of marriage preparation in West Africa. In their 1984 Plenary Meeting held in Freetown, Sierra Leone, the Catholic Bishops of Liberia, Sierra Leone and Gambia offered some recommendations and conclusions about marriage preparation in West Africa under the topic entitled: "The Pastoral Care of Marriage and Family Life"[902]. The bishops contend that this document would go a long way in fulfilling the demands of the Catholic Church as regards the canonical and pastoral activities of marriage preparation and be of immense benefit to those concerns with marriage ministry. The document when used properly would

901 Cfr. B.A. Okodua, Coping with Irregular Marriages in the Light of the Magisterium: A Pastoral Suggestion for Yorubaland – Nigeria, Rome 1985, p.43.

902 Cfr. AECAWA, "The Pastoral Care of Marriage and Family Life", Ghana 1986, pp.1-56.

also help the entire Catholic faithful for the enrichment of the Christian life in different dioceses in West Africa by living a wholesome life of the conjugal bond and the enhancement of a more vital family life[903]. We shall now briefly look at some of the themes they discussed in this very document.

6.1. Reasons for the Policy Regarding Pastoral Preparation for Marriage

The bishops acknowledge that the most pressing needs of the church in West Africa as well as other parts of the world is preparing the Christian faithful more adequately for marriage. Marriage and family life as such should be particularly involved in this maternal concern and solicitude because of the sacredness of the vocation by which husband and wife not only meet each other but in doing so they meet Christ and their union of intimacy in all its ramifications brings out the loving covenant that exists between Christ and his bride the church[904]. In order to protect and safeguard the sacred character of marriage and foster the rich traditions of family living in West Africa they insist on the proper and adequate pastoral preparation of spouses for the sacrament of matrimony and the sacrament of their willingness and readiness to carry out their responsibilities in their married and family life[905].

AECAWA maintains that Christian marriage forms the foundation of the family which itself is considered as the basis of all well-ordered society and as such the family has an important task and mission in the church, since it rests on her the duty of imparting first hand education to the children, shaping their personalities and consciences and at the same time inculcating life values to them. The Christian family is the centre of the church community and the guarantee of its future purposes. It nurses and fosters vocations, marriage and parenthood. When marriage and Christian families are strengthened the cultures of our people and the nation in its entirety are greatly enriched[906].

The institution of marriage involves the interpersonal relationship between two individuals. "Sacramental marriage involves a deep, abiding commitment of two people to each other. In God's plan, marriage always has strong erotic and emotional overtones; but also by His will, marriage is fundamentally a matter of the human intention, the act of will of two people to live together and bring up a new family; to support, sustain and cherish each other; and indeed to help sanc-

903 Cfr. AECAWA, "The Pastoral Care of Marriage", p.vii.
904 Cfr. Ibid; p.1.
905 Cfr. Ibid.
906 Cfr. Ibid; p.2.

tify each other and their children for the rest of their lives on earth. Our vision of marriage therefore implies serious values and principles to be lived out day by day. It is a sacred and beautiful personal vocation for the men and the women; and it is a sacrament not only for the couple but even for the whole church community as it helps to build up the Body of Christ"[907].

The bishops unfold the meaning of the sacrament of matrimony by describing marriage as a mutual bond of human warmth, intimacy and love, which strengthens the eternal alliance between Christ and his bride, the church. It needs a sense of honesty and maturity that is enough to ensure the spouses' growth in the grace of God and assist them to rear their children in a befitting manner. Marriage involves the value of permanence, a proper common life of mutual respect, equally and dignity, an exclusive personal and sexual fidelity of the parties to each other, and an openness to fecundity and education of children. Therefore, spouses entering marriage should endeavour to be free from impediments of either divine or ecclesiastical law, which might be an obstacle to their union. Furthermore, the spouses should show a genuine intention of supporting each other as helpmates. They parties should also have the physical and psychological capacity to live out their reciprocal commitment and to accept in good faith the responsibilities which their marriage stipulates for themselves and their children[908].

In a bid to describe the reasons that led to their policy regarding pastoral preparation for marriage the bishops argue that in West Africa countries as in other parts of the world, there is a high rate of marital failure not only in mixed marriages but also in marriages concerning two catholic spouses. In addiction to this, there is the pastoral anguish of a low rate of people marrying, in the sense that many baptised Catholics are unwilling to contract church marriage in their adulthood. Many are reluctant to entrust themselves to a relationship that is only restrictive, binding and permanent[909]. This led credence to SECAM's[910]

907 Ibid; pp.2-3.

908 AECAWA, "The Pastoral Care of Marriage", pp.3-4.

909 Cfr. Ibid; p.4.

910 SECAM is the Symposium of Episcopal Conferences of Africa and Madagascar. Their views about the problems and challenges facing marriage in Africa were made known during their sixth Plenary Assembly held in Yaounde', Cameroon from 29th June – 5th July 1981, which has as its theme: "Christian Family Life and Marriage in Africa Today", and also another Plenary Assembly held in Midrand, South Africa, from 22nd to 28th September 1997, which also has as its theme, "The Church as Family of God". The conference highlighted some pastoral guidelines and concrete points of action like the preparation for marriage and the celebration of marriage in such a way that African Christians can live their conjugal life and family relationships as a sacramental epiphany of the alliance between Christ and the church, thereby transfiguring these fundamental human realities from within. For more details on this, see SECAM, "Recommendations and Conclusions on Marriage and Christian Family Life of Africa", in AFER, 23 (1981), p.370; P.K. Amevor, New Approaches to Marriage Preparation, p.116.

acknowledgment that notwithstanding the solidarity that characterises family life in Africa there are still problems and challenges that seek for proper instructions and preparation for marriage. These challenges range from lack of peace in many families, the neglect of parents on the education of their children, breakdown of marriages and family life, polygamy and divorces, and performing marriages that are not sacramental. It stresses that these challenges may not be unconnected to social and economic conditions of the time. Also the lack of adequate preparation for marriage is one of the main causes of these problems facing family life in Africa[911].

AECAWA points out other factors in the socio-cultural environment that contribute undoubtedly to marital instability in West Africa. Some of these factors are: the importing of unhealthy attitudes and ways of behaviour from abroad, the loss of our cultural supports for marriage and family life most especially when people move from their own areas and go to settle in other big cities. There is also the tendency to lose sense of the sacred in the marriage of man and woman, and the reluctance to face the discipline which both nature and grace instil on the human sexual function. There is this divorce mentality which brings unhealthy casualness toward any firm commitment of spouses to each other and tends to prevent the development of an enduring personal conviction and determination to make together for life. In every society in the history of the world, a pervasive casualness in sexual matters and a depreciating of family values have had disastrous personal and social consequences in the sense that marriage commitment turns less attractive and less urgent, coupled with the undermining of the nuclear and extended family system that African society is made of[912].

To remedy this situation, the bishops stress the necessity of a more vital catechesis of the sacrament of matrimony, unfolding to the people its deep richness as graced by the continuous "presence of the redeeming Christ in their midst, and holding out exciting possibilities to the couple for genuine happiness and fulfilment as they exercise their privileged sharing in the creative plans of God. Such a catechesis of the sacrament should undoubtedly make marriage a more attractive way of life for our Catholics; make them want to marry in a sacramental way. And it should help people to be less hesitant and less fearful, according as they are able to assess more confidently their personal readiness for its responsibilities, its challenges and its opportunities"[913].

---

911 Cfr. P.K. Amevor, New Approaches to Marriage Preparation, p.124.

912 Cfr. AECAWA, "The Pastoral Care of Marriage", p.5.

913 Ibid; p.6.

It is in accordance with the Papal and Church's statements[914] on marriage and family as well as the prescription of the revised Code of Canon Law[915] in directing bishops and pastors of souls to provide for the Christian faithful the assistance which they need to preserve the sacred character of the married state and of Catholic family life that the bishops of the Inter-Territorial Episcopal Conference of Liberia, Sierra Leone and the Gambia issue these reasons for this policy regarding pastoral preparation for marriage. They are fully convinced that the implementation of the accompanying guidelines will help develop a fuller, profound grasp of the meaning, significance, and implications of the marriage sacrament. It will assist not only prospective couples but also those already married as ongoing support for them in their married life, and also the whole Christian community[916]. In this way, our pastoral responsibility "to assist at a marriage in the name of the Church, is balanced by our responsibility to safeguard the sanctity and integrity of the Christian sacrament. The precarious condition and even outright failure of so many marriages threaten this sanctity and integrity, to which they belong, and of the community and the nation as a whole"[917].

Having enumerated and explained in details the reasons for the policy regarding pastoral preparation for marriage in West Africa, AECAWA goes on to issue some guidelines for the Catholic marriage policy. Some of these guidelines are what we shall look into now.

6.2. Guidelines for the Catholic Marriage Policy

6.2.1. Time for Preparation

Turning to period of preparation, the bishops admonish that spouses must show themselves in good time to their parish priest. The time allotted for this is three months before the intended date of wedding so as to give enough time to prepare for the sacrament, for a mature assessment of the couple's readiness to marry and

914 Paul VI, HV, 30. "We implore you to give a lead to your priests who assist you in the sacred ministry, and to the faithful of your dioceses, in devoting yourself with all zeal to safeguarding the holiness of marriage, the better to guide married life to its full human and Christian perfection. Look upon this mission as the most important work and responsibility committed to you"; John Paul II, FC, 65 §3. "Therefore, it must be emphasised once more that the pastoral intervention of the Church in support of the family is a matter of urgency. Every effort should be made to strengthen and develop pastoral care for the family, which should be treated as a real matter of priority, in the certainty that future evangelization depends largely on the domestic Church".

915 Cfr. C.1063 CIC/1983.

916 Cfr. AECAWA, "The Pastoral Care of Marriage", p.8.

917 Ibid; p.9.

for any unforeseen complications that may emerge during the preparation process. They contend that except in extraordinary cases, priests should not waive or shorten this time period, unless it is rest assured that the necessary preparatory sessions can be done with in a shorter period of time[918].

6.2.2. Involvement of Other Priest or Parish

Addressing the involvement of other priest or parish by the intending marriage couple other than their own parish priest, or parish during the preparation program, the bishops make it clear that the parish priest of the catholic party should be notified and in time so as to furnish any necessary information that may be at hand with regard to the couple intending to enter into marriage with each other. As a matter of priority, the priest who will be assisting at the marriage of this couple will also be responsible for the pastoral preparation of the couple. He has to make sure that he carries out this function of preparing the couple unless it is proven beyond reasonable doubt that proper pastoral preparation of this couple in accordance with the norms of the church has already been carried out[919].

6.2.3. Criteria for Assessment of Readiness to Marry

AECAWA points out that the assessment of readiness to marry extends to three areas of concern. It covers spiritual or religious assessment, personal assessment, and canonical assessment[920]. It is the duty of the parish priest to note this three-

918 Ibid; p.11.

919 Ibid.

920 Ibid; pp.12-13. Under Spiritual-Religious Assessment, minimal readiness includes, among other things, the acceptance of the church as the community of faith, and the practice of that faith by at least one of the marriage partners, namely the Catholic. It includes also an acceptance of the religious character of marriage, with what this implies in terms of permanence, fidelity, children, and a common life. In the Personal Assessment, there is no yardstick that is completely reliable or fool proof by which to measure the maturity of a couple for purposes of marriage. But the following criteria will be found useful and sufficient. The parties must be mature enough to marry freely and deliberately, and having married, be capable of exercising the rights and of fulfilling the responsibilities associated with the conjugal commitment. They should be capable of normal coping with the stresses of life in their own environment. They must be able to make decisions, both as individuals and in consort with another person. They should have a healthy self-sufficiency, coupled with generosity and a capacity for unselfishness in their relationships. They should be able to communicate, and be willing to co-operate and compromise together in undertaking and carrying out the obligations of matrimonial life. The Canonical Assessment is a universal requirement of the church for every marriage; it may never be omitted. It is primarily an investigation to determine both the freedom and the capacity to

fold assessment together with the accompanying information for marriage form and register them in the parish books or records[921].

6.2.4. Content of Marriage Preparation

Under the general heading of the "Content of Marriage Preparation"[922], the bishops recount how the law of the church places the responsibility of assisting married people to live a holy, fruitful and happy married life on the bishops and priests. They remind priests concerning how the law obliges them to teach the couples about the holiness and obligations of their state, in the understanding of the marriage liturgy, what marriage is, as an act of the public worship of God in a conjugal manner. In other words, the couples ought to be taught and supported in their bid to safeguard, protect and better their conjugal covenant with each other so as to arrive at a holier and fuller living of a happy family life[923]. They draw up a special program in form of a resource book for the enrichment and nourishment of those already married and those intending to marry. The content of this resource book is: "- the role of prayer and religious practice in home and family; – the meaning of "sacrament of grace" as applied to marriage; – what it means to be "ready" for marriage; – communication and compromise in marriage and family living; – what the scriptures and the Church mean by "two in one flesh"; – mutual helpfulness and sharing the burdens of life; – personal development of man and woman through mutual help; – what equality of the spouses means and does not mean in marriage; – children as blessing and responsibility; – planning one's family in right ways and wrong ways; – the marriage partnership in our African setting; – the healthy, normal exercise of conjugal sexuality; – sexual morality in marriage; – the special implications of fidelity and safeguards for preserving it; – the extended family and in-laws; – management of income, budgeting and financial planning; – implications of the civil law for domestic relations; – the meaning of trust among the partners and how to foster it"[924].

While reemphasizing what the canon says about consulting men and women of proven experience and skill to assist on the preparation of couples for marriage[925], the bishops recommend that it will be appropriate to enlist the assistance of some

marry according to the Church's doctrine and the demands of canon law. It seeks to establish that no known impediments, of divine, ecclesiastical or civil law, are present. The Canonical Assessment will be done with the help of the specially provided Pre-nuptial Investigation Form and will usually be made toward the end of the couple's period of preparation for marriage.

921 Ibid; p.11.

922 Cfr. AECAWA, "The Pastoral Care of Marriage", p.13.

923 Cfr. Ibid.

924 Ibid; p.14.

925 Cfr. C.1064 CIC/1983.

qualified persons in the parishes in drawing up specific programme of executing the guidelines for marriage preparation and enrichment. Where it is within reach, especially in the cities and towns, preparing the couples in groups might be the best option and through this method, many people who are willing to help from several parishes could be gathered together. They go further to emphasise that some private sessions of the canonical prenuptial investigation are to be drawn up between the parish clergy, priests or deacons and the intending marriage couples themselves. The prenuptial investigation, if so desired, could be spread over several sessions of the programme[926].

6.2.5. Format of Programme

AECAWA envisages six pre-marital sessions that are not optional, and the first and last of these sessions should be with the priest or deacon, as the case may be, in the parish, unless, by wish, the priest or the deacon has to take part in all the sessions of the programme[927]. They continue to express that: "The couple should be helped to understand better the essential human and Christian aspects of their marriage, and be made more fully aware of the implications and challenges involved. Even the most normal people are somewhat frightened of taking the marital step, and it is well to bear in mind that the couple need support and understanding from the church representatives who are helping them to get ready"[928]. They reiterate the need to incorporate successful and happy married spouses in the marriage preparation process and also engage and utilize the talents of trained professional lay people to serve as "a source of inspiration, instruction and encouragement to those entering the married state – or indeed for those already living in marriage"[929]. The bishops stress that it is pertinent to observe that one approach alone will not meet the demands of the diverse requirements and conditions of the people or attend to the desire of every member of the parish clergy. This is the reason why a kind of adaptation and pastoral creativity will always be mentioned in terms of content and format of the programme[930].

926 Cfr. AECAWA, "The Pastoral Care of Marriage", p.15.
927 Cfr. Ibid.
928 Ibid.
929 Ibid; p.16.
930 Ibid.

6.3. Conclusion

All along we have been examining how the Catholic Church in West Africa has implemented through their particular laws and structures, canon 1063 of 1983 Code and all that concerns the pastoral care of marriage preparation. The Bishops of the Inter-Territorial Episcopal Conference of Liberia, Sierra Leone and the Gambia issued this pastoral policy regarding marriage preparation in West Africa. They are convinced that the implementation of these guidelines will in no doubt go a long way toward developing a fuller and deeper grasp of the meaning and implications of marriage sacrament. It will assist both those intending to marry and those already married.

As a matter of fact, one would have thought that the statement policy and the guidelines would mean more to various dioceses of the West African countries and the Episcopal Conferences of West African Bishops to enhance and attach more seriousness to the issue of marriage preparation, but regrettably, the policy and the guidelines concerning pastoral preparation for marriage remain unused in so many countries and dioceses in West Africa. Besides, there is no detailed directives and programmes with regard to marriage preparation. AECAWA concentrated more on the statement of policy and guidelines almost to the exclusion of the stages in marriage preparation and the manner in which prospective couples are to go about their preparation for marriage.

7. Conclusion of Chapter Four

This chapter reviewed the Igbo worldview, their traditional marriage procedures as well as marriage preparation in Igbo tradition and culture. As we have seen, various factors contribute to the Igbo Weltanschauung (worldview). Religion permeates in the life and culture of the Igbo people, that there is no rigid dichotomy between the sacred and the profane. It enters into the social life of the Igbo people in politics, social life, economics, and even in education. One can categorically say that religion and culture rule the day to day life of the Igbos.

How marriage is viewed by the Igbo people is also considered in this very chapter. Marriage in Igboland is seen as a consortium or partnership between the extended family relations of each of the couples intending to marry. Marriage, for them is not a covenant between two individuals but also between two family groups or kindred. This contributes immensely in holding the two family groups together and ensures the stability of the married union of the couple. The understanding of marriage in Igbo perspective cannot be overemphasised.

Obiagwu affirms this when he writes: "Marriage in Igbo is looked upon as sacred duty that every one must perform. Marriage is seen as a God-given gift and the Igbo believes that it is God himself who commanded people to get married and transmit life to continue his work of creation. So to live is to transmit and care for life which is the highest good a man can have"[931]. Hence, marriage has meaning with the presence of children in Igboland for the continuity of the family lineage.

We considered also the essential requirements in Igbo traditional marriage system. One of such elements is the payment of bride wealth. There cannot be any serious marriage negotiation in Igboland without the bride wealth payment. It is one of the last ceremonies that cement the marriage contract. The bridegroom and his bride are fully recognised traditionally as husband and wife only when it is paid. The bride wealth payment is common in African societies and it is recognised customarily as an essential requirement for a valid customary marriage. Iwuji confirms this when he opines: "Customary law recognises the payment of bridal-price as a necessary requirement for a valid contract of marriage, and makes a formal seal of the marriage contract. Its payment and acceptance testifies to the consent of the prospective spouses and their parents to the union. It is indicative of the fact that there will be no obstruction to the formal handover of the bride to the husband"[932]. So bride wealth does not entail a commercial negotiation as the European writers would say, since the girl in question is not projected as a commodity or property to be sold. But that does not make it free from abuse as some parents and extended family members of the bride nowadays sometimes use it to immerse wealth for themselves.

Consent also constitutes marriage and it is one of the essential elements in Igbo traditional marriage. In Igbo traditional society when consent has been given, it is taken that there are no obstacles to the normal celebration of marriage. Consent for marriage as we have seen is two dimensional in Igbo system of marriage: the consent of the parties and the consent of the parents, and sometimes, that of members of the extended family. The consent of the parents does not actually obstruct marriage but only serves as guardianship to the welfare of the spouses and to protect their marriage from ruin.

We also considered the Igbo traditional marriage preparation. A serious marriage preparation is compulsory because of the very high value and premium placed on marriage in Igboland. The roles play by parents in preparing their children for marriage right from childhood period to adulthood cannot be overemphasised. They try to educate their children from infancy as regards marriage and what it is all about. "Child education in an Igbo family is an integral process,

931 M.C. Obiagwu, Healthcare of the Sick among the Igbos of Nigeria vis-à-vis the Healing Ministry of the Church, Rome 2000, p.42.
932 E. Iwuji, Marriage Form in Nigeria, p.21.

a process whereby marriage preparation that combines sex education, physical training with character building, and manual activity with intellectual training. The aim is to build a strong character in the individual. Accordingly, Igbo parents aim at the child's character formation while preparing a child for marriage"[933]. Thus, parents train and educate their children on values and morality that are essential for marriage and its stability.

The community also play a vital and significant role in the marriage preparation. The community forms a living factor in uniting prospective couples and making sure they do not make mistake in their marital life. The community sometimes chooses within its ambience those who will take part in instructing prospective couples especially the female ones on the rules governing marriage and what makes for its stability.

We reviewed various initiation rites in Igboland that help prepare the young people for marriage and make them to be adults ready to assume responsibility as married and family people. Because of Christianity and civilization some of these rites of passage are no longer invoke, though some communities in Igboland still practice them as they serve as means of preparing the youth adequately for marriage.

Finally, we reviewed AECAWA policy and guidelines regarding pastoral preparation for marriage in West Africa. The Bishops of these Anglophone countries promulgated a small document concerning the pastoral care of marriage and the family. This document offers guidelines for marriage preparation. Its specific objectives are to uphold the natural right to marry in all ramifications especially where the partners show proof of the needed maturity and seriousness, and to safeguard and protect the sacredness of the sacrament and the dignity of marriage by elevating the prerequisites for its reception to a level which is considered to be suitable for the right appreciation of the spiritual and human dimensions that are involved in the marriage union and so forth[934] .

While we consider their policy and guidelines as encouraging, we must not fail to say that the bishops have given only very general policy and guidelines. They only opted for national policy and guidelines. There is still much to be done at a diocesan level. The need to work out a comprehensive diocesan policies and guidelines that will take into account the situation in particular churches about marriage preparation calls for attention. When this is done, it could then be supported by general policies at the Bishops Conferences. The bishops also concentrated much on the immediate preparation of the intending couples without taking cognisance of the other stages of marriage preparation.

933 E. Okonkwo, Marriage in the Christian and Igbo Traditional Context, p.21.
934 Cfr. AECAWA, "The Pastoral Care of Marriage", p.25.

Chapter Five: Proposed Marriage Preparation Guidelines and Programmes for the Igbo Dioceses and the Need for Inculturation

1. Proposed Marriage Preparation Guidelines and Programmes

The 1983 Code of Canon Law precisely canon 1063[935] obliges pastors of souls with the task of seeing to it that their own church community provides spouses with the necessary assistance needed in preparing adequately for marriage and living out well a Christian marriage. In line with this task canon 1064 encourages the local ordinary to formulate guidelines and programmes for proper implementation of canon 1063 regarding marriage preparation and pastoral care for marriage. In likewise manner according to canon 1067[936] the Episcopal Conference is to lay down norms regarding the examination of the partners' freedom to marry, their capacity to marry, their understanding of the responsibilities and rights of marriage, and their ability to embark on those responsibilities and exercise those rights[937].

Also in their resolution on marriage preparation the 1980 Synod of Bishops obliges the Episcopal Conferences and Dioceses to issue norms and guidelines for marriage preparation[938]. And taking explicit recognition of what the bishops of the 1980 Synod said, Pope John Paul II maintains the need for Bishops Confer-

935 C. 1063 CIC/1983: "Pastores animarum obligatione tenetur curandi ut propria ecclesiastica communitas christifidelibus assistentiam praebeat, qua status matrimonialis in spiritu christiano servetur et in perfectione progrediatur. Haec assistentia imprimis praebenda est:
1° praedicatione, catechesi minoribus, iuvenibus et adultis aptata, immo usu instrumentorum communicationis socialis, quibus christifideles de significatione matrimonii christiani deque munere coniugum ac parentum christianorum instituantur;
2° praeparatione personali ad matrimonium ineundum, qua sponsi ad novi sui status sanctitatem et official disponantur;
3° fructuosa liturgica matrimonii celebratione, qua eluceat coniuges mysterium unitatis et fecundi amoris inter Christum et Ecclesiam significare atque participare;
4° auxilio coniugatis praestito, ut ipsi foedus coniugale fideliter servants atque tuentes, ad sanctiorem in dies plenioremque in familia vitam ducendam perveniant".

936 C. 1067 CIC/1983: "Episcoporum conferentia statuat normas de examine sponsorum, necnon de publicationibus matrimonialibus aliisve opportunis mediis ad investigations peragendas, quae ante matrimonium necessaria sunt, quibus diligenter observatis, parochus procedure posit ad matrimonio assistendum".

937 Cfr. L.A. Robitaille, Commentary on Canons 1063-1072, p.1265.

938 Cfr. Synod Secretariat, The Synod Propositions, 3, 165.

ences to issue a directory for marriage preparation guidelines and pastoral care of the families. According to him "it is to be hoped that the Episcopal Conferences, just as they are concerned with appropriate initiatives to help engaged couples to be more aware of the seriousness of their choice and also to help pastors of souls to make sure of the couples' proper dispositions, so they will also take steps to see that there is issued a Directory for the Pastoral Care of the Family"[939].

It is to be noted that since the emergence of Familiaris Consortio of John Paul II in 1981, many dioceses and parishes are not leaving any stone unturned with regard to marriage preparation and pastoral care of the families. John Paul II made reference to this in his message to the Pontifical Council for the Family during the 20th anniversary of Familiaris Consortio, when he asserts: "It can be said that after the publication of Familiaris Consortio, the church's interest in the family increased, and the pastoral care of families has become the priority of countless dioceses and parishes. Pro-family and pro-life associations and movements are spreading"[940].

In supporting what John Paul II said about the great improvement in the area of pastoral care of the family in countless dioceses and parishes and how pastoral care of the family is at work in the testimonies presented during this congress commemorating the 20th anniversary, the Pontifical Council for the Family says: "These experiences, that came from all the continents, show us how many Christian homes are motivated by the love of the truth about the family"[941]. Still on the progress made during these past 20 years, the Congress contends that "one of the most important fruits of Familiaris Consortio is the renewal of the pastoral care of the family in the Bishops' Conferences, dioceses, parishes, and apostolic movements throughout the Church. In this area considerable progress has taken place in the past 20 years"[942].

However, inspite of all the achievements recorded in the areas of family and pastoral care of the family as it pertains to preparation for marriage for prospective couples and the support giving to those already married, there are still many dioceses and parishes lagging behind in the pastoral care of marriage and fami-

939 FC, 66 §9.

940 John Paul II Message to the Congress of the Pontifical Council for the Family on the 20th Anniversary of FamiliarisConsortio,23November2001,no.4. http//www.vatican.va/holy_father/john_paul_ii/speeches/2001/November/documents/hf_jp-iispe_2001 1123_card-trujillo-family_en.html. (Accessed: 2.11.2011).

941 Pontifical Council for the Family conclusions of the theological-pastoral congress on the theme:"Twenty years since "Familiaris Consortio": The Anthropological and Pastoral Dimension", 20 December 2001, Introduction.
http//www.vatican.va/roman_curia/pontifical_councils/family/documents/rc_pc_family_doc_2001 1220_xx-familiaris_en.html. (Accessed: 2.11.2011).

942 Ibid. no. 8.

lies. Thus, the Pontifical Council insists: "Despite all that has been achieved, there is still much to be done. There are still many dioceses in which the pastoral care of families lacks adequate structures"[943].

It is interesting to point out that the observation made by the Council about many dioceses' lack of structures as regards marriage preparation and pastoral care of families is a welcomed task to the bishops of the Igbo dioceses as well as the Episcopal Conference of the Nigerian bishops to put priority attention to the pastoral care of marriage and families by drafting a suitable pastoral guidelines and instructions on marriage preparation that will meet this demands.

It is against this background that we intend to propose pastoral guidelines and programmes on marriage preparation in the dioceses of Igbo region in Nigeria. Hence, the part one of this very chapter is made up of three sections. Our main thrust in the first section is to set up canonical and pastoral guidelines on marriage preparation for the Igbo dioceses. Our attention will then be directed to the stages of marriage preparation of what needs to be done during each particular stage so as to prepare the engaged couples properly for marriage in Igboland. In this second section also under the immediate stage of preparation, we will channel our mind to variety of preparation programmes and some suggested topics in each of the stages designed to pastorally guide the prospective couples prepare adequately for marriage. Section three will concern itself with situations and circumstances that need urgent attention in Igbo dioceses.

One thing is clear in this proposal. It is not to be taken as a must-take-blueprint document for the dioceses of Igbo region to adopt at all cost, rather it should serve as a reference point to developing policies and guidelines for marriage preparation and pastoral care of marriage and families in the Igbo dioceses in particular and the Nigerian dioceses as a whole.

1.2. Aim and Purpose of the Guidelines

In the preceding chapter we examined traditional Igbo marriage preparation to see how the Igbo people prepare their young ones traditionally for marriage. We x-rayed some of the many rites of passage that help usher young people into marriage in Igboland. Though some of these initiation rites do not offer the desired goal of preparing young people adequately for Christian marriage, they help shed light on what should constitute a marriage preparation process. We noticed also that the bishops of Anglophone Countries of West Africa opted only for general policy and guidelines concerning pastoral preparation for marriage in West Af-

943 Ibid. no.9.

rica without taken into account what ought to be done about marriage preparation at the diocesan and parish level. In view of this, there is the necessity to work out a comprehensive diocesan and parish guidelines on pastoral care of marriage preparation that will take into cognisance the situation in the various dioceses in Igboland.

In his apostolic exhortation, Familiaris Consortio, John Paul II asserts: "Knowing that marriage and the family constitute one of the most precious of human values, the church wishes to speak and offer her help to those who are already aware of the value of marriage and the family and seek to live it faithfully.... In a particular way the church addresses the young, who are beginning their journey towards marriage and family, for the purpose of presenting them with new horizons, helping them to discover the beauty and grandeur of the vocation to love and the service of life"[944]. Taking cognisance of the foundational importance of marriage to the church and society, it is pertinent that the church in Igboland provides the best possible guidelines and policies concerning marriage preparation for prospective spouses in Igboland planning to answer and achieve this marital vocation[945].

The aim of these guidelines is to establish general criteria in all the dioceses in Igboland for the preparation of marriage and its celebration thereby giving a pastoral orientation in order to stimulate and at the same time direct the pastoral activities of parish priests, priests, animators, and many other people involved in preparing prospective couples to worthily and fruitfully celebrate the marriage sacrament.

Pope John Paul II recognises the importance of marriage preparation in the life of the Christian faithful when he says: "The very preparation for Christian marriage is itself a journey of faith. It is a special opportunity for the engaged to rediscover and deepen the faith received in baptism and nourished by their Christian upbringing. In this way they come to recognise and freely accept their vocation to follow Christ and to serve the kingdom of God in their married state"[946].

The aim of establishing these guidelines in Igbo dioceses is also to assist pastors of souls of the Igbo dioceses in achieving and accomplishing this goal enumerated by the Pope. These guidelines will among other things help spouses approaching the Catholic Church for marriage to realise the nature of the sacredness of marriage as a sacrament and guiding them to develop a full life of permanence in the community of life and love in the world. It will equally enable them to in-

944 FC, 1 §1 and 2.

945 Cfr. Diocese of Columbus, Policies and Guidelines for Marriage Preparation, 2010, Foreword. http//www.colsdioc.org/Portals/O/Departments/CHO/Documents/Marriage Policy 2010.pdf. (Accessed: 28.10.2011).

946 FC, 51 §3.

vent and realise that their intimate relationship is sacred and their call to always stand by this union as a sign of God's prophetic love[947].

The purpose of the guidelines on the other hand, is to establish in all the Igbo dioceses an effective commitment to the well being of engaged couples and those already married, to the progress and prosperity of their intimate union and to the unity and permanence of their marriages. The guidelines will be offered in a partnership with engaged spouses and those assisting them as they embark on the vocation of marriage and family life. Through this way, they form guiding policies and principles for structuring a process of marriage preparation, education and formation for the sacrament of matrimony[948]. The guidelines will equally provide prospective couples a chance for a deep review and assessment of their relationship before marriage and to ascertain with the couple their readiness to contract a Christian marriage. It will also provide them an ample opportunity for a theological awareness of Christian marriage as a sacrament through the day to day living of the faith of the Catholic community[949].

One thing is certain about these guidelines. They are not intended to complicate the prospective couples' chances to marry in the Catholic Church in the dioceses of Igboland but they are designed to pastorally guide and direct prospective couples thereby enabling them to discern and evaluate their own relationship and strengthen it before a permanent commitment is pronounced. The main aim is to assist the prospective couples in Igbo dioceses as they prepare for a sacramental marriage, a lasting union where Christ is always present, thereby enabling the couples partake fully in Christ's love to each other and to the whole world[950].

1.3. Level of Obligation

The proposed marriage preparation guidelines shall oblige the entire ecclesial community of the Igbo dioceses. It involves directly all those who are responsible for the pastoral care of marriage in the community of the faithful. In accordance with canon 1064[951] the bishops have the primary responsibility of providing for

947 Cfr. F. Gavin, Pastoral Care in Marriage Preparation, p.166.

948 Cfr.DioceseofRichmond,CalledtoMarriage,1997. http//www.richmonddiocese.org/sites/default/files/marriage.pdf. (Accessed: 28.10.2011).

949 Cfr. F. Gavin, Pastoral Care in Marriage Preparation, p.167.

950 Cfr. Diocese of Norwish, Marriage Preparation, 2011. http//www.ccfsn.org/pdffiles/marriage-prep.2011.pdf. (Accessed: 7.11.2011).

951 Cfr. C.1064 CIC/1983: "It is up to the local ordinary to make provisions that such assistance is duly organized, even after consulting men and women of proven experience and skill, if it seems appropriate".

the many forms of initiatives of pastoral activities within the ambience of their dioceses in Igboland. The Second Vatican Council Fathers declare in Christus Dominus: "In the diocese as a whole or in its different parts, the various forms of the apostolate should be encouraged. Close collaboration and the co-ordination of all the apostolic works under the direction of the bishop should be promoted. Thus, all the undertakings and organisations, whether their object be catechetical, missionary, charitable, social, financial, educational, or any other pastoral purpose, will act together in harmony, and the unity of the diocese will be more clearly evident"[952]. So each of the bishops in Igboland has the obligation to formulate diocesan programmes for pastoral care of marriage and marriage preparation and to ensure that the assistance mentioned in canon 1063 is provided for in their various dioceses and effectively coordinated.

The obligation also binds parish priests, their assistants, deacons, and even catechists. They are to see to it that these guidelines are properly adhered to so as to achieve the goal of helping and providing the prospective couples with a solid foundation for faithful, permanent and life giving love in their sacramental union. So the parish priests, their assistants, and other team members are very important to the marriage preparation course. Their goals are to support the love of the prospective couples in their preparation for marriage and to task them to grow in their relationship and in their faith level, "to demonstrate that the Church cares for their welfare; to provide a process that enables community… to assess their spiritual and psychological readiness for marriage, to discuss and review the practical information needed to live out their commitment; and to facilitate their greater awareness of the sacred nature of marriage through an understanding and appreciation of its sacramental, liturgical, moral, and spiritual aspects"[953].

Also to be obliged by these obligations are Seminarians on one year pastoral experience and those on six weeks apostolic work. During this period they should be tasked with the responsibility of instructing prospective couples on what marriage is all about as marriage is always a major topic to be treated in the curriculum of any major seminary. The bishops of the Igbo dioceses as a suggestion could oblige them to take active in instructing and preparing engaged couples for marriage. In this way, they become part of the instructors in marriage preparation programmes. The team of reverend sisters could also be incorporated into this course. There are many reverend sisters in Igboland who specialised on marriage related courses, who could offer assistance in this area. We suggest also that the bishops through the assistance of Mother Generals of these reverend sisters' congregations could throw it open for them to see themselves as educators and instructors in marriage preparation programmes.

952 CD, 17 §1.

953 Diocese of Columbus, Policies and Guidelines for Marriage Preparation, loc.cit.

The proposed guidelines shall also bind Catholic parents, families, guardians, Godparents, teachers, educators, trained couples, and members of different pious societies in the church. It will be their task to foster among the engaged couples a lively sense of what marriage is all about by guarding them throughout their marriage preparation programmes and continued assistance after marriage. For those mentioned here, taking on this role allows them to live out their calling throughout the sacrament of marriage by being a sign to prospective couples of all that marriage is all about in good and bad times, in sickness and in good health, the ups and downs, the challenges, and everything that is in between[954].

It is also pertinent for engaged couples to avail themselves of this opportunity to participate in the marriage preparation courses as it will help them "explore their strengths and weaknesses, discuss compromises, and develop tools they can use to work through areas of difficulty before they become threats to the marriage relationship.... While marriage preparation may be just one step in the lifelong commitment to a relationship, it is a crucial one that can greatly benefit the couple throughout their marriage"[955]. Thus, prospective couples should not fail to attend to those marriage preparation programmes as these will assist them to be conscious and aware of what they are about to enter into and "become for them a cause for hope, insight and strength so that married life can be a source of wholeness and holiness for themselves, their children, the Church and society as a whole"[956].

Therefore, prospective couples in Igbo dioceses should not be exempted from participating in these programmes if we are to make any headway in this direction. Those to be exonerated are those with cogent and reasonable excuses such as sickness or those marrying at a very old age that do not have the strength to attend such programmes. In this case, permission from the parish priest or the team organiser of the programme is required to ensure that such couple are excused from participation because of their present condition. However, refusal to participate in the programmes should not warrant a refusal on the part of the parish priest for them to celebrate their marriage. The matter should rather be directed to the bishop in charge of that very diocese for proper decision[957]. The prospective couples should be made to understand that reluctance to take part in a marriage preparation programme or course can be termed as a sign of lack of commitment

954 Cfr. M. Feehan, Saying I Do: A Marriage Preparation Program, Mahwah, New Jersey 2006, p.6.

955 Ibid. P.5.

956 Diocese of Richmond, Called to Marriage, loc.cit.

957 Cfr. C.1077 CIC/1983 §1: "Ordinarius loci propriis subditis ubique commorantibus et omnibus in proprio territorio actu degentibus vetare potest matrimonium in casu peculiari, sed ad tempus tantum, gravi de causa eaque perdurante". §2: "Vetito clausulam dirimentem una suprema Ecclesiae auctoritas addere potest".

to marry in the Catholic Church. Be that as it may, it is the church's responsibility to provide proper and numerous options so that there is no reasonable hindrance to participation[958].

1.4. Drafting and Training of a Formation Team

In order to achieve the aim and purpose of marriage preparation programme and pastoral care of the family in Igbo dioceses, the formation of a diocesan commission is very crucial and important in each of the dioceses in Igboland. It is not going to be only the task of the bishops and that of the priests but the function of the entire dioceses. "The whole diocese should be involved in this task and offer the proper supports. The ideal would be to create a diocesan Commission for marriage preparation, including a group for the pastoral care of the family, composed of married couples with parish experience, movements and experts"[959]. The task[960] of the commission will be formation and to create a programme for marriage preparation that could be used in the Igbo dioceses today. They will set up a support network to take care of the young couples in a special way during the first years of their married life, but also throughout their whole married life on how to educate their children and enrich their marriage.

The commission as a matter of fact should have an overseer most importantly a priest acting in the order of a bishop. But if the commission is handled by a lay person the advice of a priest cannot be ignored since priests are responsible for seeing to it that all those participating in this commission have appropriate dispositions, sufficient and reasonable understanding of church teaching on marriage[961]. The coordinator should avail himself or herself the opportunity of briefing the bishop from time to time about the goings on.

958 Cfr. C. 213 CIC/1983: "Ius est christifidelibus ut ex spiritualibus Ecclesiae bonis, praesertim ex verbo Dei et sacramentis, adiumenta a sacris Pastoribus accipiant".

959 PCF, no.20.

960 Ibid. "The task of this diocesan commission would be formation, follow-up and coordination, in collaboration with centres on various levels involved in this service. The commission should in turn be formed by networks of teams of chosen lay persons who work together in marriage preparation in a broad sense and not only in the courses. It should have the help of a coordinator, normally a priest, representing the bishop. If the coordination is entrusted to a lay person or a couple, a priest's assistance would be advisable. All of this should enter into the organisational context of the diocese with its corresponding structures, such as possible areas headed by an Episcopal Vicar and vicars forane".

961 Ibid. no.43. "The pastoral workers and those in charge must have a solid doctrinal preparation and unquestionable fidelity to the Magisterium of the Church so that they will be able to transmit the truths of the faith and the responsibilities connected with marriage with sufficient in-depth knowledge and life witness. It is quite obvious that these pastoral workers, as educa-

The Decree on the Apostolate of the Laity, Apostolicam Actuositatem emphasises that the laity share in the threefold office of Christ. "In the Church there is diversity of ministry but unity of mission. To the apostles and their successors Christ has entrusted the office of teaching, sanctifying and governing in his name and by his power. But the laity are made to share in the priestly, prophetic and kingly office of Christ; they have therefore in the Church and in the world, their own assignment in the mission of the whole People of God"[962]. The Second Vatican Council and the Code of 1983[963] have included the laity to take active part in the threefold mission of the Church of teaching, sanctifying and serving. Therefore the formation team should be made of lay people professionally trained to carry out this task. The commission should not only be left for the priests, deacons, and catechists since the proposed guidelines will recognise that not all married couples who are willing to help prepare prospective couples for marriage are trained catechists, nor are they expected to be. While adequately trained and certified catechists are important to the marriage preparation process, the lived experience of married couples who render authentic witness to the practical realities of sacramental married life is also vital[964].

The priest who is representing the bishop should recruit trained validly married couples competent and eager to assist prospective couples prepare for Christian marriage. In other words, the selection of these married team couples should echo the diversity of prospective couples in terms of their age, faith tradition and cultural heritage. In forming and training married couples for marriage preparation course, it is pertinent that they be adequately trained in line with the teachings of the church on Christian marriage[965].

In addition to the catechists and married couples, the formation team shall be composed of a group of persons who can render from both their professional,

---

tors, will also have to be capable of welcoming the engaged, whatever their social and culture extraction, intellectual formation and concrete capacities may be. Moreover, their faithful life witness and joyful giving are indispensable conditions for carrying out their task. Based on their own experiences in life and human problems, they can offer some starting points for enlightening the engaged with Christian wisdom".

962 AA, 2§2.

963 Cfr. C. 759 CIC/1983: "Christifideles laici, vi baptismatis et confirmationis, verbo et vitae christianae exemplo evangelici nuntii sunt testes; vocari etiam possunt ut in exercitio ministerii verbi cum Episcopo et presbyteris cooperentur".

C. 774§1 CIC/1983: "Sollicitudo catechesis, sub moderamine legitimate ecclesiasticae auctoritatis, ad omnia Ecclesiae membra pro sua cuiusque parte pertinet".

964 Cfr.ArchdioceseofDenver,"WhatGodHasJoined…":Supplement,p.10. http/www.archden.org/repository//Documents/MarriageFamily/Norms/WhatGodHasJoined_Supplement.pdf. (Accessed: 10.11.2011).

965 Cfr.Dioceses of New Jersey, Section 1: The Marriage Preparation Process, p.14. http/www.rcan.org/famlife/B-MarriagePrep-Sectl.pdf. (Accessed: 25.10.2011).

ministerial and personal experiences and knowledge. All those professionally trained in the area of psychology and other professionals like economics, medicine, law, counselling, and leaders of tradition should make up the team. All the formation team should view themselves as carrying out a special task of pastoral care for the church toward the engaged couples.

Coupled with this, the commission members should have a deep personal commitment to spiritual, moral, health and development of the prospective couples. They are to be professionals with extend hospitality and concern to the prospective spouses, able to relate to their various ages and socio-cultural origins. They are to possess proper training, information and materials. They should be ready to make out time to gather for formation most importantly to examine together about their task in the preparation process and concerning what Christian marriage and marital life are all about[966].

The activities of the commission should concentrate on the three stages of marriage preparation which include remote, proximate, and immediate preparations. It should also include on going support of those who are married. They are to provide to the engaged couples from time to time booklets, pamphlets and manuals concerning marriage preparation. For the smooth running of this commission, it is the task of the diocese to provide them with financial and moral support both for the training of their members and the day to day running of the commission. The commission should take time to visit different parishes within the diocese to see how the programme is going and then brief the bishop about the progress of the commission. If there are parishes that are not measuring up well, it is their duty to help such parishes in their areas of difficulty.

1.5. Readiness to Marry

The church establishes that the right to marry is a pertinent natural right and therefore not an unqualified right. It is important to note that the church and the state can determine its legitimate restrictions[967]. Aware of the spouses' natural right to marry the Code of 1983 decrees that all can contract marriage who are not prohibited by law[968], and that before a marriage take place, it must be evident that nothing stands in the way of its valid and lawful celebration[969].

966 Cfr. Diocese of Richmond, Called to Marriage, loc.cit.

967 Cfr. Archdiocese of San Francisco, Common Policy for Pastoral Marriage Preparation, 1992, p.5; F. Gavin, Pastoral Care in Marriage Preparation, pp. 182-183.

968 Cfr. C. 1058 CIC/1983: "Omnes possunt matrimonium contrahere, qui iure non prohibentur".

969 Cfr. C. 1066 CIC/1983: "Antequam matrimonium celebretur, constare debet nihil eius validate ac licitae celebrationi obsistere". It is pertinent to note also that the Code of 1983 urges

However, there may be cases that may prompt delay of the marriage. In view of this, the Code empowers the local ordinary to prohibit a marriage but only for a time, for a grave reason, for as long as that circumstance persists[970]. The law itself does not presume a readiness to marry from all who request it. There is the necessity to assist those engaged couples in assessing entirely their readiness for marriage. In view of this, pastors of souls should be aware of the prospective couples' intention to marry. "Beginning the marriage preparation earlier will give enough time to couples to assess their individual readiness to marry and enough time to respond to particular circumstances that may require attention especially the determination of the party's freedom to marry canonically and the issue of previous marriage"[971].

The parish priest has the responsibility to determine that nothing prohibits a person from marrying. In Igboland where polygamy is sometimes the case, the parish priest should refer the matter to the bishop for urgent and proper attention if the parish priest notices that there is a tendency on the part of the man to return to polygamy. Though "there is no single objective standard by which one can judge a couple's readiness to marry. However, special reasons may indicate a need for further assessment and growth and justify a delay in the marriage ceremony"[972]. It is until the contrary is proven the presumption of being able to marry is in favour of a couple. They are only to be refused marriage when they explicitly and formally reject what the church teaches about marriage[973].

Circumstances that may warrant a delay or refusal to witness a marriage are: Age, lack of maturity, affinity, consanguinity, drug abuse, bound by a previous marriage, pregnancy, HIV/AIDS, mental disability, polygamy, etc. The parish priest in order words should be morally certain[974] about the prospective couples'

---

the ecclesial community to provide "assistance so that the matrimonial state is maintained in a Christian spirit and makes progress toward perfection" (c.1063). The Code also directs that confirmation be received before marriage and strongly recommends that the prospective couples approach the sacraments of penance and the blessed Eucharist so that they may fruitfully receive the sacrament of matrimony (c. 1065). Therefore, the local ecclesial community has also the right and a responsibility to uphold the sacrament of marriage. Thus, the natural right to marry is not absolute. For more details, see NCCB-USCC, BCPRP, Faithful to Each Other, Washington D.C. 1989, p.62.

970 Cfr. C. 1077 CIC/1983.

971 P.K. Amevor, New Approaches to Marriage Preparation, p.215.

972 Archdiocese of San Franscisco, Common Policy for Pastoral Marriage Preparation, p.5.

973 Cfr. Diocese of Dallas, A Pastoral Directive and Instruction on Marriage Preparation, 2007, p.2.

974 The moral certainty here includes: 1) Both parties understand and accept the sacredness of marriage by knowing fully well that if they are both baptised, then it is a sacramental union. 2) Since marriage in the church is first a religious and spiritual commitment, it is not to be entered into lightly or in the state of sin. 3) That the sacrament of Marriage unites a Christian man and

capability to enter a valid and lawful marriage. The parish priest has to embark on prenuptial investigation so as to protect both parties preparing to enter into marriage and the faith community.

The prospective couples who are Catholics should as a matter of fact present their baptismal certificates from their churches of baptism. Other baptised persons who are not Catholics should also present baptismal certificates or other official baptismal records from the churches they were baptised. Both baptised Catholics and other baptised persons should endeavour to present affidavits from parents or guardians or siblings confirming their freedom to marry. In this case, prospective couples who are not ready to enter marriage at that moment are not to be merely dismissed but are to be given every proper assistance and support they need so as to enter marriage in due course in a fruitful manner. If there is any impediment that will necessitate delay or refusal because of its non-dispensability, the problem must be sought out immediately or referred to the bishop for urgent solution. But the prospective couples are required to say the truth about the situation and the realistic prospect of its solution[975].

During the investigation period and the priest finds out or discovers a major obstacle to marriage and he decides to delay the marriage, he must endeavour to assist the concerned prospective couple come out of the particular situation that prompted the delay. In other words, the priest should be understandable, sensitive, and conscious with the couple so that they will not be disappointed about the decision to delay the marriage. For him to know exactly and judge accurately when the problem is amicably resolved and then put a date for the wedding means he should be ready to meet the concerned couple from time to time in order to evaluate and discern their progress in the marriage preparation process. However, if the prospective couple should meet another priest during this delay period for him to wed them, the priest in question may not continue with the wedding without contacting the parish priest who opted for the delay in wedding them[976].

---

woman in an indissoluble bond. It lasts until death and no human authority can break it. 4) The parties are to practice their faith, which means belonging to a parish, attending regularly Sunday mass, practicing a life of prayer, having received Holy Communion and Confirmation. 5) That the engagement period is a time spiritually dedicated to prepare for the life-long commitment. There is need for them to abstain for sexual activity reserved for marriage. If they have not been keeping that, they should be reconciled immediately by the sacrament of Reconciliation with a firm amendment to remain chaste prior to the wedding. For more understanding of the moral certainty, cfr. St. Thomas Aquinas Church, Charlottesville, Virginia, Preparing for the Sacrament of Matrimony, 2007, p.3. http//www.St.thomas-aquinas.org/documents/marriage/preliminary_information.pdf. (Accessed: 28.10.2011).

975 Cfr. Diocese of Dallas, A Pastoral Directive and Instruction, p.2.

976 Cfr. Archdiocese of San Francisco, Common Policy for Pastoral Marriage Preparation, p.7.

It is vital to recognise that the parish priest or priest in this period of discernment is not called upon to be a judge or a psychologist, but he is called upon to exercise his pastoral experience and training as a priest by making a true and prudent judgment on the situation at hand whether there are certain conditions attach to it or not. The priest can opt for a certain procedure that will help him make this prudent decision when he discovers an obstacle to marriage. He could follow the steps of consulting, evaluating, deciding, and appealing[977]. Above all, any serious issues concerning the prospective couple's readiness to marry are to be recorded on the prenuptial inquiry forms for proper assessment and necessary solution.

When it is certain that the wedding should be delayed because of the availability of impediments, the parish priest is to urge to exercise gentle persuasion to dissuade the prospective couple from wedding. He should use pastoral advice to let them know the reasons for the delay or refusal. A process of appeal exists to protect the right of a spouse to marry and to safeguard the priest or deacon's right either to delay the wedding or to refuse to witness the wedding because the right to marry is a natural law. A resolution that is informal is recommendable on the part of the priest and the prospective couple. But if all things fail, recourse to the marriage tribunal can be sought to[978].

1.6. Notification of Marriage

In giving notification for marriage prospective couples should approach their parish priest at least six months before their anticipated wedding date. This period of time is to accommodate the time needed to complete all that is necessary for the marriage preparation, for an adequate evaluation of the couple's readiness to marry, a prudent assessment of their level of faith and for any unforeseen circumstances which may come up as the preparation process continues. This time frame should not be discarded or shortened except in extraordinary situations when it is assured that the necessary preparatory stages can be finished in a short period of time[979].

The engaged couples in Igboland should be encouraged to contact the parish and the parish priest immediately they become engaged. The earlier the engaged spouses make this contact to arrange for their wedding the more advantageous and beneficial the marriage preparation process will be for them. It should be

977 Cfr. Ibid. p.6.

978 Cfr. Diocese of Dallas, A Pastoral Directive and Instruction, pp. 8-9.

979 Cfr. AECAWA, The Pastoral Care of Marriage, p.11.

noted that the notification period is not intended as a waiting period but it should be considered as one of preparation. The procedure of such preparation should begin at the first meeting with the parish priest. It is highly recommendable for the engaged couples to complete all the stages of the preparation at least two months before the date of the wedding[980].

The parish priest, other priest or deacon or even a catechist designated for this function should endeavour to meet with the engaged couple immediately after the initial contact with the parish so as to establish understanding and rapport by discussing in detail the marriage preparation process and to answer any question the prospective couple may posit in order to be on the known. This vital section of the preparation process should be handled with pastoral consciousness and sensitivity. The parish priest or his assistant or deacon may fix a tentative date for the wedding during this period of initial contact but only when the prospective couple must have completed their marriage preparation programme will the final date of the wedding be fixed and made open[981].

1.7. The Parish Church

In accordance with paragraph one of canon 1118 of the Code of 1983, the proposed guidelines establish that the parish of either the bride or bridegroom, if both of them are Catholics, be the appropriate place for the wedding. A marriage between a Catholic and a baptised non-catholic should take place in the parish church of the Catholic party with exceptions being granted only for serious pastoral reasons[982]. The parish where the wedding will take place will be responsible for the marriage preparation process.

A wedding between a Catholic party and an unbaptised party may be celebrated in a church or in another suitable place[983]. In this regard, the officiating priest should act prudently in line with the sacred character of ceremony, notwithstanding the fact that the diocesan bishop's permission is not required. Dispensation from disparity of cult should be obtained from the bishop or the vicar general for the purpose of validity.

980 Cfr. Archdiocese of San Francisco, Common Policy for Pastoral Marriage Preparation, p.1.

981 Cfr. Diocese of Shreveport, Sacramental Guidelines, 2004, p.128. http//www.dioshpt.org/OnlineDocs/SacramentalGuidelines.pdf. (Accessed: 16.11.2011).

982 Cfr. C. 1118 §1 CIC/1983: "Matrimonium inter catholicos vel inter partem catholcam et partem non catholicam baptizatam celebretur in ecclesia paroeciali; in alia ecclesia aut oratorio celebrari poterit de licentia Ordinarii loci vel parochi".

983 Cfr. C. 1118 §3 CIC/1983: "Matrimonium inter partem catholicam et partem non baptizatam in ecclesia vel in alio convenienti loco celebrari poterit".

When a Catholic marriage is to take place outside the parish church just as in the case of combining traditional Igbo marriage with that of the Catholic Christian marriage, permission is required from the diocesan bishop[984]. The diocesan bishop or Episcopal Conference of Bishops could equally permit the parish priest to celebrate such a marriage just as it is the situation in Germany where the parish priest is given the permission to celebrate inter-religious marriages.[985] In this case, the parish priest and the team of the marriage commission should participate and be involved till the whole wedding process elapses. The elders of the two communities and the extended family members should also be incorporated into the wedding plan as they have credibility in speaking to the prospective couple concerning the realities of married life and permanence in such a union.

If, however, the prospective couple do not reside within the ambience of the parish, there is no strong obligation for the parish priest to allow the wedding in that parish church unless at least one of the engaged spouses is enrolled in that parish. When they are living in a rural parish but will be wedded in another diocese, the preparation in this regard will take place within the rural parish and under the supervision of the Catholic party's parish priest. It is also possible that the prospective couple might be capable of completing their preparation for marriage in another diocese under the supervision of the priest or deacon who is to witness the wedding ceremony[986].

1.8. Conclusion

This section reviewed the general overview of the proposed guidelines for pastoral care of marriage and marriage preparation in the dioceses of Igboland. The aim of the guidelines as we have seen is to establish a procedure for marriage preparation and assist prospective couples in Igboland prepare effectively for marriage. The purpose is to offer the parishes in the Igbo dioceses and the pastoral ministers a base for designing and conducting both urban and rural marriage programmes most especially as it touches the engaged couples preparing to enter into marriage for effective commitment on what they are about to enter into.

---

984 Cfr. C. 1118 §2 CIC/1983: "Matrimonium in alio convenienti loco celebrari Ordinarius loci permittere potest".

985 Ausführungsbestimmungen der DBK v.23.9.1970 zum MP "Matrimonia mixta" v. 31.3.1970 über die rechtliche Ordnung konfessionsverschiedener Ehen, abgedruck in: AKathKR 139 (1970) 538-548, hier: S. 541, n. 1.a). Diese Ausführungsbestimmungen sind in die Partikularnormen der DBK von 1989 übernommen worden. For more details, see, R. Sebott, Das neue Kirchchliche Eherecht, 3., völlig neu beaarbeitete Auflage, Frankfurt a. M 2005, p. 191.

986 Cfr. Diocese of Dallas, A Pastoral Directive and Instruction, p.4.

We envisaged that the propose policy shall oblige the whole ecclesial community in the Igbo dioceses. The priest or the deacon will be responsible for the whole marriage preparation process. He is obliged to help prospective couples to understand the meaning of Christian marriage in its canonical, sacramental, human and spiritual aspects and assist in directing them throughout their preparation process. He also has the responsibility to evaluate the couple's readiness for marriage and their level of faith in a prudent manner.

Married couples are also obliged to be witness to the holiness of the prospective couples' sacramental lives of intimacy, love and commitment and to support them in preparing them for their marriage. The parents, extended family members, elders of the community, teachers, catechists, seminarians, reverend brothers and sisters also share in this obligation.

The engaged couples should also avail themselves of this ample opportunity of participating in the marriage preparation course as that will make them to know how to handle problems relating to marital issues.

We said in order to carry out these marriage preparation activities successfully a marriage formation team should be constituted in the various dioceses in Igboland. Such formation team should be composed of a priest, deacon, catechists, married couples and professionals in different fields of human endeavours. Their task will be formation and coordination and to formulate programmes for the engaged couples in preparing them for marriage. They are to work hand in hand with the existing diocesan department for marriage and family life.

The right to marry is a natural right and therefore prospective couples are not to be refused marriage or have their wedding delayed unless when they explicitly and formally reject what the church teaches concerning marriage and in this case, the parish priest or his assistant or deacon should prudently notify them in time and in a peaceful accord.

The notification of the intention to marry in the church should be made known to the parish and parish priest by the engaged couple at least six months prior to the wedding so as to allow for an adequate time to prepare and complete all the necessary documents needed for the wedding to take place. The place of the wedding should be in the Catholic Church unless otherwise stated or for some pastoral reasons.

2. Stages of Marriage Preparation

2.1. Introduction

The envisaged stages of marriage preparation in Igbo dioceses will follow the outline of the stages of marriage preparation described in Familiaris Consortio of Pope John Paul II, canon 1063 of the Code of 1983, and expatiated in the Pontifical Council for the Family's preparation for the sacrament of marriage[987]. The periods are not rigidly defined since they cannot be defined with particular reference to the age of the person participating in the marriage preparation programme or with regard to their duration. However, it is important to be familiar with them as a working tool most especially as it concerns the content to be transmitted to the various individuals[988].

Marriage preparation as a gradual and continuous process is marked by the following periods: Remote, proximate, and immediate stages of preparation. There is also pastoral care of those already married. We are going to consider each of them to know how best they will help in promoting adequate and effective marriage preparation in Igbo dioceses of Nigeria.

2.2. Remote Preparation

In keeping with the instruction of the Pontifical Council for the Family, this stage of marriage preparation starts in the womb in the atmosphere from where the new life is being waited for and welcomed by its parents most importantly through the mother's loving dialogue with her child[989]. It proceeds through infancy, childhood, adolescence and unto the period of engagement. "It includes all those family as well as other environmental factors that influence and prepare the person in positive and negative ways for marriage. Every individual is constantly being prepared, for better or for worse, for a positive future married life from the first moment of her or his existence in this world"[990].

The positive influences and their effects with regard to remote preparation include:

"– A wise family training that leads children to discover themselves as being endowed with a rich and complex psychology, together with a particular personality having its own strengths and weaknesses;

987 Cfr. FC, 66; C. 1063 CIC/1983; PCF, nos. 21-59.

988 Cfr. PCF, n. 21.

989 Cfr. PCF, n. 23.

990 NCCB-USCC, BCPRP, Faithful to Each Other, p.10.

- A general formation of the young person's character that, among other goals, instils esteem for all authentic human values, enhances skills in interpersonal and social relationships, develops an understanding and correct use of one's inclinations, and promotes a proper regard for and ability to mix with the opposite sex;
- Solid spiritual and catechetical training that pictures marriage and parenting as a true vocation and mission, without in any way minimizing the vocation and mission to the priestly or religious life"[991].

The very foundation of remote preparation is the witness of the parents' own married love, and with the help of early moral training, parents can inculcate the child into the mysteries of faith the essence of being a Christian through the every day-use at home of the church's sacramental, by family prayers, and by answering simple curious Christian questions in view of lifting the child's mind to the goodness of God, his providence, and what patterns to married and family life[992]. The Catechism of the Catholic Church in speaking about the role of parents in this remote stage of marriage preparation says: "It is in the bosom of the family that parents are by word and example… the first heralds of the faith with regard to their children. They should encourage them in the vocation which is proper to each child, fostering with special care any religious vocation"[993].

It is important to say here that for suitable remote preparation in the Igbo dioceses the parents, guardians, extended family members, and elders in the village community should through the effective use of folklores, proverbs, riddles, songs, Igbo names, and biblical stories instil moral values to the children and young people that will guide them to grasp the full meaning of conjugal love and married life. Since they are the primary educators of their children "they have an inalienable duty to teach children and form them in the positive cultural and Christian values of marriage. The family as the basic cell of the Church, through family pastoral programmes must give guidance and help so that these children and young people may grow up to understand the culture of marriage, that is, the beliefs and prohibitions about marriage"[994].

During this period children and young people should be taught good Igbo and African values such as:

- The cultural values and the beauty of life to include, respect for elders; solidarity, cooperation, participation, sincerity and discipline;

991 Ibid.

992 Cfr. B.K. Nwakonobi, Igbo System of Kinship and Family, p.216.

993 CCC, n. 1656.

994 P.K. Amevor, New Approaches to Marriage Preparation, p.221.

- Commitment and responsibility. The children and the youth to understand their individual or personal responsibilities, that is, respect for others and a concept of vocation;
- Their commitment to the community to enable them make right decision;
- The role of prayer and religious practice in home and family; the meaning of "sacramental grace" as applied to marriage; what it means to be ready for marriage;
- Communication and compromise in marriage and family living.
- What the scripture and the Church mean by "two in one flesh";
- Mutual assistance and sharing the burdens of life;
- Personal development of man and woman through cordial help;
- What equality of the spouses means and does not mean in marriage;
- Children as blessing and responsibility;
- Planning one's family in right ways and wrong ways, the marriage partnership in our Igbo and African sense[995].

Imparting the truth and the glamour of Christian marriage to all is crucial. Communicating to people concerning the sacrament of marriage is the responsibility of the entire ecclesia community. The seeds of this message are planted in the activities of day to day life as children witness how their parents work to live out their commitment of marriage life. And while parents are the primary educators of their children throughout infancy, childhood and adolescence, they need proper assistance in fulfilling their roles. The church, schools, and the society at large play increasing roles in preparing youth for marriage[996]. Canon 803 §2 of the new Code states that: "It is necessary that the formation and education given in a Catholic school be based upon the principles of Catholic doctrine; teachers are to be outstanding for their correct doctrine and integrity of life"[997]. Hence, in Catholic schools and in religious education courses, instruction suitable to different grade levels should gradually introduce young people to a formal appreciation of the marriage sacrament[998].

The church also has an important role to play during this stage of marriage preparation as it is not only the priority of the parents, guardians and teachers in the school. During Sunday masses, periodic explanations about what Christian

995 Cfr. A.O. Gbuji, The Pastoral Care of Marriage, pp. 50-51.

996 Cfr. Archdiocese of Denver, "What God Has Joined…", Particular Norms for Christian Marriage, p.4. http//www.archden.org/repository//Documents/MarriageFamily/Norms/WhatGodHasJoined.pdf. (Accessed: 10.11.2011).

997 C. 803 §2 CIC/1983: "Institutio et educatio in schola catholica principiis doctrinae catholicae nitatur oportet; magistri recta doctrina et vitae probitate praestent".

998 Cfr. Dioceses of New Jersey, Pastoral Policies and Guidelines for Marriage Preparation, p.4. http//www.rcan.org/famlife/A-Overview&Intro.pdf. (Accessed: 28.10.2011).

marriage is all about should enumerate why the church treasures the marriage preparation process as an opportunity to work with prospective couples. Even beyond the family, the school and other institutions of higher learning, the children and the youth need to be hearing often what marriage entails from the pulpit. Pastoral ministers especially priests and deacons should take such opportunities at times when the scriptures lend themselves to the topics about marriage and married life and affirm the Christian vision of married life to the hearing of the children and the youth. Such themes as polygamy, the plight of widows, the uncertainty of the dispossessed, broken homes, may be used by priests and deacons to uplift so many hearts endangered by families separated by failed marriages, by the tensions of living together with couples who no longer love themselves. In all these, faith in the Word of God concerning marriage needs to be proclaimed with conviction[999].

The church should also utilize the means of mass media in speaking out and highlighting the ideals of Christian marriage as today's mass media exerts a strong influence on children and young people. Sex education should not be left out in this stage of marriage preparation. The parents, the school, and the church should endeavour to highlight what sex education is all about and not treat it as "untouchable". The healthy normal exercise of human sexuality and sexual morality in life should be imparted on the children and the youth.

2.3. Proximate Preparation

Giving the high rate of pregnancy among the youth and trial marriages in Igboland, as well as the urgent need for young people to better comprehend the institution of marriage as a sacrament this period of marriage preparation is crucial to the efforts being made by the church and is of special concern to pastors of souls and religious educators in Igboland. This stage of marriage preparation builds on remote preparation through formal catechesis and religious formation, and is understood to comprise of adolescence and young adulthood. It is known to be the period of engagement, the maturing sexuality of an individual and the individual's development of an awareness and exercise of authentic human values and good interpersonal relationship skills and ability[1000]. Starting at a proper age, normally during the time of puberty, it comprises through suitable catechesis a more specific preparation for and rediscovery of the sacraments[1001]. The adoles-

999 Ibid.

1000 Cfr. Diocese of Columbus, Policies and Guidelines for Marriage Preparation, loc.cit.

1001 Cfr. NCCB-USCC, BCPRP, Faithful to Each Other, p. 24.

cents should be integrated into the religious formation and their preparation for marriage as spouses[1002]. This period comprises a process of evangelization and a journey of faith similar to that of catechumenate, giving an opportunity for the prospective couples to rediscover and deepen their faith which they received in baptism[1003].

During this stage, marriage in Igbo dioceses should be seen as an interpersonal relationship between a man and a woman in search of a continual development. The adolescents and the prospective couples who are involved in this period of proximate preparation will need to study the concept of conjugal sexuality and responsible parenthood with the important medical and biological knowledge in line with it. It must cover the foundational requisites for a good family living such as commitment, communication, sensible administration, management of finances, and efficient housekeeping. At this period, the young people in our Igbo dioceses should be given a vision of their well-ordered responsibility to reach out to others and also provide for them the rich resources available in the church and in the various communities where they come from in order to sustain a well-ordered family life[1004].

The period itself should include a call to conversion that ushers the prospective couples in Igboland to a deeper encounter with God into whose body they have received baptism. They must be made to know of the profound mystery of Christian marriage through a proper catechesis, doctrinal formation, and in the teaching about the natural requirements of Christian marriage comprising the following topics: The sacramentality of Christian marriage, unity and indissolubility of marriage, the conjugal act, consent, procreation and education of children, the excellence of the life of chastity, and the good of the spouses[1005]. In other words, the prospective couples should be sensitized to the deep mystery of Christian marriage through a catechesis that is explicit in order that they will feel a need to prepare adequately for it by embracing the plan of God. In this case, they will require a true conversion through this catechesis as "only by starting with conversion… can catechesis, strictly speaking, fulfil its proper task of education in the faith"[1006].

Imparting education is paramount in this stage of proximate preparation and among such organs of education the Second Vatican Council gives priority to

1002 Cfr. Ibid.

1003 Cfr. Archdiocese of Denver, "What God Has Joined….", Particular Norms, p. 6.

1004 Cfr. NCCB-USCC, BCPRP, Faithful to Each Other, p.24.

1005 Cfr. Prince of Peace Catholic Church, Marriage Preparation Policies, Proximate Preparation. http//www.images.acswebnetworks.com/1/1059/MarriagePreparationPolicies.pdf. (Accessed: 22.11.2011).

1006 Cfr. GDC, n.62.

school[1007]. The function of the Catholic school is to assist young people grow in the new life they received during baptism. Although the example the parents give their children through process and integration and the effort they exert will help bear fruit in the marriage of Christians and family life of the young people, and although the parents, guardians, and family members continue to be involved in the formation of good relational skills and attitudes of their children, it is also the responsibility of the pastors of souls, school teachers, educators, and counsellors to provide process and integration to the religious formation of young people with their life preparation as a spouse[1008]. Amevor captures these religious and moral values that should be integrated into the activities of the school when he asserts: "Serious religious and value-systems should be integrated into the activities of the schools and other youth programmes. This means that teenage programmes should be drawn up so that while still at school, especially in the final years of schooling, young people may be presented with the biological, medical, legal, traditional, cultural and evangelical aspects of marriage such that even in the midst of a highly secularised and fast changing African society, these young adults will have some basis for this very important institution of marriage that many of them will eventually find themselves"[1009].

In the course of this proximate preparation period, those responsible should provide the youth and the prospective couples quality text books that deal with marriage as a sacrament in particular and other sacraments and similar topics as a whole. The books should cover also treatment of the different contemporary experiences relating to marriage which the younger generation face nowadays. The publishers and writers of such helpful books should continue in their efforts of writing new ones and always improving on the old ones for this particular purpose of imparting the young people with the knowledge of what Christian marriage is all about.

The need for sex education[1010], in the family and in schools is very crucial during this very period of proximate preparation. Contemporary issues such as abor-

1007 Cfr. GE, 5.

1008 Cfr. USCCB, An Analysis of Diocesan Marriage Preparation Policies, 2004. http//www.usccb.org/issues-and-action/marriage-and-family/marriage-preparation/mpanalysis.cfm. (Accessed: 22.11.2011).

1009 P.K. Amevor, New Approaches to Marriage Preparation, p. 222; G.K.Nukunya, Tradition and Change in Ghana: An Introduction to Sociology, 2nd Ghana Universities Press, Accra 2003, p.155.

1010 Here we stress the basic and pervasive need for more intelligent and efficient preparation of our youth for the sexual period of their lives. No mere classroom instruction in physiology can suffice for this. The sciences, both social and psychological, have shown us in recent years how much our thinking on sexual matters is currently formed. Some of the sexual beliefs and attitudes, even actions and ways of doing things, are not dictates of nature but learned dictates of different cultures. This is remarkable when we consider the great variety of sexual

tion, the sex-related health problem of AIDS, the question of teenage pregnancies, and the use of contraceptives should be treated as topics in schools. In this way the young people will be able to acquaint themselves with useful and helpful information concerning these contemporary issues and know how to handle them before marriage. Such issues like deliberate expulsion of an unborn baby from the mother's womb should be properly spoken against in our various schools. Through this way, our young people will refrain from engaging themselves in such an act. The Bishop Conference of Nigeria in condemning the issue of legalising abortion in Nigeria as some in the corridors of power are proposing it opines: "Throughout history this act has been recognised by almost all peoples of the earth as a grave crime against both God, the Author of human life, and man, its protector. They have made strong laws against it.... But in recent years many industrialized peoples, concerned increasingly with material pleasure above all else, have legalized abortion as a way of preventing undesired births while retaining sexual indulgence. Often they resorted to abortion when other types of birth control... failed them. Today in our country some Nigerians and others, even educated and prosperous, are petitioning Government to introduce this foreign importation. We call upon our people to withstand this attempt with all courage and purposefulness. It violates the most sacred values of Nigerian life"[1011]. What the Nigerian Catholic bishops said concerning the legalization of abortion in Nigeria has all along been the authentic position of the Church that legalizing it is simply the destruction and killing of unborn human life and it contradicts the fundamental law of God and the basic reason for the existence of the society.

Sex education courses in our schools should teach our young people sexual restraint and it should be geared towards the institution of marriage. Our teachers in these schools should not be afraid of using such words like modesty and chastity and they should show examples of good behaviour by the way they act and by the ideals and convictions they must be eager to convey to the students[1012]. Thus, parents, church authorities, and school teachers should endeavour to tell

customs and habits around the world. And adequate sexual education must reflect the social and psychic, the religious and moral, and the cultural as well as the physiological dimensions of sexuality. The Church continues to teach the inseparability of sex and marriage, and also the due openness to generation of all sexuality in marriage. We continue to point to the evident harmfulness, social as well personal, of any other course. The ability to follow and observe the Church's teaching is indeed an issue of cooperating with God's grace, but also a matter of proper and effective training, enlightenment and example. The Church cannot abandon what it sees to be good because different sexual abuses publicly require further abuses to sustain themselves. For more understanding on this, see CBN, Family Planning and Population Control: Stand of the Catholic Church, Lagos 1989, pp. 40-41.

1011 CBN, Family Planning and Population Control, p. 30.

1012 Cfr. W.J. Benett, "Sex and the Education of Our Children", Address to National School Boards Association, Washington D.C. 1987, pp. 124-125.

young people the truth in the sex education courses that the best possible way of avoiding AIDS is to desist from sexual intercourse until they reach adulthood to be ready to establish a mutually faithful monogamous union. This sex education, if guided by these basic principles, could assist protect and safeguard our younger generation from this terrible disease[1013].

The pastoral ministers should endeavour to use Sunday masses as an opportunity to preach about marriage and sex education. Even occasional sermons, bulletins and articles being advertised in the church's premises can proclaim the notion of Christian marriage and what it entails. Also involving young people as readers, mass servers, gift bearers helps establish contact with the youth and motivate them to be constantly near the church. Such themes on marriage should also be taught during the weekly youth meetings and Mary league meetings in our various parishes. Even during the wedding ceremonies, affirming those already married for their efforts in being faithful to each other during an age contrary to commitment and fidelity, emphasising the importance of love, dialogue, communication among others, and forgiving one another during homily are also ways of reaching the young people who are present during the wedding in addition to wedding spouses[1014].

To ensure that this period of preparation is serious, thoughtful and truly proximate all marriage preparation process should start six to twelve months prior to the prospective couple's awaiting wedding date and conclude not less than eight weeks before that date. The prospective couple must be assisted to view their psychological or emotional weaknesses that should be resolved before entering into sacramental marriage and the different aspects of their personalities that may influence cordial compatibility in the marriage. They should be taught how to preserve and enhance open mutual communication within the ambience of marriage and family life[1015].

The proximate preparation in Igbo dioceses should generally comprised of five sessions:

Section 1: Initial Meeting with the Parish Priest
Section 2: Pre-nuptial Inquiry
Section 3: Review of Pre-nuptial Inquiry or Inventory
Section 4: A Three-day Instructional Workshop
Section 5: Natural Family Planning.

1013 Cfr. W.J. Benett – C.E. Koop, "Statement on AIDS Education, Washington D.C. 1987, in NCCB-USCC, BCPRP, Faithful to Each Other, p.26.

1014 Cfr. NCCB-USCC, BCPRP, Faithful to Each Other, pp. 53-54.

1015 Cfr. Prince of Peace Catholic Church, Marriage Preparation Policies, Proximate Preparation, loc.cit.

Section 1: Initial Meeting

To assure proper time for marriage preparation as we suggested in the notification for marriage, prospective couples desiring to marry need to contact the parish and their parish priest at least 6 months prior to the provisional date of their wedding. The needed contact is designed to assure adequate time for assessment of readiness to marry and a proper catechesis for the celebration of the matrimonial sacrament[1016]. Each of the prospective couples is to have an initial interview with the parish priest or his assistant as it is always the case in Igbo dioceses when the parish priest is not around to conduct this interview, or the deacon who is working in this very parish as soon as possible or after the initial contact. The aims of this initial interview are:

- to determine the eligibility of the prospective couple according to the Catholic Church law;
- to start developing a warm, welcoming, and congratulatory relationship with the prospective couple;
- to start to discover the couple's attitudes, beliefs, expectations concerning themselves and their yearning for marriage in the Catholic Church;
- to explore any special circumstances that may affect their marriage, for instance, age, cultural background, pregnancy, polygamy, levels of faith and religious issues, physical or emotional problems, etc;
- to start the process of evaluating their readiness for marriage;
- to explain the marriage preparation process;
- to explain to the prospective couple what is involved in their proximate and immediate preparation for the sacrament and in this way assist them in preparing and planning accordingly for the wedding;
- to set a provisional date for the wedding[1017].

The goals of this initial interview will allow for flexibility and for a reasonable and just cause, with the prudent and reasonable judgment of the parish priest or his assistant or the deacon as the case may be, marriage preparation can be properly completed. Thus, the prospective couple should participate in all the stages of these guidelines most especially the one that strictly apply to them. The task of the parish priest, his assistant, deacon, catechist, and even the Marriage Advisory Council is to assist the prospective couple in: a) identifying and discerning their personal gifts, strengths and weaknesses, b) dealing with any areas of problems and difficulties in their relationship, c) recognizing that marriage is essentially

1016 Cfr. Diocese of Shreveport, Sacramental Guidelines, p.128.

1017 Cfr. Diocese of Fort Worth, Guidelines for the Preparation and Celebration of the Sacrament of Marriage, p.9. http//www.fwdioc.org/worship/Documents/sacramental_guidelines_holy_orders.pdf. (Accessed: 23.11.2011).

characterized by unity, indissolubility, fidelity and an openness to fecundity, d) participating in evaluation and preparation, e) attending a formal marriage preparation programme, and f) taking part in premarital evaluation and counselling when suggested and recommended[1018].

A provisional wedding date may be given at the time of this first contact with the parish priest and only when the prospective couple have completed the marriage preparation process and are free to marry without any impediment or obstacle prohibiting them to marry will the final date for the wedding be given[1019]. After this initial interview of the prospective couple by the parish priest, communication between pastoral ministers and the engaged couple is urgently required for a proper and clear understanding on when the prenuptial questionnaire will be completed and how the preparation programme will be conducted and those who will be involved in it in preparing this prospective couple adequately for it.

Section 2: Prenuptial Inquiry

The Code of 1983 directs the Bishops Conference to establish norms regarding the examination of the parties and other necessary means of carrying out appropriate investigations before a marriage is to be celebrated[1020]. This Code also states that before a marriage is validly and lawfully celebrated, it must be known that nothing stands in its way[1021]. In line with this, the prenuptial investigation should be led by the parish priest or his assistant as the case may be. The completion of the prenuptial inquiry is of a legal requirement and even more than that since it is an opportunity for the Catholic Church to pastorally assist the prospective couple in achieving their aim of coming together as one body in this sacramental union[1022]. The goals[1023] of this prenuptial inquiry are to question the

1018 Cfr.DioceseofHouma-thibodaux,MarriagePreparationPolicyandProcedures. http//www.ht-diocese.org/fm/marriagePreparation/tabid/332/Default.aspx. (Accessed: 23.11.2011).

1019 Cfr. Diocese of Shreveport, Sacramental Guidelines, p. 128.

1020 Cfr. C. 1067 CIC/1983.

1021 Cfr. C. 1066 CIC/1983.

1022 Cfr. NCCB-USCC, BCPRP, Faithful to Each Other, p.95.

1023 AECAWA, The Pastoral Care of Marriage, pp. 28-29. "The purpose of this new Pre-nuptial Investigation form is as follows:

1. To make sure, in so far as human judgment can do so, that the parties are not only free to marry but also capable of marrying according to current Catholic teaching and the provisions of the new canonical norms;
2. To make emphatic, in the general context of the couple's wider pastoral preparation, the seriousness and the long-term consequences of the step they are taking:
3. To ascertain the effectiveness of the programme of preparation the couple are following, so as better to assess their readiness for the Christian sacrament; also, to gauge the extent of their understanding of the meaning and implications of marriage as taught by the Catholic Church;

parties as to their freedom to marry and to ensure that nothing stands in their way of a valid and lawful marriage.

During this prenuptial investigation, the prospective couple should be interviewed separately in order to allow complete freedom in each of their answers. It is a self-diagnostic instrument like the one being administered in "FOCCUS"[1024] and other marriage preparation inventory. It should be noted that the FOCCUS inventory is not a test for marital success or failure but a means to foster and enhance the engaged couple's communication. In other words, it is a self-evaluation tool designed to assist prospective couples in learning more about themselves and each other's strengths and weaknesses[1025].

It is the responsibility of the parish priest or the priest with canonical right to assist at marriages in the parish so as to make sure that the important marriage preparation and prenuptial inquiry are executed correctly. The completion of the investigation by the parish priest or his delegate who will preside over the wedding

---

4. To provide an orderly parish record of all the steps which led up to the marriage, which record may have considerable value later if the marriage partners should be in need of help in pastoral counselling, or if the marriage itself has to be subjected to canonical scrutiny.

The Pre-Nuptial Investigation should normally come towards the end of the couple's period of pastoral preparation for marriage. Indeed, it must be regarded as an integral part of this preparation, enlivening it with new meaning and vitality and opening up new vistas of personal reflection for the people. This new form sets out the main areas of canonical enquiry. But it seeks to do more than this, by indicating the whole range of reflection which the couple should be undertaking. From this point of view, the Pre-Nuptial Investigation can be used, if one so wishes, as the actual framework for a complete pre-marriage catechesis. One can envision, for instance, dividing it into parts or sections, taking the various questions and making them the basis of discussion and instruction in a series of preparatory sessions".

1024 FOCCUS is a self-diagnostic inventory designed to help couples learn more about themselves and their unique relationship. It is not a test or predictor of success or failure in marriage. It is a tool to help couples identify and work through issues before marriage. FOCCUS provides individualized couple feedback on where each party stands regarding topics important to marriage. The results of the inventory point to issues that may need to be addressed. FOCCUS is designed to be used at three levels. The first level of FOCCUS occurs when the individuals read and respond to the FOCCUS statements. The second level of FOCCUS occurs with the help of a facilitator. Using the couple report, the facilitator works with the couple to look at patterns in their responses, discuss issues and solve problems. The third level of FOCCUS involves referrals of two kinds. The first referral, specialized assistance, is not needed by every couple. The second referral, to educational or skills-training programmes and processes, builds in the awareness couples have after completing the first two levels of FOCCUS. These educational and formation processes can be recommended as appropriate. FOCCUS is very adaptable and can be used in a wide-variety of models: self-standing, group or individual processes, in conjunction with mentor or educational programmes. A facilitator's role is to empower the couple to discuss the issues and more toward awareness and problem solving. The facilitator also helps couples identify and affirm their strengths. Cfr. http/www.foccusinc.com/sections/focus_content-aspx?PKID=6. (Accessed: 23.11.2011).

1025 Cfr. Dioceses of New Jersey, Section 1: The Marriage Preparation Process, p.11.

should not be omitted. Thus, making sure it is completed "can enhance the relationship between the couple and the one who will lead their liturgical celebration. It also supplies that individual with insights and information that will prove helpful in the final preparation of the ceremony, especially in the development of the homily"[1026].

Depending on the situations and conditions, a copy of this prenuptial inquiry questionnaire could be provided to each party beforehand, for them to study and reflect on it during the preparation period. They should be encouraged and assisted to comprehend not only the words on the form but also the purpose and implications of the questions, in a way adaptable to their own situations and abilities. One thing is obvious; the questionnaire cannot be treated in the same manner with every individual[1027].

Since the forms for the prospective couple are essentially identical, the following questions could be applied[1028]:

Question 1: Personal Data:

a. Surname – Given Names

b. Present Address

c. Occupation/Employment

d. How long living at present location?

e. Where have you lived previously?

f. Where will you live after Marriage?

g. Father's name and place of residence

h. Mother's name and place of residence

i. Date of birth

j. Date and place of baptism

k. Consent of Parents, if under legal age.

Question 2: Have you ever been previously married in any form? Customary? – Religious? – Civil?

Question 3: Is there any blood relationship between you and your proposed spouse? – Affinity? – Fosterage? – Adoption?

Question 4: Do you know of any other obstacle or impediment between you?

Question 5: How long have you known your partner? – Have you been cohabiting together? If so, for how long? – Any serious dissensions or disagreements? – Any formal engagement or betrothal?

Question 6: Is there any circumstance whatever, or any person, putting pressure on you to marry? Do you consider yourself completely free in your choice of partner? In the timing of your marriage now?

1026 NCCB-USCC, BCPRP, Faithful to Each Other, p.96.

1027 Cfr. AECAWA, The Pastoral Care of Marriage, pp. 29-30.

1028 The content of these questions is largely drawn from AECAWA, The Pastoral Care of Marriage Preparation, pp.31-55.

Question 7: Do you understand and accept that marriage is not only a natural union, but a sacred institution established by God the creator? Do you understand and accept that Christ the Lord raised marriage to a new and greater dignity as a sacrament which constantly gives grace and help to you? Do you realise that your marriage has a lot to do with the eternal salvation of yourself and your future spouse, and also of your children?

Question 8: To what extent have you considered together the responsibilities of married life and their lifelong implications? What do you consider the major responsibilities of matrimony, of you to your partner and of your partner to you?

Question 9: Do you accept that you and your partner undertake to give yourselves to each other alone, to the exclusion of all other sexual partners, in a bond of loving and caring for each other?

Question 10: What is your understanding of "love" or "intimacy" in marriage?

Question 11: Do you understand and accept that your giving of yourselves to each other is directed to your own personal happiness and contentment and that of your partner as "helpers" to each other in the biblical sense: and also the founding of a family of your own if God so wills?

Question 12: Do you understand that the companionship of marriage means that you will live together in a common life in which you will be equal partners before God? That you will seek to establish a home for which both of you will share responsibility? That you will exchange all the marital rights in a reasonable and dignified way? And that you will mutually support each other always in the struggle of life?

Question 13: Do you understand and accept the role of sacramental "Grace" in marriage, where you will meet Christ Jesus with His help in all the acts of your common life, binding you to carry out the obligations you have so generously assumed?

Question 14: Do you understand and accept that, when you and your partner exchange your marital consent, you actually confer this sacrament on each other and in so doing you set up between you a binding, life-long union in Christ?

Question 15: Do you understand and accept that the bond of marriage is not something that restrains you and limits your freedom, but a beautiful relationship with another human being that frees you to reflect in your home the everlasting fidelity of God to His people and of Christ to His Church?

Questions 16 and 17: To what extent have you discussed children in your marriage; and the demands of responsible parenthood? Do you or your partner have any "outside" children who will be brought into the marital home? If so, have you discussed the integration of these children into your marriage and their relationship with each of you?

Question 18: Are there any personal relationships in your past life which place continuing responsibilities upon you, and which your partner does not know about?

Question 19: Do you feel reasonably confident that you and your partner are, here and now, capable with the grace of God and your own mutual assistance to each other of assuming and discharging the duties and responsibilities of Christian marriage as taught by the Catholic Church?

Questions 20 and 21: Do you promise with God's help always to give a good Christian example in your home? Do you promise also to invoke the blessings of God upon your marriage, not only in the ceremony of its celebration but also in family prayer and religious practice, for the duration of your married life together?

The prenuptial inquiry questionnaire should be appropriately filed in the parish archives. It should be made known that only the prenuptial inquiry is a canonical prerequisite and the necessary information for marriage procedure is not any way a matter of public record[1029].

It is pertinent to note that the questions in this prenuptial inquiry form can immensely assist the prospective couple to know about themselves very well and to understand properly the meaning of marriage as sacrament and an intimate union between a man and a woman which is instituted by Christ. A large number of engaged couples today attempt marriage without properly understanding what they are committing themselves to. Thus, proper and specific instruction must be given on the meaning and implications of the canonical promises of unity, indissolubility, and openness to offspring to make sure that engaged couples desire the intention of the Church about marriage[1030].

Section 3: Review of Marriage Prenuptial Inquiry or Inventory

This particular section can be taken up by the parish priest, assistant parish priest, deacon, catechist, or even a lay minister who presided over the inventory. It is also an ample opportunity to seek the assistance of properly trained married couples to help in preparing the prospective couples for marriage. The purpose of this section is to discuss the results of the prenuptial inquiry form, the strengths and weaknesses of the prospective couple's communication process, and to review with them the results of the FOCCUS inventory or any other method used. The prospective couples should be assured by the parish priest or his delegate that the FOCCUS inventory used as the case may be is not a test to assess their success or failure in married life but is intended to be a proper guideline designed to assist

1029 Ibid. p.30.

1030 Cfr. Archdiocese of Denver, "What God Has Joined…", Particular Norms, p. 2.

them learn more about themselves and their intimate union. It has to be properly explained to them that the results of the prenuptial inquiry are being discussed in a bid to identify in them their strengths and weaknesses so that they can live their lives together as husband and wife without any problem[1031].

Another purpose of this section is to examine the sacramental aspects of the couple's human covenant. The Vatican II Council Fathers in speaking about married love emphasise that: "Authentic married love is caught up into divine love and is directed and enriched by the redemptive power of Christ and the salvific action of the Church, with the result that the spouses are effectively led to God... "[1032]. The love the Council Fathers are talking about involves the good of the entire person, the couples themselves, and the whole Church, as marriage is not only for the couples who are entering into it, but also for the entire ecclesial community. This stress in the theology of marriage is consistent with the beliefs of contemporary sociology that this is the first age whereby people marry not just for marrying sake, but they marry and remain in their marriage because of the love they have for each other. Therefore, there is this stress on the mutual exchange of love as constituting the sacrament of marriage, on married love as the foundation of the institution of marriage, and on the necessity for growth in this love so as to bring this marriage sacrament to its full realization[1033].

The purpose also is to confirm the unique gifts each of the couple brings to the relationship and assist them to resolve any problem that arises. If the issues of trial marriage, polygamy, premarital sex or pregnancy before marriage have not yet surfaced, it should be discussed as part of the prenuptial inquiry or the inventory, the parish priest should evaluate the general readiness of the prospective couple so as to proceed with the normal process of marriage preparation. If on the other hand, the session is executed by a catechist, a married couple, or other qualified lay minister, the necessity for mutual collaboration with the parish priest or assistant parish priest or even deacon should not be discarded[1034].

On some occasions, reviewing the inventory properly in one session may not be realistic because of the many serious issues discovered. In view of this, additional sessions should be organised as necessity demands. A very effective and successful approach to have adequately trained married couples coordinate the review in their various homes for about three meetings, as required. The knowledge and experience of established married couples that are actively living the faith as married couples give an invaluable witness to the prospective couples[1035].

1031 Cfr. Diocese of Columbus, Policies and Guidelines for Marriage Preparation, loc.cit.

1032 GS, 48 §2.

1033 Cfr. Diocese of Shreveport, Sacramental Guidelines, p. 132.

1034 Cfr. Archdiocese of Denver, "What God Has Joined...", Particular Norms, p.13.

1035 Cfr. Ibid. pp.13-14.

Experience has shown in this regard, the worth of the witness of married couples, who live their vocation in light of the Gospel, in preparing prospective couples for marriage. When they speak out of their own conviction and from their own personal experiences concerning God, Church, sacrifices, love, commitment, prayer, stewardship, service and forgiveness, they render a powerful witness[1036].

Section 4: A Three-day Instructional Workshop

In this section, the prospective couples are advised to fulfil this part of proximate preparation by seizing the opportunity to attend a three days instructional workshop in their parishes which will be organised by the marriage preparation team or the Marriage Advisory Council as the case may be and hosted by the parish priest or assistant parish priest as circumstances permit. The three days workshops or sessions are for the prospective couples who are being married for the first time in the parish.

This instructional workshop will be held on a regular basis during the year in different locations of the parishes in each of the dioceses in Igboland. It will all be dependent on when each of the dioceses in Igboland will be organising such workshops. The motive of this workshop is to guaranty all prospective spouses an opportunity to attend a marital course in their own parish.

The first day will address such topics like: marriage as a sacrament, family of origin, communication, and decision-making. It avails the prospective couples the opportunity to understand the church's teaching on God's plan for marriage thereby reawarekening their faith and emphasising the importance of making Christ the foundation of their marriage[1037]. The engaged should be made to know that an authentic and loving marriage provides in a unique manner a daily opportunity to respond to the baptismal call of promoting God's kingdom in their lives and in the lives of others around them. In this intimate partnership of marriage they expose themselves in their strengths and weaknesses to each other. They strive to breakdown the barriers that could stand in their way of their relating to each other with greater honesty, empathy and humility. In creating deeper communion with each other they are opening themselves to greater communion with God. In permitting God to reign in their marital bond and in their family, they are fortifying the institution of marriage and family, the foundations of human society[1038].

This section also provides an opportunity for the prospective couples to have an overview of the biblical teachings on marriage by drawing essentially from

1036 Cfr. Dioceses of New Jersey, Section 1: The Marriage Preparation Process, p.14.

1037 Cfr. Archdiocese of Denver, "What God Has Joined…", Particular Norms, p. 14.

1038 Cfr. W.P. Roberts, "Christian Marriage a Divine Calling", In T.A. Salzman – T.M. Kelly – J.J. O' keefe, eds. Marriage in the Catholic Tradition, New York 2004, p. 103.

Genesis 1-3, Matthew 19, and Ephesus 5. The facilitators have to explain to them the aim of God's plan for marriage as to show that God is the author of marriage, his plan is to do us good, to show that without God's involvement in marriage it can not be blessed, and to show that access to such blessings is through Jesus Christ who raised this union to a sacrament[1039]. They have to also explain to them the meaning and importance of the commitments made in the exchange of the vows[1040].

The second day of the workshop will treat such themes as marital intimacy, human sexuality, conflict resolution, finances and spirituality. In this second day workshop, prospective couples should be made to understand that Christ modelled for us how to be in relationship to the one we love in marriage by giving his life to his spouse, the church. But God does not ask them to give their life for their partner, but to focus on each other. When they focus on each other in love, the result is joy. They have to understand that learning to give themselves to each other is as imperative as learning to receive their partner's gift of self. When they give to the best of their ability and receive graciously and passionately, they have the power to make their relationship move beyond bound. In this case, no outside influence can penetrate a union where both of them focus on each other in love[1041].

Also such theme like sexuality has to be made clear to them that sex is intimately connected with our personal identity. Our sexuality transcends beyond the physical and incorporates everything we tend to be. And if sex is part of our entire being, it becomes part of our communication and as such, it exists in all our daily lives and not just confined to a one-way traffic. If this truth is accepted, the engaged couple should be "sexually active with their partner every day by communicating deeply with each other all day long[1042].

So the human sexuality draws from the biblical foundation already laid to present the beauty and goodness of God's plan for sexual relationship. The aim is to explain the reasons behind the meaning of Catholic teaching in a manner that will make sense to people of today. Particular awareness will be allotted to the imperative moral distinction between contraceptive and natural family planning as we are going to see in section five of the component of this proximate preparation[1043].

The third day of the workshop will focus on such interesting topics like unity and indissolubility, procreation and education of children, consent, divorce, trial

---

1039 Cfr. R. Sanders – O. Sanders, Walking in Abundance for Life: Marriage Enrichment and Preparation Course, Indiana 2009, p. 2.

1040 Cfr. Archdiocese of Denver, "What God Has Joined…", Particular Norms, p. 15.

1041 Cfr. M. Feehan, Saying I Do, pp. 34-35.

1042 Cfr. Ibid. pp. 30-31.

1043 Cfr. Archdiocese of Denver, "What God Has Joined…", Particular Norms, p. 15.

marriage, polygamy, as they affect us and remain challenges that face us in Igboland and Africa as a continent. During this section, the engaged couples should be aware of the fact that openness to welcoming children and training them is central to the sacrament of marriage. The gift of children enables them to experience the enriching contributions that children inevitably make when a couple become a family. Children are signs of their love for each other and God's love for them[1044]. At the same time, they have to know that it is God who gives child and when it does not come, they should take it in good faith and waits for the appropriate time for it to come. They should not device foul means in order to get children born from such marriage.

The decision to have children is an important one for couples. It is an act of faith for the future generation. The prospective couples should know that there is much more to having children. It is a total commitment to raising these children until they are capable of living on their own and to care about them for the rest of their lives[1045]. The eagerness to adopt a child should always be a joint decision of both couple. It is always a good idea to discuss on this type of issue together and not to make assumptions concerning what your marriage partner is having in mind or thinks about it[1046].

Section 5: Natural Family Planning Instruction

In accordance with the proposed guidelines for the Igbo dioceses, prospective couples preparing for marriage in Igboland should be introduced to Natural Family Planning (NFP). The NFP is an educational course that helps spouses organise the size of their families. The method is based on observations of the naturally occurring signs and symptoms of the fertile and infertile phases of a woman's menstrual cycle[1047]. It teaches them to observe, record, as well as interpret female body changes related to ovulation[1048].

The marriage covenant according to the Church's teaching is ordered by its own very nature to the well-being of the spouses and to the procreation and upbringing of children[1049]. Hence, there is a fundamental connection between children and marriage since openness to children is an essential element of marriage.

1044 Cfr. M. Feehan, Saying I Do, pp. 34-35.

1045 Cfr. J.L. Thomas – D.M. Thomas, eds. Beginning Your Marriage, Chicago 1994, p. 127.

1046 Ibid. Pp. 132-133.

1047 Cfr.DioceseofSacramento,NaturalFamilyPlanning.http//www.diocese-sacramento.org/family_youth_young_adult/natural_family_planning.html. (Accessed: 28.11.2011); Catholic Wedding Help, Preparing for a Lifelong Marriage. http//www.catholicweddinghelp.com/wedding-planning/03-marriage-prep.htm. (Accessed: 28.11.2011).

1048 Cfr.ArchdioceseofLosAngeles,AboutNaturalFamilyPlanning. http//www.archdiocese.la/prayer/sacraments/family/nfp/index.html. (Accessed: 28.11.2011).

1049 Cfr. C. 1055 §1 CIC/1983.

In the most extensive treatment of this topic, Pope Paul VI affirms: "Marriage, then, is far from being the effect of chance or the result of the blind evolution of natural forces…. As a consequence, husband and wife, through that mutual gift of themselves, which is specific and exclusive to them alone, seek to develop that kind of personal union in which they complement one another in order to co-operate with God in the generation and education of new lives"[1050] In view of this, assisting couples to deepen their conjugal love and in doing so achieve responsible parenthood is part of the church's pastoral care of family to engaged and married couples.

Instruction in Natural Family Planning is one of the most practical ways that the church can assist spouses conform to the will of God in their married lives. It examines the dignity of the human person with the ambience of marriage and family in human sense of it should not use drugs, devices or surgical procedures to avoid pregnancy[1051].

In explaining the ambiguity of the word "Family Planning", the Catholic Bishop Conference of Nigeria says: "Unfortunately "family planning" is an ambiguous expression. For some people it simply means what it says, like responsible parenthood; a family plans, or spouse's plan, for the proper development of the family, including the likely number and spacing of children who can be properly provided for, the due size of the family in one's circumstances, and so on. Not only can there be no objection to family planning in this sense, but indeed every husband and wife, all parents, are morally responsible before God to use their intelligence in family leadership, to plan their families in accordance with their abilities and competence. Irresponsibly producing more children than can be properly provided for is immoral before God and man"[1052].

The increasing rate of irresponsible bearing of more offspring than can be adequately cared for from married couples in Igboland leaves much to be desired. There are parents who not having enough to care for themselves not to talk of their children goes about giving birth to ten to twelve children as the case may be. As a result of this, the children born in such homes suffer a lot without being provided for of their daily bread.

Therefore, one of the best ways for spacing out children is by going through the Natural Family Planning programme. It is natural, highly effective and medically safe. It can foster spiritual, intellectual, emotional and physical intimacy between couples[1053]. This is very imperative considering the fact that most of the

---

1050 HV, 8 §2.

1051 Cfr. Diocese of Columbus, Policies and Guidelines for Marriage Preparation, loc.cit; Diocese of Sacramento, Natural Family Planning, loc.cit.

1052 CBN, Family Planning and Population Control, p.37.

1053 Cfr. J.L. Thomas – D.M. Thomas, Beginning Your Marriage, p. 136.

homes in Igboland are over populated with children without properly caring for them.

We suggest therefore, that couples should learn to recognise and appreciate the fertility signs in their own body. "The information should enable them to monitor the signs of the woman's body during her menstrual periods to determine times of fertility and infertility. This will help them to achieve or postpone pregnancy without considering abortion"[1054]. It is worthy to know that when couples follow this process of NFP, they "respect the inseparable connection between the unitive and procreative meanings of human sexuality, they are acting as "ministers" of God's plan and they "benefit from" their sexuality according to the original dynamism of "total" self-giving, without manipulation or alteration"[1055].

However, care must be taken not to equate family planning with the use of contraception[1056] to control and regulate pregnancy, because "deliberate interven-

1054 P.K. Amevor, New Approaches to Marriage Preparation, p. 233.

1055 FC, 32 §5.

1056 CBN, Family Planning and Population Control, pp. 37-39. "However, the expression "family planning" often, indeed usually, means the use of some contraceptive or other techniques to prevent the generation of children. Thus, some family planners refuse to consider abortion and sterilization as proper techniques, whereas others cite abortion as the perfect birth preventive and sterilization as the perfect contraceptive; some include periodic abstinence (the use of menstrual cycle rhythm), others do not.... The Catholic Church, as indeed all other Christian churches previously and some still today, insist that interference with innocent prenascent life (abortion) and interference with the natural functioning of the sexual faculties (contraception) are incompatible with personal dignity and sexual integrity.... We first wish to allude to the intimate, almost inevitable connection between contraception and abortion. Many family planners like to propose contraception as the best way to reduce or eliminate abortion. Thus they justify it as a moral action. But the fact is that every country which has expanded contraceptive practice has soon been forced to relax or abandon its abortion laws. The reason is two-fold: the undependability and unsatisfactoriness of many kinds of contraceptives or many kinds of people; and the contraceptive mentality, which is usually unwilling to tolerate a lapse in contraceptive effectiveness. Thus when contraception fails, as happens very frequently, the result is quite often resort to abortion. Instead of curtailment of abortion being an argument for the use of contraceptives, its great increase constitutes a major objection to it. A recent study of the pro-contraception, pro-abortion Population Council in America showed that almost every woman now using contraceptives would have at least and probably more abortions before the end of her child bearing life. Contraception itself is an unworthy action, a denial of the very meaning of the marital act. The marital union is an expression of the two spouses complete commitment to each other as life-long partners in parenthood, support and companionship. Contraception is denied of that completeness. By definition the sexual act is the natural union of male and female generative elements. But contraception affirms the coming together of male and female, but blocks the completion of the very generative union which makes the coming together possible. It implies the sufficiency of sex without its openness to generation. If sex can legitimately have such anti-generative meaning, there is no reason why it need be limited to marriage. Precisely because it is treated this way do we have such a variety of pre-marital, extra-marital and contra-marital types of sexual misuse".

ing, by the use of contraceptive practices, to close off an act of intercourse to the possibility of procreation is a way of separating the unitive meaning of marriage from the procreative meaning. This is objectively wrong in and of itself and is essentially opposed to God's plan for marriage and proper human development. It makes the act of intercourse signify, or speak, something less than the unreserved self-gift intended in the marriage promises. The language of the body that is meant to express self-gift becomes mixed with another message, a contrary message- namely, the refusal to give oneself entirely. Thus the unitive meaning of that language is falsified"[1057].

Natural Family Planning, as we are suggesting should be introduced into the programmes for marriage preparation in each of the dioceses in Igboland. It is an educational process that tends to understand an imperative biological process that many women in Igboland as well as other parts of the world are not aware of, and it allows couples to function in consonant with the will of God and to remain open to life. It is not "the rhythm method" that is focused on calendar calculations of the woman's typical menstrual cycle. It rather relies on the couple's observation of variations in the woman's temperature and the characteristics of cervical mucus[1058].

Therefore, for NFP to be effective in our dioceses trained instructors are required to ensure the proper instruction of all prospective couples preparing for marriage. Profitable as it is, every parish in our dioceses should endeavour to have its own certified Natural Family Planning instructor or married couple well at home with the method. With a collaborative effort on the part of the parish priests, assistant parish priests, deacons, catechists, and other lay faithful to promote and foster NFP at the parish and diocesan level and recruit more instructors, this will be a goal that is realistic and achievable[1059].

2.4. Immediate Preparation

The immediate preparation for the marriage celebration in the Catholic dioceses of Igboland should take place at least three months before the actual wedding so as to render new meaning, content, and form to the prenuptial inquiry needed by canon law[1060]. It comprises of the final preparatory meetings between the prospective couple, the parish priest, the catechist, members of the formation team, and also the family members of the engaged couple. The goal is to strengthen the

1057 USCCB, Marriage: Love and Life in the Divine Plan, Washington D.C. 2009, p.18.
1058 Cfr. Catholic Wedding Help, Preparing for a Lifelong Marriage, loc.cit.
1059 Cfr. Archdiocese of Denver, "What God Has Joined...", Particular Norms, p.16.
1060 Cfr. FC, 66 §7.

formation received during remote and proximate preparation periods, prepare the liturgy for the wedding, and put final preparations so that the prospective couple will be worthy for the celebration of their matrimonial sacrament. It is also to evaluate and assist in accomplishing the readiness of the prospective couple to confer upon each other and then worthy to live the marriage sacrament[1061].

The immediate preparation programme in Igboland should include these three sequences of events:

Section 1: Final meeting with the parish priest and review of previous preparation.
Section 2: A two-day retreat as an opportunity for reconciliation
Section 3: Planning of the wedding liturgy.

Section 1: Final Meeting with the Parish Priest and Review

In this phase, it is pertinent to remember that the process of this stage of preparation for marriage is an ample opportunity to deepen and strengthen an engaged couple's understanding of sacramental marriage, educate them in skills, enhance their awareness and personal growth through the discovery of their unique qualities, strengths and weaknesses, while rendering witness to the support of the church[1062]. Hence, it is recommendable that the parish priest or his assistant witnessing the marriage meet with the prospective couple at least three times during the period of immediate preparation to review and synthesize their previous preparation and receive catechesis on the liturgical actions and texts of the Marriage Rite. He should also be ready to answer any last-minute questions the prospective couple are going to pose concerning the church's vision of marriage and their final preparation for the sacrament. This in no doubt will help the couple to engage in full and active participation in their wedding.

The parish priest should during this final meeting employ suitable methods to assist the prospective couple start a process of discernment about their understanding and disposition toward the marriage sacrament and their overall readiness for marriage and family life. He will use this opportunity to put the prospective couple in contact with other married couples who will assist them in planning their wedding liturgy.

If the parish priest or assistant parish priest who will witness and officiate at the wedding liturgy cannot be available during this last meeting, a priest from the parish where the wedding will take place carries out this function of reviewing their previous preparation with the couple. Even when the marriage is to take

1061 Cfr. Archdiocese of Denver, "What God Has Joined...", Particular Norms, p. 17; Diocese of Columbus, Policies and Guidelines, loc.cit.
1062 Cfr. Diocese of Columbus, Policies and Guidelines, loc.cit.

place before another priest other than the ones mentioned already, through a dispensation from canonical form, a priest or deacon supplies this component of immediate preparation for the prospective couple[1063]. The wisdom and experience of a formation coordinator or of a lay married couple can assist the parish priest at this stage of immediate preparation.

Section 2: A Two-day Retreat as an opportunity for Reconciliation

There should be at least two days retreat for prospective couples in our different dioceses who are preparing for their wedding. Where it is possible, we recommend that these two days retreat should start on the evening of Friday and ends on Sunday after mass celebration. The retreat will offer the engaged couples effective tools and practical insights that will aid them as spouses in their married and family life. During the retreat they will learn ways to maintain and nurture their love for each other. The retreat will enable them to come away better able to face, cope with and overcome the unavoidable troubles and crises of marital life with determination and trust. It will provide them with experiences that will assist them grow in knowledge and understanding of each other and deepen their love and commitment to each other[1064].

During this section, the prospective couples should be invited to receive the sacrament of penance and be encouraged to pray together on daily bases during this stage of immediate preparation. In light of the current waves of polygamy, trial marriage, and premarital sexual activity in Igboland, it is basically imperative for prospective couples to be reconciled with Christ, the church, and one another prior to the celebration of the sacrament of matrimony. In this case, pastoral sensitivity will meet the suitable ways of encouraging the couples to set aside time for prayer and reception of the sacrament of Reconciliation[1065].

Therefore, it is the responsibility of the parish priest, his assistant, deacon, catechist, even the parents of the prospective couples to encourage them to receive the sacrament of Reconciliation in advance before the wedding day. Announcing the presence of the sacrament of Reconciliation during the retreat often affords the engaged and others a privileged opportunity to receive the grace of the sacrament of Reconciliation and to deepen and strengthen their knowledge of the sacred character of their soon to be made marriage covenant[1066].

It is pertinent during this retreat to emphasize on the interconnectivity between the sacraments of Marriage, Reconciliation, and the Eucharist. Also the wisdom and experience of a married couple or formation team can also be of

1063 Cfr. Diocese of Richmond, Called to Marriage, loc.cit.

1064 Cfr. Ibid.

1065 Cfr. Archdiocese of Denver, "What God Has Joined…", Particular Norms, p.18.

1066 Cfr. Dioceses of New Jersey, Section1: The Marriage Preparation Process, p. 17.

great service in assisting the prospective couples learn how to pray together and form the spirituality of marriage. At the end of this retreat, the couples will be able to evaluate their readiness to marry and verify for themselves what they have achieved during this retreat and reconciliation period.

Section 3: Planning of the Wedding Liturgy

The planning of the wedding liturgy is also included in the stage of immediate preparation for the celebration of the sacrament of matrimony. In planning the wedding liturgy in Igbo dioceses, parish priest, assistant parish priest, deacon, catechist, liturgist, and other important pastoral workers should dedicate suitable time with the prospective couples so as to ensure their active and informed participation in the liturgy. The wedding liturgy itself should encourage the participation of the ecclesial community in worship, express the faith and commitment of the prospective couple and of the assembly of the ecclesial, and invite the faith community prayer for the prospective couple to serve as a support in their married and family life[1067].

The Rite of Marriage urges that the prospective couples should be furnished with a review of the bases of Christian doctrine. "This may include instruction on the teachings about marriage and the family, on the rites used in the celebration of the sacrament itself, and on the prayers and readings. In this way, the bridegroom and the bride will receive far greater benefit from the celebration"[1068]. The Code of 1983 emphasises a grace-filled and appropriate liturgical celebration of marriage that will teach that "the spouses signify and share in that mystery of unity and of fruitful love that exists between Christ and the Church"[1069].

The Rite of Marriage establishes various options for the readings, prayers, and the ceremonies of the wedding liturgy. As marriage preparation is based more on the lifetime experiences of a couple than the single event of wedding, the preparation of a wedding liturgy itself is also a pertinent part of the celebration process. Hence, a parish preparation course for marriage should support the active participation of the prospective couple, their parents, extended family members, communities and their guests in the wedding ritual[1070]. The prospective couples should be offered the availability of a musician, pastoral minister, sponsor couple, catechist, or a parish member who is properly trained in liturgical planning and

1067 Cfr. Diocese of Beaumont, Guidelines for the Sacrament of Matrimony, 1996, p.5. http//www.dioceseofbmt.org/resources/resources/sacrament-celebration/marriage.html.(Accessed: 28.10.2011).

1068 Rite of Marriage, Nuptial Blessing, no. 121. In NCCB-USCC, BCPRP, Faithful to Each Other, p. 114.

1069 C. 1063, 3° CIC/1983.

1070 Cfr. Dioceses of New Jersey, Pastoral Policies and Guidelines for Marriage Preparation, p. 6.

who is familiar with the rural church's interior schedules and design. Such assistance may be important in a discussion of all aspects and selections for their wedding liturgy with due consideration to the proposed guidelines and the Rite of Marriage[1071] .

The parish priest or his delegate or even the formation team who are working with the prospective couples should familiarize the engaged with the Rite of Marriage. By so doing, the pastoral effectiveness of such a celebration will be heightened if the texts of readings, prayers and songs correspond to the needs of the religious and spiritual preparation, and the aptitude of those participating.

Planning of the wedding liturgy leads the prospective couple to the marriage celebration. In this regard, the wedding ceremony should echo the distinctive quality of Christian faith, with special emphasis given to the celebration of the Word, the exchange of vows by the spouses promising to live together in love and fidelity, and the nuptial blessing[1072].

It is appropriate for each of the dioceses in Igboland to have a policy with regard to wedding music. This policy about the wedding music should be communicated to the prospective couples in time as part of their preparation so as to avoid last minute crises and misunderstanding involve in the marriage celebration[1073]. The music itself should be suitable to the liturgy and help the community to pray. It is integral to the sacramental celebrations and cantor and members of the church choir should assist the congregation to take active part in the singing during the wedding. Music is very important in that it helps to bind the congregation of worshipers together and facilitates their expression of joy and of support for the prospective couples. It should allow the congregation to express and share their faith in the church assembly[1074].

The importance of music in the marriage celebration cannot be over-emphasised. "Music, when used in the liturgical rites of the church, is a servant-art. It serves the Word of God and the sacramental action. Its purpose is to glorify God and to transform God's people. Music should assist the assembled believers to express and share, to nourish and strengthen their interior commitment of faith as that faith is experienced in life. It should heighten the texts so that the meaning is uncovered more fully and more effectively"[1075].

The parish priest, the liturgist, the choir master of the parish should assist the engaged couples to select good and appropriate songs for their wedding. The

1071 Cfr. Dioceses of New Jersey, Section 1: The Marriage Preparation Process, p. 16.

1072 Cfr. Ibid.

1073 Cfr. NCCB-USSC, BCPRP, Faithful to Each Other, p. 120.

1074 Cfr. Diocese of Beaumont, Guidelines for the Sacrament of Matrimony, p. 5.

1075 Diocese of Fort Worth, Guidelines for the Preparation and Celebration of the Sacrament of Marriage, p. 19.

stress here should be on liturgical songs, most importantly the ones whose texts are drawn from scriptural sources that are contextual to the sacrament of matrimony. In selecting these songs, care must be taken so that the selection does not hinder the natural flow of the wedding liturgy. A parish choir master should function as a song leader so that the congregation will feel secure and comfortable during the wedding ceremony and thereby take active part in singing[1076].

Special attention should be paid when weddings are to be celebrated during the seasons of Lent and Advent. Thus, prospective couples planning their weddings during these two periods should be told of the special nature of these seasons and plan properly. For instance, selections of suitable music and antiphons, readings, and decoration of the alter and the church itself should be done in accordance with the season. If a visiting priest is to officiate the wedding mass, a copy of the parish marriage policy and guidelines should be sent to him in time prior to the wedding date so that he will take time to go through it and know what is involved in the celebration of the marriage sacrament in such a parish[1077].

The date and time for the rehearsal should be set to ensure that everything is well mastered before the actual celebration itself. It is very important that all those taking part during the wedding liturgy are present during this rehearsal so as to familiarize themselves with the church's activities and to receive instructions suitable to their role during the wedding ceremony. This should also provide an opportunity for the parents, and other members of the two parties to meet and know exactly how they are going to take part in the wedding liturgy and what is expected from them. In this case, the prospective couples are encouraged to make the proper introductions of their parents and family members to the parish priest or his assistant or any other priest delegated to conduct the rehearsal[1078].

2.4.1. Marriage Preparation Programmes

2.4.1.1. Introduction

Marriage today in Igboland as well as other parts of the world faces a variety of challenges in all facets of life. The proposed marriage preparation programmes under the period of immediate preparation will help prepare engaged couples for many of these challenges and equips them with appropriate tools they can use in their day to day lives that will help them live a loving, happy and long lasting marriage covenant. The programmes normally take different forms, but their goal is to assist engaged couples discuss about issues that may not have come up while

1076 Cfr. Ibid. p. 20.

1077 Cfr. Dioceses of New Jersey, Section 1: The Marriage Preparation Process, p. 16.

1078 Cfr. Ibid. p. 17.

they were dating, and it provides them with proven strategies for overcoming their challenges in married and family life.

One thing is clear about these programmes. They are important aids to prospective couples, but they are not to be substituted for the private sessions with the parish priest or his delegate. We suggest that prospective couples seeking to enter into marriage in the Igbo dioceses should participate in one of the programmes. That will give them room to take stock of themselves and prepare well to tackle their challenges that are inevitable in marriage. The programmes will be designed to take place during the three months period of immediate preparation in all the dioceses.

2.4.1.2. Parish Pre-Cana Programme

The Pre-Cana programme is a one day marriage preparation programme designed to help prospective couples in preparing for their life-long marriage. The name "Cana" was the name of the town where Jesus Christ attended a wedding and performed his first public miracle by turning water into wine (John 2: 1-11). Hence, the name "Pre-Cana" means "before marriage". It will be a time for the prospective couples to focus entirely on their union with each other, with God and with his Church. It should be also a time to study, review, and then learn the truth and the joy about God's plan for marriage[1079].

The parish marriage formation team will be responsible for this programme in their various parishes. This formation team will comprise mainly of married couples and the parish priest or his assistant. Single persons with expertise in some professional fields could also be incorporated. The programme should be offered on various Saturdays throughout the year at the parish centre. The programme may begin at 9.00 am and concludes at 4.00pm. It should be a day-long marriage programme.

The day-long programme will consist of a series of presentations giving essential instruction on the nature of Christian marriage, the essential elements of marriage, its ends, God's plan for marriage and family life, polygamy and divorce, responsible parenthood and natural family planning, to mention but a few. There will be also time allotted for couples discussion and a question-and-answer session to help them promote good dialogue between themselves. At the end of this programme a liturgical mass celebration should be used to conclude it.

1079 Cfr.DioceseofPeoria,DiocesanPrograms–PartOne:Pre-CanaConferences. http//www.cdop.org/pages/AOfficeFamilyMarriage.aspx.(Accessed: 30.11.2011).

2.4.1.3. Diocesan Pre-Cana Programme

The Pre-Cana programme should also be offered at the diocesan level just like that of the parish level. The diocesan Pre-Cana programme is an option for prospective couples whose parish has no Pre-Cana formation team or their own programme and that of the parish programme do not coincide. The diocesan presenting team will comprise primarily of married couples and a priest serving as a Pre-Cana team coordinator or chaplain. The programme will begin with mass as it is on Sunday at 10.00 am and ends at 5.00 pm in the evening of that Sunday.

The full day programme will enable the engaged couples to discuss their strengths and weaknesses, the sacrament of marriage, family life, communication, family finances, sexuality, their role in the church and society, children, parenting and natural family planning. At the end of each topic, there will be time for sharing of thoughts and feelings by each engaged couple to help them make the beauty of the marriage doctrine a living reality.

2.4.1.4. Engaged Encounter Weekend

The Engaged Encounter Weekend is a weekend retreat led by a team of married couples who share their own stories and life experiences in their married lives. There will be also the presence of a priest, usually the parish priest to coordinate the encounter. This programme offers the prospective couples an ample opportunity to look at their commitment to each other in a deeper manner as they prepare for a sacramental marriage. This weekend encounter is designed to give spouses preparing for marriage the opportunity to open dialogue concerning various aspects of their planned life together. Here, the engaged will be giving time to talk about their strengths, weaknesses, desires, ambitions, money, family, attitudes about children, and their role in the church and community. Such a weekend will be structured so that the engaged couples hear topics and then spend an ample time to write and to discuss them. But it will not be a group sharing format[1080].

The members of the formation team will discuss these topics in the context of their own experience while sharing their own personal stories. The primary goal is to provide time for the prospective couples to reflect privately and discuss the issues at hand. The weekend programme will avail the couples the opportunity to move away from the pressures and anxieties of work and wedding plans and spend the whole weekend with one another while focusing on their relationship as a couple, with God and his Church. The emphasis of the weekend is on Christian

1080 Cfr. Diocese of San Jose, San Jose Catholic Engaged Encounter. http//www.dsj.org/being-catholic/marriage-in-the-catholic-church/san-jose-catholic-engaged-encounter. (Accessed: 30.11.2011).

marriage and not the wedding itself. They will use this Weekend Encounter to get to know other couples and make family friends. Also the opportunity to take part in the sacraments of Reconciliation and Eucharist, make such a weekend a complete one[1081]. At the end of the Engaged Encounter Weekend, the couples who participated in this programme will leave the retreat with a certificate of completion that the officiating priest may need as part of the parish marriage preparation.

2.4.1.5. Sponsor Couple Programme

The Sponsor Couple Programme is a mentor programme. In this programme a married couple will be trained primarily for this task and assigned in the parish to administer and shoulder this responsibility. The sponsor couples are basically married couples who act as friends and mentors to the prospective couples, furnishing them with support and tips as they prepare for their marriage. They should be available to the prospective couples in their preparations for the wedding liturgy and be also available during their wedding. They should also continue to be present to the couple even after the wedding to direct them in their early stage of married life.

Normally the prospective couple preparing for marriage do their homework first by studying the meaning of Christian marriage and the skills of such a marriage. They will then meet with their sponsors in the home of the sponsor couple. This allows the sponsor couple the opportunity to use their own experiences to confirm, coach and even challenge the prospective couple to learn and practice more appropriate and effective marriage qualities[1082].

The sponsor couples, when formed in the different dioceses in Igboland will help provide encouragement and example to the prospective couples, assisting them to recognize the challenges of marriage and family life and leading them to face those challenges. They will assist them to understand and realize that marriage formation is a gradual and on going process which help sustain and develop their life and love throughout the whole course of their marriage[1083]. This programme when considered and used, will no doubt, help to keep a closer, more personal and continuous contact with the prospective couples in Igboland.

1081 Cfr. Diocese of Peoria, Diocesan Programs – Part One: Engaged Couple Encounter, loc.cit.

1082 Cfr.USCCDE,"MarriagePreparationProgrammes,AretheyWorking?". http//www.ourcatholicmarriage.org/parishes/importance/Do-Marriage-Prep-Programs-Work.pdf. (Accessed: 30.11.2011).

1083 Cfr. Diocese of Richmond, Called to Marriage, loc.cit.

2.5. Ongoing Support after Marriage

Marriage preparation starts at infancy and continues after the marriage must have taken place. Pope John Paul II places the duty of this ongoing support after marriage upon the members of the local church community to assisting the newly married couples to find out and live their new married life and mission[1084]. There should be a mutual exchange between newly married couples and those with experience in marital union[1085]. Such assistance from family-to-family creates a model of collaboration and mutual connectivity. "Thus, within the ecclesial community – the great family made up of Christian families – there will take place a mutual exchange of presence and help among all the families, each one putting at the service of others its own experience of life, as well as the gifts of faith and grace. Animated by a true apostolic spirit, this assistance from family to family will constitute one of the simplest, most effective and most accessible means for transmitting from one to another those Christian values which are both the starting point and goal of all pastoral care"[1086]. Even the new Code recognises such assistance to be giving to those who have entered marriage so that they may achieve a spiritual and whole family life[1087].

Therefore, the pastoral care after marriage should be introduced, if it has not already started, to all the dioceses and parishes in Igboland. Each of the parishes should endeavour to develop other creative means to assist sustain a special bond between young married couples and the ecclesial community. Through this way, the young married couples will know the encouragement and companionship of such ecclesial community. The new weds will be able to share with the community the joys and achievements of their new life together and be able to look up to the community for guidance and understanding as their new life as married couples progresses[1088].

The parish sponsored-support and enrichment for newly married couples in Igboland is as important as the preparation they will receive before the celebration of their marriage in the church. Thus, "there is urgent need of a broad catechetical effort regarding the Christian ideal of conjugal communion and family life, including a spirituality of fatherhood and motherhood. Greater pastoral attention must be given to the role of men as husbands and fathers, as well as the responsibility which they share with their wives for their marriage, the family, and the raising of their children"[1089].

1084 Cfr. FC, 69 §1.
1085 Cfr. FC, 69 §2.
1086 Ibid.
1087 Cfr. C. 1063, 4° CIC/1983.
1088 Cfr. Diocese of Richmond, Called to Marriage, loc.cit.
1089 CA, 46.

Such associations in the Igbo Catholic dioceses like Christian Fathers Association (CFA), Christian Mothers Association (CMA), other pious associations in the church, and the so-called August Meeting where our Catholic women gather once every year in August (home and abroad) to discuss about the development and progress of the parish are perfect occasions to provide support for the newly young married couples. Such occasions can help young couples fit into their new role. By reaching out to them, encouraging their active participation in these associations, engaging them in discussions and showing them hospitality can assist them to feel at home in their new state of life and in the parish in which they belong instead of isolating themselves until during the presentation of their first child for baptism.

Also individual and groups participation in the pastoral care after marriage is very crucial and vital in the dioceses and parishes in Igboland. In this regard, parents, grand parents, extended family members, elders of the community, should contribute towards helping the newly married couples. Also in-laws, married daughters from the same community, age grades, and the Umunna should play significant roles to assist young couples in their new state of life. As individuals and groups, they should show deep concern and affection towards the newly married and then become part of the instruments to bring about fulfilment in their lives as married partners.

As an aid to the pastoral care after marriage, a series of marriage enrichment programmes such as Marriage Encounter Weekend, Newly Married Ministry, Married Couple Support, Sponsor Couple Enrichment Group designed basically to nurture good marriages should be formed in the different dioceses of Igboland. Such enrichment programmes for the newly married couples should mix up elements of practical nature to assist spouses adjust to married life with ongoing instruction in the church's teaching on marriage and conjugal love. It should also involve opportunities for socialization and stress the need for personal involvement in the parish community[1090]

Anniversaries in the parish church such as silver jubilee, golden or diamond jubilees which ritualize a major occasion in the lives of the people and bring out the importance of marriage should be used as opportunities to speak on important issues of concern for married young couples. Also homilies that treat about aspects of married and family life should be encouraged during week days and Sunday masses. The young married couples need to hear words concerning taking time for each other, understanding the true meaning of love, fidelity, indissolubility, rearing of children and developing a spirit of mutual forgiveness[1091]. All these efforts on the ongoing support after marriage for married couples are investments

1090 Cfr. Archdiocese of Denver, "What God Has Joined…", Supplement, p. 21.
1091 Cfr. NCCB-USSC, BCPRP, Faithful to Each Other, p. 137.

in the future of our families in Igboland and when carried out successfully will bear abundant fruit for generations to come in Igboland.

2.6. Conclusion

All along we have been dealing with the three stages of marriage preparation, trying to establish how they are going to be carried out in the dioceses and parishes of Igboland in preparing prospective couples properly for marriage. Remote preparation starts at the period of infancy and involves the family and other environmental issues that influence and prepare the person for married life. While recognizing that parents in this stage are the primary educators of their children throughout infancy and adolescence, they require proper assistance from the church, school and other larger community. Through this way, they play an important role in preparing their children for future marriage.

We also established that proximate preparation starts during the earliest days of the engagement period and continues till the final weeks before the proper marriage celebration. In this stage, the parish priests, their assistants, and deacons are encouraged to establish guidelines that will incorporate the marriage preparation process into the life of the parish. The proximate preparation programme in the dioceses should consist of five sections. These include: initial contact with the parish priest, prenuptial investigation, review of marriage prenuptial inventory, a three-day Instructional Workshop, and the Natural Family Planning instruction. Hence, preparation at this period is geared toward an evangelization and catechesis that enable engaged couples to embrace consciously and freely what the Church teaches about the marriage sacrament.

The immediate preparation comprises of the final meetings between the prospective couples and the pastoral ministers and workers. It takes place in the months and weeks immediately before the actual wedding. It should be a journey of faith, similar to that of catechumenate and it should incorporate such elements as a deeper understanding of grace and the responsibility of Christian marriage, a fuller awareness of the mystery of Christ and the Church, and a practical preparation for taking active part in the rites of the marriage liturgy[1092].

The three sections in this stage are: final meeting with the parish priest and review of the previous preparation, a two-day retreat as an opportunity for reconciliation, and planning of the wedding liturgy. A thoughtful, prayerful planning and participation in the Catholic wedding bring joy and blessings to the married life.

1092 Cfr. Ibid. p.58.

We also x-rayed some useful programmes that when establish in the dioceses, will assist the engaged couples as they prepare for their sacramental marriage. Such programmes are Parish Pre-Cana programme, Diocesan Pre-Cana programme, Engaged Encounter weekend, and Sponsor Couple programme.

Finally, we treated the support that should be given to the newly married couples after marriage. Right from the beginning of their immediate preparation, spouses should be urged that their formation in marriage does not end with their wedding. They should realize that need will arise for which the ecclesial community will continue to support them and be at their service for stability and permanence in their married life.

3. Areas of Special Circumstances

3.1. Introduction

The prospective couples contacting the church for marriage in Igbo dioceses may find themselves in conditions that affect the quality of their life experiences and also the lawfulness and validity of marriage. "Part of what a successful marriage requires of a couple is to be mature, responsible, and free. Christian marriage requires that the dimension of faith also be present in a couple's relationship. Since each couple is unique, there is no single, objective standard by which one can judge a couple's readiness to marry, nor guarantee the success of their marriage. However, specific, identifiable special circumstances may be present which indicate a need for further assessment and growth before the final decision is made to proceed with the marriage"[1093].

These special circumstances are rooted in the 1983 Code of canon law which establishes that "all persons not prohibited by law can contact marriage" (c.1058), and that "before marriage is celebrated, it must be evident that nothing stands in the way of its valid and licit celebration" (c.1066). The Code also empowers the local ordinary to "prohibit marriage, but only for a time for a serious cause and as long as that cause exists" (c.1077). The prospective couples in Igboland today visit the church with a wide range of backgrounds and family difficulties and most often parish priests in our various parishes encounter such circumstances that require special care and attention.

1093 USCCB, An Analysis of Diocesan Marriage Preparation Policies, 2005. http//www.usccb.org/issues-and-action/marriage-and-family/marriage-preparation/mpanalysis.cfm.(Accessed: 22.1.2011).

So in this section we intend to highlight some of these special circumstances that require special concern and pastoral care which the church should give these couples to ensure stability in their married and family life.

3.2. Age

The Code of 1983 stipulates that without special permission from the local ordinary, no one is to assist at a marriage of an under age when the parents are unaware of the marriage or are opposed to it for reasonable cause[1094]. In Igboland most people especially girls marry in their teen age either because of undue family pressure arising from parents who do not have money and want their daughters to marry early so as to assist in carrying the burden of the family or due to early pregnancy. In the Eastern States of Nigeria (Igboland), the age of marriage is 16 years for both male and female. Any marriage between or in respect of persons either of whom is under this age of sixteen is nullified. Therefore, marriages of minors in the Igbo dioceses must be vehemently discouraged.

Marriage preparation in which one or both of the parties is under the required age in Igbo dioceses requires that the party be assisted in evaluating their own personal maturity and the quality of their relationship with each other and that will afford them the opportunity to appreciate really the dangers of marrying too early and reconsider their plan[1095].

The Catholic Church in Igboland has the responsibility to ensure that prospective couples understand the sacred nature of marriage as a lifelong commitment. Most of our teenagers are not sufficiently mature to carry out successfully the obligations and responsibilities of marriage in contemporary Igbo society. Enough time is needed for our teenagers to acquire the spiritual, emotional, and intellectual development and balance required to make the commitment of married life. Clear proof of immaturity, especially when assisted by parental opposition, requires that the parish priest counsel the party to delay their marriage[1096].

Hence, the preparation process in Igbo dioceses should be age appropriate. The parish priest should endeavour to establish an audience not only with the young parties, but also with the parents so as to discern very well the strength of the marriage commitment. He is challenged to show special care and concern and to

1094 Cfr. C. 1071, 6° CIC/1983: "matrimonio filii familias minoris, insciis aut rationabiliter invitis parentibus".

1095 Cfr. Dioceses of New Jersey, Section III: Special Circumstances in Marriage Preparation, p. 48. http//www.diometuchen.org/medin/files/familylife/marriage-prep/family_life_marriage_prep-special_circumstances.pdf. (Accessed: 28.10.2011).

1096 Cfr. Archdiocese of Denver, "What God Has Joined…", Supplement, p. 13.

demonstrate utmost respect and sensitivity with any couple in which one or both are under age. He is not necessarily to suggest that the marriage should be put off but he is to urge that they do so according to canon 1072 of the 1983 Code. When finally the couple rejects the parish priest's admonitions, then the matter should be referred to the local ordinary so that he will make the final decision. Care must be taken as to not allow parents to pressure their daughters to marry at early age because of financial benefits.

3.3. Older Couples

Special care and consideration should be offered to older persons during the marriage preparation process when both couples are requesting for marriage for the first time. Notwithstanding the general notion in Igboland that older couples need less preparation presumably because of their maturity and experience, there are also many special cases unique to older persons that require discussion. Such cases like polygamy, previous relationships most especially divorced or widowed men and women, and other marriage related cases need to be carefully explored. The Church in Igboland should be aware that age does not automatically assure readiness for marriage. Hence, the marriage preparation process should be adapted to the age and maturity of the spouses as well as assist them in integrating their past experiences and evaluate their future together in terms of their vocation to marry.

The dioceses in Igboland must be careful not to assume that a prospective couple is ready for marriage in the church just because of the simple fact that they are older. They should know that many marriages of older couples have failed in recent past and continue to fail because of the inability of these couples to compromise individual independence with the cordial interdependence of the marriage relationship[1097].

3.4. Mixed and Inter-religious Marriages

A mixed marriage is the marriage of two baptised persons, one of whom is a Catholic with the other partner who is not a Catholic[1098]. Permission from the

1097 Cfr. Ibid. p. 18; Diocese of Columbus, Policies and Guidelines for Marriage Preparation, loc. cit.

1098 Cfr. C. 1124 CIC/1983: "Matrimonium inter duas personas baptizatas, quarum altera sit in Ecclesia catholica baptizata vel in eandem post baptismum recepta, quaeque nec ab ea actu

competent authority is needed for such a union which, in a valid marriage, is seen as a sacrament. An inter-religious marriage is a marriage between a baptised Catholic and a non baptised person of another religion such as Islam or Traditionalism, as it is the case in Igboland, and such a marriage is never regarded as a sacramental union by the church. For validity on such a marriage a dispensation from the impediment of disparity of worship is important for any marriage between a baptised Catholic and a non baptised non-catholic[1099].

In such an inter-religious marriage and also in a mixed marriage the Catholic partner must make the following promise in order to be faithful to the Catholic Church and bring up his or her children in the Catholic faith. Thus, according to canon 1125, 1° of the 1983 Code, "the catholic party is to declare that he or she is prepared to remove dangers of defecting from the faith, and is to make a sincere promise to do all in his or her power in order that all the children be baptised and brought up in the Catholic church"[1100]. Also the same canon, 2° says: "the other party is to be informed in good time of these promises to be made by the catholic party, so that it is certain that he or she is truly aware of the promise and of the obligation of the catholic party"[1101].

It is pertinent to know that under the current law of the new Code, the party who is not a catholic is required not to make an agreement or sign any promises, but he or she must be made to know that his or her catholic partner must do so. Hence, the couple should be informed of the reality of the generous efforts needed for a successful inter-religious marriage in order to think about their differences and to decide how to raise their children in a religious manner. Encouragement should be given to the prospective couples who are involved in this inter-religious marriage in the Igbo dioceses to grow in their awareness of, respect and sensitivity for their partner's faith tradition. The parish priest or his delegate, and the formation team involved in marriage preparation process should ensure that each of the parties enjoy total freedom concerning their own beliefs and practices. Developing their shared faith life and appreciating the positive aspects of their married union are to be encouraged in the church[1102].

Therefore, there should be adequate instruction given to the couples of inter-religious denominations during their preparation for marriage so that they understand the catholic partner's obligation to continue in the practice of his

formali defecerit, altera vero Ecclesiae vel communitati ecclesiali plenam communionem cum Ecclesia catholica non habenti adscripta, sine expressa auctoritatis competentis licentia prohibitum est".

1099 Cfr. C. 1086 CIC/1983.

1100 C. 1125, 1° CIC/1983.

1101 C. 1125, 2 CIC/1983.

1102 Cfr.DioceseofSanDiego,GuidelinesforMarriagePreparation,2010,pp.3-4.http//www.diocesesdiego.org/Handbook/Handbook_PDFs/Marriage.pdf. (Accessed: 28.11.2011).

or her faith[1103] and shared with the children through baptism in the Catholic Church[1104].

3.5. Pregnancy before Marriage

Pregnancy prior to marriage is one of the most difficult circumstances to be addressed with regard to marriage preparation in Igboland. This issue should be treated with a sense of wisdom and a caution to marriage as against a reason to hasten up the wedding liturgy[1105]. This is because of the obvious fact of interference with a person's capability to consent to marriage freely. Hence, the Bishops of Anglophone of West Africa emphasise: "The circumstances of a pregnancy does not per se constitute an adequate justification for a hasty marriage, but must be weighed in the light of all other considerations of the couple's suitability for each other and their state of readiness for a sacramental union"[1106]. Inspite of the pressures coming from the family members, in-laws, members of the extended family, and even outside the family circle, it is very necessary to slow down the wedding process so that the best possible decision can be made.

In a case like this, the parish priest has the obligation to teach and counsel the couple to be aware of the fact that the church does not immediately expect them to marry because of the pregnancy. The pregnancy itself can influence their sense of commitment to each other. Therefore, the parish priest should assist in inquiring whether they are committed toward marriage or toward the child in the womb. However, the parish priest should also consider their courageous decision not to abort the child and therefore has an obligation to give pastoral care and support to the engaged couple even if they are not married eventually[1107].

1103 FC, 78 §2,6,7. "In the first place, attention must be paid to the obligations that faith imposes on the Catholic party with regard to the free exercise of the faith and the consequent obligation to ensure, as far as possible, the Baptism and upbringing of the children in the Catholic faith.... – It is of the greatest importance that, through the support of the community, the Catholic party should be strengthened in faith and positively helped to mature in understanding and practicing that faith, so as to become a credible witness within the family through his or her own life and through the quality of love shown to the other spouse and the children. Marriage between Catholics and other baptised persons have their own particular nature, but they contain numerous elements that could well be made good use of and developed, both for their intrinsic value and for the contribution that they can make to the ecumenical movement. This is particularly true when both parties are faithful to their religious duties. Their common Baptism and the dynamism of grace provide the spouses in these marriages with the basis and motivation for expressing their unity in the sphere of moral and spiritual values".

1104 Cfr. F. Gavin, Pastoral Care in Marriage Preparation, p.177.

1105 Cfr. Diocese of Columbus, Policies and Guidelines for Marriage Preparation, loc.cit.

1106 AECAWA, The Pastoral Care of Marriage, p. 18.

1107 Cfr. Dioceses of New Jersey, Section III: Special Circumstances in Marriage Preparation, p. 52.

It is pertinent also to request the assistance of the parents of the couple in the counselling process as they will be of help in knowing some of the background of their daughter's pregnancy and the degree of the relationship between the two parties. It will also be very necessary to ascertain if the pregnancy is the major factor pushing them to marry at that particular time.

3.6. Previous Marriage

Pastoral care and concern are needed in the dioceses of Igboland to meet the special demands of spouses requesting for sacramental marriage after a previous union in the church. The parish priest or his assistant must be careful to find out that both spouses are canonically free to marry before continuing with the marriage preparation and to make sure that the children born from the previous marriage receive the proper care they deserve (c.1071 §1, 3°).

At the initial contact with the prospective couple the parish priest should determine that both couple are free to marry in the church. A certificate of death is needed if the couple from a previous marriage is dead. Thus, a decree establishing the freedom to marry in the church as a church annulment from the Catholic Church is needed for any marriage in which the previous spouse is still alive. Marriage preparation in the dioceses should not begin and no date should be set for the wedding until after these obligations are satisfactorily met. The parish priest should also address resolution of grief of separation from the previous union[1108].

One thing is clear. The parish priest should avoid the tendency of presuming that persons marrying for the second time do not need a great deal of marriage preparation since they are familiar with the institution of marriage. He should make them to know that marriage preparation is not only based on the institution of marriage, but is also about them preparing very well for it together and then make fruit out of it[1109].

The bishops of West Africa in discussing about this previous union opine: "The new relationship calls for a careful assessment of readiness, even though the same intensity or length of preparation may not be required. Pastors must use their own discretion, based on their knowledge of the couple's background, in

1108 Cfr. Archdiocese of Denver, "What God Has Joined…", Supplement, p. 15; Dioceses of New Jersey, Section III: Special Circumstances in Marriage Preparation, p.54; Diocese of Columbus, Policies and Guidelines for Marriage Preparation, loc.cit.

1109 Cfr. Dioceses of New Jersey, Section III: Special Circumstances in Marriage Preparation, p. 54.

determining the degree and kind of preparation that is called for in such cases"[1110]. So special care and attention are required to assist those couples understand how a previous union may effect their new marriage.

3.7. Convalidation

There are many couples in Igbo dioceses as well as in other parts of the world who marry invalidly outside the church and want to convalidate their marriages in the Catholic Church. "The effect of a convalidation is to establish a canonical marriage where there was previously only a civil marriage"[1111]. When such a situation arises, the parish priest has to treat each couple on a case-by-case basis. Discovering the reason for the marriage outside the church will likely suggest what type of preparation and precautions are to be implored to each of the couple. The couple's preparation should be like any other couple who desires to marry in the church[1112].

There are numerous reasons that push couples to seek the convalidation of their union. "It is hoped that a request is born of the couple's or the Catholic party's desire to return to the active practice of the faith. Their initiative may arise because an impediment to a valid marriage has now been removed.... It is not uncommon for a convalidation to be sought for reasons that may jeopardize the valid celebration of the new marriage. For example, a husband or wife may seek a marriage in the church to remedy a troubled relationship. This is to be addressed adequately, lest the convalidated marriage result in separation"[1113].

It is very pertinent for couples in Igbo dioceses seeking regularization of their invalid marriages to prepare properly and have time to reflect on what they are seeking for before marrying in the church. The parish priest has to explain to the couple about their making a new act of consent before the validity of their marriage (cc.1156-1160). They must be made to know that their previous marriage was invalid right from the beginning. The parish priest must make them understand that their new act of consent brings marriage into being. It will not be proper to inform them "that convalidation is simply the blessing of marriage"[1114].

It is considered very necessary for the parish priest to help the couple in finding out issues that are not yet resolved that may be inherent in the couple's marriage and find ways of resolving them before their marriage.

1110 AECAWA, The Pastoral Care of Marriage, p. 20.
1111 Dioceses of New Jersey, Section III: Special Circumstances, p. 40.
1112 Cfr. Diocese of Dallas, A Pastoral Directive and Instruction, pp. 11-12.
1113 Dioceses of New Jersey, Section III: Special Circumstances, p. 40.
1114 Ibid.

3.8. Cohabitation

There are many couples who approach the church for marriage in Igbo dioceses that are already living together. This presents a lot of challenges to the parish priest, his assistant and those in charge of marriage preparation in the dioceses. Such couples should be treated with absolute care. The parish priest or his delegate "should be welcoming and see this as opportunity for evangelization, yet at the same time they must uphold in absolutely clear terms the church's teaching that sexual intimacy is only made authentically in the context of valid marriage"[1115].

Pope John Paul II in his Apostolic Exhortation, Familiaris Consortio, gives a general approach toward couples who are cohabiting. He recommends that: "The pastors and the ecclesial community should take care to become acquainted with such situations and their actual causes, case by case. They should make tactful and respectful contact with the couples concerned, and enlighten them patiently, correct them charitably and show them the witness of Christian family life, in such a way as to smooth the path for them to regularize their situation"[1116]. Such cohabiting couples in Igbo dioceses need to take the gospel message of commitment and faithfulness very seriously as they need to be welcomed in the church with the gospel values of love, awareness, and acceptance.

There are two extremes to be avoided when dealing with cohabiting couples. The issue of cohabitation when noticed from a couple seeking to marry in the church, should not be ignored, and at the same time, acting so passively as if it was of no consequence or even confronting and condemning a couple because they are cohabiting should not come up[1117].

Therefore, a couple in the dioceses of Igboland may not be denied marriage in the church for their living together prior to their request of being wedded in the church, but additional time is needed to address their issue of cohabiting as the parish priest, his assistant, or those in charge of marriage preparation in the parish or diocese work with the couple in preparing them for the sacrament of marriage.

3.9. Persons with Disabilities

Prospective couples with physical, emotional or intellectual disabilities in the various dioceses of Igboland need special attention in their preparation for mar-

1115 Diocese of Columbus, Policies and Guidelines for Marriage Preparation, loc.cit.

1116 Cfr. Chapter Three above.

1117 Cfr. Dioceses of New Jersey, Section III, Special Circumstances, p. 37.

riage. The parish priest should demonstrate particular care and sensitivity when disabled persons request for marriage in the Catholic Church. This involves evaluating their ability to enter a valid marriage. After the assessment of the couple's ability to give consent a determination should be made with both the family of the disabled couple and professionals who can evaluate the person's ability to make a permanent commitment[1118]. The parish priest or his delegate should be open to the couple's willingness to share their feelings and thoughts concerning how this disability may affect or contribute to their union.

3.10. HIV/AIDS

While acknowledging the fact that HIV/AIDS is not an impediment to marriage and also the fact that canon law does not list it as such, it has serious consequences for the natural right to marry. "Sexual intercourse when one or both parties is/are HIV infected could place the other partner or any child that would be conceived in serious danger to life and health. While HIV/AIDS is not a canonical impediment to marriage, it has serious implications for the natural right to marry and for the decisions that a man and a woman must make. The church has, at times and for grave reasons, accepted the validity of a marriage in which the couple freely agrees to abstain from sexual relations throughout their marriage"[1119].

It is very important that persons living with HIV/AIDS in the Igbo dioceses be open to disclose to their prospective spouse concerning their status as HIV/AIDS positive carriers. The parish priest and his assistant should make sure that persons affected with this disease receive adequate counselling so as to not to delve into marriage. They should refer these persons for counselling and spiritual direction as that will help them in their decision to stop anything concerning marriage. This is very important as attempting to marry could place the other partner or any child that would be conceived in danger to life and health.

3.11. Conclusion

We have seen some areas of special circumstances that need special attention and care. There are still many others but we have limited ourselves to the ones that most importantly affect the church in Igboland. These special circumstances offer the officiating priest or the deacon the opportunity to show concern, care,

1118 Cfr. Archdiocese of Denver, "What God Has Joined…", Supplement, p.17.
1119 Ibid. P. 44.

and attention to the prospective couple's particular situation, to discuss about the church's teaching in this regard and when required, because of their situation, to refer such couple to professionals who specialize in that area of special circumstance for assistance and counselling that will eventually help them assess their ability to enter into marriage.

4. Igbo Traditional Marriage: Towards Inculturating the Sacrament of Marriage.

4.1. Introduction

In the previous section of this very chapter we concentrated on the proposed guidelines and programmes for marriage preparation in the Igbo Catholic dioceses to see ways in which marriage preparation programmes could be adequately organised in the diocesan. In this last section we shall look how best to inculturate the Christian marriage with Igbo traditional marriage such that it will not be a double celebration of one marriage and double expenditure for the engaged couples in Igboland.

The church today enjoys a wide range of cultural diversity. Most cultures like Igbo cultures carry with them some traditions that reflect their history. This is the reason why the revised marriage ritual and Pope John Paul II consented to use of suitable elements of local cultures in the wedding liturgy. Hence, the Pope stresses that church authorities can include in the liturgical celebration "such elements proper to each culture which serve to express more clearly the profound human and religious significance of the marriage contract, provided that such elements contain nothing that is not in harmony with Christian faith and morality"[1120].

A good number of Catholics in Igbo dioceses consider themselves married only through their customary marriage. They sometimes consider the Christian marriage as less important and as such, do not take the marriage instruction programme very seriously. They start to live together after their traditional marriage and would remove any idea of being wedded in the church from their mind. Amevor in trying to give reasons for this reluctance in marrying in the church asserts: "However, some dioceses in Africa resolve to do just that but the point remains that in Africa the church has not in any critical way been able to raise the traditional African marriage into church marriage. What actually takes place in Africa can be described as a reality of customary marriage to which a subsequent

1120 Cfr. FC, 67§2.

church marriage or blessing, as it is usually called, is added as a trimming, for the purpose of solemnity. The situation remains so because most Catholic faithful in Africa, on the other hand, feel no need of, and are often in no harmony for a church marriage since customary marriage in their mind is a real marriage which appeals to their values"[1121].

We also discussed in chapter four how the Igbo people prepare their children and youth traditional for marriage. Boys and girls went through an intensive initiation course that was meant specifically to prepare them adequately for marriage and family life. But this system of preparing the youth for marriage has almost disappeared. The traditional ways are not all that suitable for today's society. Marriage preparation in accordance with the Christian tradition has to be synchronized with the traditional marriage preparation to deal with the new situation. This is an urgent task facing the church in Igboland.

It is against this background, we intend to find a solution to the pastoral problem concerning traditional marriage among the Igbo people of Nigeria by inculturating it with the Christian marriage. It is not possible as such to inculturate the whole nature of Igbo traditional marriage rites; this will need more years of examination. Be that as it may, this work will start with the inculturation of the pre-marital preparation and solemnization rites. So only these rites are presented for inculturation in this work.

4.2. The Meaning of Inculturation

Every culture in itself has the ability and the resources of accepting and interpreting Christianity by making it meaningful to the people of that very culture. Pope John Paul II used the term "Inculturation" to refer to "the incarnation of the gospel in autonomous cultures into the life of the church"[1122]. He goes on to define it "as an intimate transformation of the authentic cultural values by their integration into Christianity and the implantation of Christianity into different human cultures"[1123]. According to Schineller: "Inculturation is the incarnation of Christian life and of the Christian message in a particular cultural context, in such a way that this experience not only finds expression through elements proper to the culture in question, but becomes a principle that animates, directs and unifies the culture, transforming and remarking it so as to bring about a new creation"[1124].

1121 P.K. Amevor, New Approaches to Marriage Preparation, pp.248-249.
1122 SA, 21.
1123 RM, 52.
1124 P. Schineller, A Handbook on Inculturation, New York 1990, p.6.

The church has always recommended that if the gospel message is to have any meaning and understanding on people, if it is to become Good News for the people who receive it, it has to be rooted in the culture of different people as Jesus Christ took flesh in the culture of the Jews. The Second Vatican Council insisted that Christians in different churches should "borrow from the customs, traditions, wisdom, teaching, arts and sciences of their people everything, which could be used to praise the glory of the Creator, manifest the grace of the saviour, or contribute to the right ordering of Christian life"[1125]. That means, it is through inculturation that the values of the Christian Gospel are to be transmitted to the different cultures and the good elements that already exist in these cultures at the same time, are inculturated by the Gospel renewed from within[1126].

Inculturation itself appeared as one of the five sub-themes of the Synod of Bishops for Africa, which took place in 1994. During this Synod, the African bishops saw inculturation from the perspective of incarnation and emphasised that authentic inculturation should include the entire Christian existence – theology, liturgy and structures[1127]. Hence, the Synod sees the task of inculturation as a matter of priority that needs urgent attention in the African Church. In his address to the bishops of Kenya on the 7th of May, 1980, Pope John Paul II told the bishops that the inculturation he means "… is no question of adulterating the Word of God, or of emptying the cross of its power (cf. 1 Cor 1:17), but rather of bringing Christ into the very centre of African life and of lifting up all African life to Christ. Thus not only is Christianity relevant to Africa, but Christ, in the members of his Body, is himself African"[1128]. Also in his address to the bishops of Ghana, the Pope had this to say: "…the Bishops must carry on the task of inculturation of the Gospel for the good of each people…. In this process, cultures themselves must be uplifted, transformed and permeated by Christ's original message of divine truth, without harming what is noble in them. Hence worthy African traditions are to be preserved. Moreover, in accordance with the full truth of the Gospels and in harmony with the Magisterium of the church, living and dynamic African Christian traditions are to be consolidated"[1129]. Therefore, for inculturation to be meaningful it has to pay attention to the rule of faith, the Christian doctrines and the important connectivity between the local and the universal church.

For incarnation of Christian life and Christian message to permeate into the Igbo culture and also through it develop an Igbo theology that is Igbo, the work

1125 AG, 22.

1126 EN, 20.

1127 Cfr. Ecclesia in Africa, 59 and 78.

1128 John Paul II, Address to the Bishops of Kenya, 7 May 1980, AAS 72 (1980), p.497.

1129 John Paul II, Message to Bishops of Ghana, 9 May 1980, AAS 72 81980), p.515..

of inculturation has to be promoted in the Igbo dioceses especially in the area of marriage. John Paul II lays credence to this very fact when he opines: "It is earnestly to be hoped that theologians in Africa will work out the theology of the church as family with all the riches contained in this concept, showing its complementarity with other images of the church"[1130]. Also in his address to the bishops of Nigeria in his second visit to Nigeria, the Pope called on the Nigerian Church to ensure that inculturation is offered its normal position in evangelization. Thus, he urged the bishops to do all they can in liturgy, theology, and administration, "so that your people will feel more and more at home in the church and the church more and more at home in your people"[1131].

It is pertinent to note that, in the process of this inculturation, there are two extremes to be avoided. "The rejection of all elements of local culture, as evil or against the natural law, a mistake which has been made in the past, and the pretence to inculturate the whole Christian message, as something which is entirely out of the context of local culture"[1132].

4.3. Inculturating the Sacrament of Marriage

It is well observed by many that the conflict between the Christian marriage and traditional marriage is the main problem of Christian life, which has affected the growth of the church in Igboland. Many engaged couples in Igboland view the duplication of giving their consent as something that is not necessary. In this regard, they prefer marrying in accordance with the traditional rite and start bearing their children until they acquire enough money to wed in the church. There are many couples today who attend masses in the church but do not receive the sacrament of the Eucharist because they are prohibited by the church not to receive the sacrament because of the fact that they are not yet wedded in the church.

The Igbo traditional marriage (Igba Nkwu Nwanyi) is what seals the marriage contract traditionally. Without it the marriage contract is not taken as valid. Ndiokwere puts it this way: "Generally in Igboland the marriage contract is not recognized as valid if Igba Nkwu Nwanyi is not done. In some extreme cases the young man is denied certain rights and privileges in the community and could be ostracized. It is an obligation, a duty that must be accomplished. And its social importance cannot be underrated. One can often see couples who had lived together for over ten years celebrating the Igba Nkwu at such late hour"[1133]. The

1130 EA, 63.

1131 John Paul II, Message to the Nigerian Bishops, 23 March 1998, n.5.

1132 L. Policarpo, Customary Marriage in Zambia in the Light of Canon Law, Rome 1986, p.61.

1133 N.I. Ndiokwere, The African Church, Today and Tomorrow, vol. II, Enugu 1994, p.132.

Igbo traditional marriage is valid and lawful as any other marriage in different countries with their cultures. The consideration of any other marriage after the traditional marriage is most often seen by the Igbo people as well as the Africans as unnecessary.

The Christian marriage on the other hand, is primarily a sacramental union between a man and a woman, which is of its nature, a permanent partnership of life with openness to fecundity and rearing of children. Also the deliberate and free consent of the parties brings about the institution of marriage and gives validity to the marriage contract between them.

Hence, in order to avoid accepting one form of marriage and rejecting the other, and then relieve the prospective couples and their families from financial burden of celebrating double marriage ceremonies, it is important to inculturate the Christian marriage and the Igbo traditional marriage. This, no doubt, will solve the problem of the spouses living together unlawfully after their traditional marriage ceremony and will also solve the problem of pre-marital relationship in Igboland. This will also favour both the church and the traditional community since both the church and the traditional community do not recognize a marriage entered into in which the two celebrations are not done.

During the 1980 Synod of Bishops, the African bishops presented certain pastoral solutions to the discrepancy between traditional marriage and Christian marriage. As a solution to this dichotomy, they offered a suggestion that the church should recognize and Christianize the celebration of "monogamous traditional and customary marriage". They said consent in customary marriage should be given in the presence of a priest and elders of the Catholic Church. The blessing of the couple could take place later at the celebration of the mass. A course for catechesis according to them should be prepared for married people formation. They also suggested that marriage counselling and spirituality programmes for Christian family be introduced everywhere[1134].

It is pertinent to know that before the Code of canon law, the church had desired that marriage should take place in the church and while there was this desire, there were no strict restrictions against marriages being celebrated outside the church premises[1135].

The 1983 Code of canon law removes the requirement of an extra-ordinary case and a just cause to ensure the celebration of marriage outside the church premises. All that is needed to enter into marriage in any appropriate place is

1134 Cfr. P. Dery, Christian and Customary Marriage in Ghana, in AFER, p.38; P.K. Amevor, New Approaches to Marriage Preparation, p.250.

1135 Cfr. P. Gaspari, Tractatut Canonicus de Matrimonio, (Typis Polyglottis Vaticanis, 1932), n. 1064, In J.C. Atado, African Marriage Customs and Church Law, p.82.

the authorization of either the local ordinary or the proper parish priest[1136]. Thus, there is no general policy concerning the determination of the appropriate place for marriage celebration, but the local ordinary can establish policy for the suitability of the place. To avoid discrepancies, the Episcopal Conference is empowered to establish norms with regard to the granting of dispensations from the form[1137]. Such norms could be the official witness with a new dispensation required for any change[1138].

It is to be noted that the Rite of the Catholic Church gives credence to the celebration of marriage in any other suitable place when it says: "Among people where marriage ceremonies customarily take place in the home, sometimes over a period of several days, these customs should be adapted to the Christian spirit and to the liturgy. In such cases, the Conference of Bishops according to the pastoral needs of the people may allow sacramental rite to be celebrated in the home"[1139].

But the pertinent questions arising from this provision are: Is the home of the bride or bridegroom suitable for the solemnization of marriage contract? If not, where then could be more suitable outside the church to celebrate the sacrament of marriage between two Christian couple? In other words, will the celebration of marriage outside the church constitute danger to what marriage in the church really means? When couples marry, they call upon God who instituted and raised marriage into sacrament to be their witness so that what they are celebrating may receive his blessing. So is marriage outside the church among an ecclesial community and in the presence of a priest who is to witness and bless the marriage bond acceptable.

What we are saying in actual fact is that traditional marriage should be celebrated along with the Christian marriage so that it becomes monogamous for the couple on spiritual and canonical grounds. But celebrated under traditional rite alone favours polygamy which is against the monogamous Christian type of marriage, and for the fact that traditional marriage is not a civil marriage, it can be dissolved by customary courts that have jurisdiction over such marriages and this constitute a danger to the Christian marriage[1140].

1136 Cfr. CC. 1115 and 1118 CIC/1983.

1137 Cfr. C. 1127 §2 CIC/1983: "Si graves difficultates formae canonicae servandae obstent, Ordinario loci partis catholicae ius est ab eadem in singulis casibus dispensandi, consulto tamen Ordinario loci in quo matrimonium celebratur, et salva ad validitatem aliqua publica forma celebrationis; Episcoporum conferentiae est normas statuere, quibus praedicta dispensation concordi ratione concedatur".

1138 Cfr. M.O.C. Kalu, Evaluation of the Canonical Form of Marriage in Canon 1180 in the Light of Igbo Traditional Marriage, Port Harcourt 1993, p.60.

1139 The Rite of the Catholic Church, New York 1976, p.538, n.18.

1140 Cfr. J.U. Gangwari, Church State Relations in Marriage in Nigeria, Jos 1994, pp.43-44.

Based on the above positions, there is need for the bishops of Igbo dioceses to exercise the power given to them by the church canonically by establishing norms necessary for the inculturation of traditional marriage and Christian marriage and also allow for a suitable place for the celebration of the two marriages together.

4.4. Proposed Rite of Preparation and Celebration

The Ordo Celebrandi Matrimonium of 1969 and the refomed Ordo Celebrandi of 1991 have empowered the local churches to enrich the Roman Rite with their cultural values and rituals. Such local rituals must possessed the Christian spirit and retain the exchange of consent before the assisting minister. The permission for inculturation of the rite of marriage is derived from the constitution on the Sacred Liturgy. It encompasses the church's wish to preserve and foster those elements of the cultural heritage of the people that are "not indissolubly bound up with superstition and error"[1141].

Canon 1120 of the Code of 1983 gives support to this when it states that: "The Episcopal Conference can draw up its own rite of marriage, in keeping with those usages of place and people which accord with the Christian spirit; it is to be reviewed by the Holy See, and it is without prejudice to the law that the person who is present to assist at the marriage is to ask for and receive the expression of the consent of the contracting parties"[1142]. Therefore, in order that the Christian marriage rite is inculturated into the traditional marriage rite, it must get to the home of the culture. The wedding could take place in the home of the bride as local customs demand. It is important that before this celebration, the first element of inculturation should take place immediately after the traditional prenuptial inquiry (Iju Ese Nwanyi) by the family of the bridegroom. From the very moment the choice of a partner is confirmed, the engaged couple and their families have the duty to inform the parish priest or his assistant of their intention to marry. The parish priest once informed has the pastoral obligation to assist them made a mature judgement concerning their marriage. He is also to assist in the prenuptial investigation process so as to help in the discernment of the couple's readiness to marry if at all there is any reason that could prevent them from marrying each other.

The church can also play a vital role in the stages of the traditional marriage process. In terms of the pressure coming from the parents and members of the

1141 SC, 37.
1142 C. 1120 CIC/1983.

extended families on who to marry, the elders of the ecclesial community who are at home with the engagement of the young people can call the attention of the parents and the extended family members not to interfere or in anyway influence the young people in the choice of their own partners in marriage as consent cannot be supplied by any human power except the two persons who mutually bestow it on each other. This lasting bond of bestowing consent should be seen from a theological and juridical point of view. The consent in other words, should be personal, because it is an act of will which is exchanged between two persons, and not between two families (c.1057 §1).

It has to be acknowledged also that nowadays, though the parents may give their consent on whom to marry which may or may not be accepted by the person marrying, but there is no force to enter marriage with anybody suggested by the parents or members of the extended family. There is no interference as such on who to marry, but they only show concerns in the couple's welfare and to assist them in difficult times.

Since there is also provision for pre-marital instructions in the Igbo traditional marriage preparation whereby the parents and the community are involved in preparing the child for marriage right from the infancy to adulthood, the elders of the Christian community who are also very rooted in the cultures of the community could be called upon to take the responsibility of instructing the young people about the Christian doctrine concerning marriage and family life as well as their traditional culture with regard to marriage thereby assisting them to integrate Igbo marriage values into Christian marriage and family.

The pre-marital instruction will be likened to fattening seclusion of girls and the initiation of boys into age grade which are traditionally both proximate and immediate preparations of marriage. Fattening Seclution (Iru Mgbede) as we saw in chapter four of this work refers to a period of marriage preparation in the early days when a girl was kept in a fattening room before marriage, where she was trained to meet up with the demands of womanhood and marriage life. Initiation of boys into age grade or adulthood (Iwa Akwa) refers to the period before marriage whereby boys of the same age grade are drilled in the requirements of adulthood, marriage and family life. This type of marriage preparation among the boys still takes place till today. Therefore, if the period of marriage preparation is inculturated in view of what already exists in the Igbo culture, it would enhance and foster the marriage partnership in our Igbo and African settings, and promote a better understanding of the Christian marriage values.

To prevent the marriage of the prospective couple from being invalidated, the parish priest or his delegate should ensure that no impediment is taken for granted. During this stage, the publication of banns in the church should be announced and more inquiry about the couple be made among the local community.

The celebration rite we are suggesting should begin in the home of the bride in the normal traditional manner. Canon 1108 of the Code of 1983 demands the presence of two witnesses as part of the form that makes marriage valid since the couples themselves are the main ministers of the marriage sacrament. In that case, the officiating priest and other church members especially the person who is also the custodian of the community culture should be present to represent the church. The middle man (Onye aka-ebe) who serves as a mediator between the bride and the bridegroom in Igbo traditional marriage culture, who is also an active member of the church could also be drafted as one of the two witnesses for the marriage.

During the ceremony, it is pertinent to allow the parents and the elders of the community to question prospective couple in line with traditional rite to know their readiness to marry each other. The priest who is present to solemnize the union starts with an opening prayer after the interrogation by the parents and elders of the bride to be. It will be followed by the readings for the wedding ceremony which will usher in homily from the priest witnessing the marriage ceremony. The priest homily should centre on such themes like the theology of marriage, the essential elements of marriage, and its ends as it concerns the well-being of the couple and the procreation and education of children.

The priest should call upon the father of the bride or her guardian, if her father is no longer alive, as it is sometimes the case, to hand over the bride to the bridegroom and his people after the homily by the officiating priest.

The prospective couple should after the hand over ceremony face each other before the assembly to exchange their consent in an audible manner since consent is the central element in the rite of Christian marriage and also in the traditional marriage rite. And since their consent is needed to establish their marriage, the couple should express it before the officiating witness of the church that means, before the parish priest or his delegate and also the assembly of the people. This should be in accordance with canon 1108 §2 of the Code of 1983 which stipulates that: "Only that person who, being present, asks the contracting parties to manifest their consent and in the name of the church receives it, is understood to assist at a marriage"[1143]. For the avoidance of doubt about the exchange of consent and its expression, it would be pertinent for the bride and groom to make use of the formular in the liturgical rites of Christian marriage. The priest will in the name of the church receive their consent in accordance with the canonical form of the Roman rite. The couple's ring should be blessed immediately by the officiating priest after the exchange of consent. This will be followed by the parents' blessing to the couple, wishing them a happy and long-lasting union and fruits of the womb. The officiating priest then seals the wedding by inviting them to join their

1143 Cfr. C.1108 §2 CIC/1983.

right hands to each other, binding them with stole, blesses and sprinkles them with holy water.

It will be followed by the prayer of the faithful which will be spontaneous from the congregation. This prayer of the faithful will afford the assembly the opportunity to express in their own way their intentions for the church, the newly married couple and the traditional community. The conclusion of the prayer of the faithful will be said by the priest with nuptial blessing.

There will be offertory collection in which the newly wedded couple together with their families and those present will make their offertory with dance procession. The officiating priest then makes the final blessing and conclusion by praying over the new couple, members of their families, their communities and all those present for the combined wedding ceremony.

It will now be followed by entertainment, merry making, dance and donation of gifts to the newly wedded by their friends and well-wishers.

On the following Sunday, the newly married couple should attend the thanksgiving mass. They should also receive the sacrament of the Holy Eucharist if both are Catholics. It is the duty of the parish priest or his assistant to make a formal introduction of the newly married couple to the ecclesial community during the time for announcement at the end of the reception of the communion. This will allow them the opportunity to enrol themselves into the Christian Fathers and Mothers Associations respectively. The parish priest and the church community will also use this period to exchange contacts and addresses with the new couple so as to continue to support them in their newly married life so that they meet up with the demands and challenges of married and family life.

4.5. Conclusion

In this last section of chapter five we tried to see how to synchronize the Igbo traditional marriage and the Christian marriage through inculturation. We defined inculturation as the honest and serious bid to make Christ and his Gospel message of salvation evermore comprehended by peoples of different cultures, localities and time[1144].

The Church's Magisterium sees inculturation of Christianity in Africa as something that needs urgent attention. The special Assembly for Africa of the Synod of Bishops "considered inculturation as a priority… in the life of Africa's particular

1144 Cfr. V. Ifeanyi, "Inculturation and Liberation Theology: Similarities and Differences", In Nacaths Journal of African Theology, Vol.10, Owerri 2000, p.23.

churches"[1145]. The demands of inculturation in Africa has been identified as comprising "in ensuring that the followers of Christ will ever more fully assimilate the Gospel message, while remaining faithful to all authentic African values"[1146].

We also said that for Christian marriage to gain its prominence and continue to be significant to the Igbo people, it has to be synchronized with the Igbo traditional marriage through inculturation. The Igbo people love their culture and that is why traditional marriage is taken seriously by them. It is a ceremony that must be done before a bride is handed over finally to her groom and that is the final process that seals marriage traditionally. Also the church marriage is very crucial in the life of the Igbo people and there is no way of avoiding it. But because of the duplication of marriage celebrations and the financial burden attached to it, some of them see the Christian marriage as only a blessing of an already existing marriage and therefore not necessary[1147].

On account of this we suggested that there is need to emerge the two together to eliminate dichotomies and duplication of marriage celebrations so that the Igbo people can celebrate their marriages in a meaningful traditionally important ceremony that is in line with the Christian doctrine and spirituality. We did not stop at the suggestion of what is to be done but we moved a step forward to propose a marriage preparation and celebration rite that encompasses both the traditional marriage rite and Christian marriage rite. This rite, when used, will foster the blending of traditional customs with the liturgy of the church and help make Christian marriage ever more appealing to the Igbo people.

5. Conclusion of Chapter Five

Chapter five is concerned with drafting guidelines and policies for marriage preparation in the Igbo dioceses of Nigeria. This idea came up as a result of not having comprehensive diocesan and parish guidelines that will take cognisance of the situation in particular local churches in Igboland and then offer in broad ways, a united approach to the pastoral care of marriage preparation in the entire dioceses of Igboland.

The aim of the proposed guidelines is to establish a consistent marriage policy for all the dioceses of Igboland thereby assisting the church as a caring community in addressing the demands of the prospective couples and help them not just to prepare for their marriage ceremony but for their married life together.

1145 EA, 78.

1146 Ibid.

1147 Cfr. N.I. Ndiokwere, The African Church, Today and Tomorrow, p.135.

The purpose of the policy as we said earlier is to establish an effective commitment to the well being of the prospective couples in the Igbo dioceses and assist them in the growth of their relationship to each other and to God the author of the institution of marriage.

We envisaged that the proposed marriage preparation guidelines shall oblige the whole ecclesial community of Igbo extraction. The bishops are responsible for providing the many ideas of initiatives of pastoral actions within the jurisdiction of their dioceses in Igboland. The priests and deacons who plan to witness a marriage in their various parishes are responsible for the complete marriage preparation process. The ecclesial community in each parish have also the obligation to assist prospective couples prepare for their marriage. Married couples in the dioceses have a primary responsibility to participate actively in the marriage preparation of prospective couples in their various parishes. Parents also share in this obligation of responding actively in the evaluation and preparation of their children for marriage. The engaged couples should also avail themselves the opportunity by responding actively in this marriage preparation programmes.

The seminarians, reverend sisters, catechists, guardians, God parents, teachers, active members of different pious societies in the church, extended family members, and elders of the community are also encouraged to respond to the invitation to take part actively in the assessment and preparation of the engaged couples for marriage.

We emphasised the idea of forming a commission team in order to achieve the aims and objectives of the proposed guidelines and policy for the Igbo dioceses. The formation team shall take the place of the existing diocesan chaplaincy for marriage assessment coordinated by a priest. It shall have the responsibility of all marriage related cases in the different dioceses of Igboland. Each diocese in Igboland should endeavour to form this commission. The commission should be composed of mainly married couples, representing some different age groups, and those still single but professionally trained for marriage related issues. A coordinator normally a priest who represents the local ordinary should be piloting the affairs of this commission and from time to time give report of the progress of the team to the local ordinary.

We shifted our thoughts to one of the concerns that so much press upon the local ordinary, priest and those actively involved in marriage preparation process, and that concern is the readiness of the engaged couple for marriage. Since marriage as a sacrament requires the presence of faith on those who request it, we suggested that pastors of souls in Igbo dioceses should know the engaged couples' intention to marry and help them in assessing their readiness to marry each other.

In giving notification for marriage the dioceses of Igbo region we suggested, will require prospective couples to contact the parish at least six months before a date can be set for wedding. This will allow the prospective couple's time to be beneficiaries of the marriage preparation programmes and fulfil all the important requirements.

Marriage is typically to be celebrated in the parish of either the bride or the bridegroom. Also the marriage of a Catholic and a baptised non-catholic should be celebrated in the parish church of the Catholic party with exception being granted only for serious pastoral reasons. The parish where the celebration will take place shall be responsible for the marriage preparation process.

We proposed that stages of marriage preparation will toe the line of that envisaged by Familiaris Consortio, explained in the Code of 1983 and the Pontifical Council for the Family. In this regard, we envisaged three stages of marriage preparation. They are: remote, proximate and immediate preparation. We also talked about the on going support after marriage.

The remote marriage preparation embodies each person's personal development from infancy and childhood till early adolescence period. Parents are both educators and models of their children in this period. The proximate stage coincides with the period of engagement. Here we proposed five sections which include: a) initial contact with the parish priest, b) pre-nuptial inquiry, c) review of marriage prenuptial inquiry or inventory, d) a three-day instructional workshop, e) and natural family planning. The five sections should be taken seriously for any meaningful marriage preparation in the dioceses. The immediate marriage preparation comprises of the final preparatory meetings between the parish priest, marriage formation team members, and the prospective couples themselves during the last three months before the wedding itself. The three sequences of events for this stage includes: a) final meeting with the parish priest and review of prior preparation, b) completion of a retreat as an opportunity for reconciliation, c) and planning of the wedding liturgy.

The aim of this immediate preparation is to deepen the formation acquired from remote and proximate preparations. It is an opportunity for the prospective couples to meet and reflect together on their vocation to marry as husbands and wives and then look on to the ecclesial community as an important context for their future marital union[1148].

We x-rayed four varieties of marriage preparation programmes under immediate preparation that can help the prospective couples prepare adequately for their marriage. The programmes could assist them in discussing issues that may not have emerged while they were dating and then help them to overcome the challenges of married life. We suggested that prospective couples in Igbo

1148 Cfr. Diocese of Richmond, Called to Marriage, loc.cit.

dioceses should take part in one of the programmes before their actual wedding.

The on going support for married couples in the Igbo dioceses should be encouraged. This support will no doubt assist married couples to stablize their marital union and cultivate a spirituality of marriage and that of the family. This pastoral care after marriage must reach out to those married couples who find themselves in particularly difficult conditions and situations especially in the rural areas of Igboland.

Guidelines are also offered to some various special circumstances that demand special pastoral care or more adequate preparation in Igbo dioceses. The guidelines if followed properly may help the prospective couples and the parish priest or his delegate working with them to assess their situation in a realistic and responsible manner[1149].

We engaged ourselves into finding ways of synchronizing the Igbo traditional marriage with the Christian marriage through inculturation. We posited that for Christian marriage to be rooted in the lives of the Igbo people, it has to be fused into the Igbo traditional marriage. Since it is not possible to inculturate the whole nature of Igbo traditional marriage rites, the first thing would be to inculturate the preparation and the solemnization rite. In this view, we suggested emerging the two marriages together to avoid duplication of consent, since it cannot be given two times by the same couple and for the same particular purpose, and also to prevent the duplication of marriage celebrations and help the prospective couples especially the-not-well to do ones come out of the financial burden they will incur after going through the two marriage ceremonies. This will definitely help our people come to terms with Christian marriage and then understand it the more as an intimate union between a man and a woman which is instituted by God and raised to the dignity of a sacrament.

1149 Cfr. Dioceses of New Jersey, Pastorial Policies and Guidelines for Marriage Preparation, p.2.

General Conclusion

The main point of departure in this work has been to explore the norms of the Code of 1983 especially that of canon 1063 on marriage preparation and pastoral care for marriage in connection with the preparation of marriage in the traditional Igbo society as a prerequisite for assistance in the drafting of policies, guidelines and programmes for canonical marriage preparation in the Igbo dioceses of Nigeria.

The 1917 Code of Canon Law has added a number of requirements in its jurisdiction that meant to safeguard a valid and licit celebration of marriage. In addiction to this the Code was also interested in other matters with regard to marriage preparation. The parish priest who had the right and duty to make the investigation before the marriage celebration was responsible in assisting at the marriage celebration[1150]. Due consideration was given to assure that nothing stood in the way of its valid and licit celebration[1151]. There were precisely two canons in the Code of 1917 that treated broadly what could be termed as marriage preparation. Canon 1018 treated the parish priest's general catechesis which he was obliged to provide for the people as regards the sacrament of marriage and its impediments, while canon 1033 dealt with the parish priest's role in instructing prospective couples concerning the sanctity of the sacrament of marriage, the mutual obligations of spouses and parents, and sacramental preparation (penance and Eucharist) before the celebration of the wedding.

However, the Code of 1917, on echoing the Church's tradition on marriage put on legislation which in time diminished and some how supplanted a pastorally-oriented marriage preparation. In this way, pastoral care for marriage preparation became a way of simply fulfilling the necessary criteria for a valid and lawful marriage[1152]. As a result of this, there were yearnings for a more intense preparation for the sacrament of marriage. So the need to revise the old legislation was felt in the preparatory stage of the Second Vatican Council.

The work emphasised the two instructions of 1921 and 1941 which was issued by the Congregation for the Discipline of Sacraments, which were a repetition of those norms as contained in canons 1018 and 1033 of the Code of 1917. They were to serve as preliminary acts to be completed prior to a celebration of marriage.

1150 Cfr. C.1020 §1 CIC/1917.

1151 Cfr. C.1019 §1 CIC/1917.

1152 Cfr. B.D. Hajovsky, Marriage Preparation and Pastoral Care, pp. 21-22.

The Congregation believed in the observation of these general and particular instructions so as to protect the sacrament of marriage.

We turned our attention to some elements of the response of the Church on marriage preparation by looking to some Popes who contributed immensely to the topic about marriage preparation. Pope Pius XI's encyclical Casti Connubii brought out in a very systematic manner the Church's teaching on marriage preparation. The encyclical went on to admonish those desiring to contract marriage and those whose responsibility is to educate the young people to take into account of the future by preparing what is appropriate in marriage preparation. Hence, marriage preparation was seen as both remote and proximate, enduring through a lifetime, and not leaving out the period immediately before the celebration of marriage. Pope Pius XII stressed in many of his addresses and allocutions the need for marriage preparation. He often drew attention to the family and the pastoral care challenges on marriage preparation. He emphasised that people had to be prepared from infancy for marriage and the responsibilities involved in it. He also stressed the need for collaboration between the entire ecclesial communities. Pope John XXIII emphasised about the Christian teaching on the importance of marriage and called for a continuous and persuasive instruction of the Christian faithful. He placed great emphasis on reaching the Christian youth who are approaching marriage that they might take more seriously the duty of religious instruction in preparing adequately for marriage.

The Second Vatican Council's decision to treat marriage first among the urgent problems facing the world during that period in time showed a desire on the part of the Council Fathers to resolve the relationship between the Church and the world. The Council presented the Church with guidelines and directives concerning marriage preparation in order to complete the important task of her renewal. The work revealed that the Pastoral Constitution on the Church in the Modern World, Gaudium et Spes urges that young people should be given proper and effective instruction on married love and life, and in addition, the document invites various organisations to set up programmes of instruction in order to strengthen and prepare young people for family and apostolic life[1153].

The study explored the 1980 Synod of Bishops' treatment on the role of the Christian Family in the Modern World. In dealing with this, they talked about the necessity for a gradual approach to marriage preparation with different stages, and the fundamental role the family and the Church community should play. There was emphasis on the need for a faith preparation for marriage and a special catechesis for the prospective couples.

We saw also repeated instances on the necessity for marriage preparation in John Paul II's apostolic exhortation, Familiari Consortio which he published in

1153 Cfr. GS, 49, 52.

1981. The document treated marriage preparation as a life-time journey of remote, proximate and immediate preparations, and it was a preparation established to include the whole ecclesial community.

Our work turned its attention to the canonical understanding of the nature of marriage in the Code of 1983 so as to provide bases to marriage preparation and pastoral care for marriage in the new Code. The teachings of the Vatican II Council concerning the nature and sacramentality of marriage in accordance with the development of Rotal jurisprudence about marital consent and the consortium totius vitae led to a new formulation of marriage as covenant in the Code of 1983[1154]. The new Code moves beyond the Code of 1917's contractual character of the notion of marriage[1155]. The intimate partnership of the whole life which the new Code establishes comprises of various goods and ends[1156]. The hierarchical structure of ends, as established in the Code of 1917[1157], was no longer taken, but procreation still remains as a finality of marriage[1158]. The study revealed that the couples mutually give and accept themselves through the irrevocable consent so as to establish marriage[1159]. The object of the covenanting consent is the partnership of the whole life, a total sharing of their lives. In this view, the new Code defines marital consent as being more than an exchange of ius in corpus as established in the Code of 1917[1160].

Reflecting the vision of the Second Vatican Council, the 1983 Code introduces the notion of pastoral care for marriage preparation into the title of the part concerning marriage preparation. In this way, there is a remarkable shift of emphasis from seeing pre-marriage preparation precisely in terms of the necessary conditions for a valid and licit marriage to emphasising the personal responsibilities and pastoral nature of pre-marriage preparation[1161]. Thus, the new legislation in contrast to the old Code offers special attention to and interest in regulating this matter when it puts together all the norms that formerly were scattered, and provides emphasis to the pastoral aspects of preparation and not just to the juridical aspects, and also when it demands a fruitful celebration of the sacrament of marriage[1162]. In doing so, there was a significant change from pre-marriage investiga-

1154 Cfr. C.1055 §1 CIC/1983; B.D. Hajovsky, Marriage Preparation and Pastoral Care, p. 37.

1155 Cfr. C.1012 §1 CIC/1917.

1156 Cfr. GS, 48.

1157 Cfr. C.1013 §1 CIC/1917.

1158 Cfr. GS, 50.

1159 Cfr. C.1057 §2 CIC/1983.

1160 Cfr. C.1018 §2 CIC/1917: "Matrimonial consent is an act of the will by which each party gives and accepts a perpetual and exclusive right over the body, for acts which are of themselves suitable for the generation of children".

1161 Cfr. B.D. Hajovsky, Marriage Preparation and Pastoral Care, p.47.

1162 Cfr. T. Ricon-Perez, Commentary on Canons 1063-1072, p.1112.

tion of the old legislation to pastoral care in marriage preparation and from the exclusive responsibility of the parish priest in marriage preparation of the Code of 1917 to the participation of the whole ecclesial community in the new Code.

The work x-rayed the significance and pastoral importance of canon 1063 of the 1983 Code, an entirely new formulation in the Code, in bringing out the broader implications of pastoral care for marriage on prospective couples and those already married. This canon places a serious obligation on pastors of souls to ensure that their own proper ecclesial community provides suitable and proper assistance to safeguarding and developing the Christian character of marriage. Although the direct obligation is on the pastors of souls, the ecclesial community is to be involved in fostering and enhancing marriage preparation and providing this support[1163].

In providing this support, canon 1063 outlines four principal ways in which this obligation is to be implemented. It points to remote preparation with particular emphasis on the meaning of Christian marriage and on the role of spouses and parents in preparing their children for marriage right from infancy. The proximate preparation is centred on the sanctity and the obligation of the engaged couples' new state of life. The immediate preparation is focused on the community aspect of marriage preparation in establishing a fruitful and effective celebration of the marriage liturgy to the prospective couples[1164]. Lastly, the canon speaks of post marriage support of those already married[1165]. The study saw that the four principal ways established by canon 1063 correspond closely with the stages of marriage preparation proposed by John Paul II's apostolic exhortation, Familiaris Consortio and further developed by the Pontifical Council for the Family.

The work also addressed some of the canonical and pastoral difficulties that are frequently encountered in preparing prospective couples for marriage and how they hinder proper and effective preparation for the celebration of marriage. Some of the difficult cases include: the right to marry and marriage preparation, the faith of the couple and marriage preparation, and the last but not the least, cohabiting couples and marriage preparation. There are many couples today who approach the Church requesting for marriage that are living together. There are those who do not have faith. While acknowledging the obvious fact about the impossibility of measuring faith and the fact that no one can judge the faith of another, the task of the parish priest is to discern in the request to enter marriage,

1163 Cfr. C.843 §2 CIC/1983: "Animarum pastores ceterique christifideles, pro suo quisque ecclesiastico munere, officium habent curandi ut qui sacramenta petunt debita evangelizatione necnon catechetica institutione ad eadem recipienda praeparentur, attentis normis a competenti auctoritate editis".

1164 Cfr. PCF, nn.21-59.

1165 Cfr. FC, 69.

a faith motivation which would make a sacramental marriage possible. He should try as much as possible to help those prospective couples grow in their faith. Also marriage cannot be denied of those living together prior to their wedding, but their consciousness should be raised. However, prospective couples could enter marriage with major problems that may lead to marital failure. The priest should be sensitive to the possible existence of such major problems.

We also examined in this work the nature of Igbo traditional marriage. Marriage is one of the most pertinent events in the life of every Igbo. Marriage has meaning in Igboland with the presence of Children. It is not only an alliance or a covenant between two individuals of opposite sex but also an alliance between two families or communities. This contributes immensely in holding the nuclear and extended families together and ensures the stability of marriage in Igbo society. The alliance means that the preparation and the celebration of marriage in Igboland involve not only the prospective couple but also the whole family members and communities where the prospective couple come from.

Preparation for marriage in traditional Igbo society was oriented towards family life. Boys and girls sometimes went through an intensive initiation programme into adulthood that was meant to prepare them for their roles in the society as husbands and wives and even as parents. The process being followed was complex but it was a real and adequate preparation for marriage that was both remote and proximate. Nowadays, the marriage preparation through initiation into adulthood has almost disappeared, even though some communities in Igboland still practice it, it is no longer suitable for today's society. The canonical marriage preparation is what is urgently needed. How can it be provided? This is an urgent task facing the Church in Igboland. The men and women who get married in Igboland, how are they prepared for it? Those are the questions we addressed in the last chapter of our work.

Also in our study we found out that in the Igbo traditional marriage procedures there are some indispensable elements that must be carried out before a marriage is contracted. They are the essential and formal requirements for the valid and lawful celebration of Igbo traditional marriage. The form includes: choice of partner, consent, inquiries, reciprocal inquiries, betrothal, bride wealth, and handover of the bride to the groom. The bride wealth ceremony seals the marriage union and symbolises the marriage covenant between a man and a woman. It legalises traditionally the marriage entered into by the two opposite sex. The payment of the bride wealth cements the marriage traditionally. In the Igbo traditional view, church marriage celebrated without prior celebration of the traditional rites is considered unacceptable notwithstanding the fact that the non-performance of these rites has no effect whatsoever on the validity of marriage canonically. The Igbo Church emphasises the full performance of the traditional rites before the celebration of the sacramental marriage in the Church.

The work x-rayed the AECAWA's overview of marriage preparation in West Africa. The bishops of the West African region in giving their reasons for this policy regarding pastoral marriage preparation acknowledge that the most pressing needs of the Church in West Africa is preparing the Christian faithful more properly for marriage. To safeguard and protect the sacred character of marriage and foster the rich tradition of family living there should be an effective pastoral preparation of spouses for the sacrament of marriage and the evaluation of their readiness to carry out their obligations in their married life[1166]. The bishops issued guidelines for the Catholic marriage policy and admonished prospective couples preparing for marriage to show themselves in good time to their parish priest so as to provide enough time for a mature and sensitive assessment of the couple's readiness for marriage and to prepare them properly for the sacrament of marriage.

Accordingly, one would have thought that the guidelines and policy by AECAWA would interest and mean more to various dioceses of the West African countries to foster and attach more seriousness to marriage preparation and pastoral care for marriage, but unfortunately, these guidelines about pastoral preparation for marriage remain unyielding and unused in some dioceses in the West African region. Besides, the bishops opted only for general policy and guidelines that take care of the national level while leaving out both the diocesan and parish level. They concentrated more on the immediate preparation of the prospective couples without taking into account of the other stages of marriage preparation.

Hence, there is the necessity to work out a comprehensive diocesan and parish policies and guidelines that will take cognisance of the situation about marriage preparation and pastoral care for marriage in particular churches like in Igbo dioceses of Nigeria.

It is interesting to point out that it is against this background of lack of comprehensive and elaborate marriage guidelines and programmes in both diocesan and parish level and the lack of structures in the dioceses of Igboland concerning marriage preparation that the study proposed a canonical pastoral guidelines and programmes on marriage preparation and pastoral care for marriage in the dioceses of Igboland. To achieve this, the work suggested that each diocese in Igboland should form a diocesan and parish commission for marriage preparation and pastoral care for marriage. The team members of this commission should set up a support network that will take care of the prospective couples and help draw policy and guidelines to be followed by the parishes in this diocese. The commission should have a coordinator most probably a priest who oversees the activities of the commission and informs the bishop on the progress of the commission from time to time. Part of their responsibility also is to provide the diocese and the par-

1166 Cfr. AECAWA, The Pastoral Care of Marriage, p.1.

ish the help in ensuring the durability and stability of marriage relationships. In carrying out this task the commission members are required to be realistic with regard to the scope of their obligation. Expectations concerning the range of their effectiveness need to be reasonable. They should also foster the establishment of other structured programmes to assist those already married who are living out their married and family life.

The work maintained that the fruits of the proposed guidelines and programmes depend mostly on the seriousness of the parish priest in carrying out this function in collaboration with the formation team. The parish priest has the pastoral obligation to assist those desiring to enter marriage to participate in the marriage preparation programmes. The serious moral and ministerial responsibilities rest on him to help the prospective couples in understanding the meaning of Christian marriage in its human, sacramental, and canonical aspects. The parish priest's positive attitude regarding those desiring to marry is the first step in pasturing the prospective couples.

The ecclesial community shares also in the pastoral responsibility to assist engaged couples prepare adequately for marriage. Married couples as we suggested should be called upon to participate actively in the marriage preparation programmes for the prospective couples as they have the credibility in helping the engaged couples understand the realities of married life and family life.

The work also recognised the unique and important role played by parents in preparing their children right from childhood for marriage as it is in the case of parental role in the traditional Igbo marriage preparation. In view of this, parents and guardians are therefore encouraged to respond to the invitation of the Church in order to participate actively in the evaluation and preparation of their children for sacramental marriage in the Church whenever the need arises.

The study also suggested that prospective couples should avail themselves the opportunity to participate actively in the marriage preparation programmes being organised in their respective dioceses and parishes. The need for marriage preparation and its usefulness for the engaged couples put it straight that prospective couples should not go without full preparation except for cogent, sensible and serious unavoidable reasons. In case there is an urgent reason that restricts their full participation prior to the wedding, proper opportunities should be organised in the various parishes in Igboland for the couples to make up for the elements of marriage preparation that they missed because of the unavoidable reasons.

We maintained in this work that the inculturation of Igbo traditional marriage and Christian marriage in the marriage celebration in the Igbo dioceses is very necessary so as to eliminate duplication of marriage celebrations and then offer the Igbo people the opportunity to celebrate their traditional marriages meaningfully as a pertinent ceremony that is also in line with the Christian doctrine. The proposed rite of marriage we suggested if looked into and considered will help foster the blending of Igbo customary values and customs with that of the Christian liturgy so as to make Christian marriage ever more appealing to the people in Igboland.

The study insisted that traditional marriage ceremonies should not be just ignored or rejected but they should be assessed and accepted as one with the Christian ceremony so that the Igbo people without losing their Igbo identity can perform them and participate in them meaningfully while keeping in line with the doctrine of the Church.

Hence, the proposed rite of marriage can meet the demands of canon law in as much as it is accepted by the Bishop Conference and approved by the Holy See in accordance with canon 1120 of the Code of 1983. The carrying out of this very canon is very crucial for the Igbo dioceses and the Igbo people who are increasingly putting greater values on their cultures and traditions. Therefore, it is a matter of priority for the bishops of Igbo dioceses to find out possible ways of resolving the dichotomy between the traditional marriage rite and that of the Christian marriage rite by inculturating the two together in order to avoid duplication of exchange of consent and marriage celebrations.

It is important to state here that the proposals in this work are not to be seen as a must-take-blueprint document for the Igbo dioceses to adopt at all cost, but as a reference point to foster and develop guidelines and policies for marriage preparation and pastoral care in Igbo dioceses of Nigeria. The work is an academic research primarily aimed at providing a canonical awareness of the provisions of the Code of 1983 regarding marriage preparation and pastoral care for marriage. It calls for the correct implementation and application of the norms regarding marriage preparation in this Code and to work out a strategic plan of action for an effective and proper marriage preparation programme in Igboland with a view to foster throughout the dioceses a solid commitment to the well-being of prospective and married couples, to the health and prosperity of their unions and to the quality and permanence of their married lives.

Finally, the proposed guidelines and policies for the dioceses of Igboland are not intended to make it hard for prospective couples in Igboland to marry or wed in the Catholic Church, but they will help to create awareness on the seriousness of marriage and the responsibility of the Church in Igboland to assist engaged couples prepare adequately and effectively for marriage and life together. Hence, the implementation and application of these proposed guidelines will demand a substantial investment of time, attention and commitment on the part of bishops, priests, deacons, religious, seminarians, catechists, formation team, parents, guardians, lay faithful, and above all, prospective couples themselves. Collaboration is, therefore pertinent to a proper and effective use of these policies and guidelines for the Igbo Church.

Abbreviations

AA	Apostolicam actuositatem, Decree on the Apostolate of the Laity, 18 November 1965
AAS	Acta Apostolicae Sedis
Abl.	Amtsblatt
Addr.	Address
AECAWA	Association of Episcopal Conferences of Anglophone West Africa
AIDS	Acquired Immune Deficiency Syndrome
AfER	African Ecclesial Review
AfkKR	Archiv für Katholiches Kirchenrecht
AKF	Arbeitsgemeinschaft für katholische Familienbildung
Anm.	Anmerkungstafeln
Apost. Const.	Apostolic Constitution
Art.	Article
Aufl.	Auflage
BCPRP	Bishops' Committee for Pastoral Research and Practices
Bd.	Band
BMS	Bigard Memmorial Seminary
BzMK	Beihefte zur Münsterischen Kommentar
c; can.	canon
CBCN	Catholic Bishops Conferences of Nigeria
cc; cann.	canons
CCC	Catechism of the Catholic Church
CCEO	Code of Canons of the Eastern Churches
CD	Christus Dominus, Decree on the Pastoral Office of the Bishops in the Church, 28 October 1965
Cf; Cfr.	Confer
CFA	Christian Fathers Association
CIC/1917	Codex Iuris Canonici of 27 May 1917
CIC/1983	Codex Iuris Canonici of 25 January 1983
CLD	Canon Law Digest
CLSA	Canon Law Society of America
CLSAP	Canon Law Society of America Proceedings
CMAC	Catholic Marriage Advisory Council

CMFCU	Center for Marriage and the Family, Craighton University
CMO	Christian Mothers Association
Comm.	Communicationes, Pontificia Commissio Codici Iuris Canonici Recognoscendo, Communicationes, Typis Polyglottis Vaticanis 1969
Const.	Constitution
CT	Ciencia Tomista
Decr.	Decree
DOL	Documents of the Liturgy
DS	Denzinger, H – Hünermann, Enchiridion Symbolorum, definitionum et Declarationum de rebus fidei et morum, (edizione bilingue) Bologna 1995
ed.	Edited or Editor
eds.	Editors
e.g.	Example
Enc; Encyl.	Encyclical
EPL	Ehevorbereitung – ein Partnerschaftliches Lernprogramm
et al.	and others
etc	et cetera
Exh.	Exhortation
f.	following page
FC	Familiaris Consortio
ff.	following pages
FLANNERY	Vatican Council II, Constitutions, Decrees, Declarations, ed. A Flannery, Dublin 1996
FOCCUS	Facilitating Open Couple Communication, Understanding and Study
Fontes	Codicis Iuris Canonici Fontes, ed. P. Gasparri (t. 1-6) and J. Seredi (t. 7-9)
GDC	General Directory for Catechesis
GE	Gravissimum educationis, Declaration on Christian Education, 28 October 1965
Gen.	Genesis
GS	Gaudium et Spes, Pastoral Constitution on the Church in the Modern World, 7 December 1965
HdbKathKR	Handbuch des katholischen Kirchenrechts, herausgegeben von Joseph Listl und Heribert Schmitz, zweite, grundlegend neubearbeitete Auflage, Regensburg 1999
HIV	Human Immundeficiency Virus
Hrsg.	Herausgegeben

HV	Humanae Vitae
Ibid	From the same book or article
i.e.	that is
IM	Inter mirifica, Decree on the Means of Social Communication, 4 December 1963
Instr.	Instructio/Instruction
Instr. lab.	Instrumentum Laboris
ITC	International Theological Commission
IusCan	Ius Canonicum
LG	Lumen gentium, Dogmatic Constitution on the Church, 21 November 1964
loc-cit.	loco citato (in the place cited: Internet sources)
MFLC	Marriage and Family Life Committee
MonEccl	Monitor Ecclesiasticus
M.p.	Motu proprio
Mt.	Matthew
NACATHS	National Association of Catholic Theology Students, Nigeria
NCCB	National Conference of Catholic Bishops
n; no.	Number
nn; nos.	Numbers
Op.cit.	Opere Citato
p.	page
par.	Paragraph
PCCICR	Pontificia Commissio Codici Iuris Canonici Recognoscendo
PCF	Pontifical Council for the Family
pp.	pages
re. ed.	Revised edition
Rev. Sch.	Revised Schema
SC	Sacrosanctum concilium, Constitution on the Sacred Liturgy, 4 December 1963
S.C.C.	Sacred Congregation of the Council
S.C.R.	Sacred Congragation of Rites
SECAM	Symposium of Episcopal Conferences of Africa and Madagascar
sess.	Session
StCan	Studia Canonica
STD	Sexually Transmitted Disease
TANNER	TANNER, N.P., Decrees of the Ecumenical Councils, 1-11, London 1990
transl.	Translated

USCC	United States Catholic Conference
Verl.	Verlag
Vol.	Volume

Bibliography

Sources and Documents

AECAWA, The Pastoral Care of Marriage and Family Life, Catholic Mission Press, Cape Coast, Ghana 1986.

AFER, Special double issue 1980 Synod of Bishops, "African Bishops Interventions", Eldoret, Kenya, Vol. 23, Nr. 1 and 2 (February-April, 1981) 15-116.

BEAUMONT: Diocese of, Guidelines for the Sacrament of Matrimony, 1996: http://www.dioceseofbmt.org/resources/resources/sacrament-celebration/marriage.html (Accessed: 28.10.2011).

Catechism of the Catholic Church, A Cassell Imprint, Geoffrey Chapman, London 1994.

Catholic Bishops' Conference of Nigeria, Particular Complementary Norms to the Revised Code, Onitsha 1985.

CBCN, Catholic Bishops Conference of Nigeria, Family Planning and Population Control: Stand of the Catholic Church, Lagos 1989.

Catholic Wedding Help, Preparing for a Lifelong Marriage: http://www. Catholic wedding help.com/wedding-planning/03-marriage-prep.htm (Accessed: 28.11.2011).

Codex Iuris Canonici, Pii X pontificis maximi iussu Digestus Benedicti Papae XV auctoritate Promulgatus, 27 May 1917, in: AAS 9 (1917) 3-521.

Codex Iuris Canonici, Auctoritate Ioannis Pauli PP II Promulgatus, 25 January 1983, in: AAS 75 (1983) 1-317.

Codex Iuris Canonici, Pii X pontificis maximi iussu Digestus Benedicti Papae XV, auctoritate Promulgatus, Praefatione eminentissimi Petri Card. Gasparri et indice analytico-alphabetico auctus, Typis Polyglottis Vaticanis, 1956.

Codex Iuris Canonici, Auctoritate Ioannis Pauli PP II Promulgatus, Codex des kanonischen Rechtes, Lateinisch-deutshe Ausgabe mit Sachverzeichnis, hg. Im Auftrag der deutschen Bischofskonferenz, der Österreichischen Bischofskonferenz, der Schweizer Bischofskonferenz, der Erzbischöfe von Luxemburg und von Straßburg sowie der Bischöfe von Bozen-Brixen, von Lüttich und von Metz, Kevelaer, 2001.

Codex Canonum Ecclesiarum Orientalium auctoritate Ioannis Pauli II Promulgatus, in: AAS 82 (1990) 1061-1363.

COLUMBUS: Diocese of, Policies and Guidelines for Marriage Preparation, Foreword,2010. http://www.colsdioc.org/portals/0/Departments/cho/Documents/MarriagePolicy2010.pdf (Accessed: 28.10.2011).
Conferenza Episcopale Italiana, Evangelizzazione e Sacramenti, Torino 1973.
Council of Trent, Decree Tametsi (de.ref.matrim.), 11 November 1963, in: TANNER, 755-759.
DALLAS: Diocese of, A Pastoral Directive and Instruction on Marriage Preparation in the Diocese of Dallas, Office of Marriage Ministries, 2007.
DENVER: Archdiocese of, "What God Has Joined..." Supplement to the Particular Norms for Christian Marriage in the Archdiocese of Denver: http://www.archden.org/repository//Documents/MarriageFamily/Norms/WhatGodHasJoined_Supplementary.pdf (Accessed: 10.11.2011).
DENVER: Archdiocese of, "What God Has Joined...", Particular Norms for Christian Marriage in the Archdiocese of Denver: http://www. archden.org/repository//Documents/ MarriageFamily/Norms/WhatGodHasJoined.pdf (Accessed: 10.11.2011).
Die Deutschen Bischofskonferenz, Auf dem Weg zum Sakrament der Ehe: Überlegungen zur Trauungspastoral im Wandel, Hrsg. Vom Sekretariat der Deutschen Bischofskonferenz, Bonn 28 September, 2000.
Die Deutschen Bischofskonferenz, Ehevorbereitungsprotokoll (Niederschrift zur kirchlichen Ehevorbereitung und Eheschließung, Amtliches Formular der deutschen Bischofskonferenz), Anmerkungstafel, no.9, Fulda 2008.
DOL, Documents of the Liturgy 1963-79, Collegeville, Minnosota 1982, 2521.
FLANNERY, Austin, ed. Vatican Council II: Vol. 1, The Conciliar and Post Conciliar Documents, New York 1988.
FOCCUS, Facilitating Open Couple Communication, Understanding and Study: http://www.foccusinc.com/sections/foccus_content.asp?PKID=6.
FORTWORTH: Diocese of, Guidelines for the Preparation and Celebration of the Sacrament of Marriage: http://www.fwdioc.org/worship/Documents/sacramental-guidelines_holy_orders.pdf (Accessed: 23.11.2011).
Gemeinsame Synode der Bistümer in der Bundesrepublik Deutschland (1971-1975), Verlag Herder KG, Freiburg in Breisgau, 1976, 411-457.
HOUMA-THIBODAUX: Diocese of, Marriage Preparation Policy and Procedures: http://www.htdiocese.org/fm/marriagePreparation/tabid/332/Default.aspx (Accessed: 23.11.2011).
JOHN XXIII, Speech to the Roman Cardinals, 25th January, 1959, AAS 51 (1959), 65-69.
JOHN XXIII, Address to the Prelates of the Sacred Rota, 13 December 1961, in: M.J. Byrnes, Papal Teachings, New York 1963, 538.
JOHN XXIII, Enc. Pacem in terris, 11 April 1963, AAS 55 (1963), 261.

JOHN XXIII, Addr. Diarium Romanae Curiae, AAS 55 (1963), 363.

JOHN PAUL II, Apostolic Exhortation, Catechesis tradendae, 16 October 1979, AAS 71 (1979), 1277-1340.

JOHN PAUL II, Address to the Bishops of Kenya, 7 May 1980, AAS 72 (1980), 497.

JOHN PAUL II, Apostolic Exhortation, Familiaris consortio, 22 November 1981, AAS 74 (1982), 81-191, in: Paulines Publications USA, Boston 1981, 95-113.

JOHN PAUL II, Slavorum apostolic, 2 June 1985, AAS 77 (1985), 779-819.

JOHN PAUL II, Redemptoris missio, 9 December 1990, AAS 83 (1991), 249-340.

JOHN PAUL II, Evangelium vitae, Liberia Editrice Vaticana, Roma 1995.

JOHN PAUL II, Post-Synodal Apostolic Exhortation, Ecclesia in Africa, 14 September 1995, AAS 88 (1996), 5-82.

JOHN PAUL II, Allocution to the Roman Rota, 2 February 2001, AAS 93 (2001), 358-365, English trans. MonEccl. 126 (2001), 4-17.

JOHN PAUL II, Homily at the Opening Mass of Synod of Bishops of Africa, in: L'osservatore Romano 15, 1336.

JOHN PAUL II, Message to the Congress of the Pontifical Council for the Family on the 20th Anniversary of Familiaris Consortio, 23 November 2001. http://www.vatican.va/holyfather/john_paul_ii/speeches/2001/november/documents/hf_jp-ii_spe_20011123_card-trujillo-family_en.html(Accessed: 2.11.2011).

JOHN PAUL II, Letter to Families, Address to the Fourth World Meeting of Families in Manila, Philippines, 25 January, 2003. http://www.vatican.va/holy_father/john_paul_ii/speeches/2003/january/documents/hf_jp-ii_spe_20030125_family-manila_en.html>> (Accessed:27.6.2011).

LEO XIII, Enc. Arcanum divinae sapientiae, 10 February 1880, AAS 12 (1879), 385-402.

LOS ANGELES: Archdiocese of, About Natural Family Planning: http://www.archdiocese.la/prayer/sacraments/family/nfp/index.html (Accessed: 28.11.2011).

National Conference of Catholic Bishops, The Role of the Christian Family in the Modern World, Washington 1979.

NCCB-USCC, Bishops' Committee for Pastoral Research and Practices, Faithful to Each Other Forever: A Catholic Handbook for Pastoral Help for Marriage Preparation, Washington D.C. 1989.

NCCB-USCC, Implementation of the 1983 Code of Canon Law, National Conference of Catholic Bishops, Complementary Norms, Washington D.C. 1991. http://www.nccbuscc.org/norms/norms.htm (Accessed: 14.10.2011).

NCCB-USCC, Marriage and Family Life Committee, "Marriage Preparation and Cohabiting Couples, Information and Report". http://www.usccb.org/laity/marriage/cohabiting.htm (Accessed: 12.9.2011).

NCCB-USCC, An Analysis of Diocesan Marriage Preparation Policies, 2004. http://www.usccb.org/issues-and-action/marriage-and-family/marriage-preparation/mpanalysis.cfm (Accessed: 22.11.2011).
NCCB-USCC, Marriage: Love and Life in the Divine Plan, Washington D.C. 2009.
NCCB-USCC, "Marriage Preparation Programs, Are the Working?". http://www.ourcatholicmarriage.org/parishes/importance/DorMarriage-Prep-Programs-Work.pdf/Accessed: 30.11.2011).
NEW JERSEY: Dioceses of, Section 1: The Marriage Preparation Process. http://www.rcan.org/famlife/B-MarriagePrep-Sectl.pdf (Accessed: 25.10.2011).
NEW JERSEY: Pastoral Policies and Guidelines for Marriage Preparation. http://www.rcan.org/fam-life/A-OverviewandIntro.pdf (Accessed: 28.10.2011).
NEW JERSEY: Section 111: Special Circumstances in Marriage Preparation. http://www.diometuchen.org/medin/files/familylife/marriage-prep/family_life_marriage_Prep-special_circumstances.pdf (Accessed: 28.10.2011).
NORWICH: Diocese of, Marriage Preparation, 2011. http://www.ccfsn.org/pdf-files/marriageprep.2011.pdf (Accessed: 7.11.2011).
Papal Committee on the Family, "The Family in the Pastoral Activity of the Church", USCC, Washington D.C. 1978.
PAUL V, Rituale Romanum, Tornaci Nerviorum, 1886.
PAUL VI, Addr. Singulari cum animi, 20 November 1965, AAS 57 (1965), 985-989.
PAUL VI, Africae Terrarum, Message to the Peoples of Africa, AAS 59 (1967), 74.
PAUL VI, Enc. Humanae Vitae, July 25, 1968, AAS 60 81968), 482.
PAUL VI, Apostolic Letter, Motu proprio, Matrimonia mixta, 30 March 1970, AAS 62 (1970), 257-263.
PAUL VI, Apostolic Exhortation, Evangelli Nuntiandi, 8 December 1975, AAS 68 (1976), 5-76.
PCCICR, "Acta Commissionis- Coetus de Matrimonio", Comm. 3 (1977) 69-81; 9 (1977), 117-146.
PCCICR, Schema Documenti Pontificii quo disciplina Canonica de sacramentis recognoscitur, Typis Polyglottis Vaticanis 1975.
PCCICR, Codex Iuris Canonici Schema novissimum iuxta placita partum commissionis emendatum atque summon pontifici praesentatum, Vatican City 1982.
PEORIA: Diocese of, Diocesan Programs- Part One: Pre-Cana Conferences. http://www.cdop.org/pages/AOfficeFamilyMarriage.aspx (Accessed: 30.11.2011).
PIUS XI, Enc. Casti connubii, 31 December 1930, AAS 22 (1930), 539-592.

PIUS XI, Enc. Divini illius magistri, 31 December 1929, AAS 22 (1930), 49-88.
PIUS XII, Enc. Summi pontificatus, 20 October 1939, AAS 31 (1939), 413-453.
PIUS XII, Address to the Women of Catholic Action, 26 October 1941, in: Discorsie Radiomessaggi di Sua Santita Pio XII, III, Milano 1944, 183-207.
PIUS XII, Allocution to the Parish Priests and Lenten Preachers of Rome, 22 February 1944, in: M.J. Brynes, Papal Teachings, New York 1963, 356.
PIUS XII, Address to the Women of Italian Catholic Action Women's Apostolate, 24 July 1949, in: Discorsie Radiomessaggi di Sua Santita Pio XII, XI, Tipografia Poliglotta Vaticana 1950, 155-163.
PIUS XII, Address to the Men of Catholic Action of Portugal, 10 December 1950, in: Discorsie Radiomessaggi di Sua Santita Pio XII, XII, Tipografia Poliglotta Vaticana 1951, 359-365.
PIUS XII, Radio Message Addressed to the Fourth Congress of Catholic Education of Central America, 5 August 1951, in: Discorsie Radiomessaggi di Sua Santita Pio XII, XIII, Tipografia Poliglotta Vaticana 1952, 203-209.
PIUS XII, Address to the Students and Teachers of Schools for Adult Education, 19 March 1953, in: Discorsie Radiomessaggi di Sua Santita Pio XII, XV, Tipografia Poliglitta Vaticana 1954, 7-17.
Prince of Peace Catholic Church, Marriage Preparation Policies, Proximate Preparation. http://www.images.acswebnetworks.com/1/1059/MarriagePreparationPolicies.pdf (Accessed: 22.11.2011).
Pontificia Commissio Codici Iuris Canonici Recognoscendo, Relatio Complectens Synthesim animadversionum, Vatican City 1981.
Pontifical Council For The Family, Preparation for the Sacrament of Marriage, Paulines Publications Africa, Kolbe Press, Limuru, Nairobi 2001.
Pontifical Council For The Family, Pontifical Council for the Family Conclusions of the Theology – Pastoral Congress on the Theme: "Twenty Years Since 'Familiaris Consortio': The Anthropological and Pastoral Dimension", 20 December 2001. http://www.vatican.va/roman_curia/pontifical_councils/family/documents/rc_pc_family_doc_20011220_xx-familianis_en.html (Accessed: 2.11.2011).
Pontifical Council For The Family, Enchiridion on the Family: A Compendium of Church Teaching on Family and Life Issues from Vatican II to the Present, Boston 2004.
Pontifical Council For Legislative Texts, Dignitas Connubii, Catholic Truth Society, London 2005.
RICHMOND, Diocese of, Called to Marriage, 1997. http://www.richmonddiocese.org/sites/default/files/marriage.pdf(Accessed: 28.10.2011).
Sacred Congregation of the Council, Decr. Ne temere, 2 August 1907, AAS 40 (1907), 525-530.

Sacred Congregation of Rites, Ordo Celebrandi Matrimonium, Typis Polyglottis Vaticanis 1969.
Sacred Congregation of Rites, Ordo Celebrandi Matrimonium, Typis Polyglottis Vaticanis, Vatican City 1991, Nos. 5-7.
Sacrae Congregatio de Sacramentis, Instructio ad Ordinarius Circa Statum Liberum ac Denunciationem Initi Matrimonii, 6 December 1911, AAS 3 (1911), 102-103.
Sacrae Congregatio de Displina Sacramentorum, Instructio ad Rev. mos Ordinarios Locorum Super Probatione Status Liberi ac Denuntiatione Initi Matrimonii, 4 July 1921, AAS 13 (1921), 348-349.
SACRAMENTO: Diocese of, Natural Family Planning. http://www.diocese-sacramento.org/family_youth_young_adult/natural_family_planning.html (Accessed: 28.11.2011).
SAN DIEGO: Diocese of, Guidelines for Marriage Preparation, 2010. http://www.diocese-sdiego.org/Handbook/Handbook_PDFs/Marriage.pdf (Accessed: 28.11.2011).
SAN FRANSCISCO: Archdiocese of, Common Policy for Pastoral Marriage Preparation, 1992.
SAN JOSE: Diocese of, San Jose Catholic Engaged Encounter. http://www.dsj.org/being-catholic/marriage-in-the-catholic-church/san-jose-catholic-engaged-encounter (Accessed: 30.11.2011).
SECAM, Symposium of Episcopal Conferences of Africa and Madagascar, The Church as Family of God: Instrumentum Laboris and Pastoral Letter, SECAM Publication, Accra 1998.
Second Vatican Council, Const. Sacrosanctum concilium, 4 December 1963, AAS 56 (1964), 97-138. English Translation, in: FLANNERY, Austin, ed; Vatican Council II: Vol. I, The Conciliar and Post Conciliar Documents, New York 1988, 20-24.
Second Vatican Council, Decr. Inter mirifica, 4 December 1963, AAS 56 (1964), 145-152. English Translation, in: FLANNERY, Austin, ed; Vatican Council II: Vol. I, The Conciliar and Post Conciliar Documents, New York 1988, 284-288.
Second Vatican Council, Dogmatic Const. Lumen gentium, 21 November 1964, AAS 57 (1965), 4-71. English Translation, in: FLANNERY, Austin, ed; Vatican Council II: Vol. I, The Conciliar and Post Conciliar Documents, New York 1988, 388-402.
Second Vatican Council, Decr. Christus dominus, 28 October 1965, AAS 58 (1966), 837-864. English Translation, in: FLANNERY, Austin, ed; Vatican Council II: Vol. I, The Conciliar and Post Conciliar Documents, New York 1988, 569-576.

Second Vatican Council, Decl. Gravissimum educationis, 28 October 1965, AAS 58 81966). English Translation, in: FLANNERY, Austin, ed; Vatican Council II: Vol. I, The Conciliar and Post Conciliar Documents, New York 1988, 725-737.
Second Vatican Council, Decr. Apostolicam actuositatem, 18 November 1965, AAS 58 (1966) 837-864. English Translation, in: FLANNERY, Austin, ed; Vatican Council II: Vol. I, The Conciliar and Post Conciliar Documents, New York 1988, 776-782.
Second Vatican Council, Decr. Ad gentes divinitus, 7 December 1965, AAS 58 (1966) , 813-862. English Translation, in: FLANNERY, Austin, ed; Vatican Council II: Vol. I, The Conciliar and Post Conciliar Documents, New York 1988, 835-840.
Second Vatican Council, Pastoral Const. Gaudium et spes, 7 December 1965, AAS 58 (1966), 837-864. English Translation, in: FLANNERY, Austin, ed; Vatican Council II: Vol. I, The Conciliar and Post Conciliar Documents, New York 1988, 949-957.
SHREVEPORT: Diocese of, Sacramental Guidelines, 2004. http://www.dioshpt.org/OnlineDocs/SacramentalGuidelines.pdf(Accessed: 16.11.2011).
Synod Secretariat, De Muneribus familiae Christianae in mundo hodierno: Lineamenta ad usum Conferentiarum episcopalium, Typis Polyglottis Vaticanis 1979, Italian Translation, Segreteria del Sinodo, "I Compiti della famiglia cristiana nel mondo contemporaneo", IL Regn. Documenti II (1979), 258-270.
Synod Secretariat, De Muneribus familiae Christianae in mundo hodierno: Instrumentum laboris ad usum sodalium Quinti Coetus Generalis, Typis Polyglottis Vaticanis 1980, Italian Translation, Segreteria del Sinodo, "Instrumentum Laboris. I Compiti della famiglia cristiana nel mondo contemporaneo", II Regno-Documenti 17 (1980), 258-270. English Translation, "The 1980 Synod on the Family", Origins 10 (1980), 226-233.
Synod Secretariat, "Le 43 Proposizioni", IL Regno-Documenti, 13 (1981), 386-397, or EV 7, 600-759, English Translation, "The Synod Propositions", The Tablet, 31 January 1981, 116-118, 7 February 1981, 141-142, 14 February 1981, 164-167.
The Rites of the Catholic Church, Vol. I, "Rite of Marriage", Introduction, n. 7, Pueblo Publishing Company, New York 1976, 534-570.
TUCSON: Diocese of, Guidelines for the Sacrament of Marriage, Tucson 30 November 1986.
WASHINGTON: Archdiocese of, "The Sacrament of Marriage", in: Sacramental Norms and Policies, Washington D.C. January 1995, 57-74.
WORCESTER: Diocese of, Pastoral Policy for Marriage Preparation, June 1997.

Books and Articles

ABBO, J.B – HANNAN, J.D; The Sacred Canons: A Concise Presentation of the Current Disciplinary Norms of the Church, II St. Louis 1960.

ACHEBE, C; Things Fall Apart, London 1958.

ACHEBE, C; Arrow of God, New York 1969.

ACHEBE, C; No Longer at Ease, London 1978.

AGBO, D.U; Traditional Love and Christian Charity in the Igbo Community, (Lateran) Rome 1982.

AKALONU, C.I; Procreation in Igbo Marriage, Inculturation of the Christian Deal, Madrid 1987.

ALESANDRO, J.A; "Marriage Legislation in the New Code: Preparation for Marriage", Washington 1980.

ALFS, R; Die außerordentlichen Formen der kanonischen Eheschließung im Licht der Lehre von der Sakramentalität der Ehe, Eine Untersuchung zur ekklesiologischen Bedeutung der Sakramentalen Eheschließung, echter, Würzburg 1960.

AMADI, E; Ethics in Nigerian Culture, Ibadan 1982.

AMEVOR, P.K; New Approaches to Marriage Preparation in the 1983 Code of Canon Law: Challenges to the Particular Church in Ghana, Doctoral Dissertation, Regensburg 2009.

ANAMEZE, L; Marriage Among Igbos, Enugu 1996.

ARINZE, F.A; Sacrifice in Ibo Religion, Ibadan University Press, Ibadan 1970.

ARTHUR, P; ed; Survey of African Marriage and Family Life, Oxford University Press, London 1953.

ASIEGBU, A.U; A Crisis of Faith and a Quest for Spirituality, Enugu 2000.

ASOQUO, C – AKPANESSIEN, N.T; "African Ancestors in the Christian Communion of Saints" in: NACATHS Journal of African Theology, Ikot Ekpene 2002, 19.

ASUQUO AKPAN, E; The Path to Holy Orders, Owerri 1999.

ASUQUO AKPAN, E; "Problems of Christian Marriage and Family Life in the Nigerian Situation", in: B. Etafo – H.O. Okeke, ed; Marriage and the Family in Nigeria, Onitsha 1993, 86-87.

ASUZU, C.C – ASUZU, M.C; Christian Courtship, The Ambassador Publications, Iperu-Remo 1994.

ATADO, J.C; African Marriage Customs and Church Law, Modern Printers Ltd; Kano 1988.

AUGUSTINE (St), De Bono Coniugali, Trans. C.T. Wilcox, The Fathers of the Church, The Catholic University of America Press, Washington, D.C. 1999.

AUGUSTINE, P.C; A Commentary on the New Code of Canon Law, London 1935.
AYRINHAC, H.A; Marriage Legislation in the Code of Canon Law, London 1932.
AWOLALU, J.O; West African Traditional Religions, Ibadan 1912.
AZNAR GIL, F.R; Derecho Matrimonial Canonico, Vol. I: canones 1055-1094, Salamanca 2001.
AZNAR GIL, F.R – OLMOS ORTEGA, M.E; La Preparacion Celebracion e inscripcion del Matrimonio en Espana, Salamanca 1996.
AZORJI, E; Some Recurrent Problems of Christian Inculturation in Nigeria with Special Reference to the Igbo People, Rome 1988.
BANARES, J.I; "Commentary on Canons 1055-1062, Marriage", in: A. Marzoa – J. Miras – R. Rodriguez-Ocana, ed; Exegetical Commentary on the Code of Canon Law, Vol. III, Montreal 2004, 1049-1107.
BAUMANN, U; Die Ehe- ein Sakrament?, B einziger Verlag, Zürich, 1988.
BAUSCH, W.J; A New Look at the Sacraments, revised edition, Twenty-Third Publications Mystic Connecticut, 1992.
BASDEN, G.T; Niger Ibos, Frank Cass & Co; London 1966.
BASDEN, G.T; Among the Ibos of Nigeria, University Publishing Co; Lagos 1982.
BEAL, J.P – CORIDEN, J.A – GREEN, T.J; ed; New Commentary on the Code of Canon Law, Theological Publication India, Bangalore 2004.
BEAL, J.P; "Marriage: Commentary on Historical Overview and Canons 1055-1062", in: J.P. Beal – J.A. Coriden – T.J. Green, ed; New Commentary on the Code of Canon Law, Bangalore 2004, 1234-1260.
BENETT, W.J; "Sex and the Education of our Children", Address to National School Boards Association, (22 January, 1987), Washington 1987, in: NCCB-USCC, Faithful to Each Other Forever, Washington D.C. 1989, 26.
BENETT, W.J – KOOP, C.E; "Statement on AIDS Education", (30 January, 1987), Washington 1987, in: NCCB-USCC, Faithful to Each Other Forever, Washington D.C. 1989, 26.
BERKMANN, B.J; Die Ehen Von/Mit Nichtkatholiken Von der Lateinischen Kirche. Dissertation, Frankfurt am Main 2008.
BIKO, S; I Write What I Like, New York 1978.
BIRKHÖLZER, H; Ehe kein Auslaufmodell: Lebensgestaltung zwischen biblisch Orientierter, christlicher Lebenssicht und Lebenskompromiss, Claudius Verlag, München 1997.
BLESKE, E; Konfliktfeld Ehe und christliche Ethik, mit einem Vorwort von Anita Mandel, Kösel-Verlag, München 1981.

BODY, A; Growing Together: The Course, A Complete Marriage Preparation Programme, Church House Publishing, London 2007.
BOUSCAREN, T.L – ELLIS, A.C; Canon Law: A Text and Commentary, Milwaukee 1955.
BUJO, B; "Polygamy in Africa: A Pastoral Approach", in: Theology Digest 32 (1985), 231.
BURKE, J; Marriage Today, Don Bosco Centre, Akure 1990.
BURKE, J; Marriage in Scripture, Society of African Missions, Ibadan 1993.
BURKE, J; Marriage and Nullity of Marriage, Society of African Missions, Ibadan 1993.
BURKE, J; The Pre-Marriage Investigation by the Priest, Lagos 1998.
BURKE, J; "Is it Advisable to Join Together in one Ceremony Traditional and Catholic Church Marriage Rites"?, in: Shalom Proclaim Peace, A Spiritual Pastoral Journal, Vol. XVI, No. I, 2001, 39-40.
BURKE, J; The Theology and Canon Law of Marriage, Society of African Mission, Ibadan 2001.
BURKE, J; Catholic Marriage, Pauline Publications Africa, Nairobi, Kenya 2006.
BURKE, J; Catholic and Fundamentalist Christian Marriages, Don Bosco Centre, Akure 2006.
BYRNES, M.J; Papal Teachings: Marriage, transl. New York 1963.
CAHILL, L.S; "Commentary on Familiaris Consortio (Apostolic Exhortation on the Family)", in: Kenneth R. Himes, et al; ed; Modern Catholic Social Teaching: Commentary and Interpretations, Georgetown University Press, Washington D.C. 2005, 363-389.
CAPRILE, G; II Sinodo dei Vescovi. Quinta Assemblea Generale, Roma 1982.
CAPPELLO, M.F; Summa Iuris Canonici, II, Romae 1934.
CAPPELLO, M.F; Tractatus Canonico-Moralis De Sacramentis, V, De Matrimonio, Taurini-Romae 1961.
CARBERRY, J; The Juridical Form of Marriage, Catholic University of America, Washington D.C. 1934.
CARLSTON, K.S; Social Theory and African Tribal Organisation, Chicago 1968.
CHIBUKO, P.C; Igbo Christian Rite of Marriage, Vol. 119, Peter Lang, Frankfurt am Main 1999.
CHIBUKO, P.C; Church Wedding and Traditional Marriage in one Ceremony, Black Belt Konzult Ltd; Enugu 2003.
CHINIGO, M; ed; The Pope Speaks: The Teachings of Pope Pius XII, New York 1957.
CLARK, E.A; ed; St. Augustine on Marriage and Sexuality, The Catholic University of America Press, Washington D.C. 1996.

CLAYTON, R; The Family, Marriage and Social Change, D.C. Heath and Company, Lexington, Massachusetts, Toronto, London 1975.
CONNOLLY, P; The Nature of Marriage as Proposed in the Codex Iuris Canonici and in the Codex Canonum Ecclesiarum Orientalium, Ottawa 1995.
CONNOLLY, P; "Contrasts in the Western and Eastern Approaches to Marriage", in: StudCan 35 82001), 357-402.
CONTON, W; The African, London 1906.
CONTRA, E – Rubin, N.N; Readings in African Law II, London 1970.
COOKE, B; Sacraments and Sacramentality, Mystic: Twenty-Third Publications, 1983.
CORCIONE, M.S; Marriage Preparation in the U.S. Implementing canons 1063-4, Licence Thesis, Pontifical Athenaeum Antonianum, Rome 2001.
CORIDEN, J.A; An Introduction to Canon Law, New Jersey, 2004.
CORIDEN, J.A; "Commentary on canons 747-833, The Teaching Office of the Church", in: J.A. Coriden – T.J. Green – D.E. Heintschel, ed; The Code of Canon Law, New York/Malwah 1985.
CORIDEN, J.A – GREEN, T.J – Heintschel, D.E; ed; The Code of Canon Law: A Text and Commentary, Paulist Press, New York/Mahwah 1985.
COVINO, P – Madden, L – Rendler, E – Buscemi, J; Celebrating Marriage: Preparing the Wedding Liturgy, A Workshop for Engaged Couples, The Pastoral Press, Washington D.C. 1988.
CUNEO, J.J; "Restriction on Marriage Following Prior Union with Continuing Obligations", Jurist 45 (1985), 324-327.
CUNNINGHAM, R.G; "Marriage and the Nescient Catholic: Questions of Faith and Sacrament", in: T.P. Doyle, ed; Marriage Studies, II, Washington D.C. 1982, 20-73.
DAIDSON, B; The African Genius, Boston 1969.
DERERRARI, R.J; ed; The Fathers of the Church: St. Augustine Treatises on Marriage and other Subjects, The Catholic University of America Press, Washington, D.C. 1985.
DEMEL, S; Kirchliche Trauung – unerlässliche Pflicht für die Ehe des katholschen Christen?, Verlag W. Kohihammer, Stuttgart, Berlin, Köln 1993.
DIETRICH VON HILDEBRAND, Marriage, Longman, Green and Co; London 1942.
DIKE, E.E; Christian Marriage and Family in Igboland: A Study of the Conflict between Igbo- Culture and Christianity, Münster 2001.
DONOVAN, J.J; The Pastor's Obligation in Pre-nuptial Investigation: An Historical Synopsis and Commentary, Washington 1938.
DOYLE, T.P; "The Individual's Right to Marry in the Context of the Common Good", StudCan 13 (1979), 246-301.

DOYLE, T.P; "The Canonical Foundations for Pre-Marriage Preparation Guidelines", in: T.P. Doyle, ed; Marriage Studies, I, Washington, D.C. 1980, 66-77.
DOYLE, T.P; "Commentary on canons 1063-1072, Pastoral Care and what must precede Celebration of Marriage", in: J.A. Coriden – T.J. Green – D.E. Heintschel, eds; The Code of Canon Law. A text and Commentary, New York 1985, 737-833.
DUNCKER, A; Gleichheit und Ungleichheit in der Ehe, Persönliche Stellung von Frau und Mann im Recht der ehelichen Lebensgemeinschaft 1700-1914, Böhlau Verlag, Köln, Weimar, Wien 2003.
EBOH, B.O; The Concept of the Human Soul in Igbo Traditional Philosophy, (Gregorian) Rome 1972.
EDEH, E; Towards an Igbo Metaphysics, Loyola University Press, Chicago 1985.
EKWURU, G; The Pangs of an African Culture in Travail, Owerri 1999.
ELIAS, T.O; Groundwork of Nigerian Law, Oxford University Press, London 1964.
ELIAS, T.O; African Indigenous Laws of Worship, Enugu 1975.
ELLIS, A; Group Marriage: A Possible Alternative? In Beyond Monogamy, recent studies of Sexual alternatives in marriage, edited and with an introductory Essay by J.R. Smith – L.G. Smith, The Johns Hopkins University Press, Baltimore and London 1974.
EPETUKU, C.B.A; Intensive Care of Married Couples, Justice and Peace Standard Press, Eku 2006.
ESTEVEZ, J.M; transl; Male and Female He Created Them: On Marriage and the Family, Ignatius Press, San Franscisco 2003.
FAGIOLO, V; In Commento al Codici di Diritto Canonica, in: P.O.V. Pinto, ed; Rome 1985, 622-624.
FAGIOLO, V; "Commentary on canons 1063-1072, De Cura Pastorali et de iis quae matrimoni celebrationi praemitti debent", in: P.V. Pinto, ed; Commento al Codici di Diritto Canonico, Libreria Editrice Vaticana 2001, 629-632.
FAGIOLO, V; "La dimensione pastorale dei Tribunali ecclesiastici per le cause matrimoniali", in: L' Osservatore Romano, Friday 13 February 1988, 6.
FAGIOLO, V; "La preparazione al matrimonio: normative Canonica per una pastorale matrimoniale Comunitario" MonEccl 119 (1994), 1-52.
FEEHAN, M; Saying I Do: A Marriage Preparation Program, Paulist Press, New York/Mahwah, New Jersey 2006.
FINN, R; "Faith and the Sacrament of Marriage: General Conclusions from an Historical Study", Marriage Studies 3 (1985), 95-111.
FLATTEN, H; "Der Eheprozess im Entwurf zum künftigen Codex iuris Canonici", in: AfkKR (1977), 36-73.
FORNES, J; Derecho matrimonial canonico, Madrid 1990.

FUMAGALLI, O; La Normatira del nuoro Codici, Brescia 1983.
GANGWARI, J.U; Civil Marriage in Nigeria, PortHarcourt 1993.
GANGWARI, J.U; Church State Relations in Marriage in Nigeria, Jos 1994.
GASPARRI, P; Tractus canonicus de matrimonio, I-II, Romae 1891, 1932.
GASPARRI, P – Seredi, G.J; ed; Codicis Iuris Canonica Fontes, Rome 1926.
GAVIN, F; Pastoral Care in Marriage Preparation (Can. 1063). History, Analysis of the Norms and its Implementation by Some Particular Churches, Editrice Pontificia Universita Gregoriana, Rome 2004.
GBUJI, A.O; The Pastoral Care of Marriage and Family Life in Nigeria, St. Paul Press Training School, Ibadan 2006.
GRAMUNT, I; The Essence of Marriage and the Code of Canon Law, Studia Canonica 25 (1991), 365-383.
GRAMUNT, I – Hervada, J – Wauck, L.A; Canons and Commentaries on Marriage, Minnesota 1987.
GREEN, T.J; "The Revision of the Code: the First Decade", The Jurist 36 (1976), 353-355.
GREEN, T.J; "The Revision of Marriage Law: An Exposition and Critique", Studia Canonica 10 (1976), 363.
GREEN, T.J; The Revised Schema De Matrimonio, Jurist 40 (1980), 60-61.
GREEN, T.J; The Church's Sanctifying Mission: Some Aspects of the Normative Role of the Diocesan Bishop, Studia Canonica 25 (1991), 267.
GROARKE, T.J; Marriage Preparation in Contemporary Theology and Canon Law, Doctoral Thesis, Lateran University, Alfonsianum Academy, Rome 1991.
GROOTAERS, J – SELLING, J.A; The 1980 Synod of Bishops on the Role of the Family, Leuven 1983.
GRUBBER, H.G; "Grundlagen und Impulse einer verantwortlichen kirchlichen Ehevorbereitung", in: Arbeitsgemeinschaft für katholische Familienbildung (Hrsg.), Liebe und Ehe. Grundlagen und Konzepte in Ehevorbereitung, Ehebegleitung und der Arbeit mit jungen Erwachsenen, AKF Berichte 36, Bonn 1999, 7-37.
GÜNTHER, H; Formen und Urgeschichte der Ehe: Die Formen der Ehe, Familie und Verwandtschaft und die Fragen einer Urgeschichte der Ehe (zweite Auflage), J. Lehmanns Verlag, München/Berlin 1941.
GYEKYE, K; African Cultural Values: An Introduction, Sankofa Publishing Company, Accra 2003.
HAJOVSKY, B.D; Marriage Preparation and Pastoral Care: A Comparison between the 1917 and 1983 Codes of Canon Law, JCL Dissertation, Catholic University of America, Washington 1984.

HALLERMANN, H; Gemeinsame Synode, in: A.V. Compenhausen – I. Riedel-Spangenberger – R. Sebott, Hgg; Lexikon für Kirchen- und Staatskirchenrecht II, Paderborn 2002, 41-44.
HAMLON, J.S; A Call to Families: Study Guide and Commentary for Familiaris Consortio, Minnesota 1984.
HÄRING, B; Marriage in the Modern World, Westminster 1966.
HÄRING, B; Free and Faithful in Christ, Moral Theology for Priests and Laity, Vol.2, St. Paul Publications, Middlegreen 1979.
HÄRING, B; "Fostering the Nobility of Marriage and the Family", in: H. Vorgrimler, ed; Commentary on the Documents of Vatican II, V, New York 1969, 239.
HASTING, A; Christian Marriage in Africa, London 1973.
HAUSER, D; Marriage and Christian Life: A Theology of Christian Marriage, University Press of America, Lanham, Maryland 2005.
HEIMERL, H – PREE, H; Kirchenrecht: Allgemeine Normen und Eherecht, Wien 1983.
HOLBÖCK, C; Handbuch des Kirchenrechtes Bd. II, Gemeinschaftsverlag, Tyrolia Innsbruck/Herder Wien 1951.
HÖPPLER, G; Nichteheliche Lebensgemeinschaften als Problem für das staatliche und kirchliche Recht, Peter Lang, Frankfurt am Main 1999.
HUIZING, P.J; "Alternativentwurf für eine Revision des kanonischen Eherechts", in: P.J. Huizing, ed; Für eine neue kirchliche Eheordnung, Düsseldorf 1975, 86.
HUIZING, P.J; Relator, Opera Consultorum: De Matrimonio, in: Communicationis 3 (1971), 71.
HUIZING, P.J; "Canonical Implications of the Conception of Marriage in the Conciliar Constitution Gaudium et Spes", in: W.P. Roberts, ed; Commitment to Partnership, New York 1987, 106-107.
HUNTER, D.G; ed; Marriage in the Early Church, Wipf and Stock Publishers, West Broadway 2001.
IDIGO, A.C; Towards Making the Igbo Traditional Marriage a Christian Marriage (Socio-Anthropological & Canonical Approach), Rome 2001.
IDOWU, B.E; African Traditional Religion – A Definition, London 1973.
IDOWU, B.E; Olodumare: God in Yoruba Belief, Ikeja 1982.
IFEANYI, V; "Inculturation and Liberation Theology: Similarities and Differences", in: NACATHS Journal of African Theology, Vol.10, Owerri 2000.
IGWE, A; "An Inquiry into African Traditional Religion and its Theological Status for Inculturation", in: NACATHS Journal of African Theology, Vol.12, Ikot Ekpene 2002, 29.
ILOGU, E; Christianity and Igbo Culture, New York 1974.
ISICHEI, E; The Igbo People and the Europeans, London 1973.

ISICHEI, E; A History of the Igbo People, London 1976.

IWUJI, E; Customary Law Marriage in Nigeria, Göttingen 1982.

IWUJI, E; Marriage Form in Nigeria, Rome 1983.

JOYCE, G.H; Christian Marriage: An Historical and Doctrinal Study, Sheed and Ward, London 1948.

KAISER, M; "Grundfragen des kirchlichen Eherechts", in: J. Listl – H. Müller – H. Schmitz, (Hrsg.), Grundriss des nachkonziliaren Kirchenrechts, Verlag Friedrich Pustet, Regensburg 1980, 536-549.

KALU, M.O.C; Evaluation of the Canonical Form of Marriage in Canon 1108 in the Light of Igbo Traditional Marriage, Masters Thesis, PortHarcourt 1993.

KASPER, W; Theology of Christian Marriage, New York, 1993.

KAYONGO-MALE, D – ONYANGO, P; The Sociology of the African Family, London 1984.

KELLY, D; "Whither Familiaris Consortio", HPR 83 (1982), 9-16.

KELLY, D; "Commentary on canons 1063-1072, Pastoral Care and the Prerequisites for the Celebration of Marriage", in: G. Sheehey, ed; The Canon Law: Letter and Spirit, Dublin 1995, 578-588.

KELLY, G; Pastoral Care of the Family – Stages, Structures, Agents, and Situations, Articles 65-72, in: M.J. Wrenn, ed; Pope John Paul II and the Family, Chicago 1983.

KIPPLEY, J.F; Marriage is for Keeps: Wedding Edition with Marriage Rite and Readings, Foundation for the Family Inc; Cincinnati, Ohio 1993.

KISEMBO, B – Magesa, L – Shorter, A; African Christian Marriage, Paulines Publications Africa, Nairobi 1998.

LACERTE, H; "Theological Reflections on Marriage as a Humanizing Experience in a Dehumanizing World", in: Marriage Studies 11, Washington 1982, 63.

LAW, B; Christian Marriage: a Covenant of Love and Life, A Pastoral Letter, Archdiocese of Boston, March 25, 1998.

LAWLER, M.G; Marriage and Sacrament: A Theology of Christian Marriage, The Liturgical Press, Minnesota 1993.

LEE, L; Contributions of Lay People Towards Preparation of Marriage: Commentary on canons 1063 and 1064, JCL Dissertation, Catholic University of America, Washington 1990.

LEHMANN, J; Ehevorbereitung in der Bundesrepublik Deutschland: Moglichkeiten der Verwirklichung anhand des Codex Iuris Canonici und der Adhortatio apostolic, "Familiaris Consortio" Papst Johannes Pauls II, München 1985.

LEONARD, A.G; The Lower Niger and its Tribes, London 1958.

LISTL, J – MÜLLER, H – SCHMITZ, H; (Hrsg.), Handbuch des katholischen Kirchenrechts, Verlag Friedrich Pustet, Regensburg 1983.

LOBO, G.V; The New Marriage Law, St. Paul Press Training School, Bangalore 2005.
LUCAS, J.O; Religions in West Africa and Ancient Egypt, Lagos 1970.
LÜDECKE, N; Genese und Exegese der Ehelehre der Konzilskonstitution "GS", in: Kanonistischer Auswertung, Echter Verlag, Würzburg 1989.
LÜDICKE, K; Codex Iuris Canonici, Kommentar für Studium und Praxis, Eherecht: Canones 1055-1165, Ludgerus Verlag, Essen 1983.
MACKIN, T; The Marital Sacrament: Marriage in the Catholic Church, Paulist Press, New York/Mahwah, New Jersey 1989.
MADU, I.A.C; Christianizing the Igbo Traditional Love and Morality Rites, Enugu 2005.
MARINELLI, T – MCDONOUGH, P; The Joy of Marriage Preparation, Resurrection Press, New Jersey 2001.
MBA, C.S; Matrimonial Consent in Igbo Marriages, Rome 1964.
MBA, C.S; "The Significance of Dowry or Bride-Wealth in the Igbo Traditional Marriage and its Implication for Christianity in Africa today", in: Lucerna (Bulletin), Vol.2, No.2, B.M.S; Enugu 1981.
MBA, C.S; "Igbo Customary Marriage and the Validation of Marriage in the Church", in: Lucerna, Vol.3, No.1, B.M.S; Enugu 1982.
MBA, C.S; A Handbook of Marriage Instruction, Enugu 1986.
MBA, C.S; "Trial Marriage in Nigeria", in: Lucerna, Vol.8, No.1, B.M.S; Enugu 1988.
MBA, C.S; "African Traditional Marriage: Its Values and Contributions to Christian Marriage", in: B. Etafo – H. Okeke, ed; Marriage and Family in Nigeria, Onitsha 1993, 8-18.
MBA, C.S; Evolving an Igbo Christian Rite of Marriage, Enugu 1994.
MBITI, J.S; Concepts of God in Africa, London 1970.
MBITI, J.S; Love and Marriage in Africa, Longman Group, London 1973.
MBITI, J.S; African Religion and Philosophy, London 1975.
MBITI, J.S; An Introduction to African Religion, London 1975.
MCAREAVEY, J; The Canon Law of Marriage and the Family, Dublin 1997.
MCCARTHY, F; Wedding Liturgies, Dominican Publications, Dublin 1989.
MEEK, C.K; Law and Authority in a Nigerian Tribe, London 1937.
METUH, E.I; Comparative Studies of African Traditional Religions, Onitsha 1987.
METUH, E.I; God and Man in African Religion, Enugu 1991.
METUH, E.I; African Religious in Western Conceptual Schemes: The Problem of Interpretation, Jos 1991.
MIDGLEY, J.M.V – MIDGLEY, S.V; A Marriage Preparation Program: A Decision to Love, Twenty-Third Publications, New London 2009.

MILLER, M; The Post-Synodal Apostolic Exhortations of John Paul II, Huntington 1998.
MORRISEY, F.G; Revising Church Legislation on Marriage, Origins 9 (1979), 213.
MOSIEK, U; Kirchliches Eherecht: Unter Berücksichtigung der nachkonziliaren Rechtslage, Freiburg 1972.
NACATHS Journal of African Theology, Vol.10, The Practice of African Theology in the Third Millennium, Owerri 2000.
NACATHS Journal of African Theology, Vol.12, African Traditional Religious Beliefs and Christian Faith, Ikot Ekpene 2002.
NDIOKWERE, N; The African Church, Today and Tomorrow, Vol.2, Inculturation in Practice, SNAAP Press, Enugu 1994.
NDIOKWERE, N; Search for Greener Pastures: Igbo and African Experience, Nebraska 1998.
NUKUNYA, G.K; Tradition and Change in Ghana: An Introduction to Sociology, 2nd Ghana Universities Press, Accra 2003.
NWAKONOBI, B.K; Consent in Igbo Christian Marriage, PortHarcourt 1989.
NWAKONOBI, B.K; Igbo System of Kinship and Family: Christian Response, A Study of One of the Important Pastoral Moral Challenges in Africa, A Dissertation, Rome 1997.
NWOGUGU, E.I; Family Law in Nigeria, Ibadan 1966.
NWOGUGU, E.I; Studies in Igbo Political System, Los Angeles 1972.
NZEKWU, O; Wand of Noble Wood, Ibadan 1971.
NZIMIRO, I; A Study of Mobility Among the Igbos of Southern Nigeria, Kinship and Geographical Mobility, London 1965.
OBI, I; "African Traditional Values in Dialogue with Christianity", in: NACATHS Journal of African Theology, Ikot Ekpene 2002.
OBIAGWU, M.C; Healthcare of the Sick Among the Igbos of Nigeria Vis-à-vis the Healing Ministry of the Church, Rome 2000.
OBIECHINA, E; Culture, Tradition and Society in the West African Novel, London 1975.
OGBALU, F.C; Igbo Institutions and Customs, University Publishing Co; Onitsha 1963.
OGBENNA, A.C; Choosing a Right Partner in Marriage, Lumen Press, Umuahia 2009.
OJEMEN, C.A; "Canonical Requirements of Matrimonial Consent in the Nigerian Context", in: B. Etafo – H.O. Okeke, ed; Marriage and the Family in Nigeria, Onitsha 1993, 24-30.
OJIKE, M; My Africa, New York 1946.

OKODUA, B.A; Coping with Irregular Marriages in the Light of the Magisterium: A Pastoral Suggestion for Yorubaland- Nigeria, Rome 1985.
OKONKWO, E; Marriage in the Christian and Igbo Traditional Context: Towards an Inculturation, A Dissertation, Peter Lang, Frankfurt am Main 2003.
OKORIE, G.M; The Integral Salvation of the Human Persons in Ecclesia in Africa: A Case Study of the Theological Implications Among the Igbo in Nigeria, A Dissertation, Peter Lang, Frankfurt am Main 2008.
OKOYE, G.M; The Sacredness of Marriage and Family Life, Enugu 1973.
OKPOKU, K; West African Traditional Religion, Accra 1978.
OLSEN, G.W; ed; Christian Marriage: A Historical Study, The Crossroad Publishing Company, New York 2001.
ONWUBIKO, O.A; The Church and the Culture in An African Community, Madrid 1987.
ONWUBIKO, O.A; African Thought, Religion and Culture, SNAAP Press, Enugu 1991.
ONYEOCHA, A.E; Family Apostolate in Igboland, Rome 1983.
ONYEOCHA, A.E; Marrying and Marriage: Insight into the Meaning and Purpose of Marriage, Asumpta Press, Owerri 1987.
ONYAGO-AJUS, P – KIURA, M.J; ed; Families First School of Christian Life, Paulines Publications Africa, Nairobi 2003.
ONYEOCHA, A.E; Family Catechesis in Nigeria in the Light of Familiaris Consortio, Asumpta Press, Owerri 1989.
OPARAUGO, B.N; Igbo Traditional Marriage Rite and the Roman "Ordo Celebrandi Matrimonium" of 1991, Rome 1994.
ÖRSY, L; Christian Marriage: Doctrine and Law. Glossae on Canons 1012-1015, The Jurist 40, 1980.
ÖRSY, L; Marriage in Canon Law, Michael Glazier, Delaware 1986.
ÖRSY, L; Marriage in Canon Law, Texts and Comments: Reflections and Questions, Michael Glazier, Wilmington, Delaware 1988.
OTTENBERG, P; The Afikpo-Ibo of Eastern Nigeria: "Peoples of Africa", in: J.L. Gibbs ed; New York 1960, 17-18.
PARRINDER, E.G; Religion in an African Society, Oxford University Press, London 1953.
PARRINDER, E.G; African Traditional Religion, Sheldon Press, London 1976.
PARSONS, M; Marriage Preparation, London 1967.
PAZHAYAMPALLIL, T; Pastoral Guide, Vol.2. New Delhi 2004.
PESCHKE, K.H; Christian Ethics, Bangalore 1992.
PETERS, E.N; The 1917 Pio-Benedictine Code of Canon Law, San Francisco 2001.

POLICARPO, L; Customary Marriage in Zambia in the Light of Canon Law, Rome 1986.

POSPISHIL, V.J; Eastern Catholic Marriage Law According to the Code of Canons of the Eastern Churches, Brooklyn 1991.

PRADER, J; Das kirchliche Eherecht in der seelsorglichen Praxis, Würzburg 1983.

PRADER, J; "Die Ehe in der kirchlichen Rechtsordnung", in: J. Listl – H. Schmitz (Hgsr.), zwei grundlegend neubearbeitete Auflage, Verlag Friedrich Pustet, Regensburg 1999, 884-904.

PROVOST, J.H; "Marriage Preparation in the New Code: Canon 1063 and the Novus Habitus Mentis", in: J.H. Provost – K. Walf, ed; Studies in Canon Law Presented to P.J.M. Huizing, Louven 1991, 173-192.

PUCHER, E; "Ehevorbereitung und Kirchenrecht", in: Österreichisches Archiv für Recht und Religion 50 (2003), 368-372.

REINHARDT, H.J.F; Todesgefahr, in: LKS+KRIII (2004), 690.

REINHARDT, H.J.F; Die kirchliche Trauung, Ehevorbereitung, Trauung und Registrierung der Eheschließung im Bereich der Deutschen Bischofskonferenz, Texte und Kommentar, Ludgerus Verlag, Essen 2006.

REYNOLDS, P.L; Marriage in the Western Church: The Christianization of Marriage During the Patristic and Early Medieval Periods, Brill Academie Publishers, Inc; Boston/Leiden 2001.

RINCON-PEREZ, T; "Commentary on Canons 1063-1072, Pastoral Care and the Prerequisites for the Celebration of Marriage", in: A. Marzoa – J. MIRAS – R. Rodriguez-Ocana, ed; Exegetical Commentary on the Code of Canon Law, Montreal 2004, 1110-1147.

ROBERTS, J.B; The Banns of Marriage: An Historical Synopsis and Commentary, Washington 1931.

ROBERTS, W.P; "Christian Marriage a Divine Calling", in: T.A. Salzman – T.M. Kelly – J.J. O'Keefe, ed; Marriage in the Catholic Tradition, New York 2004.

ROBITAILLE, L.A; "Commentary on Canons 1063-1072, Pastoral Care and those things which must precede the Celebration of Marriage", in: J.P. Beal – J.A. Coriden – T.J. Green, ed; New Commentary on the Code of Canon Law, Bangalore 2004, 1261-1271.

SANDERS, R – SANDERS, O; Walking in Abundance for Life: Marriage Enrichment and Preparation Course, Bloomington, Indiana 2009.

SCHILLEBEECKX, E; Marriage: Human Reality and Saving Mystery, Sheed & Ward, London 1980.

SCHINELLER, P; A Handbook on Inculturation, Paulist Press, New York/Mahwah 1990.

SCHÖPSDAU, W; Konfessionsverschiedene Ehe, Ein Handbuch, Kommentar und Dokumente zu Seelsorge, Theologie und Recht der Kirchen, 3; völlig neu bearbeitete Auflage, Vandenhoeck & Ruprecht, Göttingen 1995.

SCICLUNA, C.J; The Essential Difinition of Marriage According to the 1917 and 1983 Codes of Canon Law: An Exegetical and Comparative Study, University Press of America, Lanhan, New York, London 1995.

SCOTT, K – WARREN, M; ed; Perspectives on Marriage, A Reader, Oxford University Press, New York 2007.

SEBOTT, R; Das neue Kirchliche Eherecht, 2; neue bearbeitete Auflage, Verlag Josef Knecht, Frankfurt am Main 1990.

SEBOTT, R; Das neue Kirchliche Eherecht, 3. Völlig neu bearbeitete Auflage, Verlag Josef Knecht, Frankfurt am Main, 2005.

SEBOTT, R – MARUCCI, C; II Nuovo Diritto Matrimoniale della Chiesa: Commento giuridico e teologico ai can. 1055-1165 del nuovo CIC, Naples, Edizioni Dehoniane, 1985.

SHORTER, A; African Culture and the Christian Church: An Introduction to Social and Pastoral Anthropology, Geoffrey Chapman, London 1973.

SIEGLE, B.A; Marriage According to the New Code of Canon Law, New York 1986.

SKILLIN, H.D; "Marriage in the Year 2000: Canonical-Pastoral Considerations", in: CLSA Proceedings 52 (1990), 11-25.

SMITH, S.S; The Church in Nigeria: Catholic Life Among the Ibos, in: Tablet 76, 1957, 53.

SMOCK, D.R – SMOCK, A.C; Cultural and Political Aspects of Rural Transformation: A Case Study of Eastern Nigeria, New York 1972.

SPITZER, A; "Marriage", in: New Catholic Encyclopaedia, Vol. IX, 1967, 259.

TALBOT, P.A; The Peoples of Southern Nigeria, Vol.1, London 1926.

TAYLOR, G – DE BECKER, E; Parish Priests and Marriage Cases, Bangalore 2005.

THOMAS, J.L. – THOMAS, D.M; ed; Beginning Your Marriage, Acta Publications, Chicago 1994.

TYLOR, E.B; Primitive Culture, London 1871.

UCHENDU, V.C; The Igbo of Southeast Nigeria, Holt, Rinehart & Winston, New York 1965.

UCHENDU, V.C; "Concubinage Among Ngwa Igbo of Southern Nigeria", in Afer 35 (1965), 189.

UDOETTE, D – OBI, N.N; ed; Inculturation and the Nigerian Church: St. Joseph Theology Symposium Series (SJTSS, No.1), Ikot Ekpene 2000.

UGORJI, L.I; The Service of the Word: On the Practice of Faith, Enugu 2000.

UNWUEJEOGWU, M.A; An Outline of the Dawn of Igbo Civilization, Journal of the Odinani Museum Nri, Vol.1, March 1972.
WALSH, L; The Sacraments of Initiation, London 1988.
WERNZ, F.X; Ius decretalium, IV, pars. 1, ius matrimoniale Eccles. Catholicae, Prati 1911.
WERNZ, F.X – VIDAL, P; Ius Canonicum, V, Ius Matrimoniale, Romae 1946.
WIRTH, P; Das Neue Kirchliche Eherecht: Kurzer Überblick und Kritische Würdigung, Österreichisches Archiv für katholisches Kirchenrecht 26 (1975), 326.
WITTE, J; From Sacrament to Contract: Marriage, Religion, and Law in the Western Tradition, Westminster John Knox Press, Louisville, Kentucky 1997.
WRENN, M.J; ed; John Paul II and the Family, Chicago 1983.
ZAPP, H; "Eheversprechen, Vorbereitung der Eheschließung, Trauungsverbote", in: J. Listl – H. Müller – H. Schmitz (Hsgr.), Grundriss des nachkonziliaren Kirchrechts, Verlag Friedrich Pustet, Regensburg 1980.
ZAPP, H; Kirchliches Eherecht mit dem Entwurf der CIC- Reform- Kommission, 5. Auflage, Verlag Rombach, Freiburg 1981.
ZAPP, H; Kanonisches Eherecht, Verlag Rombach, Freiburg 1983.
ZAVALLONI, R; Self-Determination: The Psychology of Personal Freedom, Chicago 1962.

African Theological Studies
Etudes Théologiques Africaines

Edited by Gerhard Droesser and Chibueze Udeani

Vol. 1 Blaise Okachibe Okpanachi: Nigerian-Vatican Diplomatic Relations. Evangelisation and Catholic Missionary Enterprise 1884-1950. 2013.

Vol. 2 Fidelis Chineme Bayo Kwazu: Developing a Viable Strategy of Solving the Problems of Poverty in the Light of Human Rights. A Case Study of Igboland in Nigeria. 2013.

Vol. 3 Onyenali Rowland: The Trilogy of Parables in Mt 21:28-22:14. From a Matthean Perspective. 2013.

Vol. 4 Paulinus Chibuike Nwaigwe: Canonical Marriage Preparation in the Igbo Tradition in the Light of Canon 1063 of the 1983 Code of Canon Law. Canonical Norms and Inculturation. 2013.

www.peterlang.com